Sorry this is late.

I moved to Tokyo about eight years ago, and my dream of bringing my mother from Shiga has finally come true. Unfortunately, so far all we seem to do is fight.

—Katsura Hoshino

Shiga Prefecture native Katsura Hoshino's hit manga series *D.Gray-man* has been serialized in *Weekly Shonen Jump* since 2004. Katsura's debut manga, "Continue," appeared for the first time in *Weekly Shonen Jump* in 2003.

Katsura adores cats.

D.GRAY-MAN

VOL. 8

SHONEN JUMP ADVANCED
Manga Edition

STORY AND ART BY

KATSURA HOSHINO

English Adaptation/Lance Caselman
Translation/Toshifumi Yoshida
Touch-up Art & Lettering/Kelle Han
Design/Yukiko Whitley
Editor/Gary Leach

VP, Production/Alvin Lu
VP, Sales & Product Marketing/Gonzalo Ferreyra
VP, Creative/Linda Espinosa
Publisher/Hyoe Narita

Printed in the U.S.A.

Published by VIZ Media, LLC
P.O. Box 77010
San Francisco, CA 94107

10 9 8 7 6 5 4
First printing, February 2008
Fourth printing, October 2009

RATED T+ FOR OLDER TEEN

PARENTAL ADVISORY
D.GRAY-MAN is rated T+ for Older Teen and is recommended for ages 16 and up. This volume contains fantasy violence.

ratings.viz.com

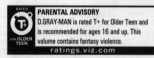

SHONEN JUMP ADVANCED MANGA EDITION

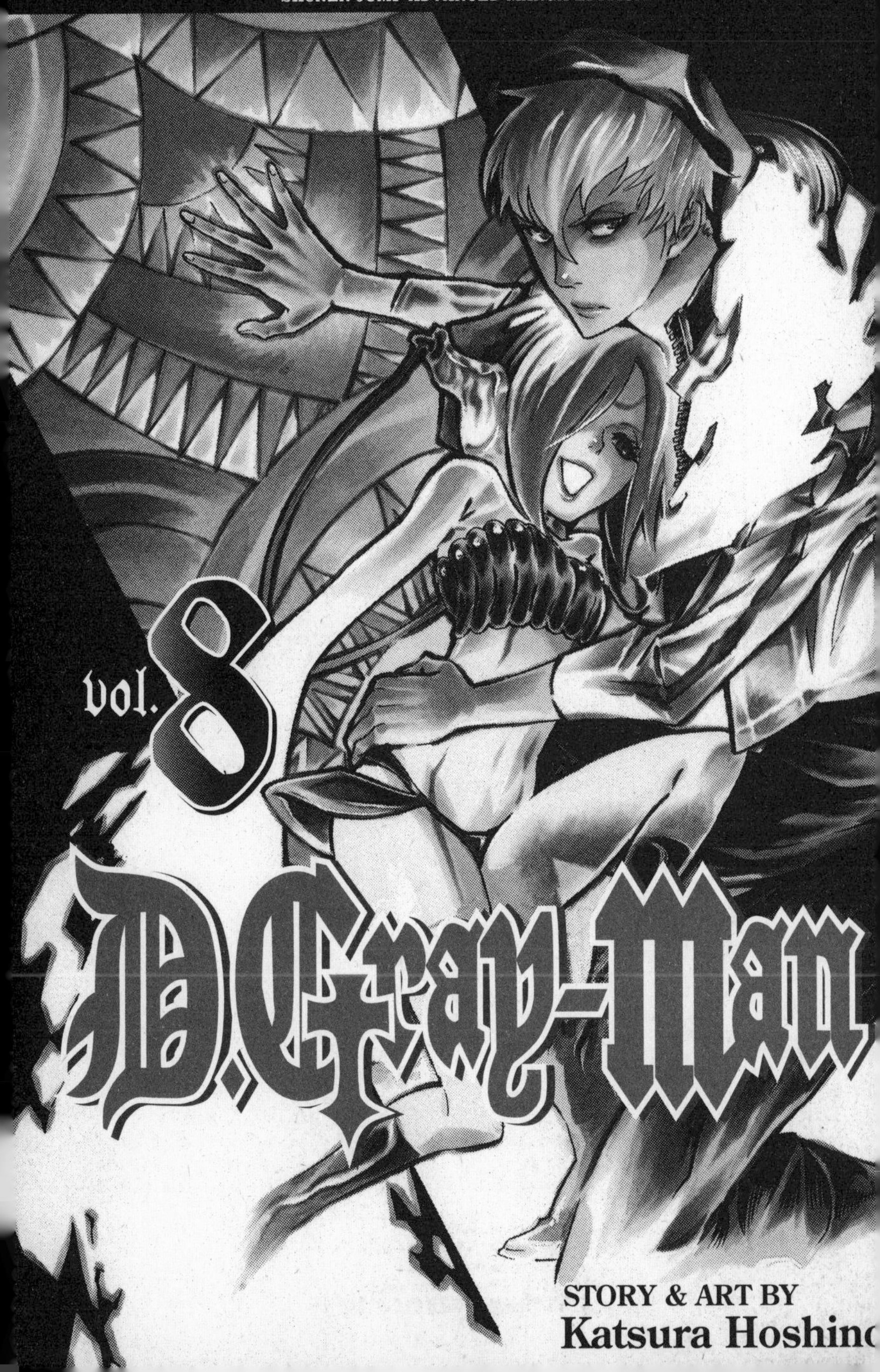
vol. 8
D.Gray-man
STORY & ART BY
Katsura Hoshino

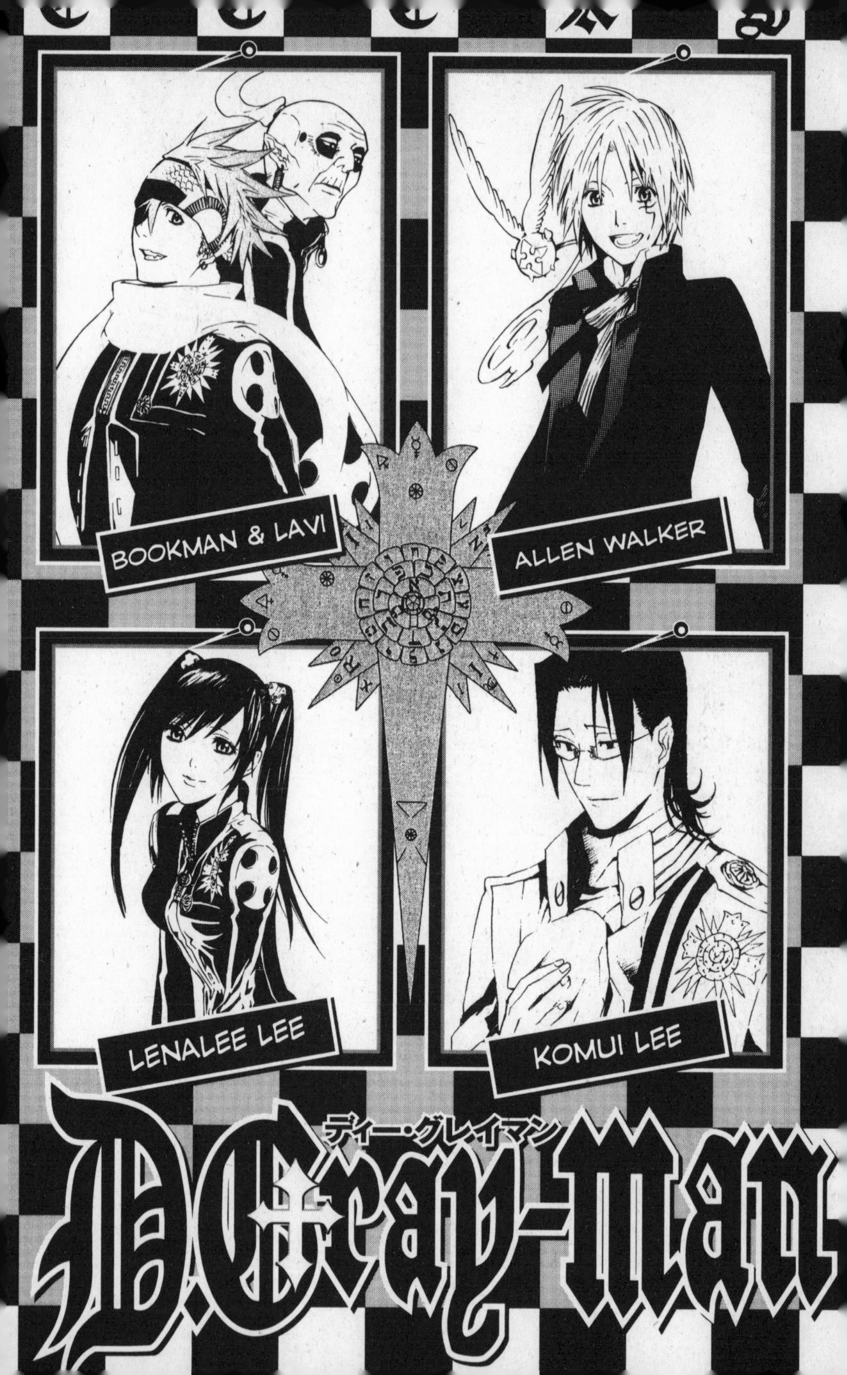
BOOKMAN & LAVI
ALLEN WALKER
LENALEE LEE
KOMUI LEE
ディー・グレイマン
D.Gray-man

CHARA

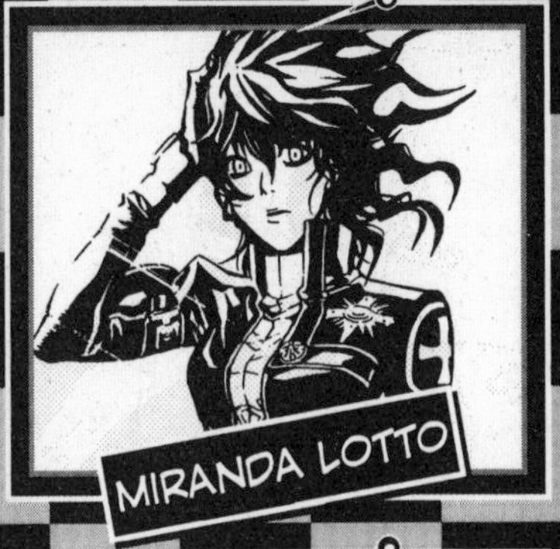
MIRANDA LOTTO

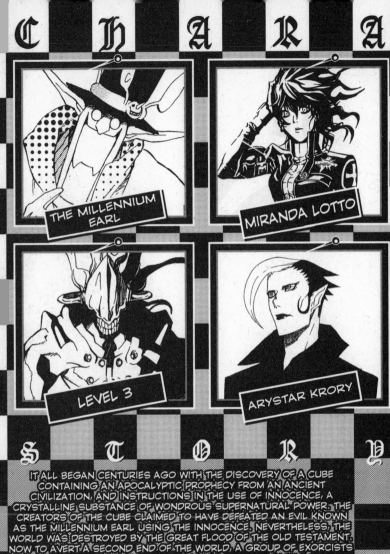

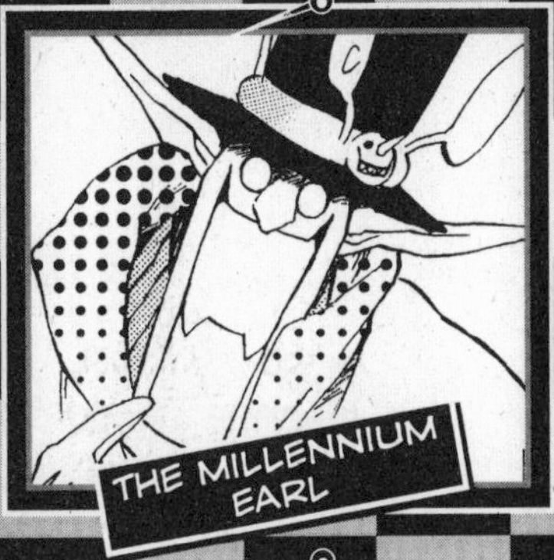
THE MILLENNIUM EARL

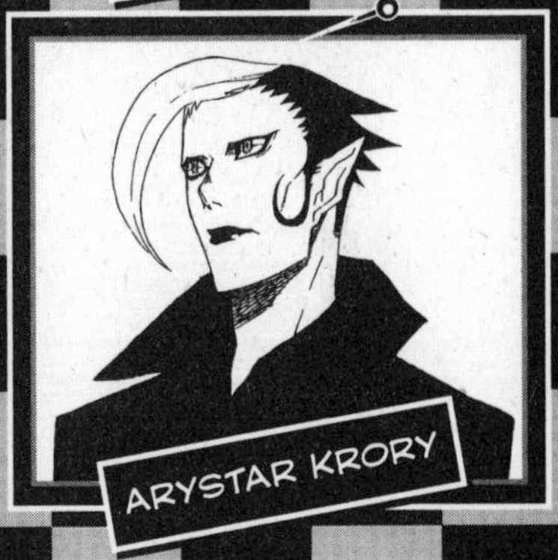
ARYSTAR KRORY

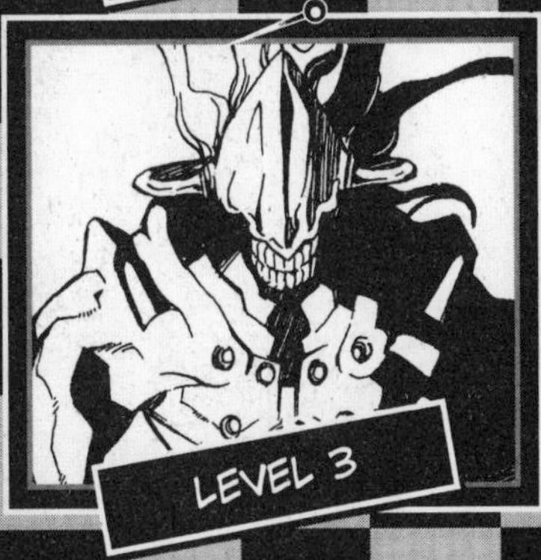
LEVEL 3

STORY

IT ALL BEGAN CENTURIES AGO WITH THE DISCOVERY OF A CUBE CONTAINING AN APOCALYPTIC PROPHECY FROM AN ANCIENT CIVILIZATION, AND INSTRUCTIONS IN THE USE OF INNOCENCE, A CRYSTALLINE SUBSTANCE OF WONDROUS SUPERNATURAL POWER. THE CREATORS OF THE CUBE CLAIMED TO HAVE DEFEATED AN EVIL KNOWN AS THE MILLENNIUM EARL USING THE INNOCENCE. NEVERTHELESS, THE WORLD WAS DESTROYED BY THE GREAT FLOOD OF THE OLD TESTAMENT. NOW TO AVERT A SECOND END OF THE WORLD, A GROUP OF EXORCISTS WIELDING WEAPONS MADE OF INNOCENCE MUST BATTLE THE MILLENNIUM EARL AND HIS TERRIBLE MINIONS, THE AKUMA.

HAVING LEFT ALLEN BEHIND IN CHINA, LENALEE, LAVI AND BOOKMAN SAIL FOR JAPAN IN HOPES OF FINDING GENERAL CROSS MARIAN BEFORE THE AKUMA DO. BUT THEIR VOYAGE IS INTERRUPTED, FIRST BY A MASSIVE SWARM OF AKUMA AND THEN BY A LEVEL 3 AKUMA OF INCREDIBLE POWER. TO SAVE HER COMRADES AND THE SHIP, LENALEE ATTACKS THE LEVEL 3 WITH EVERYTHING SHE HAS. BUT CAN LENALEE SURVIVE THE DEVASTATING POWER OF HER OWN ATTACK?

D.GRAY-MAN
Vol. 8

CONTENTS

THE 67TH NIGHT: UNKNOWN PHENOMENON

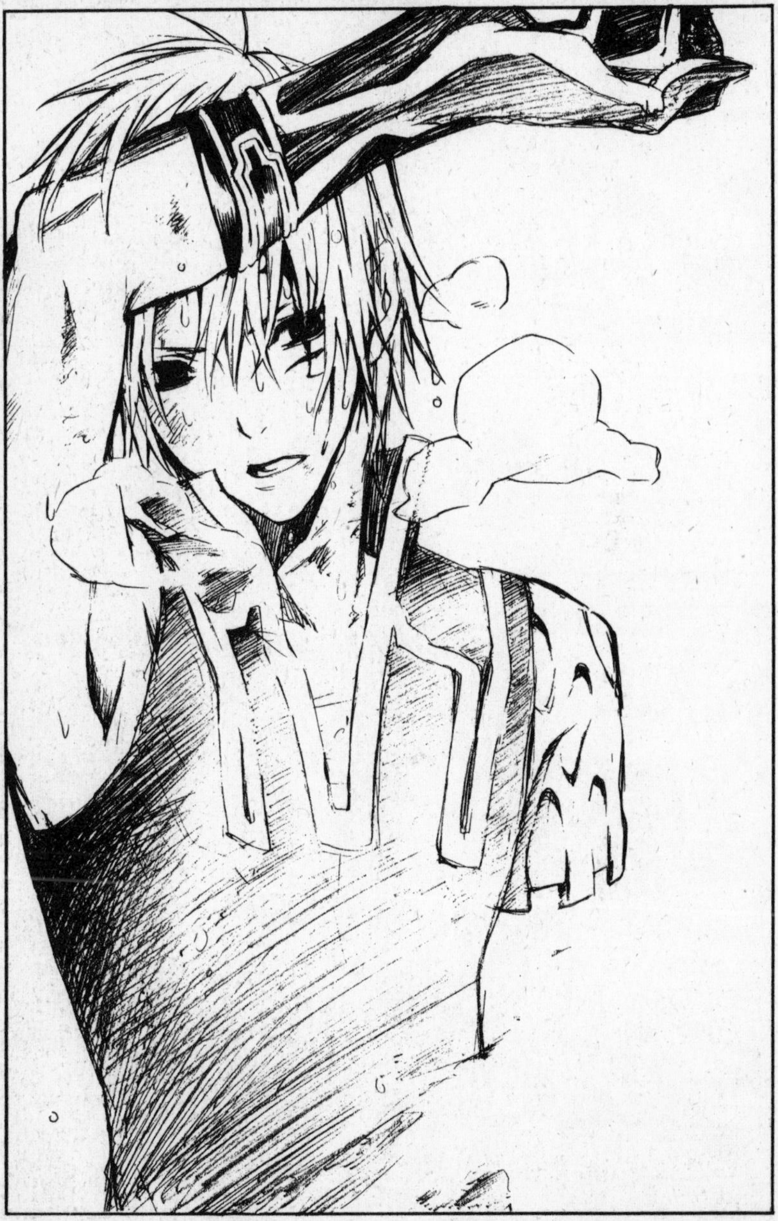

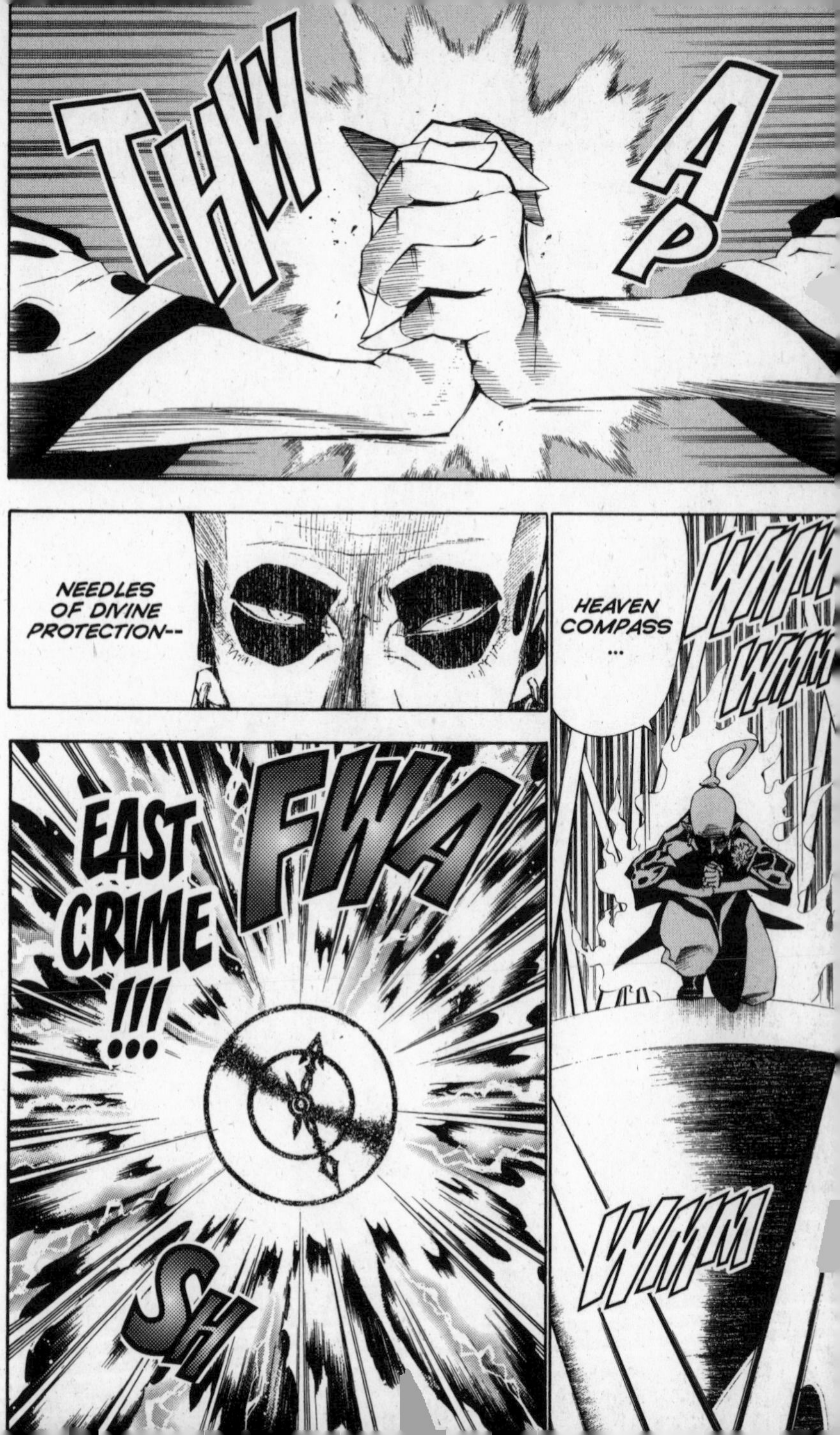
THWAP
HEAVEN COMPASS...
WMM
WMM
WMM
NEEDLES OF DIVINE PROTECTION--
EAST CRIME!!!
FWA
SH

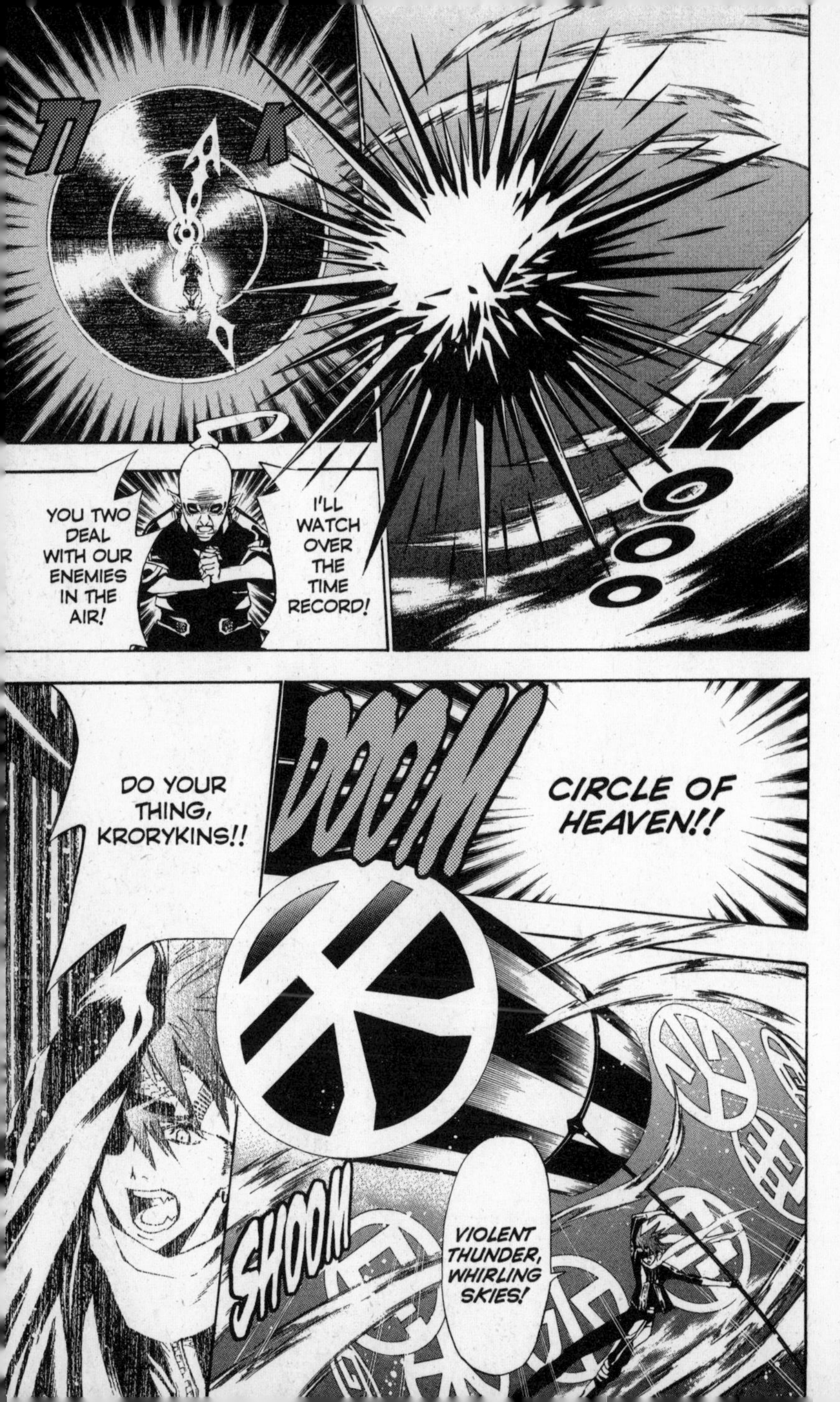
TI K
WOOOO
I'LL WATCH OVER THE TIME RECORD!
YOU TWO DEAL WITH OUR ENEMIES IN THE AIR!
CIRCLE OF HEAVEN!!
DOOM
DO YOUR THING, KRORYKINS!!
VIOLENT THUNDER, WHIRLING SKIES!
SHOOM

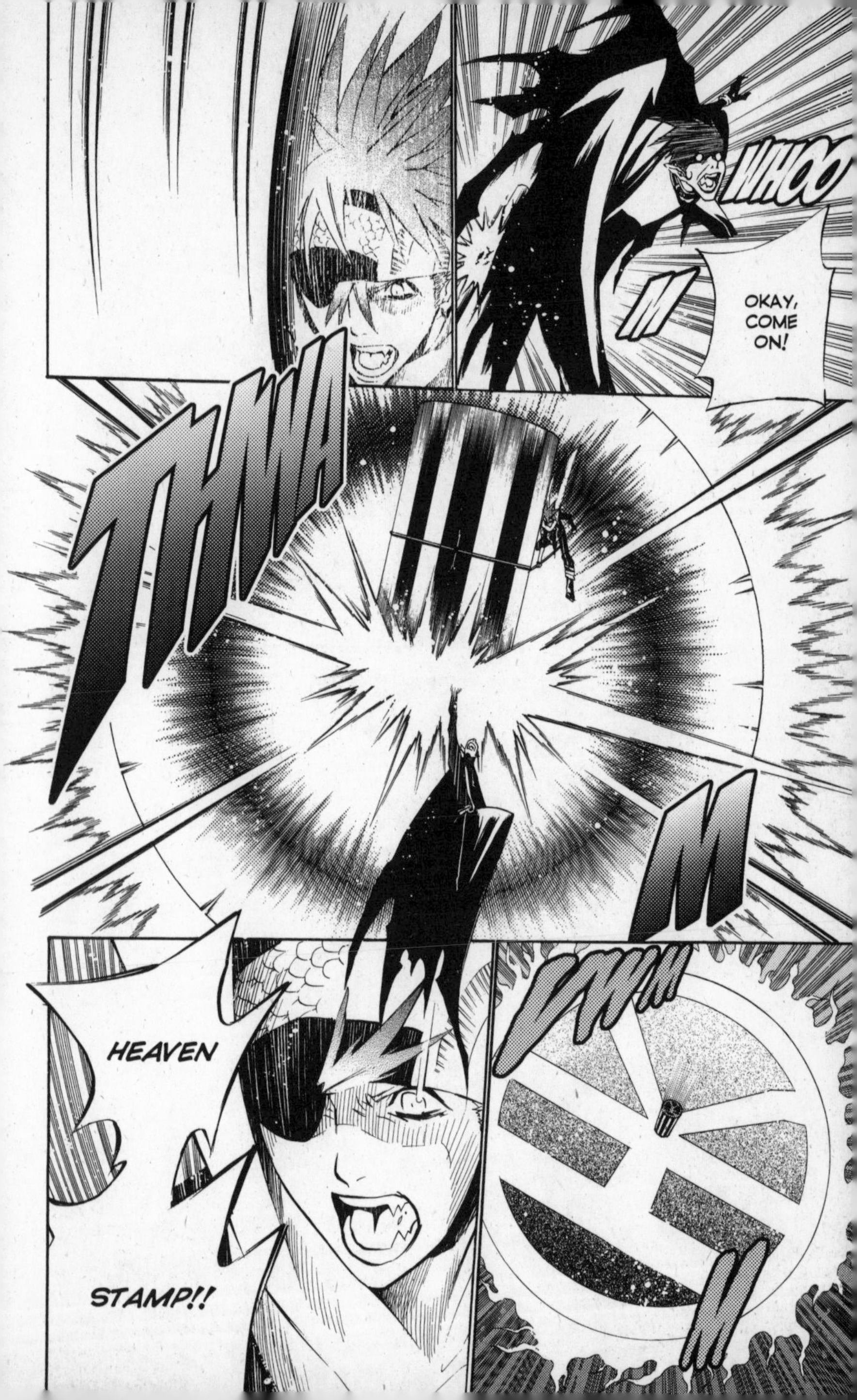
WHOO
OKAY, COME ON!
THWAM
VMMM
HEAVEN
STAMP!!

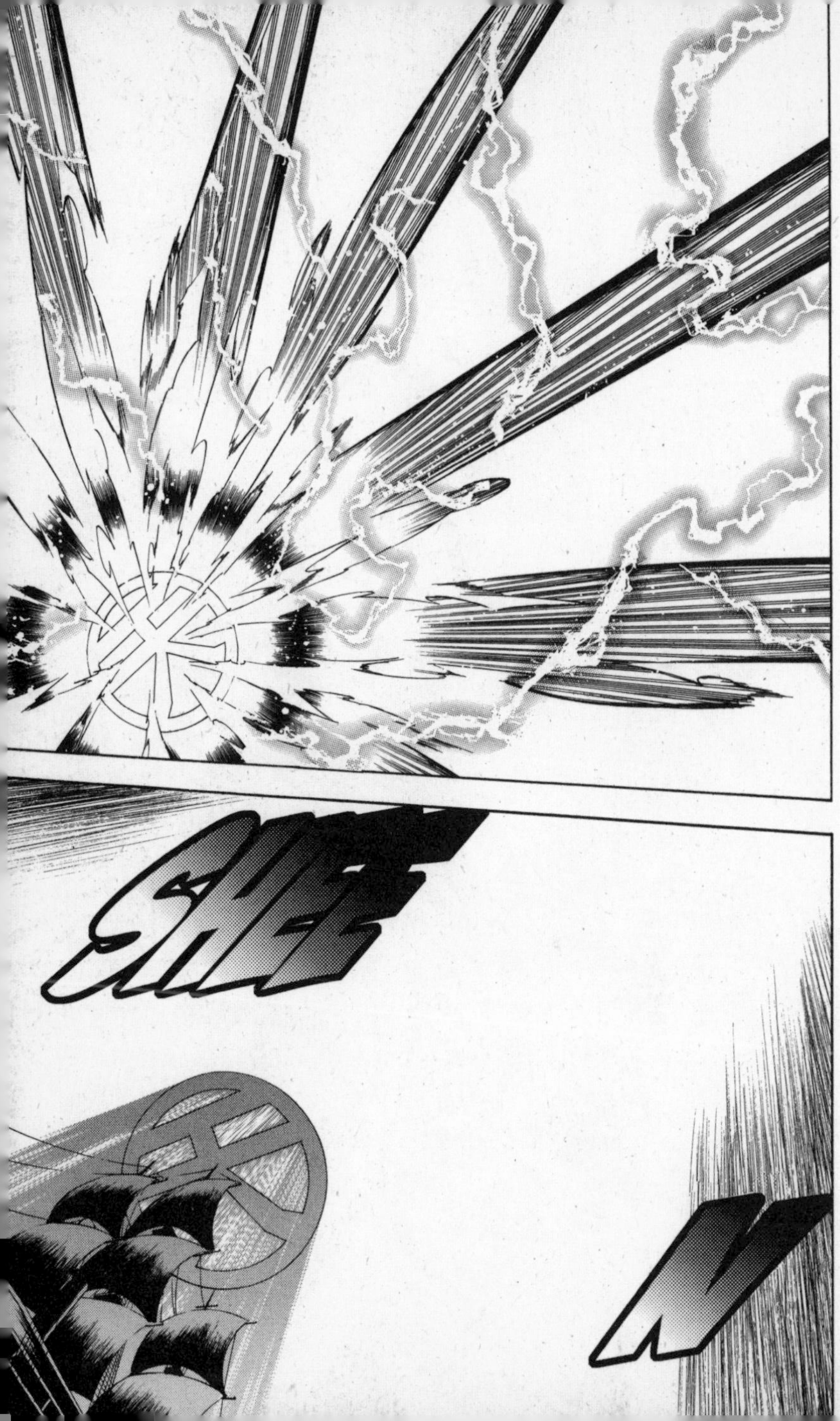
SHEE
N

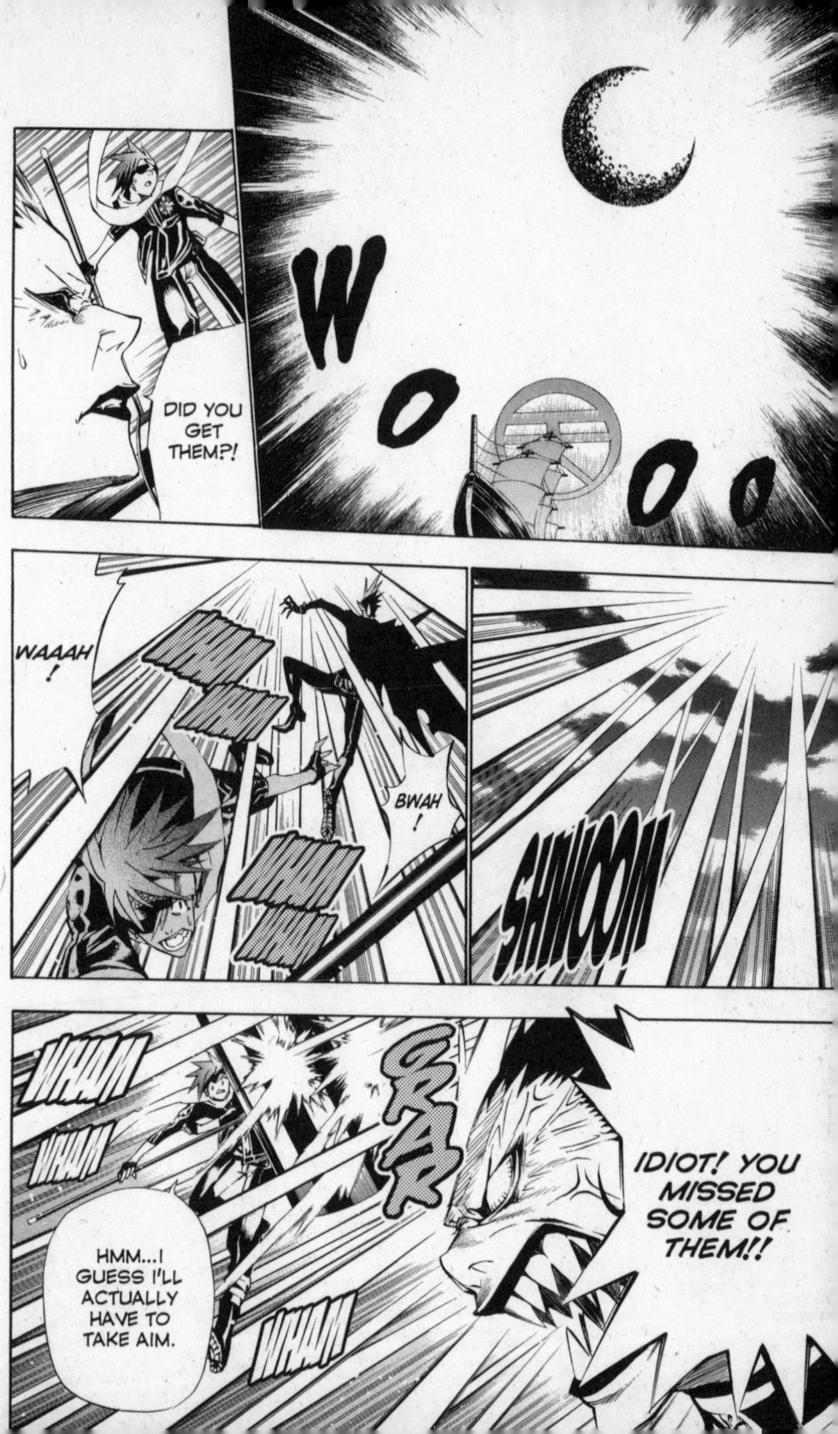
WOOOO
DID YOU GET THEM?!
SHWOOM
WAAAH!
BWAH!
IDIOT! YOU MISSED SOME OF THEM!!
WHAM
WHAM
HMM...I GUESS I'LL ACTUALLY HAVE TO TAKE AIM.
WHAM

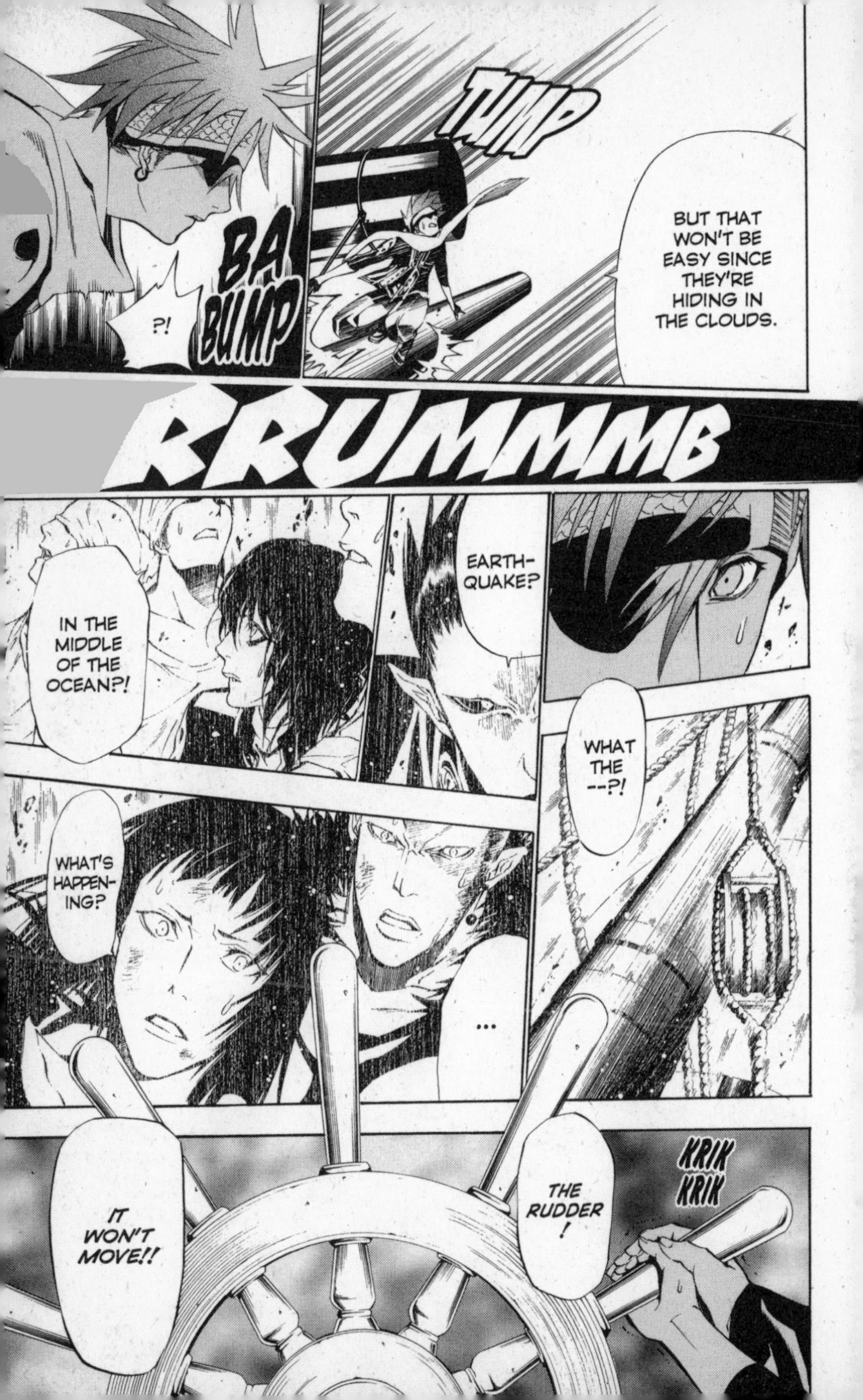
BUT THAT WON'T BE EASY SINCE THEY'RE HIDING IN THE CLOUDS.
TUMP
BA BUMP
?!
KRUMMMB
EARTH-QUAKE?
IN THE MIDDLE OF THE OCEAN?!
WHAT THE --?!
WHAT'S HAPPEN-ING?
...
KRIK KRIK
THE RUDDER!
IT WON'T MOVE!!

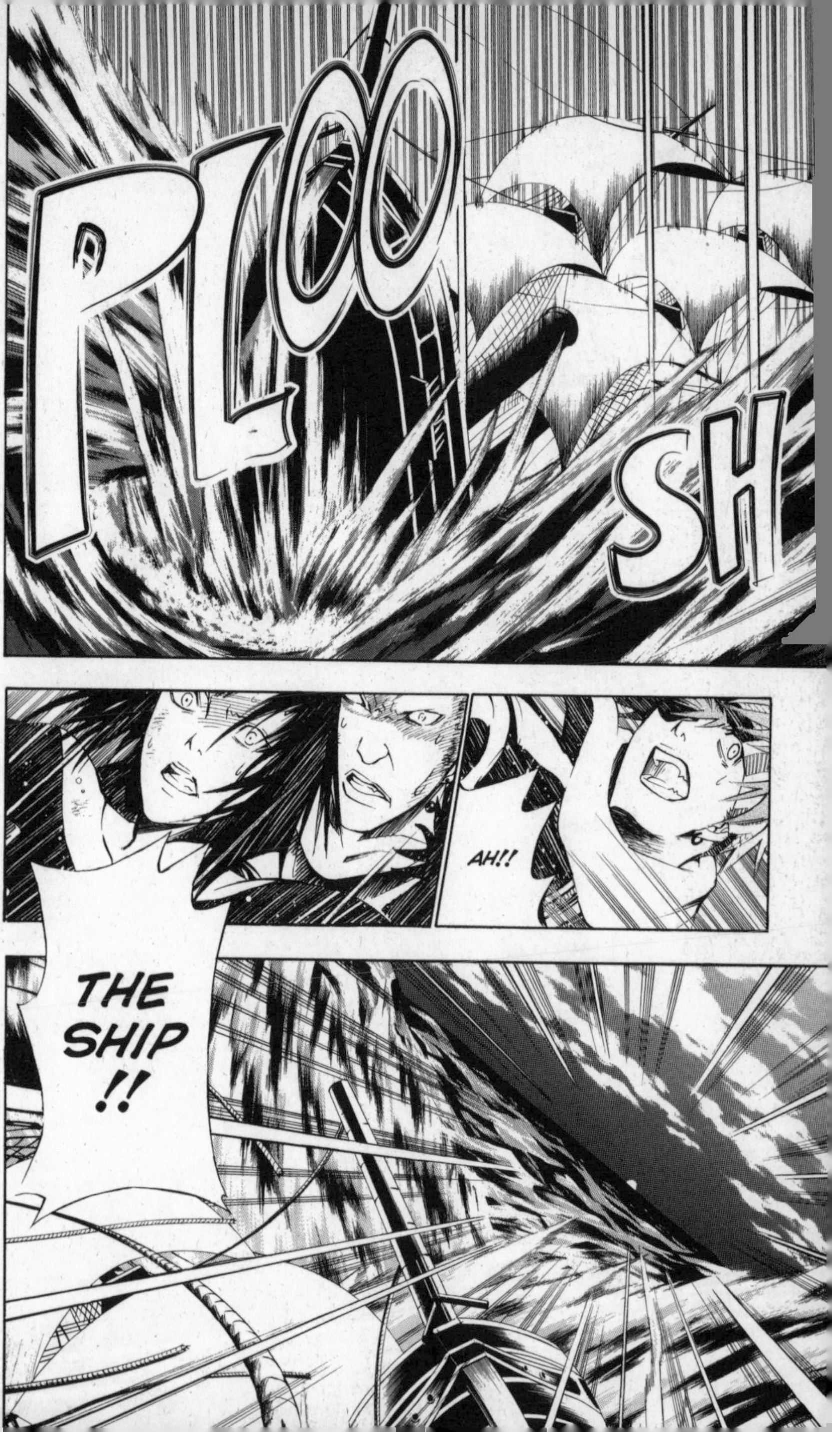
PLOO
SH
AH!!
THE SHIP !!

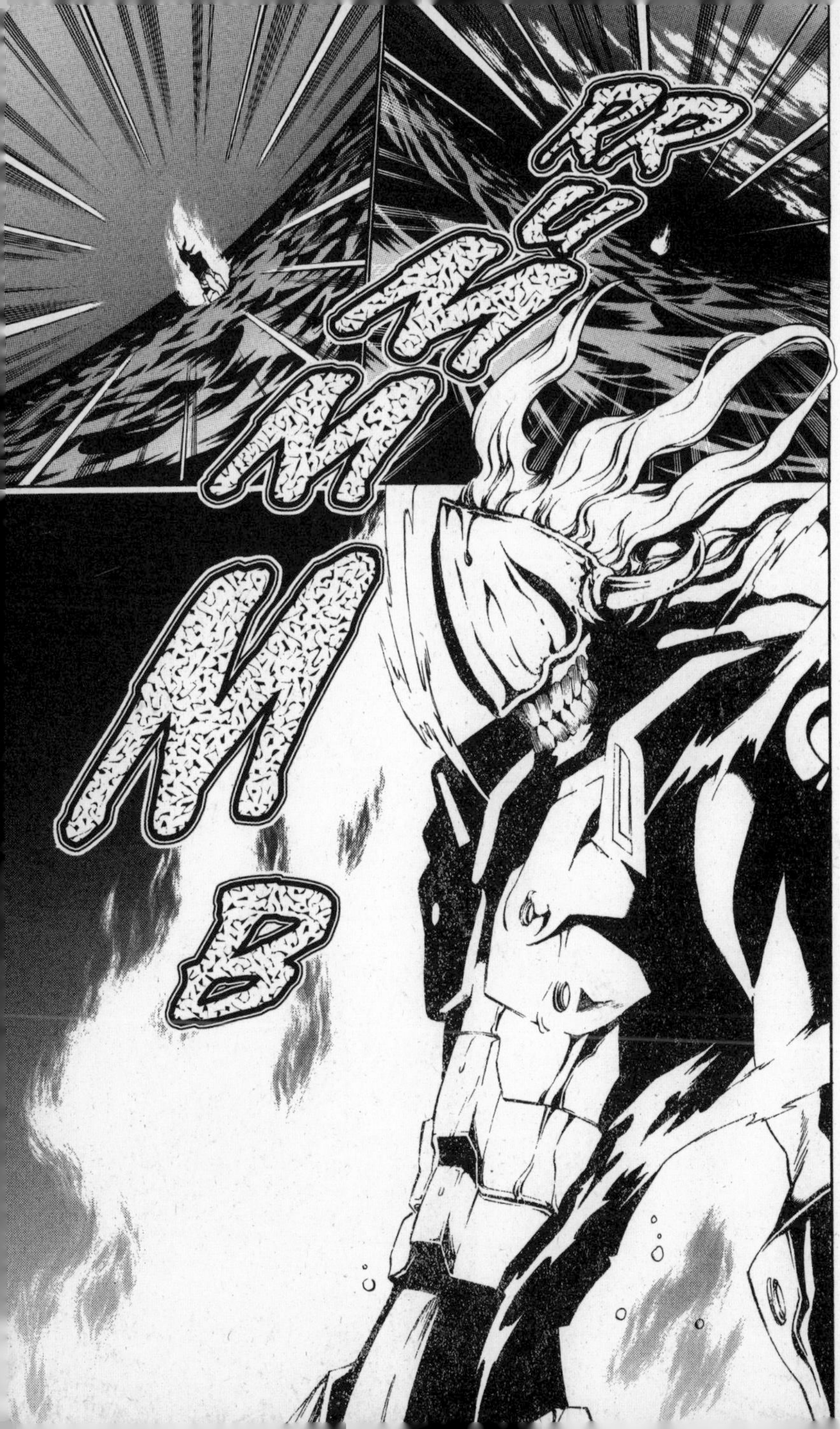
RRUMMMB

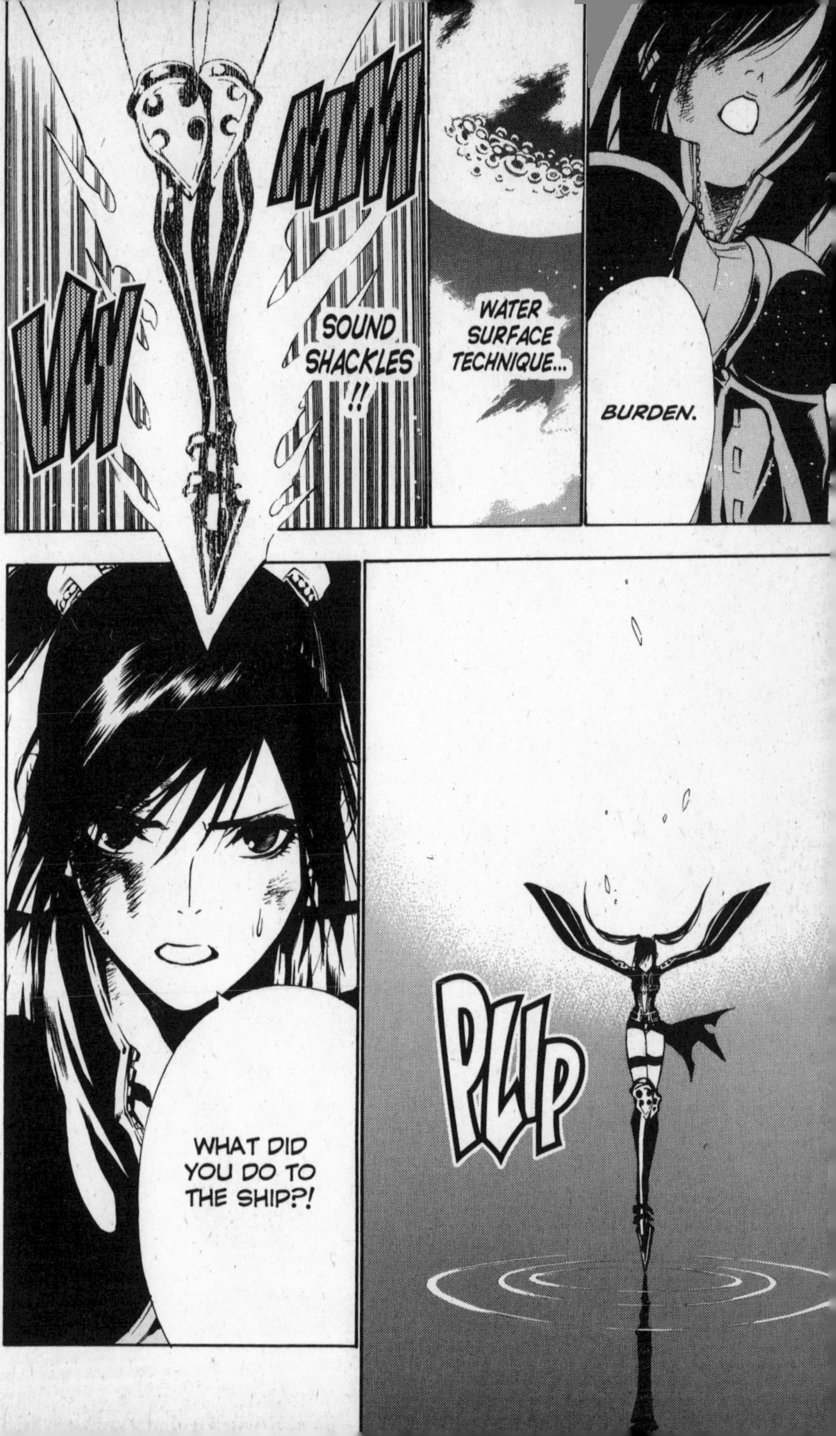
BURDEN.
WATER SURFACE TECHNIQUE...
SOUND SHACKLES!!
PLIP
WHAT DID YOU DO TO THE SHIP?!

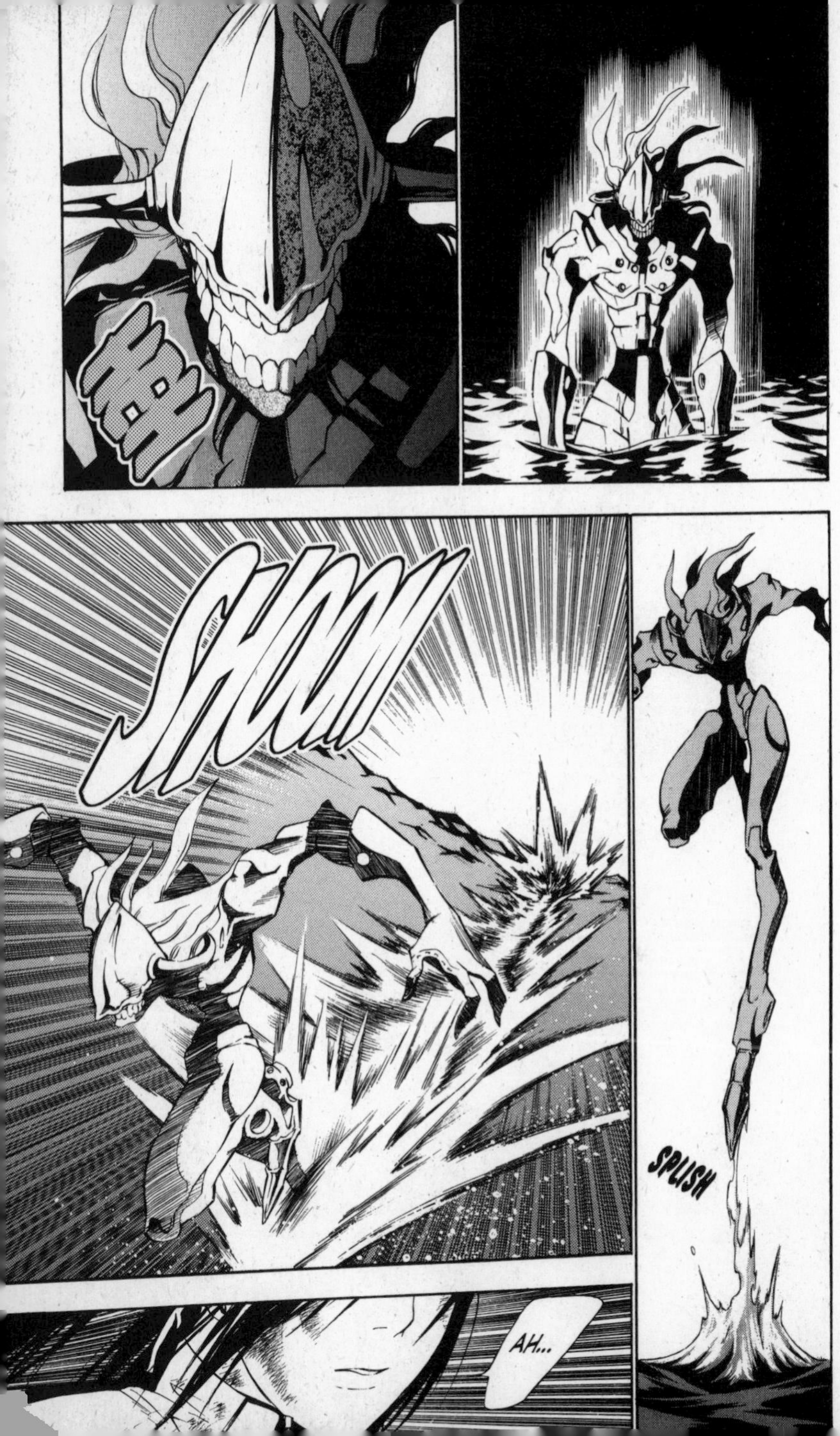
SHOOM
SPLISH
AH...

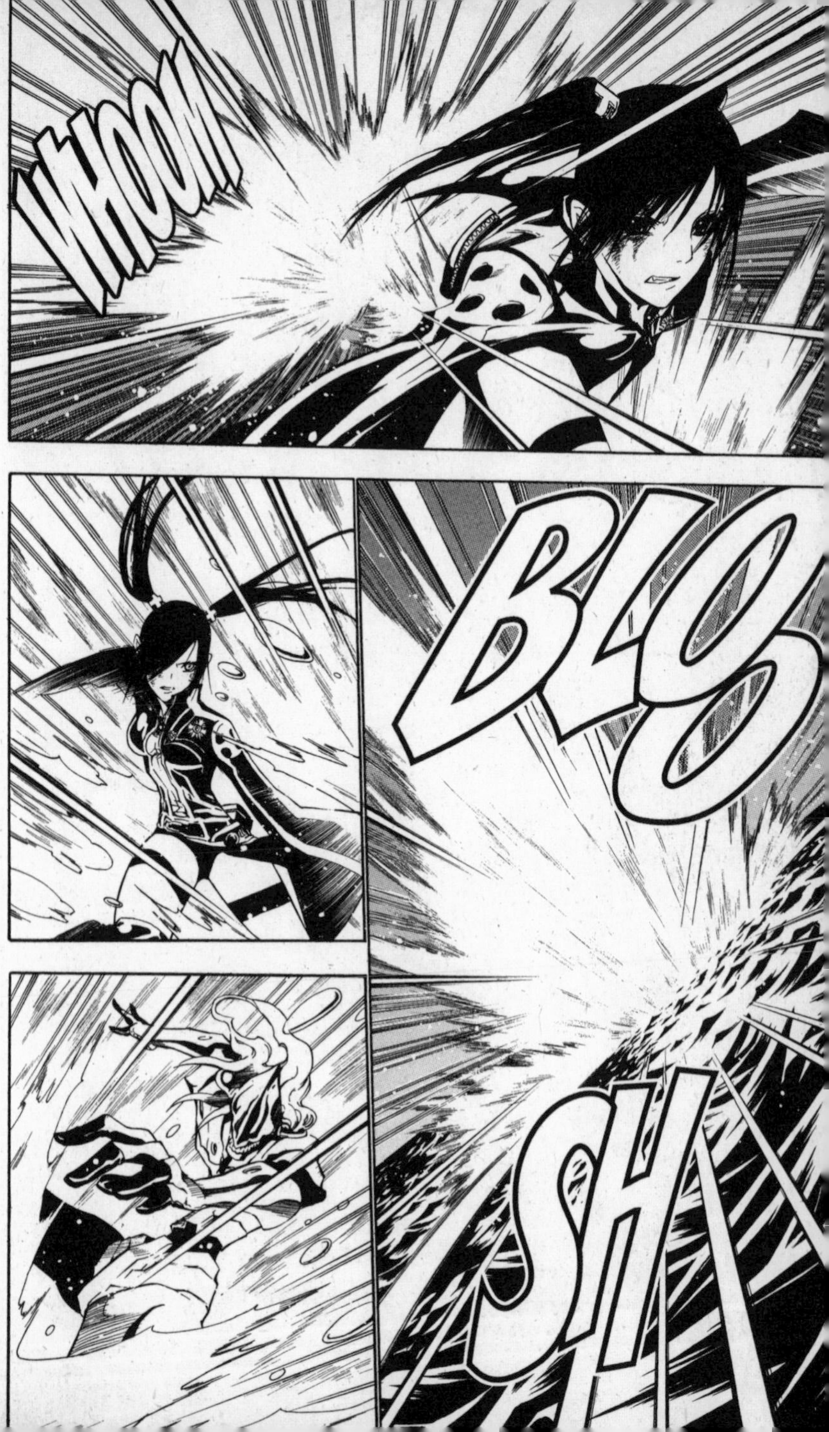
WHOOM
BLO
SH

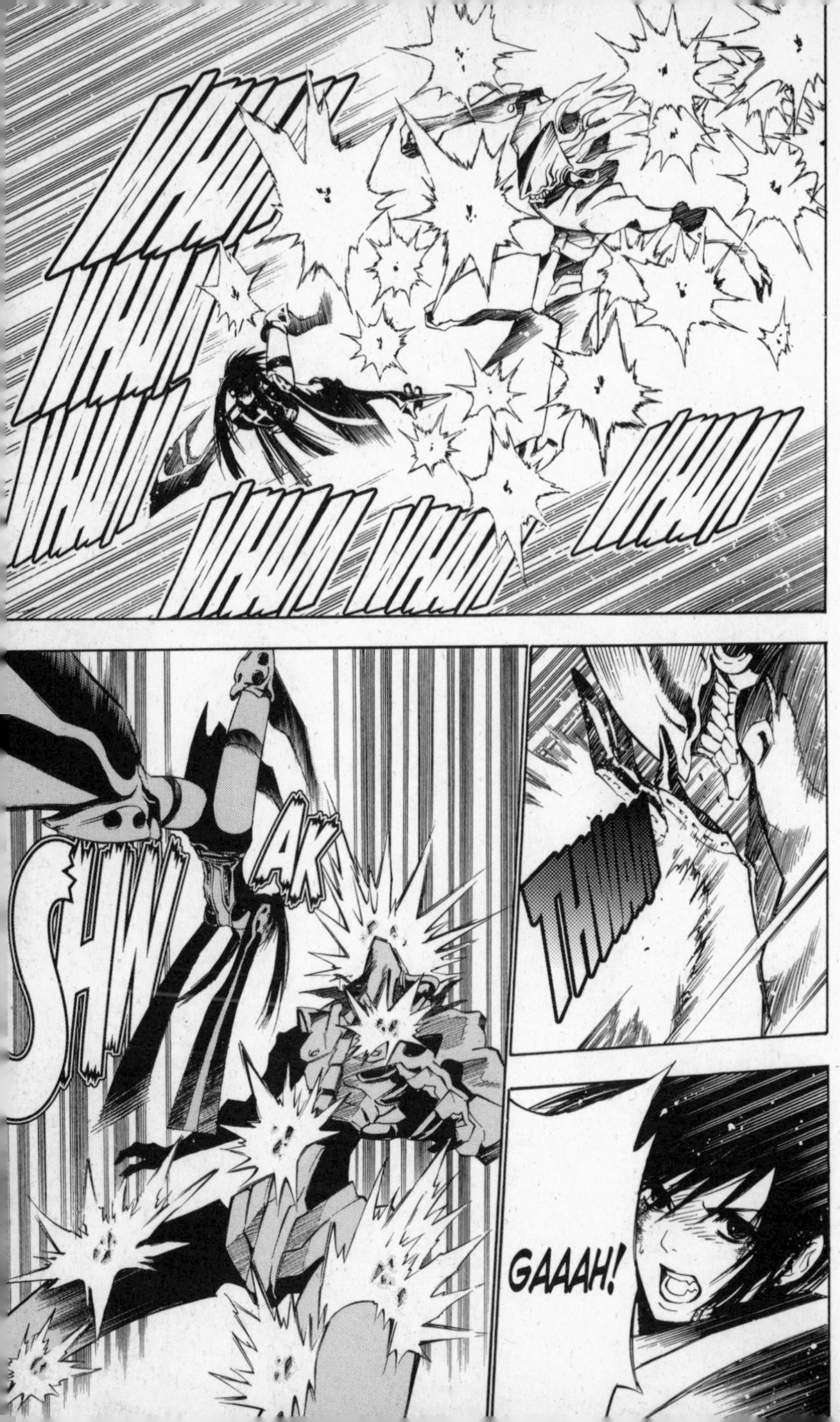
GAAAH!

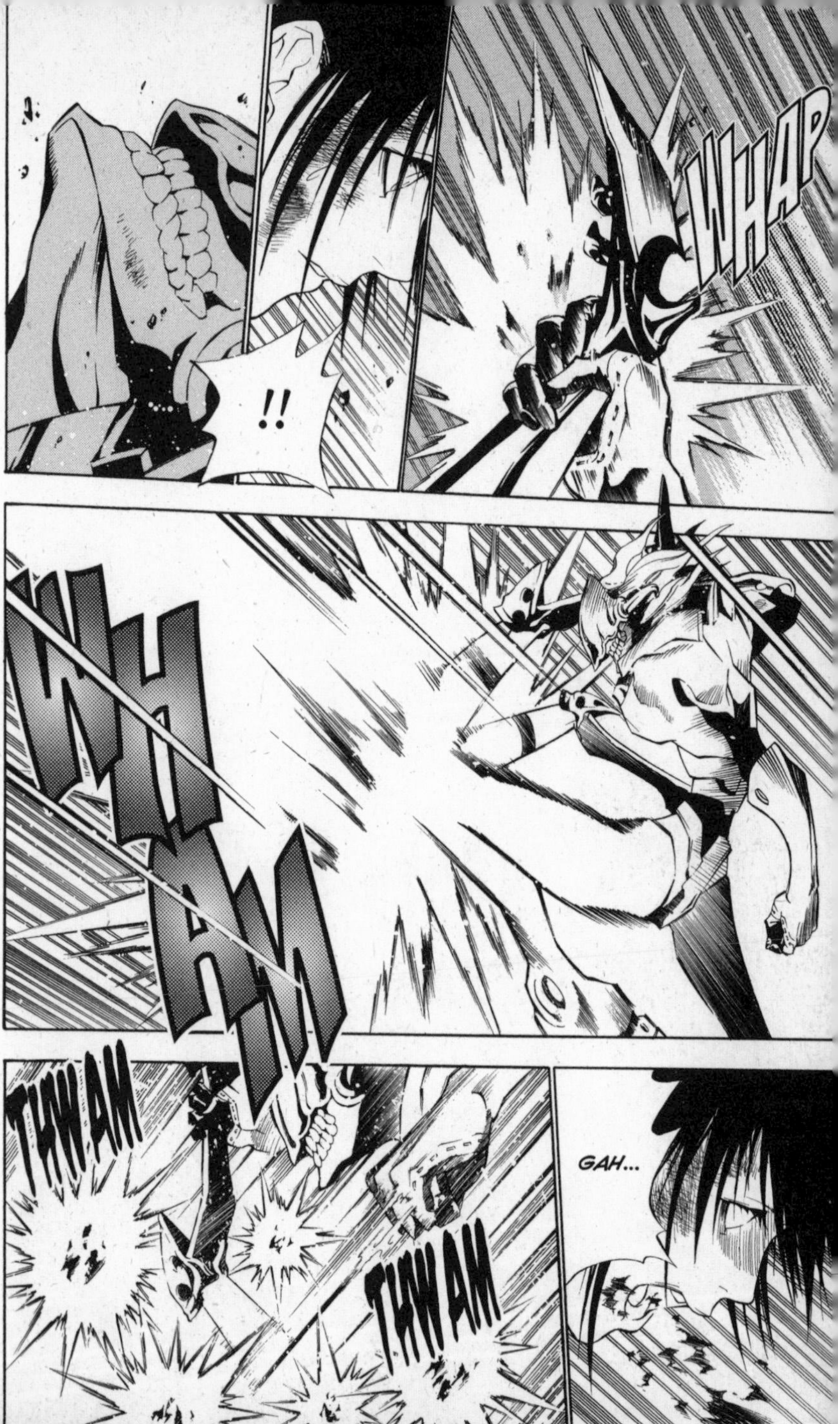
WHAP
!!
WHAM
GAH...
THWAM
THWAM

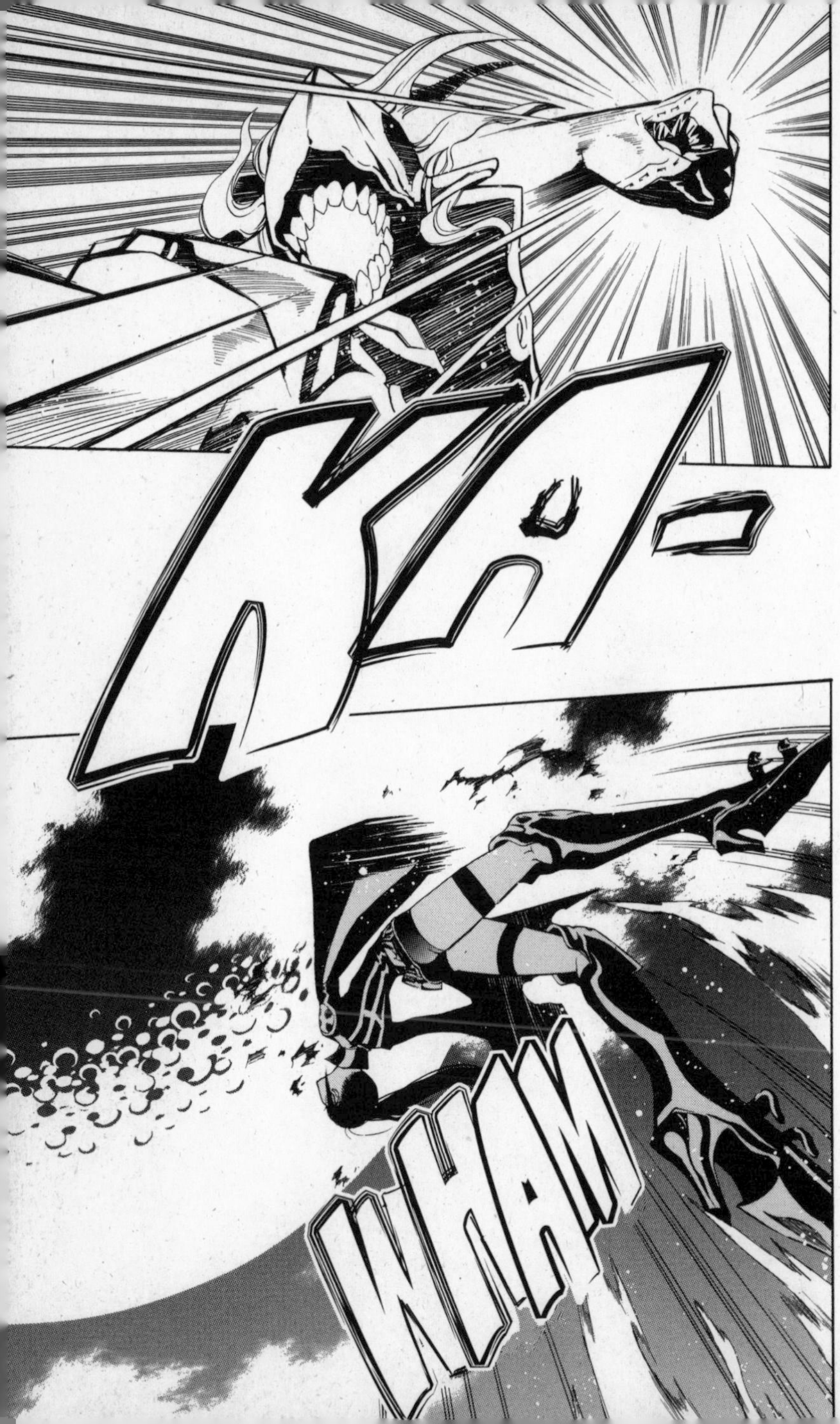
KRA
WHAM

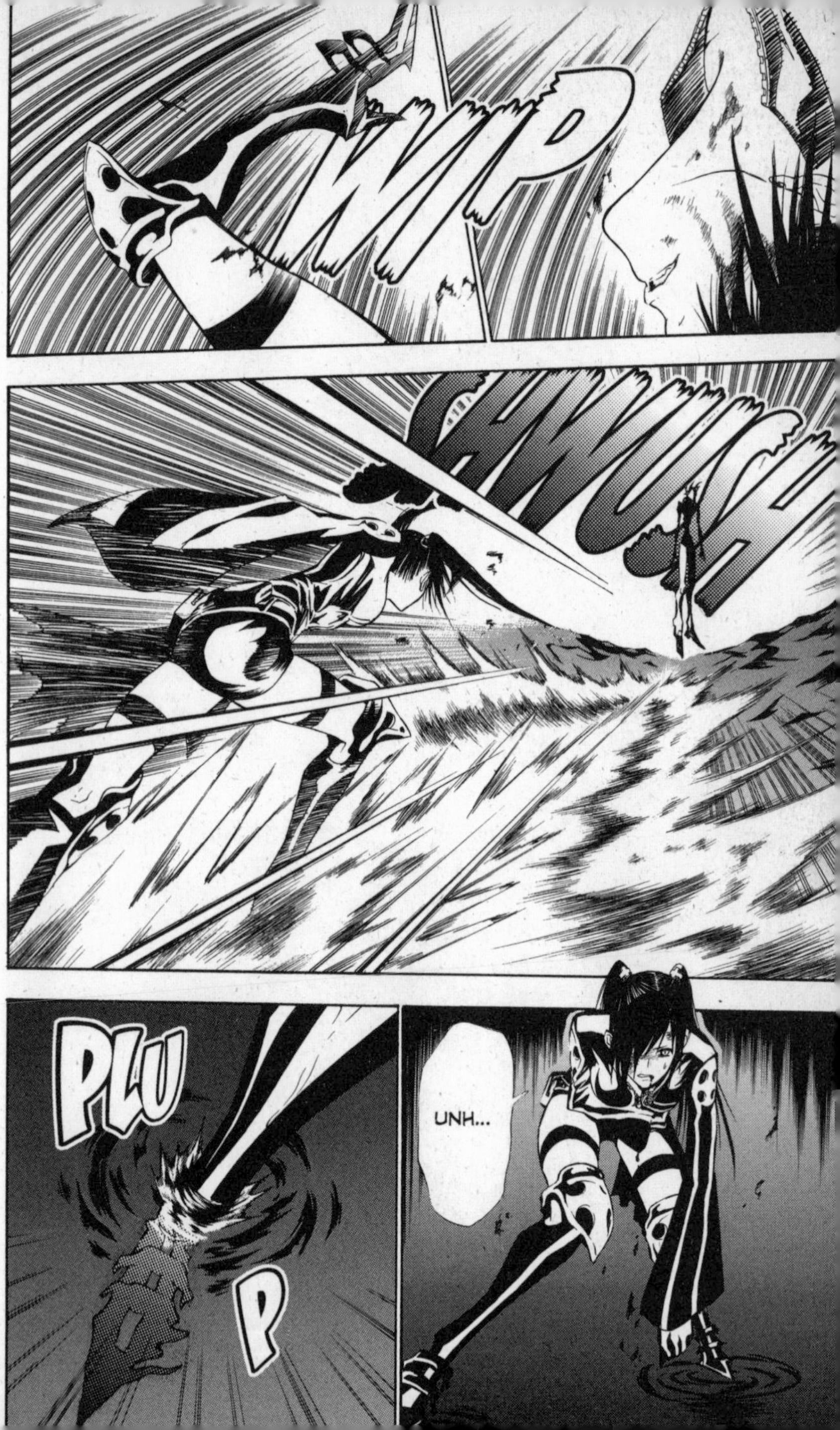
WHIP
SWUSH
UNH...
PLU
P

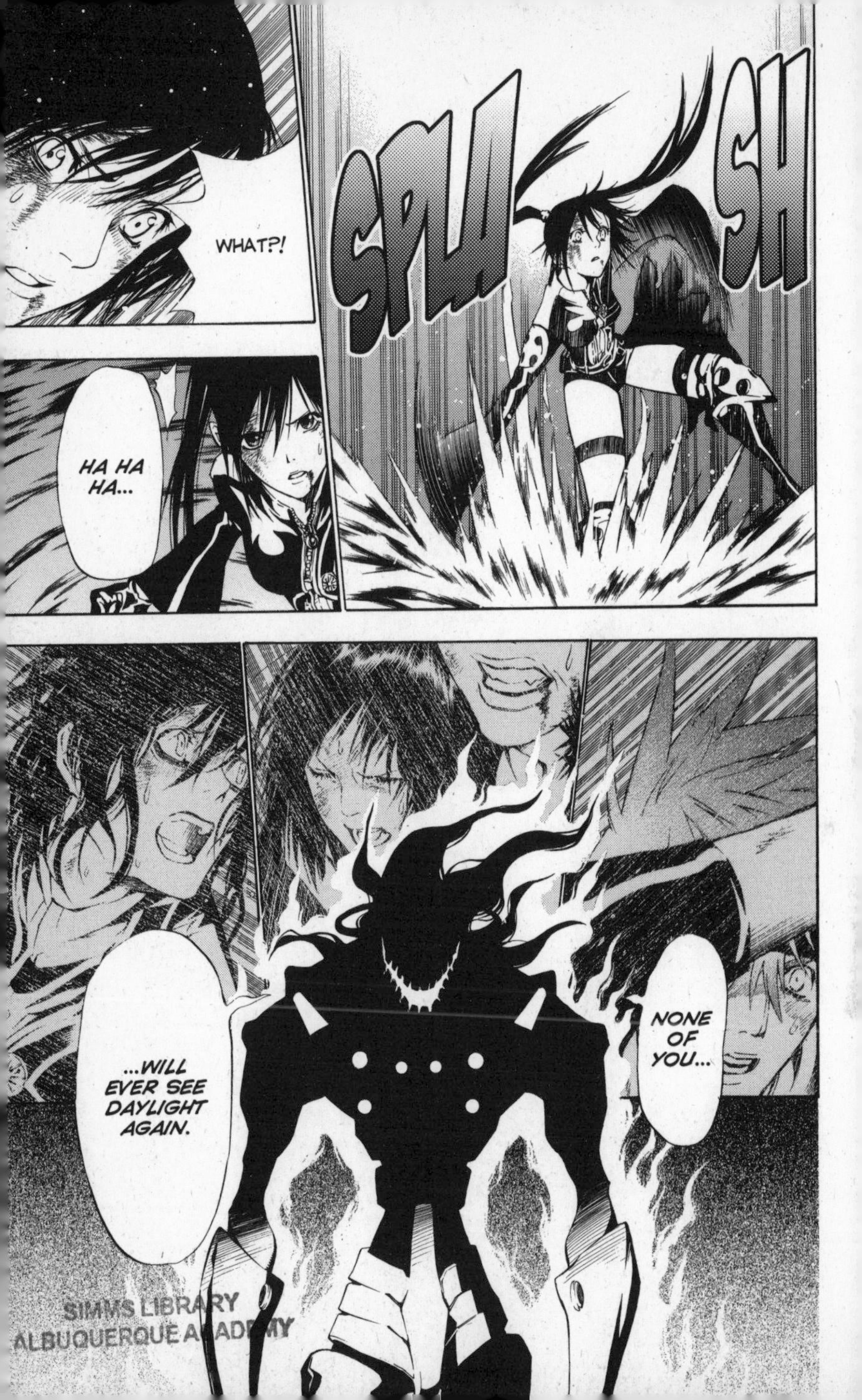
SPLASH
WHAT?!
HA HA HA...
NONE OF YOU...
...WILL EVER SEE DAYLIGHT AGAIN.

BAK CHAN

WHUP

POISON

BAK CHAN IS A CHINESE DESCENDANT OF A GERMAN WIZARD, ONE OF THE FOUNDERS OF THE BLACK ORDER.

HEIGHT: 168 CM
WEIGHT: 53 KG
BIRTHDAY: NOVEMBER 11TH (SCORPIO)
BLOOD TYPE: A

I'VE ALWAYS WANTED TO SHOW SOME OF THE BRANCH OFFICES OF THE BLACK ORDER, BUT I DIDN'T EXPECT THE HEAD OF ASIA BRANCH TO SHOW UP IN THE D. GRAY-MAN NOVELS BEFORE THE MANGA. BUT, ACTUALLY, I'M GLAD IT HAPPENED THAT WAY. WRITER KAYA KIZAKI AND I CAME UP WITH BAK CHAN TOGETHER. WE'RE VERY FOND OF HIM. AND NOW THAT WE'VE SHOWN ASIA BRANCH, I'D LIKE TO SHOW YOU THE OTHER FIVE BRANCHES. JUST KIDDING.

THE 68TH NIGHT: THE SINKING DARKNESS

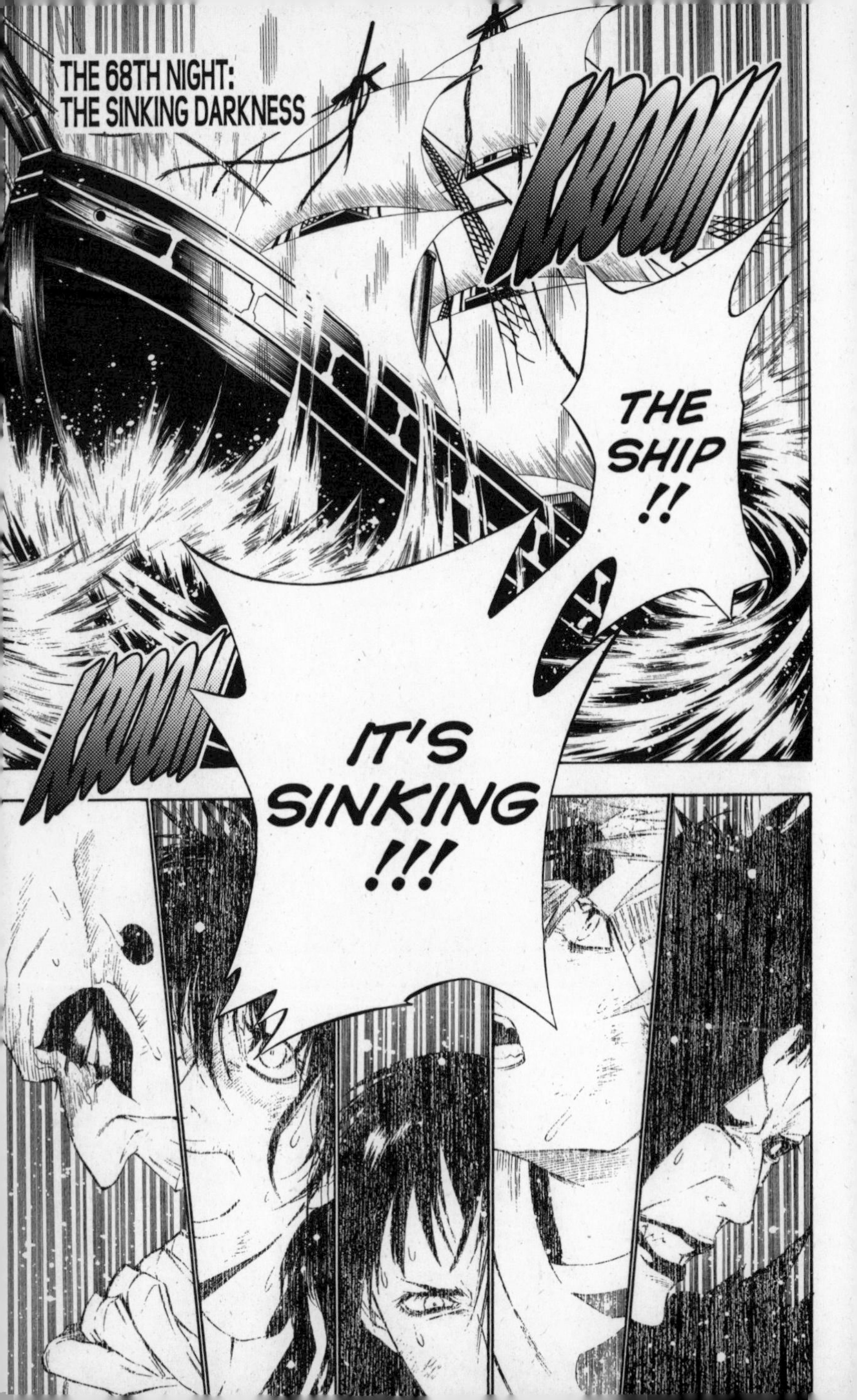
THE SHIP !!
IT'S SINKING !!!

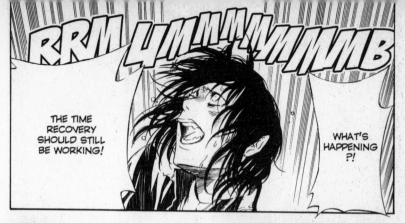

RRM UMMMMMMMMB
WHAT'S HAPPENING ?!
THE TIME RECOVERY SHOULD STILL BE WORKING!
?!
WHAT'S THIS?
OW!
BZAKK
OH, NO...

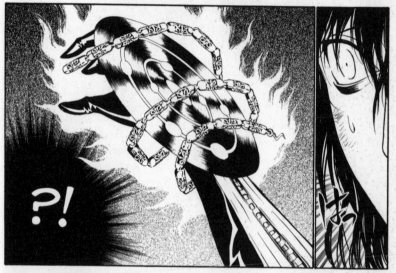

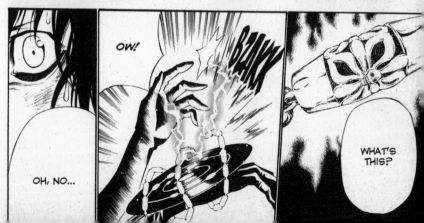

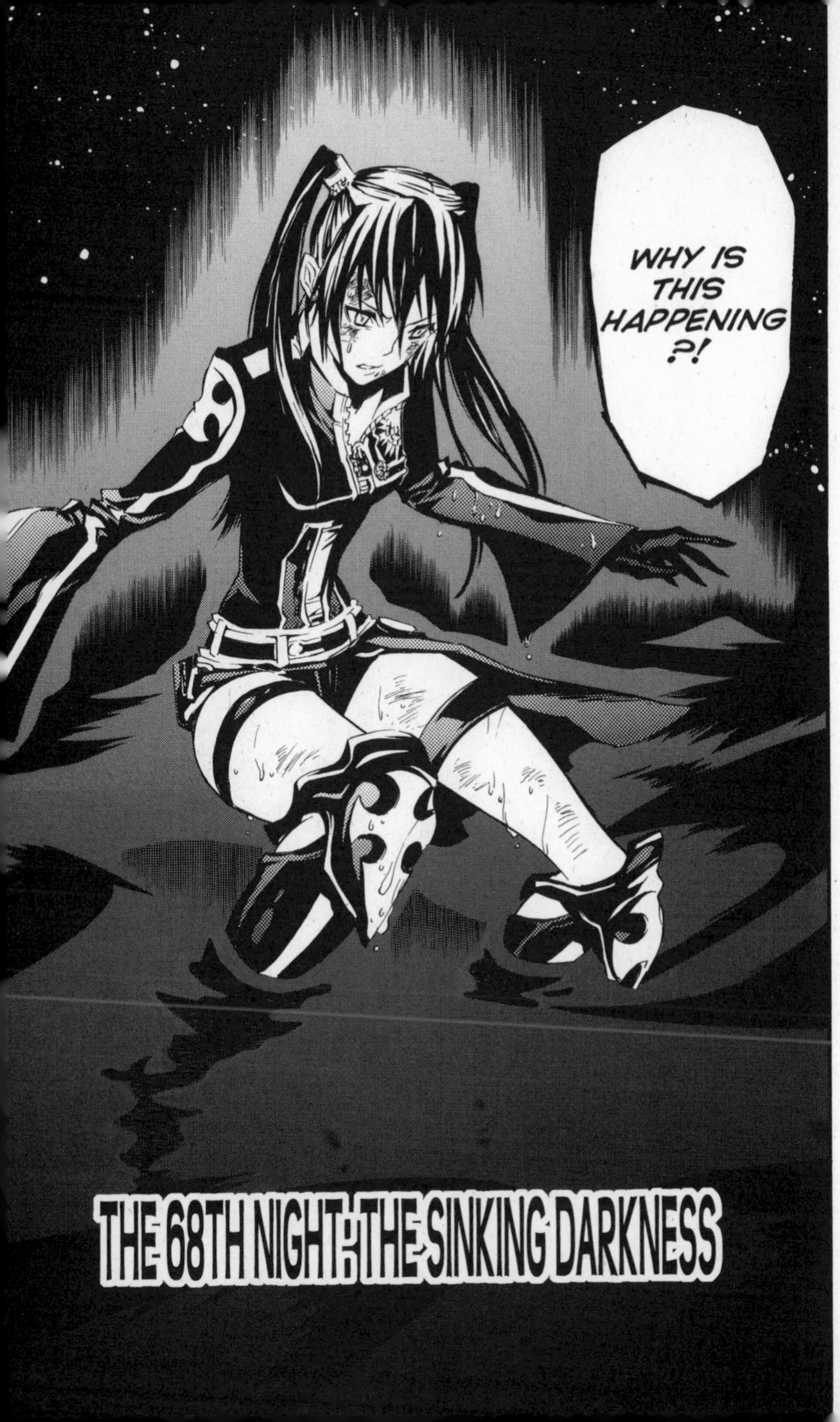
WHY IS THIS HAPPENING ?!

THE 68TH NIGHT: THE SINKING DARKNESS

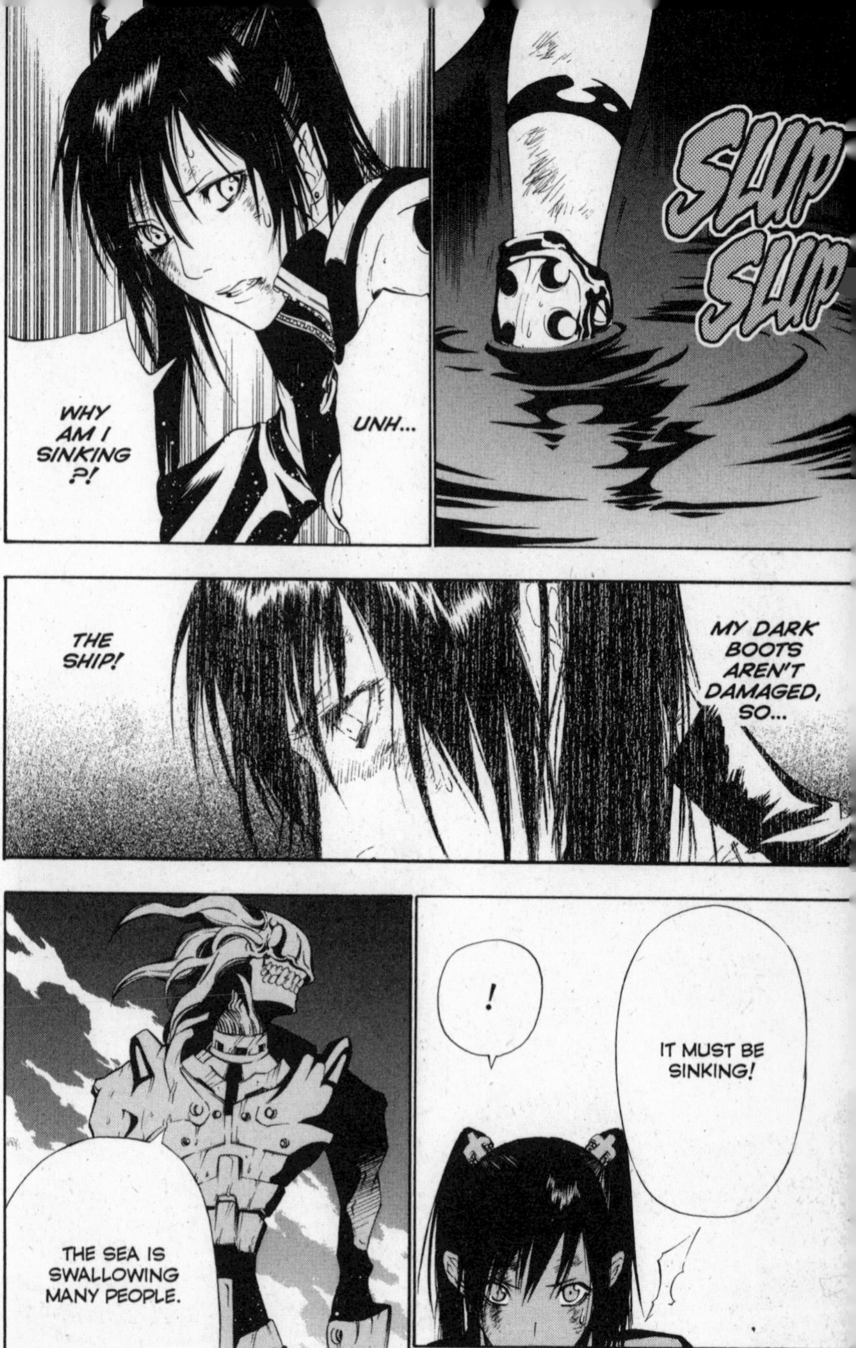
SLUP SLUP
UNH...
WHY AM I SINKING ?!
MY DARK BOOTS AREN'T DAMAGED, SO...
THE SHIP!
IT MUST BE SINKING!
!
THE SEA IS SWALLOWING MANY PEOPLE.

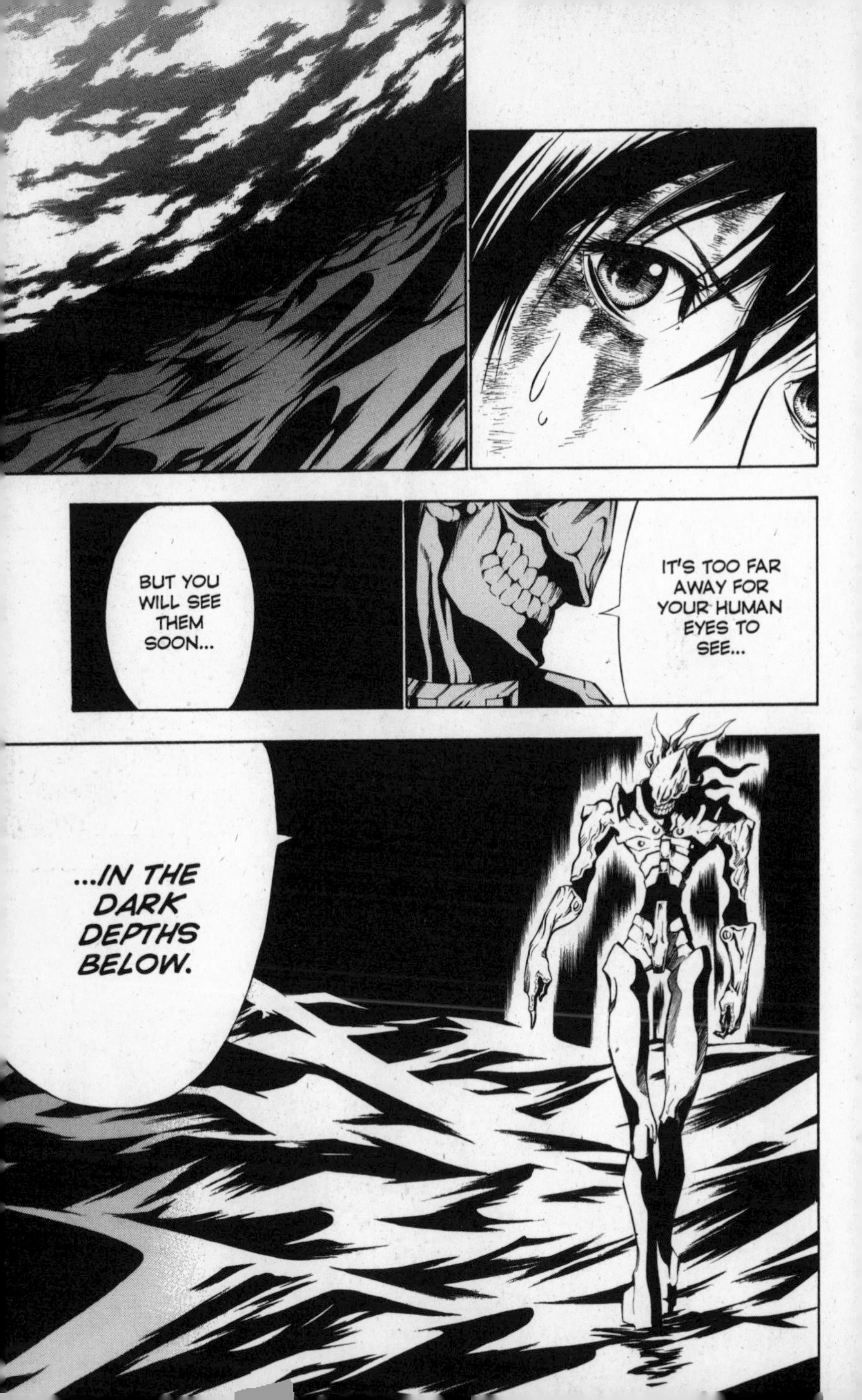
IT'S TOO FAR AWAY FOR YOUR HUMAN EYES TO SEE...
BUT YOU WILL SEE THEM SOON...
...IN THE DARK DEPTHS BELOW.

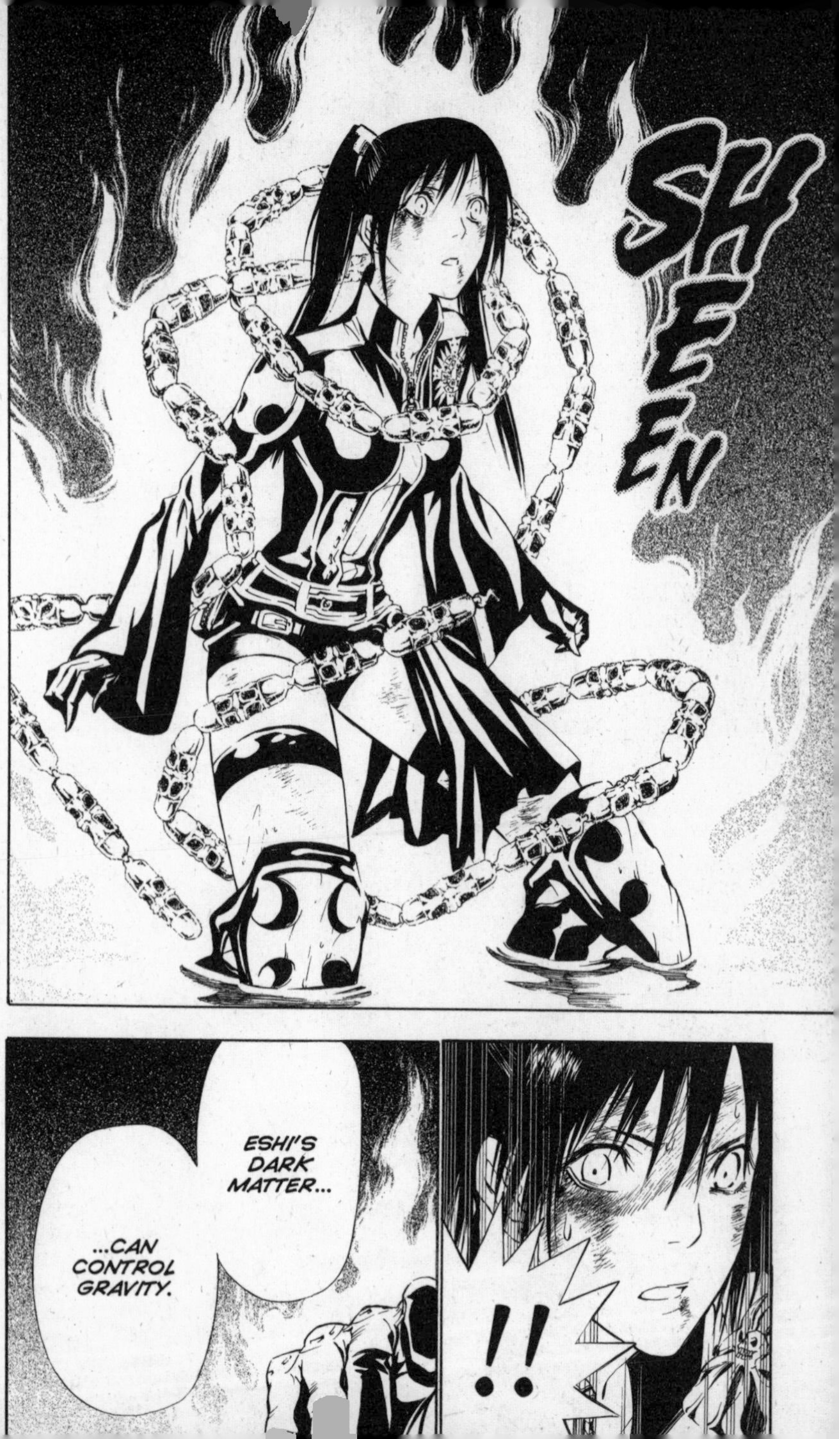
SHHEEEN
ESHI'S DARK MATTER...
...CAN CONTROL GRAVITY.
!!

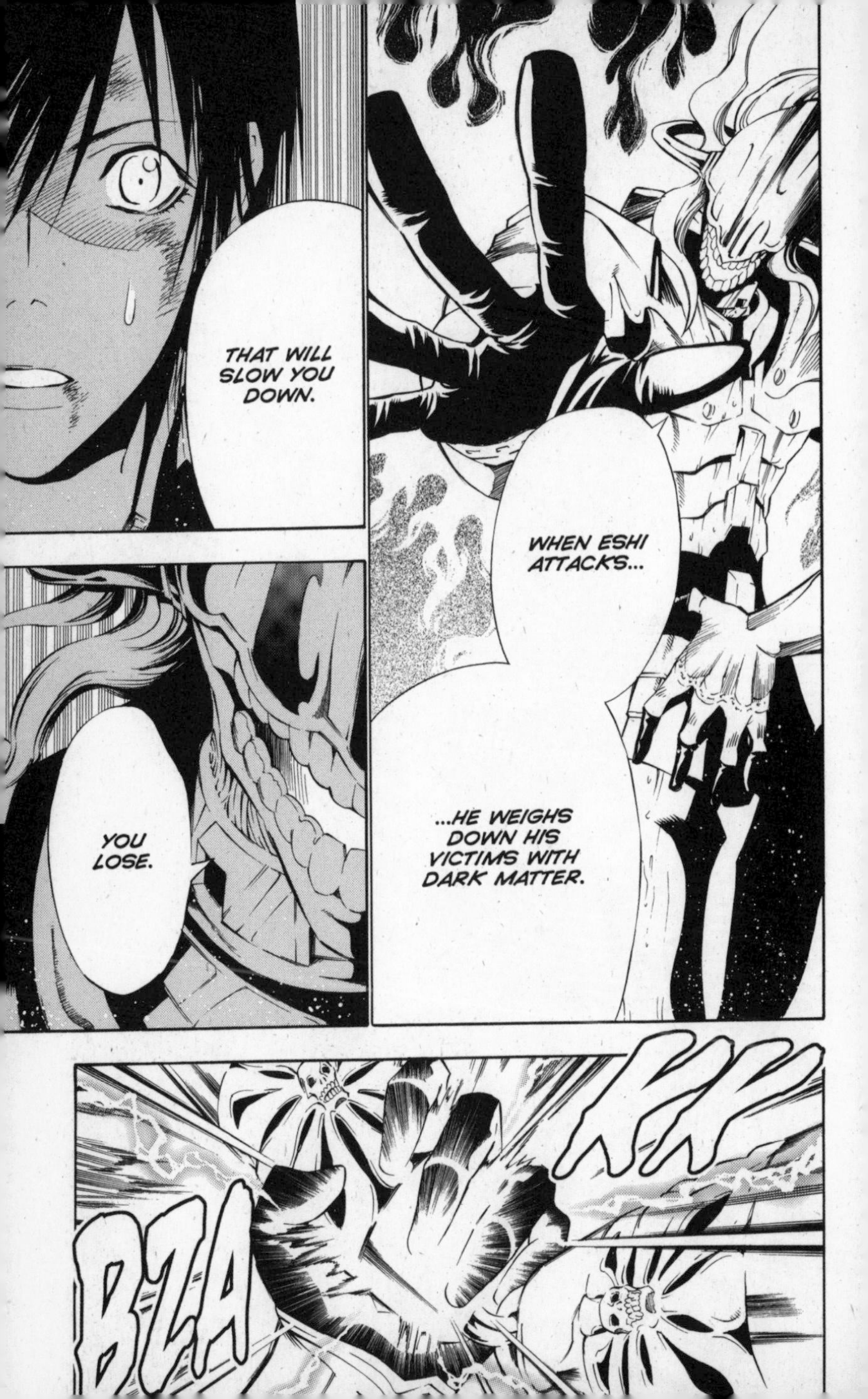
WHEN ESHI ATTACKS...
...HE WEIGHS DOWN HIS VICTIMS WITH DARK MATTER.
THAT WILL SLOW YOU DOWN.
YOU LOSE.
BZA

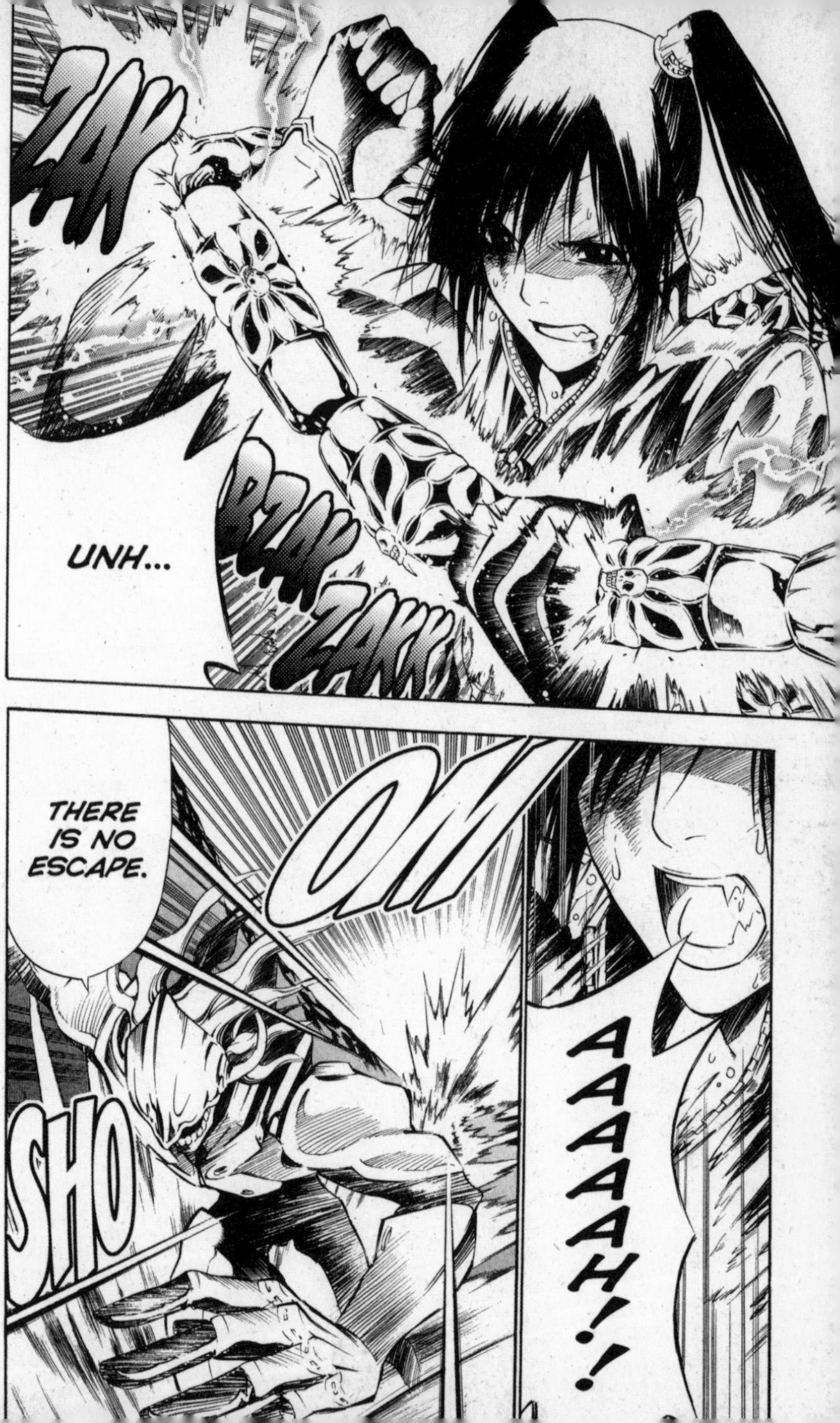
ZAK
UNH...
ZAKK
AAAAAH!!
THERE IS NO ESCAPE.
SHO

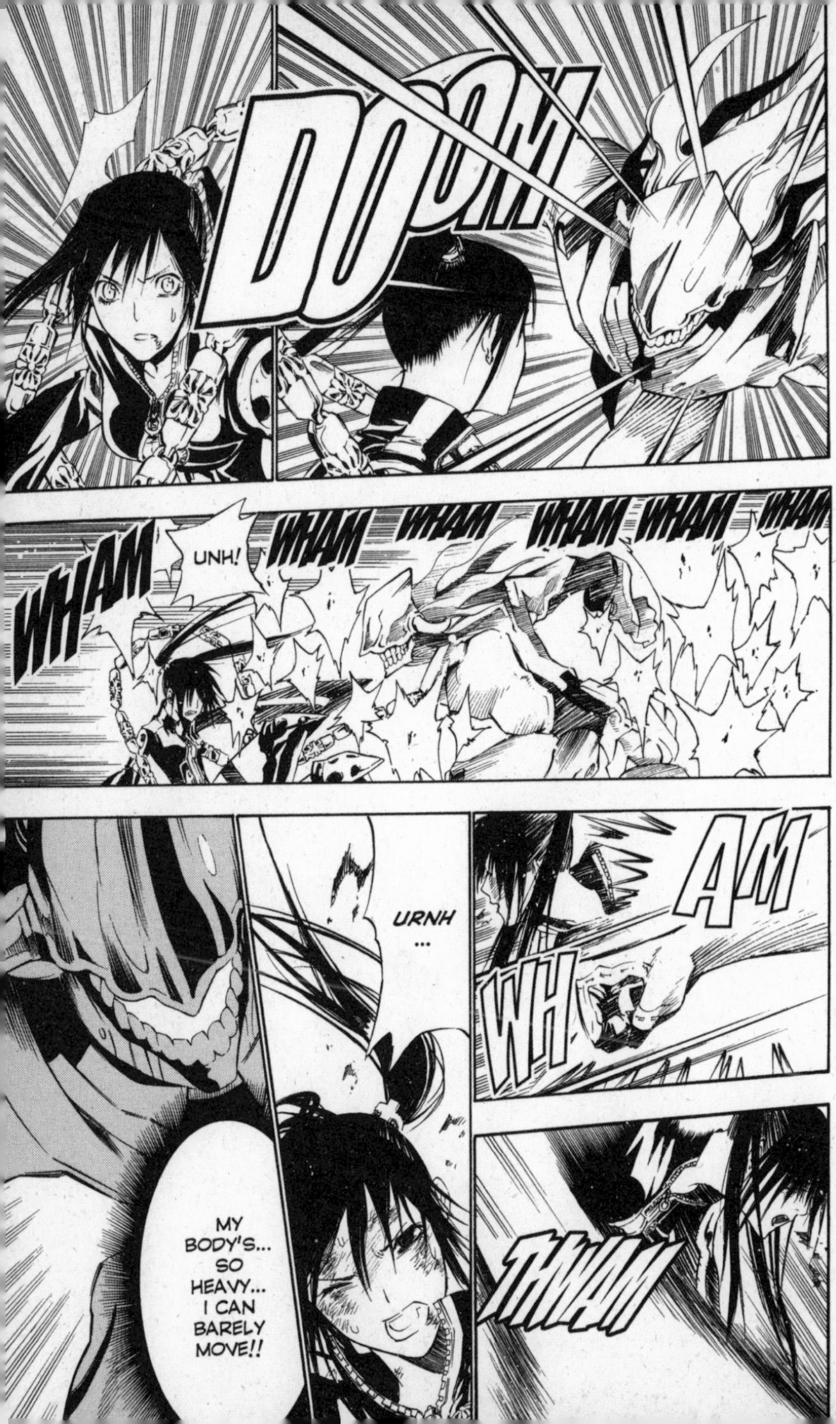
DOOM
WHAM
WHAM
WHAM
WHAM
WHAM
UNH!
WHAM
WHAM
THWAM
URNH ...
MY BODY'S... SO HEAVY... I CAN BARELY MOVE!!

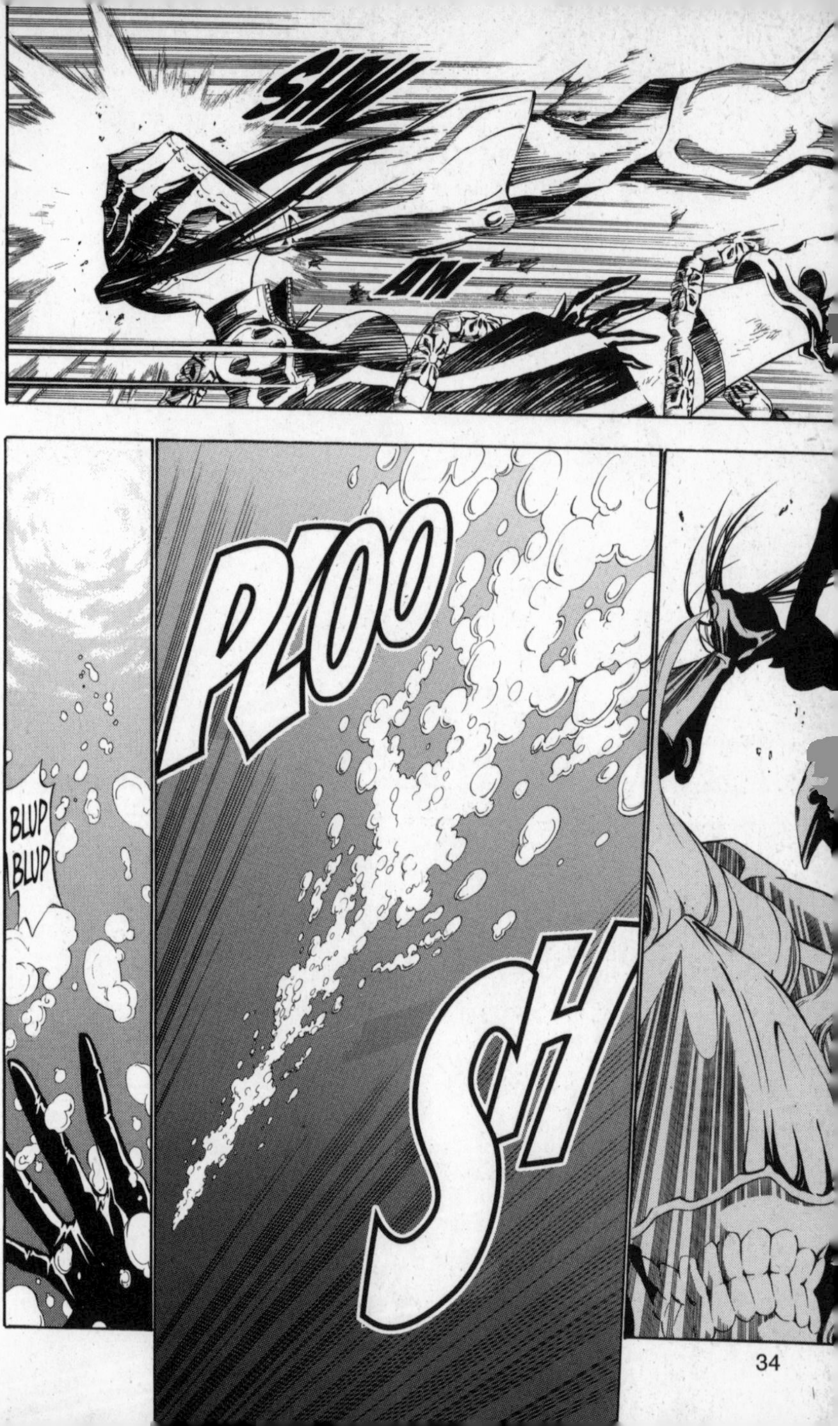
SHW
AM
PLOO
SH
BLUP BLUP

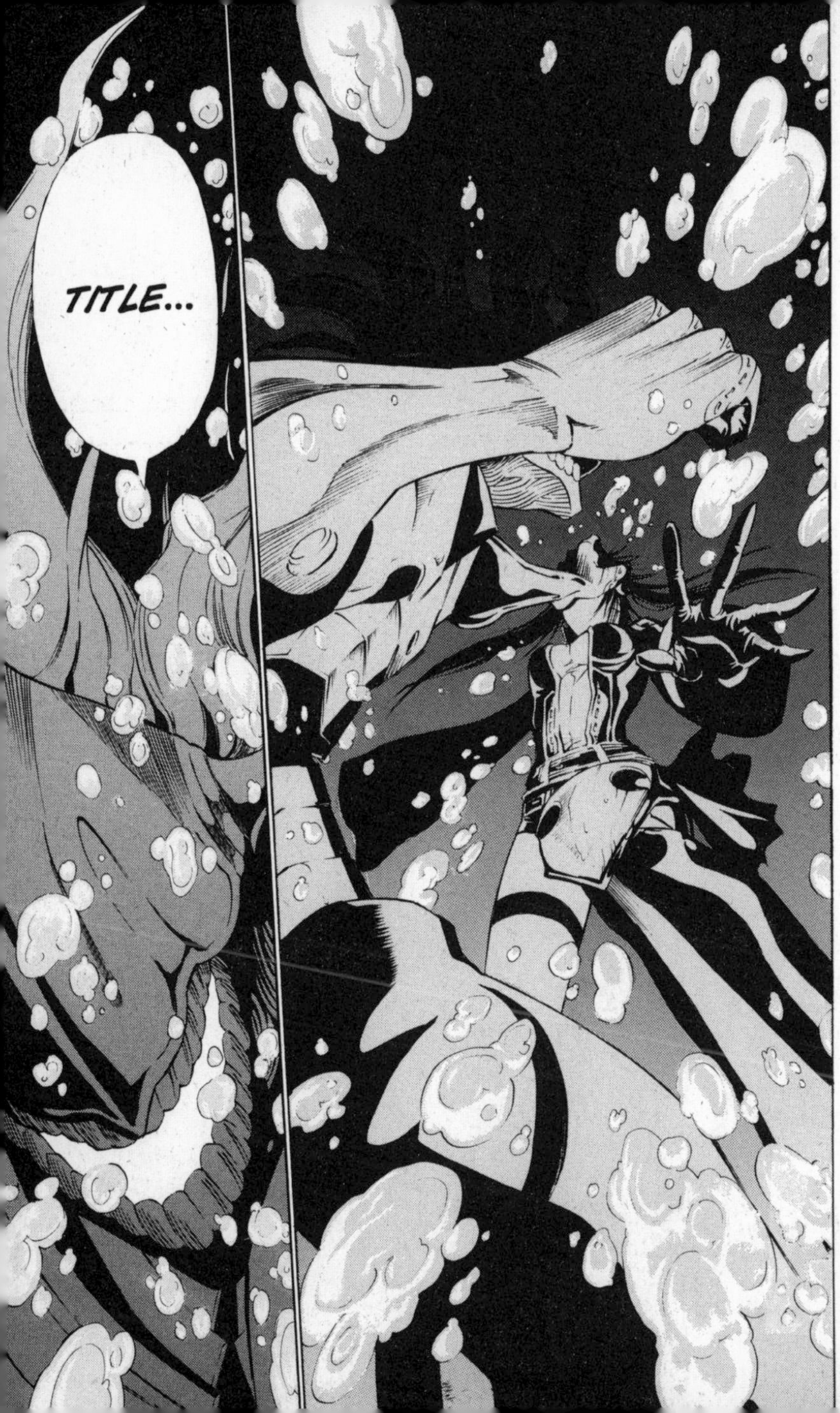
TITLE...

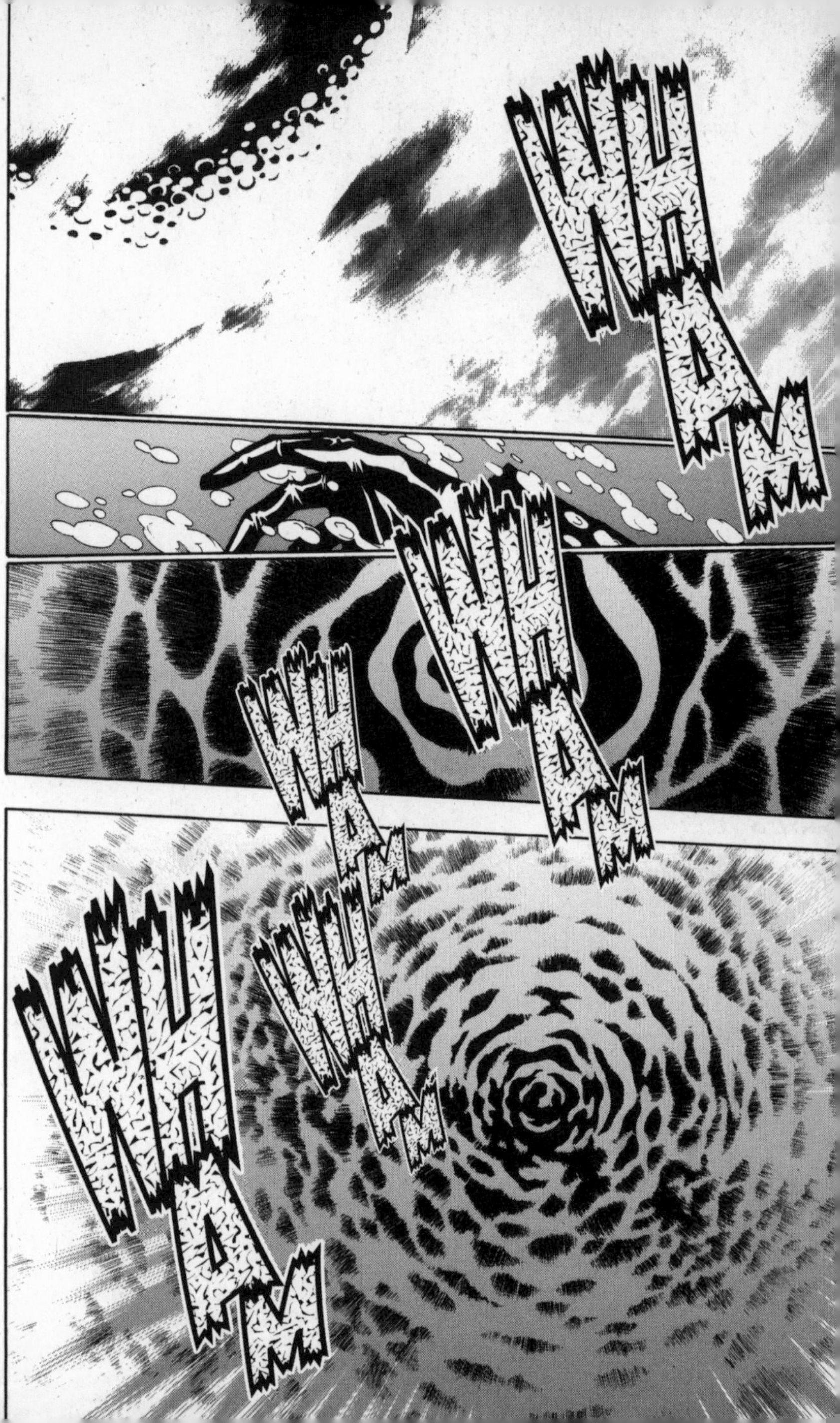
WHAM
WHAM
WHAM
WHAM
WHAM

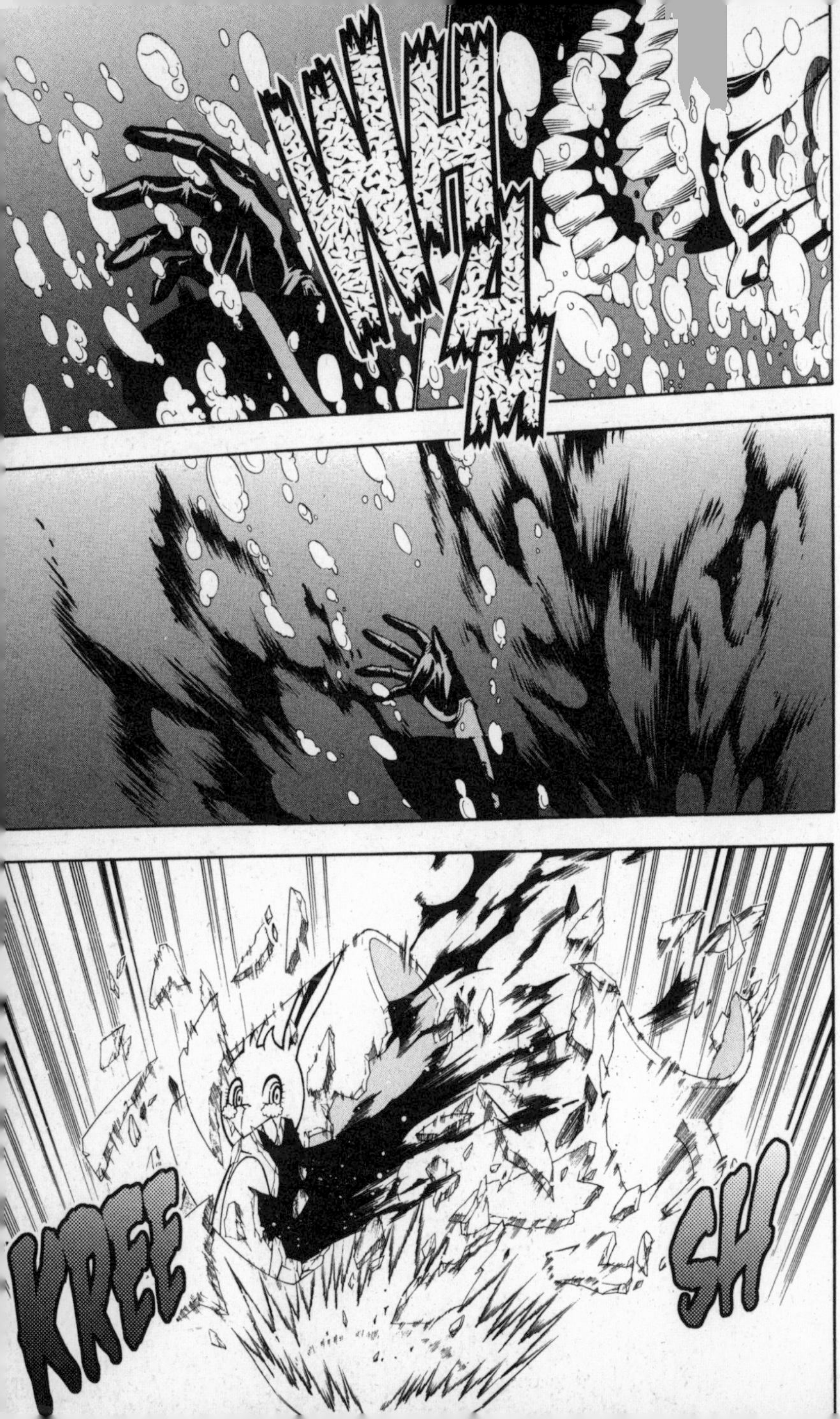
WHAM
KREESH

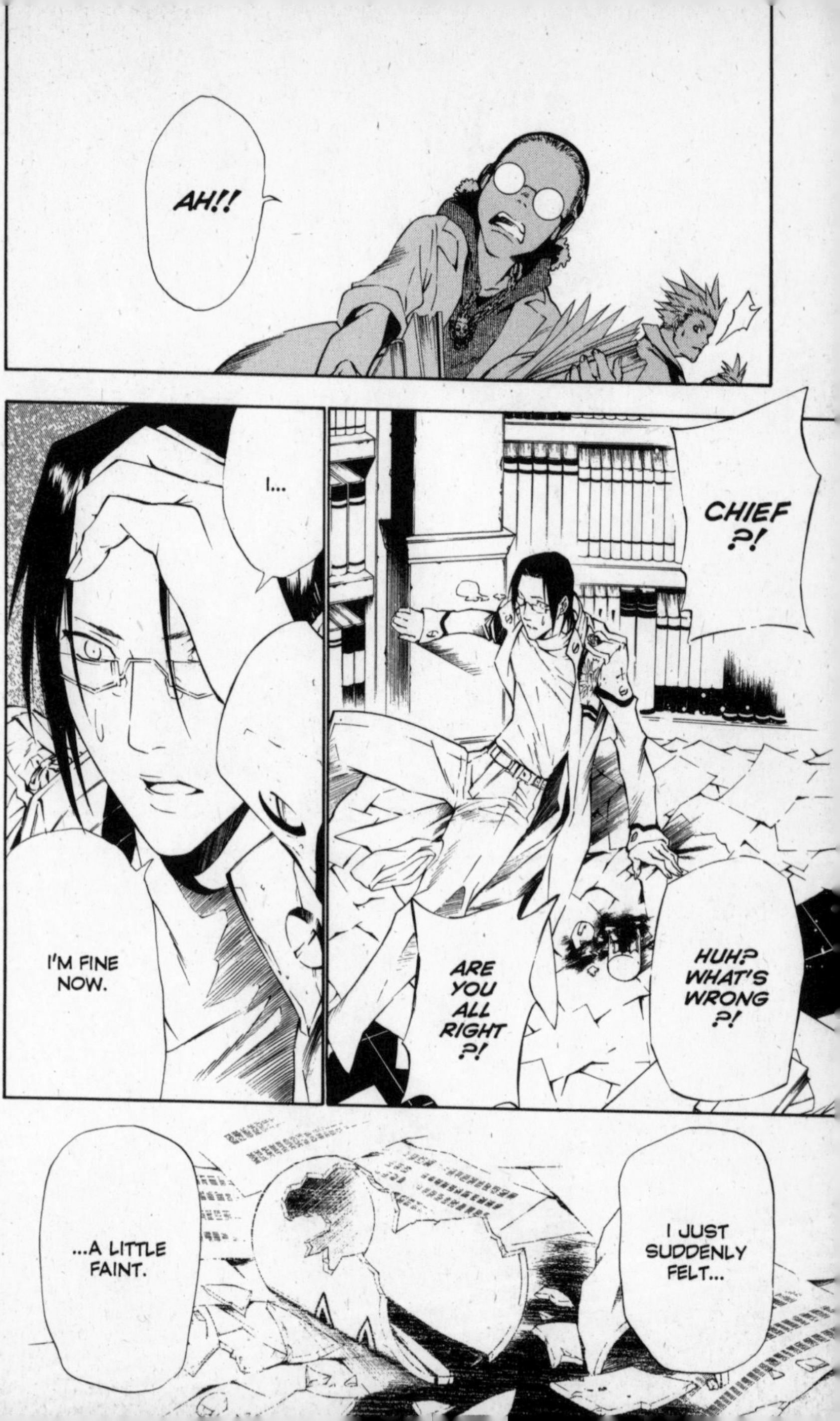
AH!!
CHIEF ?!
HUH? WHAT'S WRONG ?!
ARE YOU ALL RIGHT ?!
I...
I'M FINE NOW.
I JUST SUDDENLY FELT...
...A LITTLE FAINT.

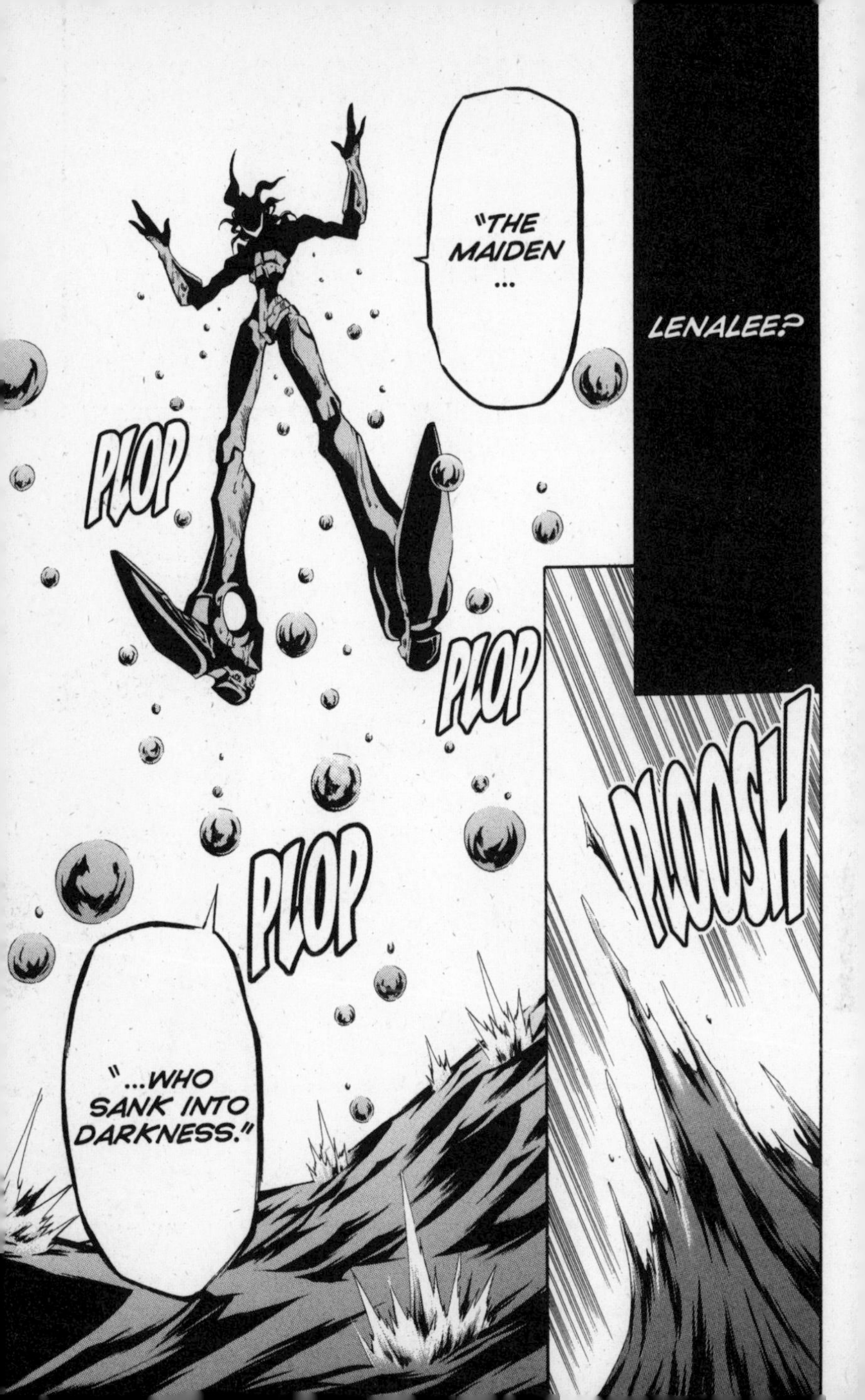
LENALEE?
PLOOSH
"THE MAIDEN ...
PLOP
PLOP
PLOP
"...WHO SANK INTO DARKNESS."

KOMUI'S DISCUSSION ROOM, VOL. 1

(KANDA) HMPH.

(ALLEN) WELL, HERE WE ARE WITH ANOTHER SEGMENT OF KOMUI'S DISCUSSION ROOM, WHICH KOMUI NEVER SHOWS UP FOR. I'M CARRYING OVER FROM VOLUME 7 AND THIS TIME I'M JOINED BY KANDA, WHO HAS HIS HAIR STYLED LIKE A GIRL'S.

(KANDA) WHAT DID YOU SAY?

(ALLEN) KANDA, I SUGGEST WE THINK OF THIS AS AN UNPLEASANT DUTY AND GET IT OVER WITH AS QUICKLY AS POSSIBLE. I DON'T LIKE THIS ANY MORE THAN YOU DO. SEE? MY HANDS ARE TREMBLING SO MUCH THAT I'M ABOUT TO SPILL MY JUICE.

(KANDA) WELL, I'M ABOUT TO SHATTER MY TEA CUP!!

(ALLEN) CALM DOWN. I'M A GENTLE STREAM OF WATER. NOTHING CAN UPSET ME...

(KANDA) YOU'RE REALLY STARTING TO IRRITATE ME.

Q: DO THE NAMES OF THE CHARACTERS HAVE ANY INTERESTING STORIES BEHIND THEM?

(ALLEN) NOT THAT I KNOW OF. THE CREATOR JUST MAKES THEM UP ON THE SPOT. HOSHINO DOESN'T EVEN REMEMBER HOW HE CAME UP WITH MY NAME. WHAT ABOUT YOU, KANDA?

(KANDA) HMPH. HE GOT MY NAME FROM THE MAIN CHARACTER OF A COMIC HE DID EARLY IN HIS CAREER THAT NEVER GOT PICKED UP.

(ALLEN) SO, BASICALLY, YOU'RE LEFTOVERS.

(KANDA) DID YOU JUST SMIRK?!

(ALLEN) OF COURSE NOT.

ZAK ZAK ZAK ZAK

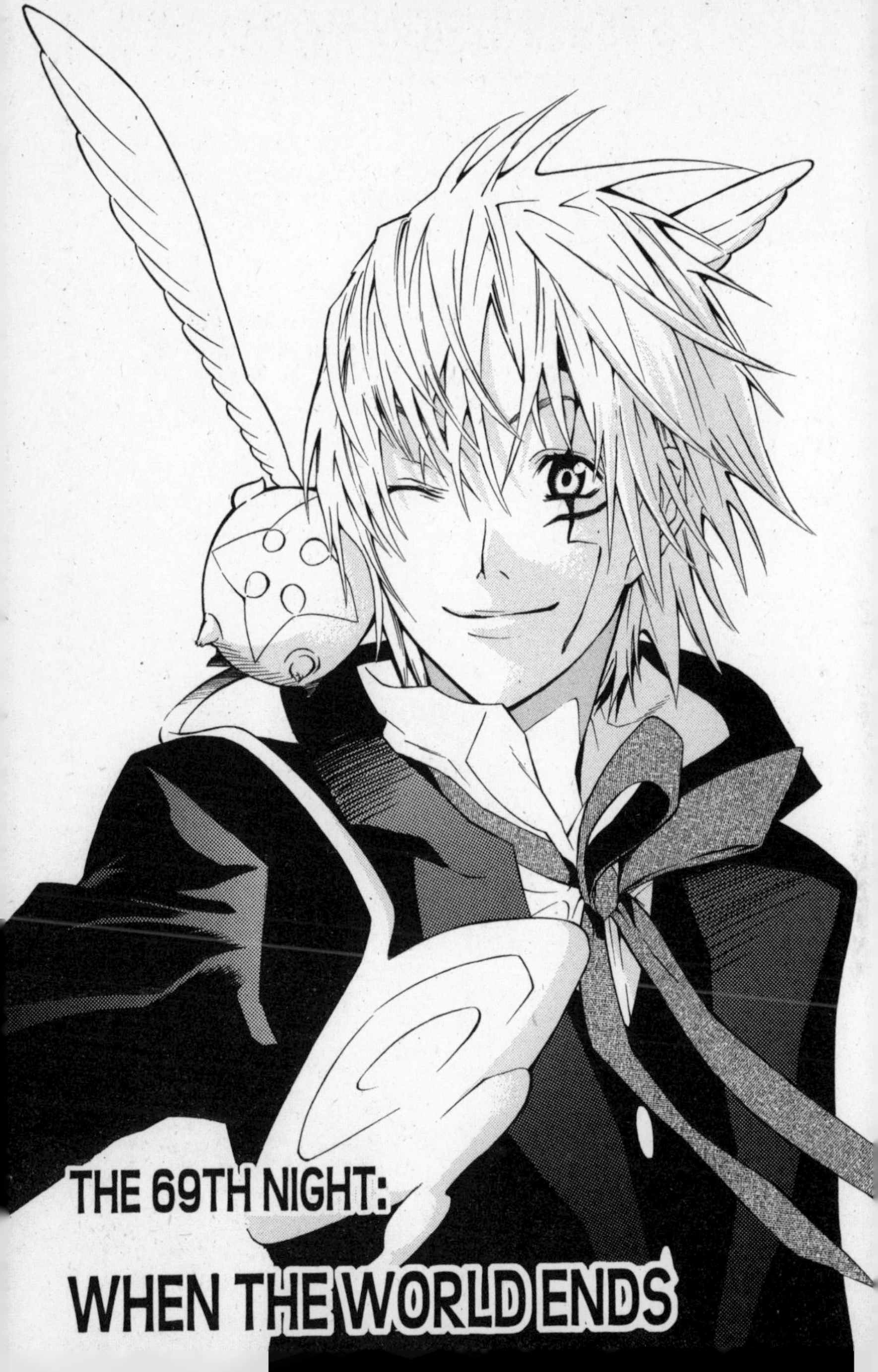
THE 69TH NIGHT:
WHEN THE WORLD ENDS

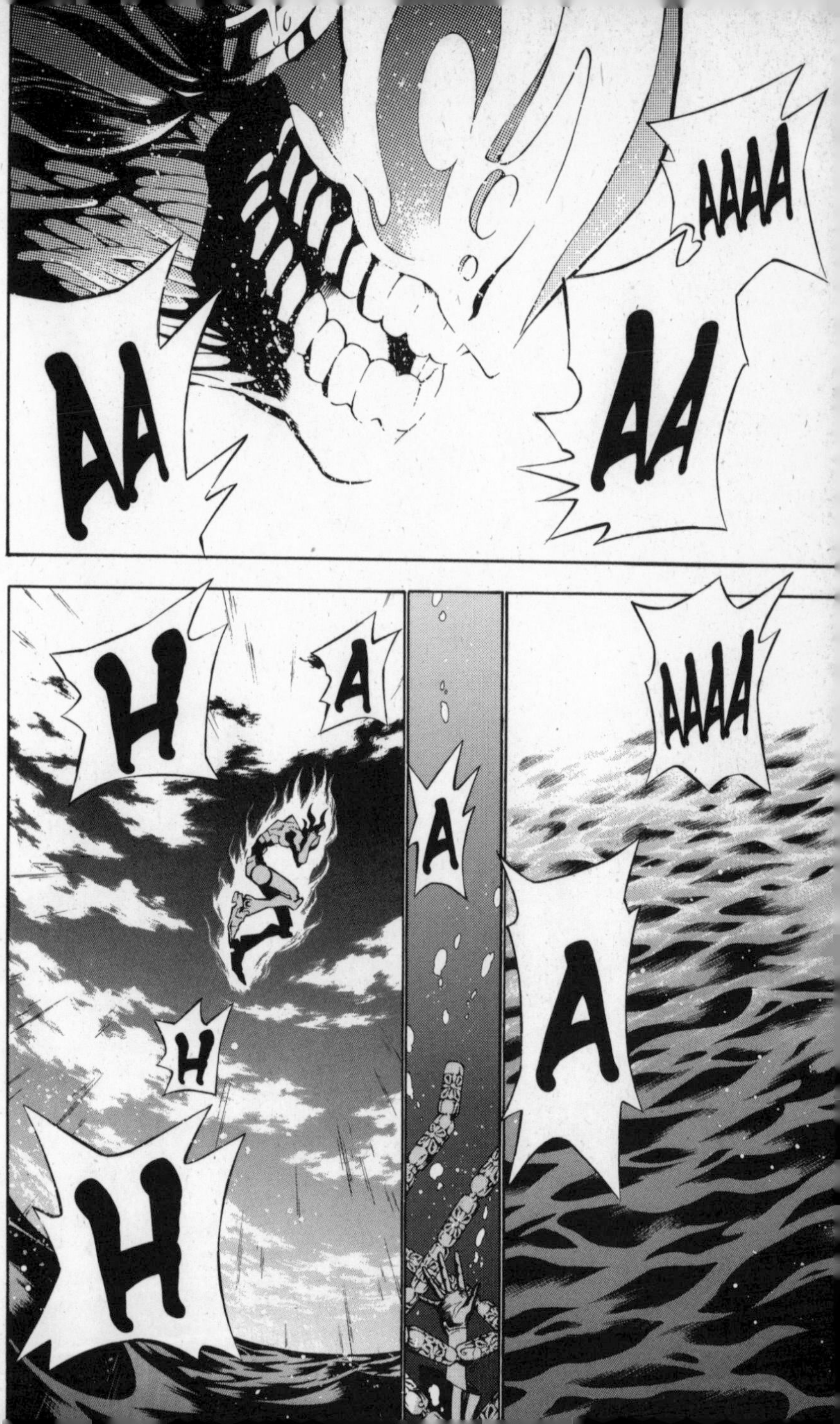
AAAA
AA
AA
AAAA
A
A
A
H
H
H

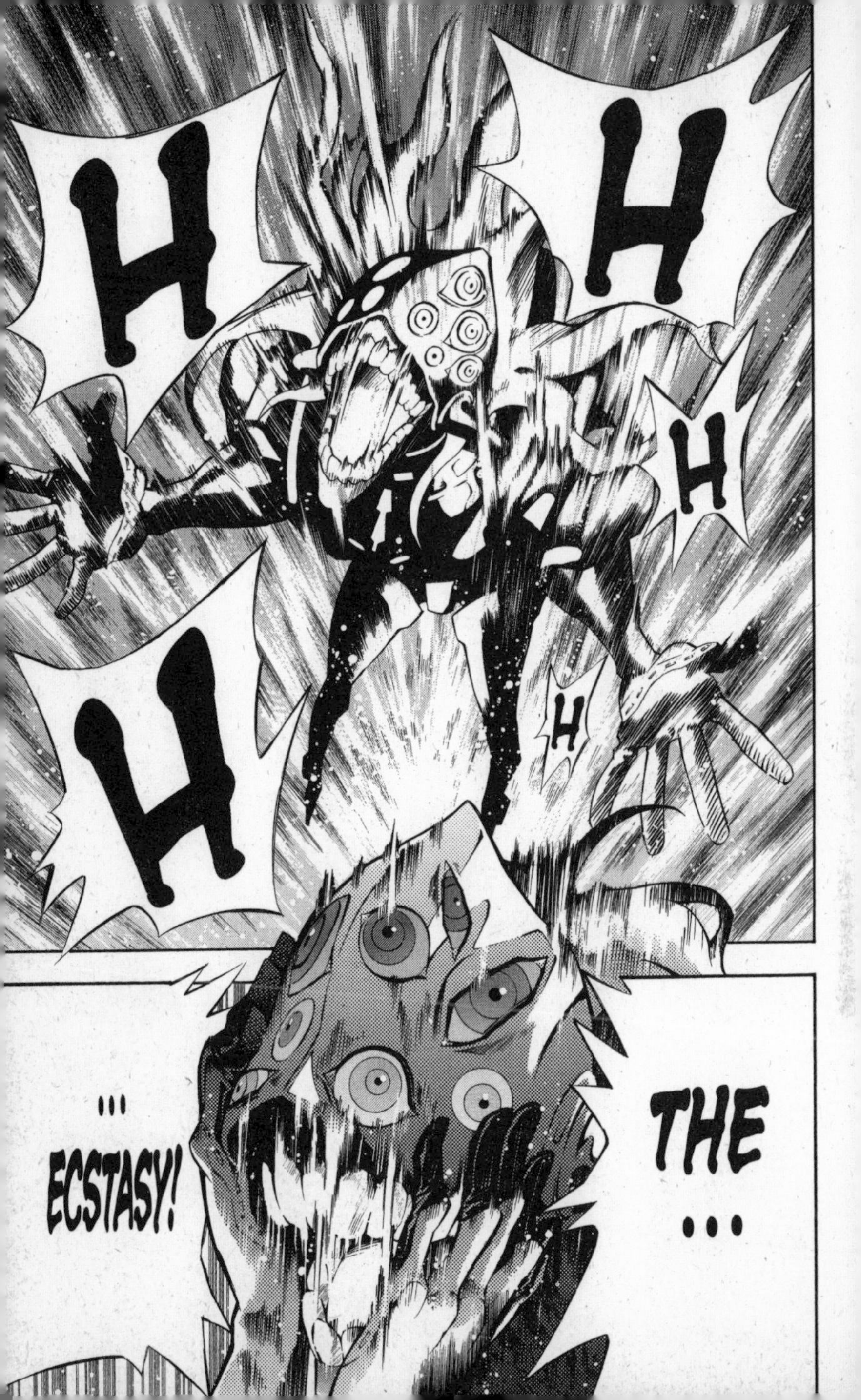
H
H
H
H
H
THE...
...ECSTASY!

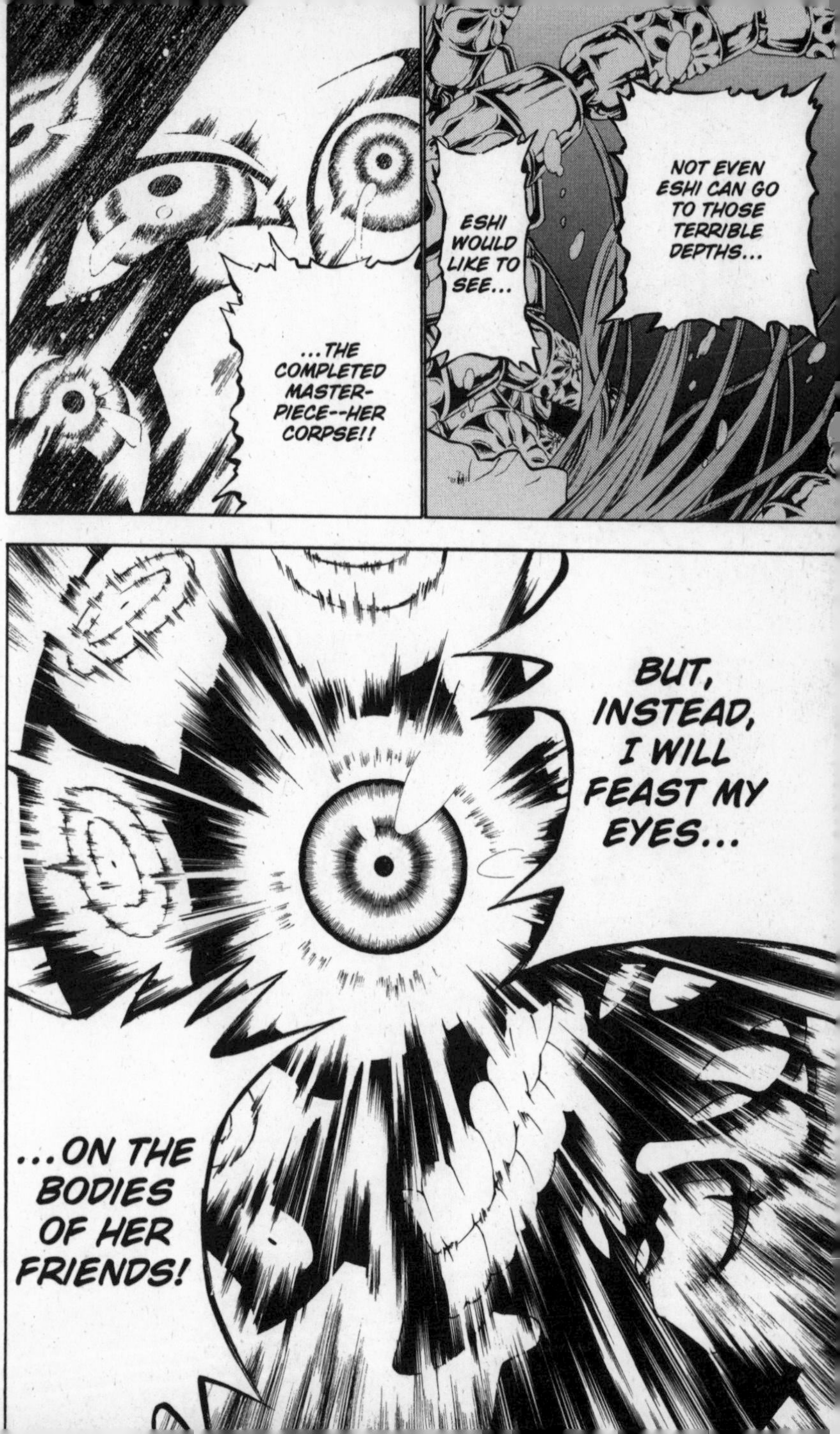
NOT EVEN ESHI CAN GO TO THOSE TERRIBLE DEPTHS...
ESHI WOULD LIKE TO SEE...
...THE COMPLETED MASTER-PIECE--HER CORPSE!!
BUT, INSTEAD, I WILL FEAST MY EYES...
...ON THE BODIES OF HER FRIENDS!

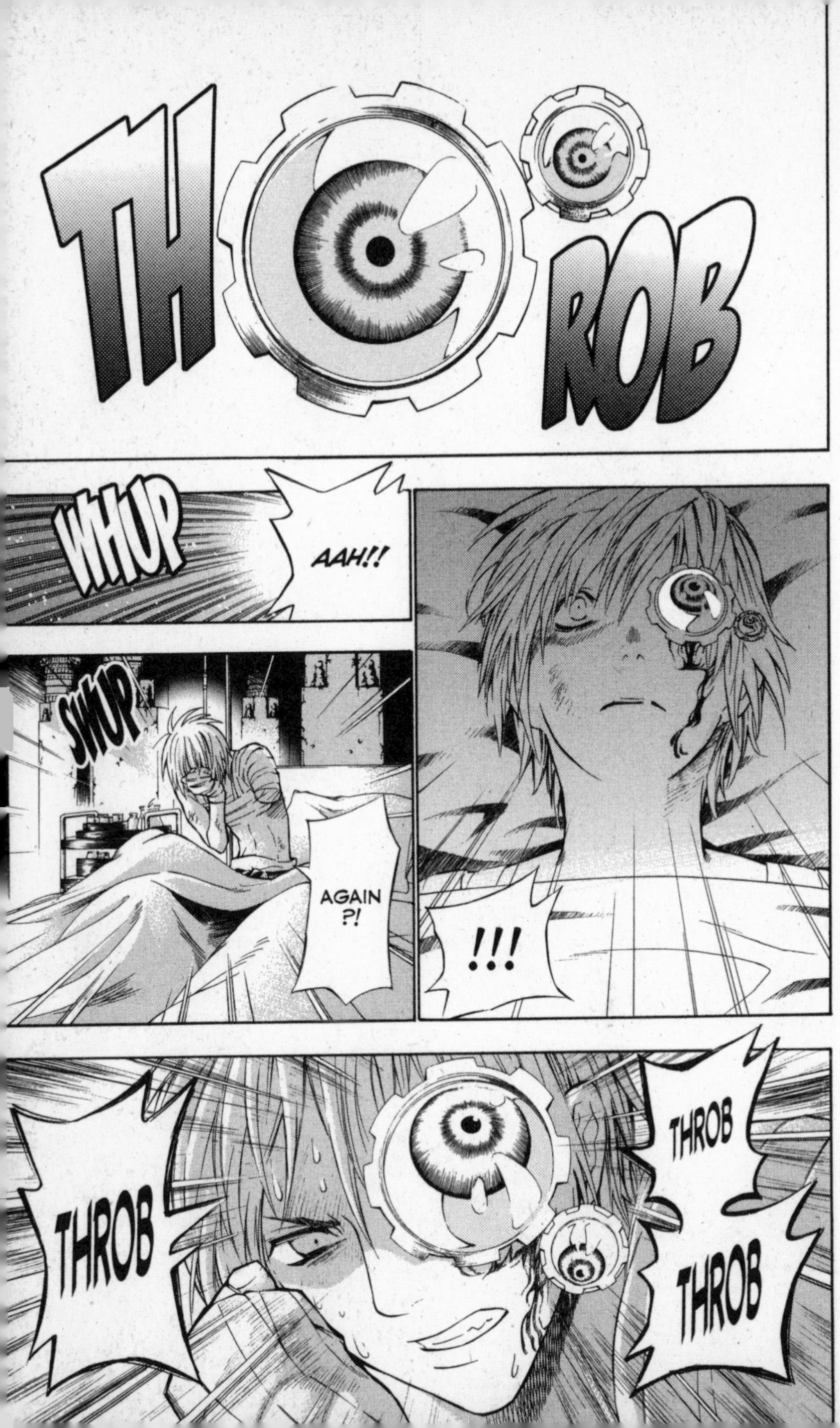
THROB
!!!
WHUP
AAH!!
SWUP
AGAIN ?!
THROB
THROB
THROB

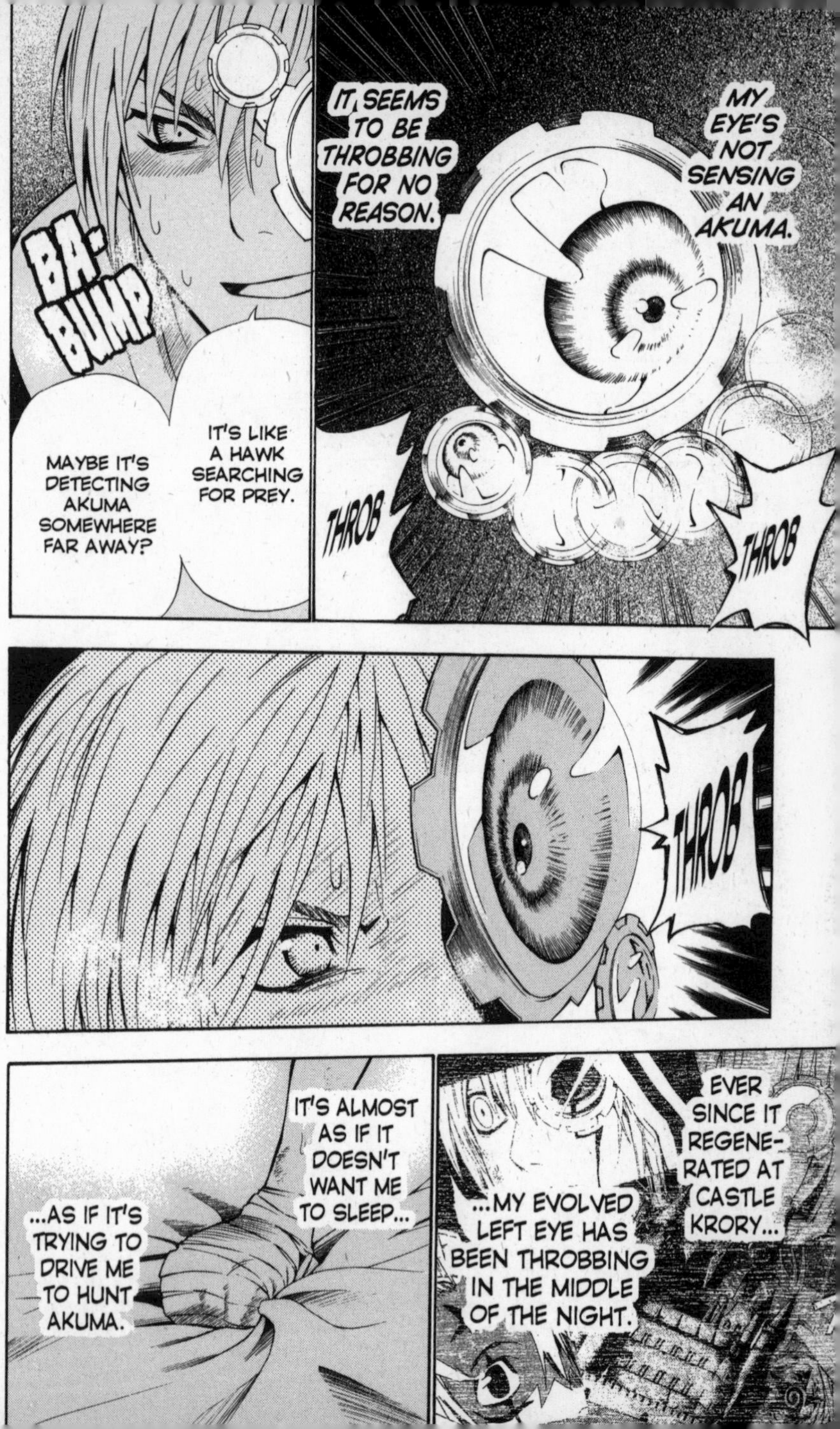
MY EYE'S NOT SENSING AN AKUMA.
IT SEEMS TO BE THROBBING FOR NO REASON.
THROB
THROB
BA-BUMP
IT'S LIKE A HAWK SEARCHING FOR PREY.
MAYBE IT'S DETECTING AKUMA SOMEWHERE FAR AWAY?
THROB
EVER SINCE IT REGENE-RATED AT CASTLE KRORY...
...MY EVOLVED LEFT EYE HAS BEEN THROBBING IN THE MIDDLE OF THE NIGHT.
IT'S ALMOST AS IF IT DOESN'T WANT ME TO SLEEP...
...AS IF IT'S TRYING TO DRIVE ME TO HUNT AKUMA.

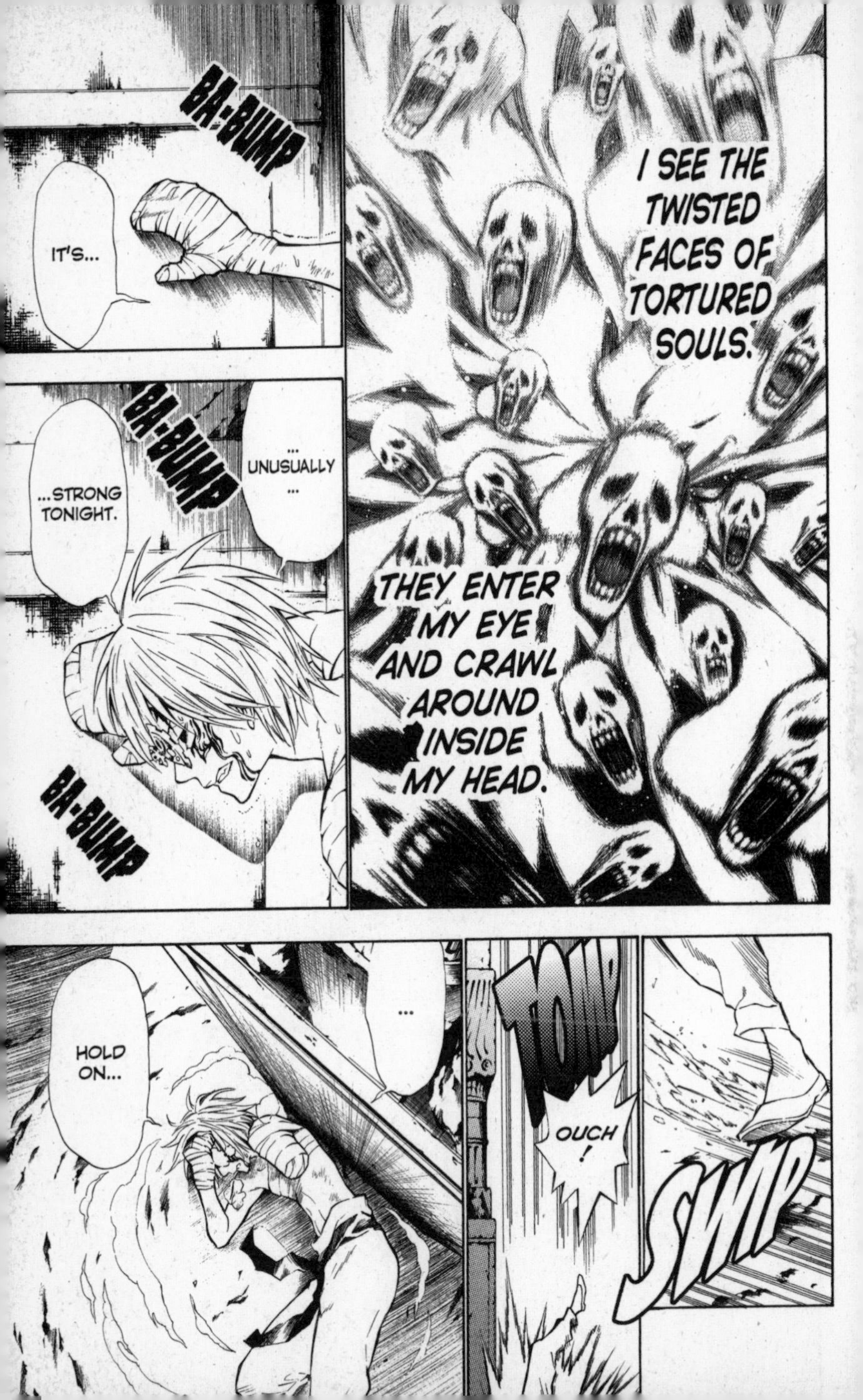
I SEE THE TWISTED FACES OF TORTURED SOULS.
THEY ENTER MY EYE AND CRAWL AROUND INSIDE MY HEAD.
BA-BUMP
IT'S...
BA-BUMP
...UNUSUALLY...
...STRONG TONIGHT.
BA-BUMP
SWIP
OUCH!
...
HOLD ON...

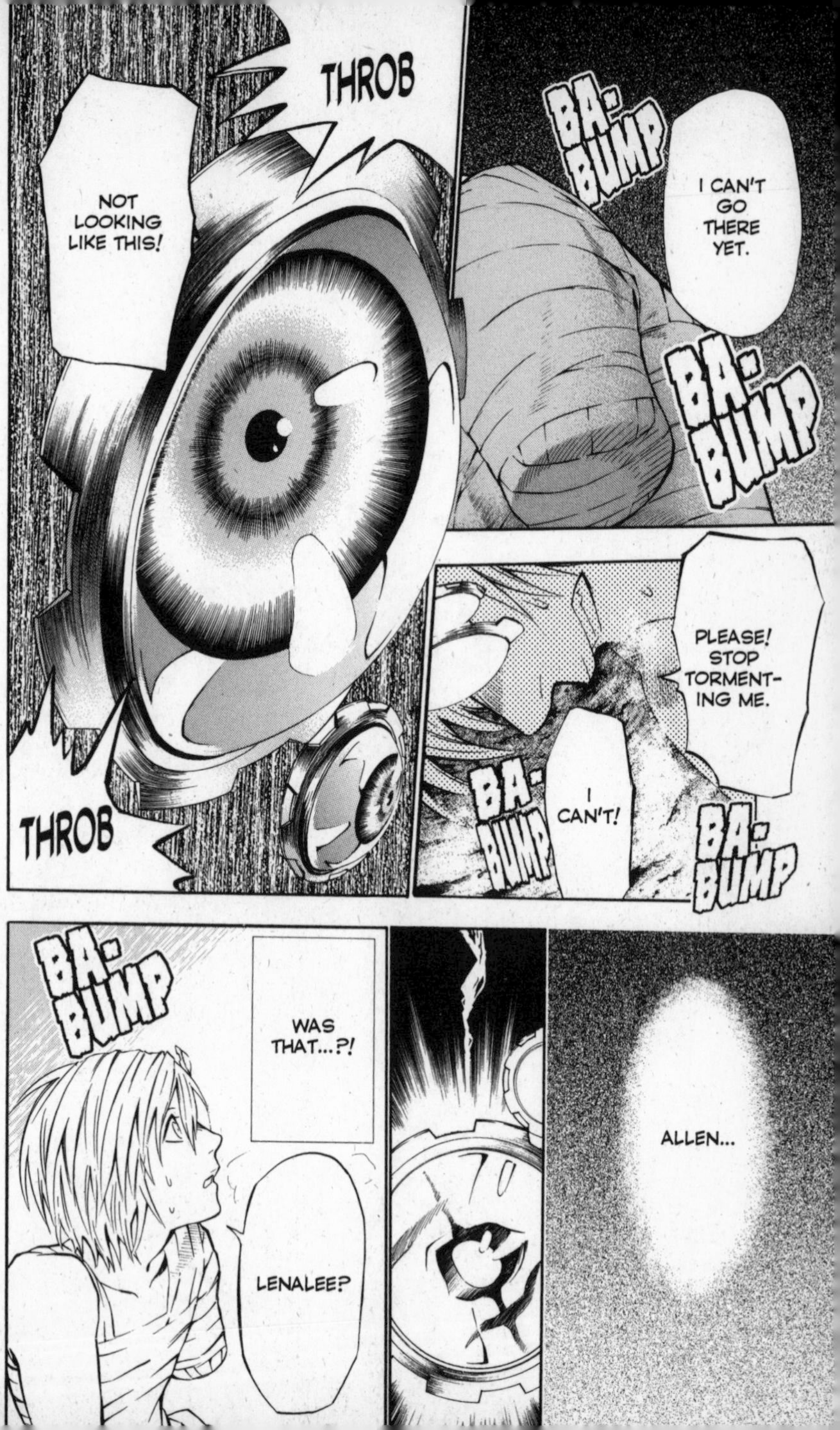
BA-BUMP
I CAN'T GO THERE YET.
BA-BUMP
PLEASE! STOP TORMENT-ING ME.
BA-BUMP
I CAN'T!
BA-BUMP
THROB
NOT LOOKING LIKE THIS!
THROB
ALLEN...
BA-BUMP
WAS THAT...?!
LENALEE?

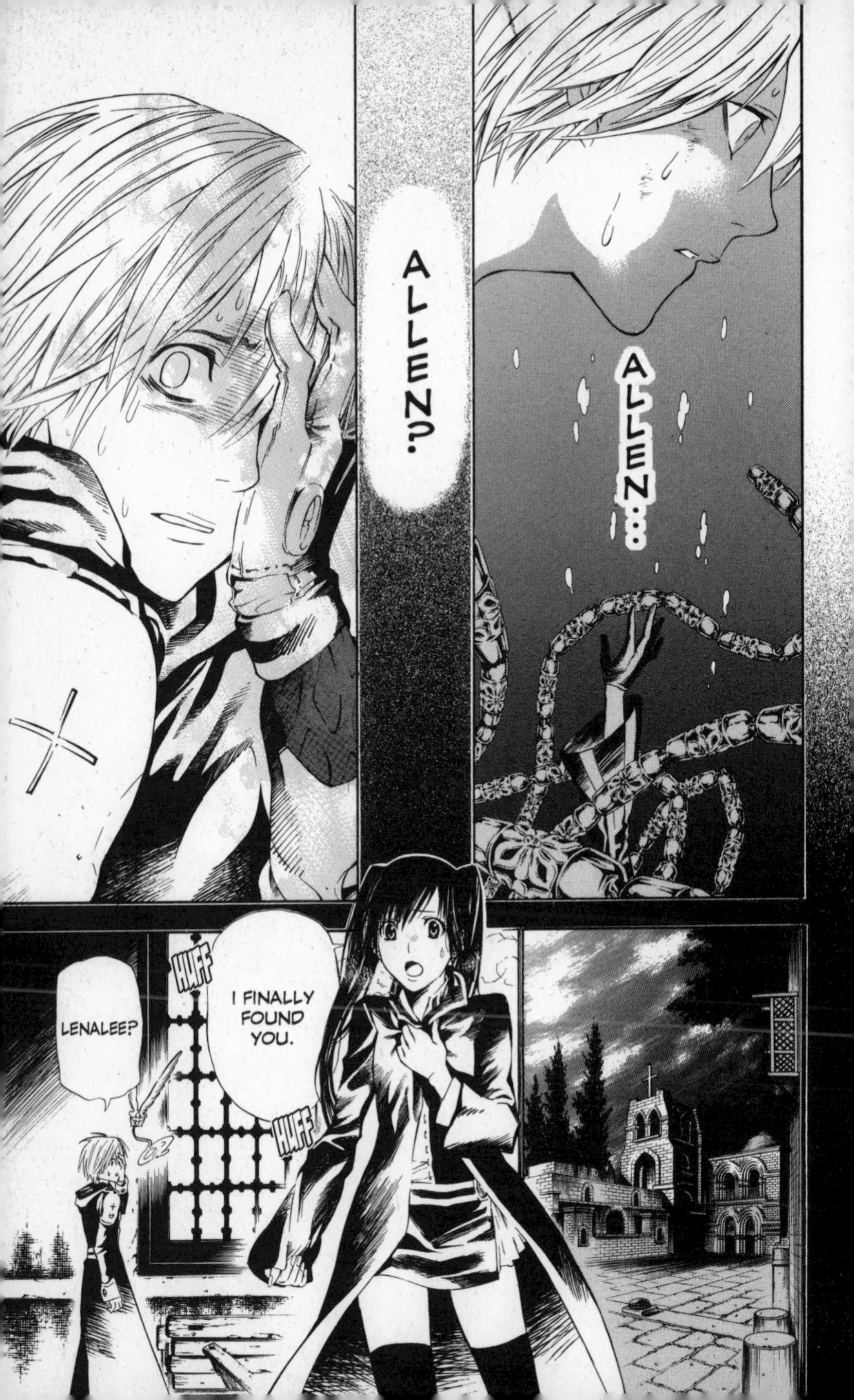
ALLEN...
ALLEN?
I FINALLY FOUND YOU.
HUFF
HUFF
LENALEE?

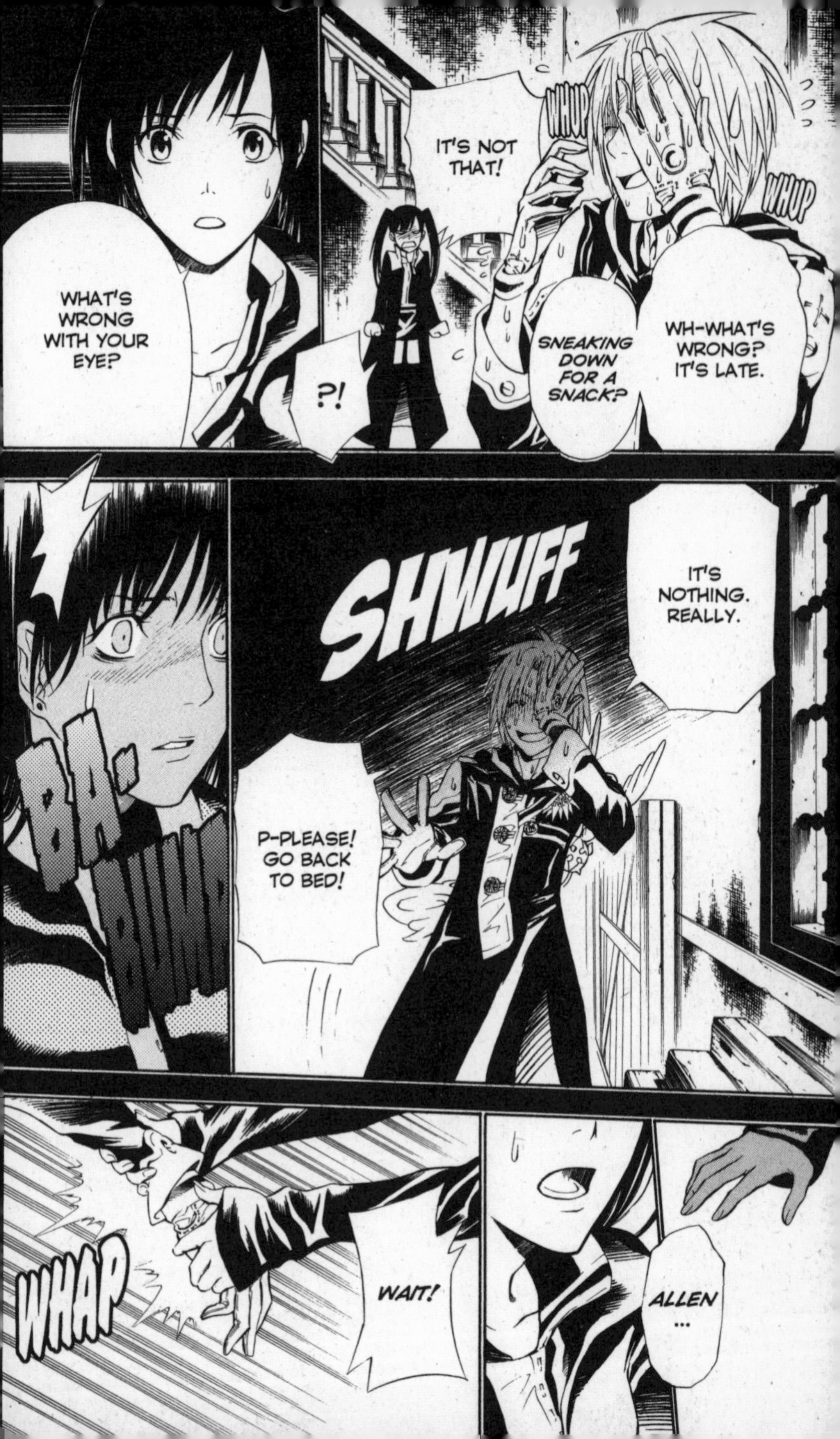
WHUP
WHUP
WH-WHAT'S WRONG? IT'S LATE.
SNEAKING DOWN FOR A SNACK?
IT'S NOT THAT!
?!
WHAT'S WRONG WITH YOUR EYE?
IT'S NOTHING. REALLY.
SHWUFF
P-PLEASE! GO BACK TO BED!
ALLEN ...
WAIT!
WHAP

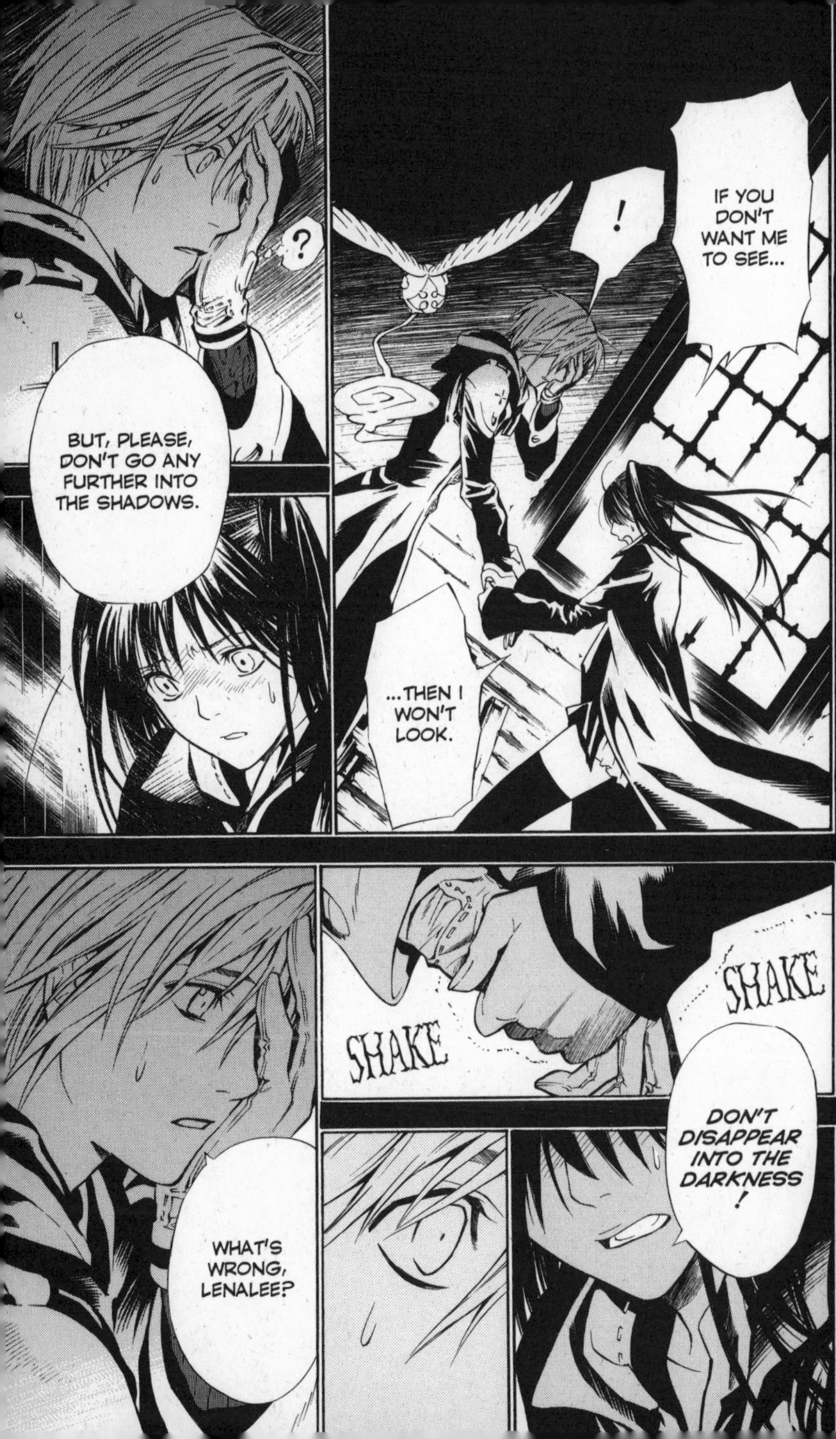
IF YOU DON'T WANT ME TO SEE...
!
...THEN I WON'T LOOK.
?
BUT, PLEASE, DON'T GO ANY FURTHER INTO THE SHADOWS.
SHAKE
SHAKE
DON'T DISAPPEAR INTO THE DARKNESS!
WHAT'S WRONG, LENALEE?

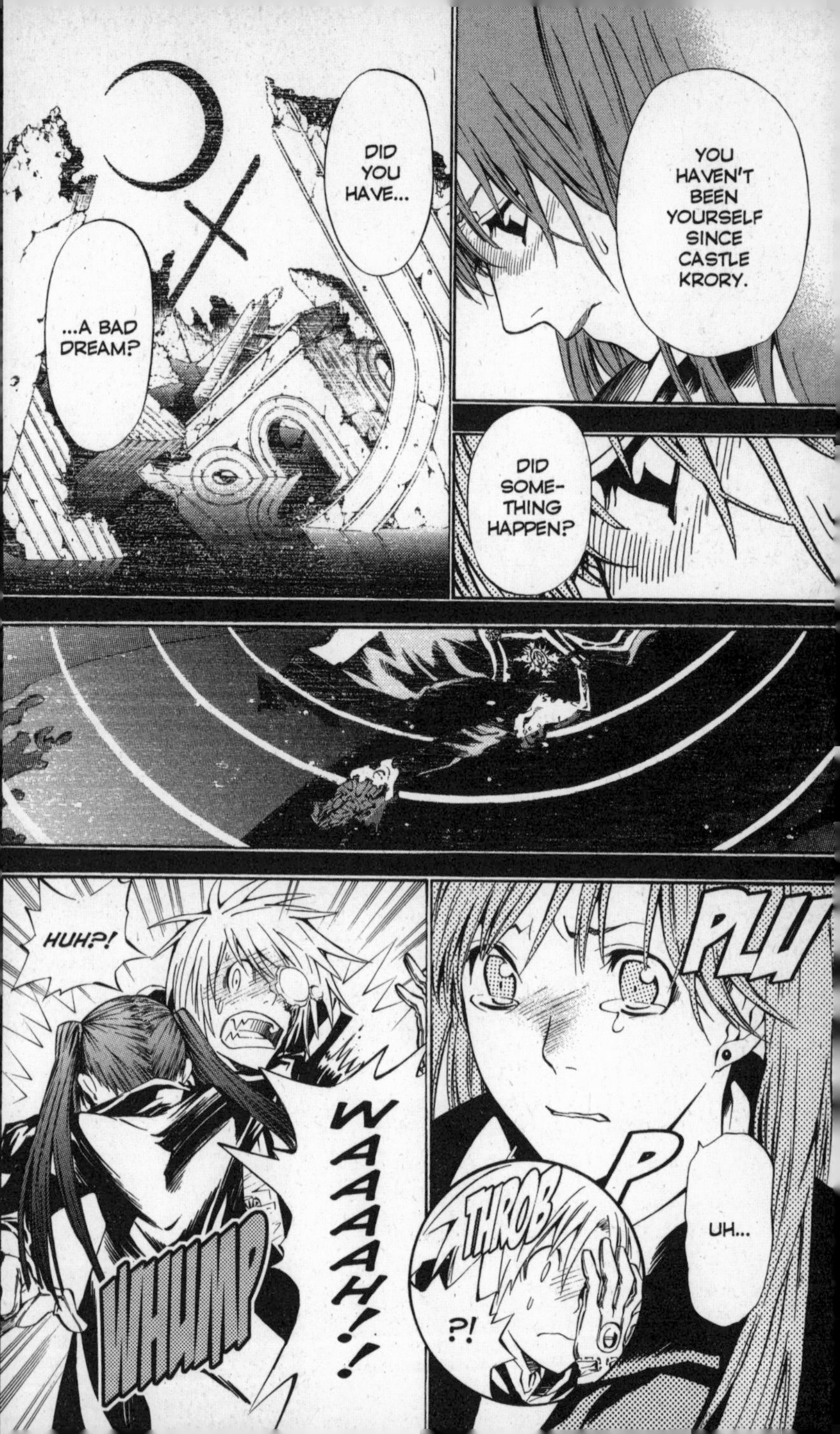
YOU HAVEN'T BEEN YOURSELF SINCE CASTLE KRORY.
DID SOME-THING HAPPEN?
DID YOU HAVE...
...A BAD DREAM?
PLU
P
UH...
THROB
?!
HUH?!
WAAAAAH!!
WHUMP

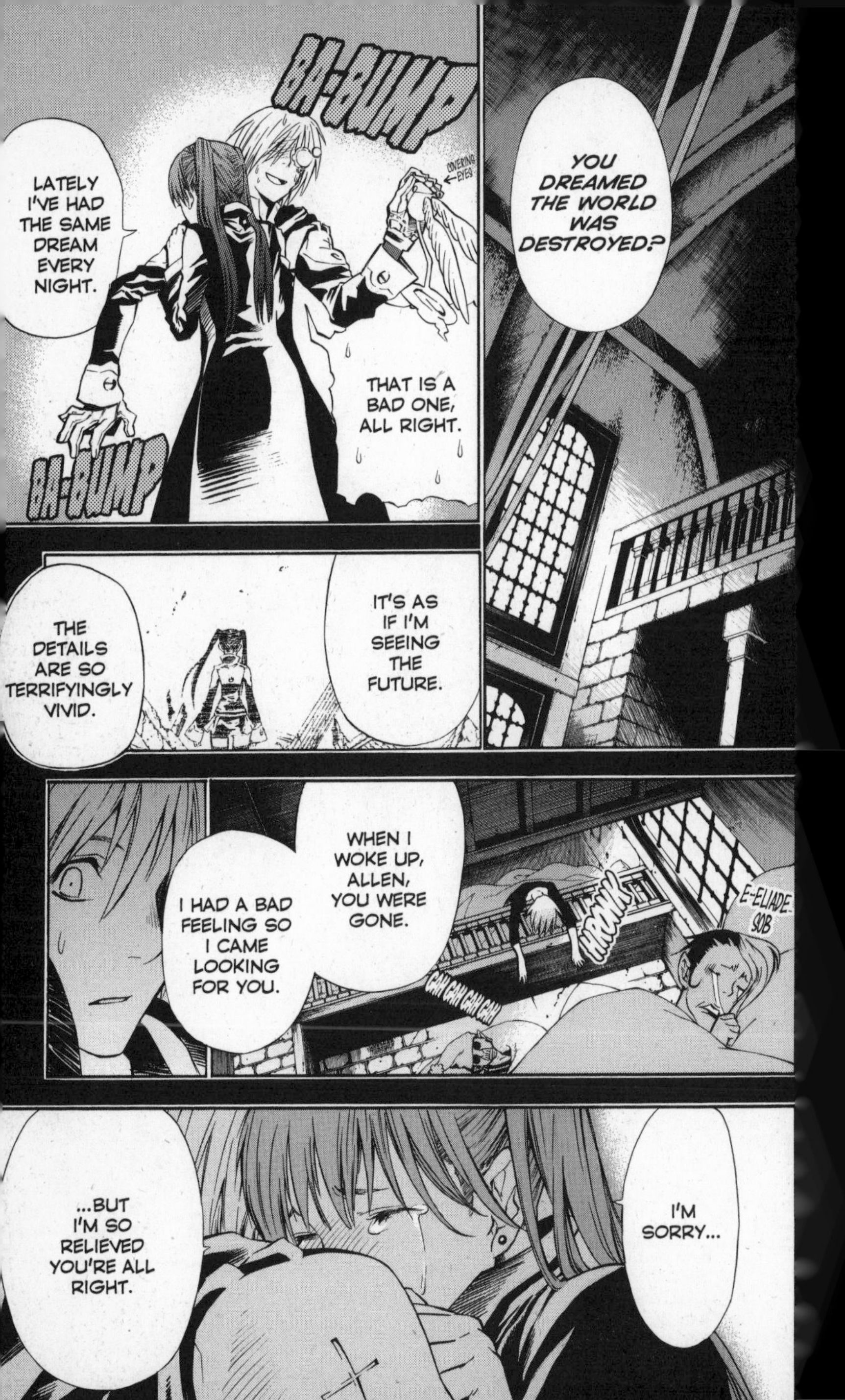
YOU DREAMED THE WORLD WAS DESTROYED?
BA-BUMP
COVERING EYES
LATELY I'VE HAD THE SAME DREAM EVERY NIGHT.
THAT IS A BAD ONE, ALL RIGHT.
BA-BUMP
IT'S AS IF I'M SEEING THE FUTURE.
THE DETAILS ARE SO TERRIFYINGLY VIVID.
E-ELIADE-
SOB
KRONK
WHEN I WOKE UP, ALLEN, YOU WERE GONE.
GAH GAH GAH GAH
I HAD A BAD FEELING SO I CAME LOOKING FOR YOU.
I'M SORRY...
...BUT I'M SO RELIEVED YOU'RE ALL RIGHT.

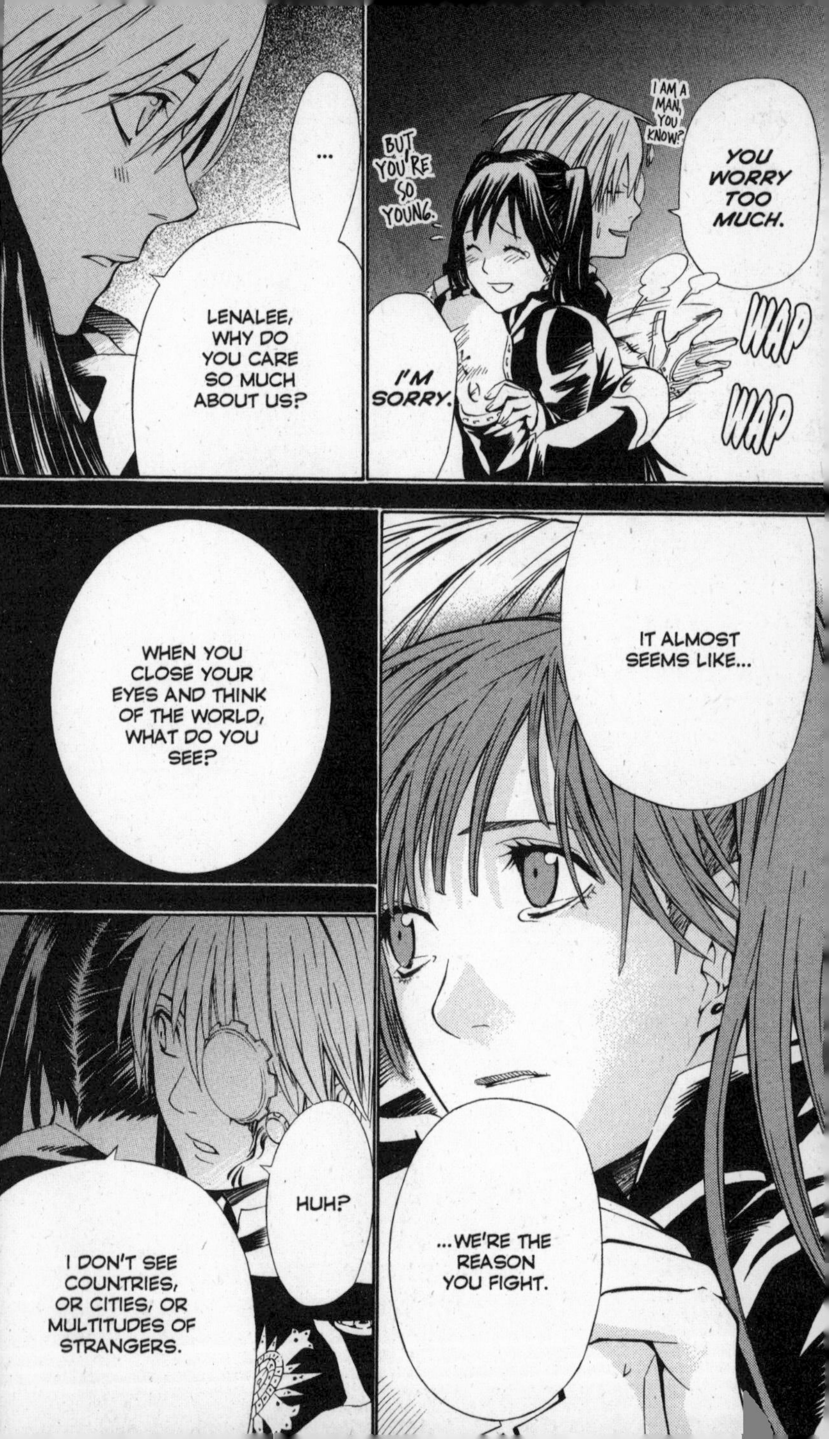
YOU WORRY TOO MUCH.
I AM A MAN, YOU KNOW?
WAP
WAP
BUT YOU'RE SO YOUNG.
I'M SORRY.
...
LENALEE, WHY DO YOU CARE SO MUCH ABOUT US?
IT ALMOST SEEMS LIKE...
...WE'RE THE REASON YOU FIGHT.
WHEN YOU CLOSE YOUR EYES AND THINK OF THE WORLD, WHAT DO YOU SEE?
HUH?
I DON'T SEE COUNTRIES, OR CITIES, OR MULTITUDES OF STRANGERS.

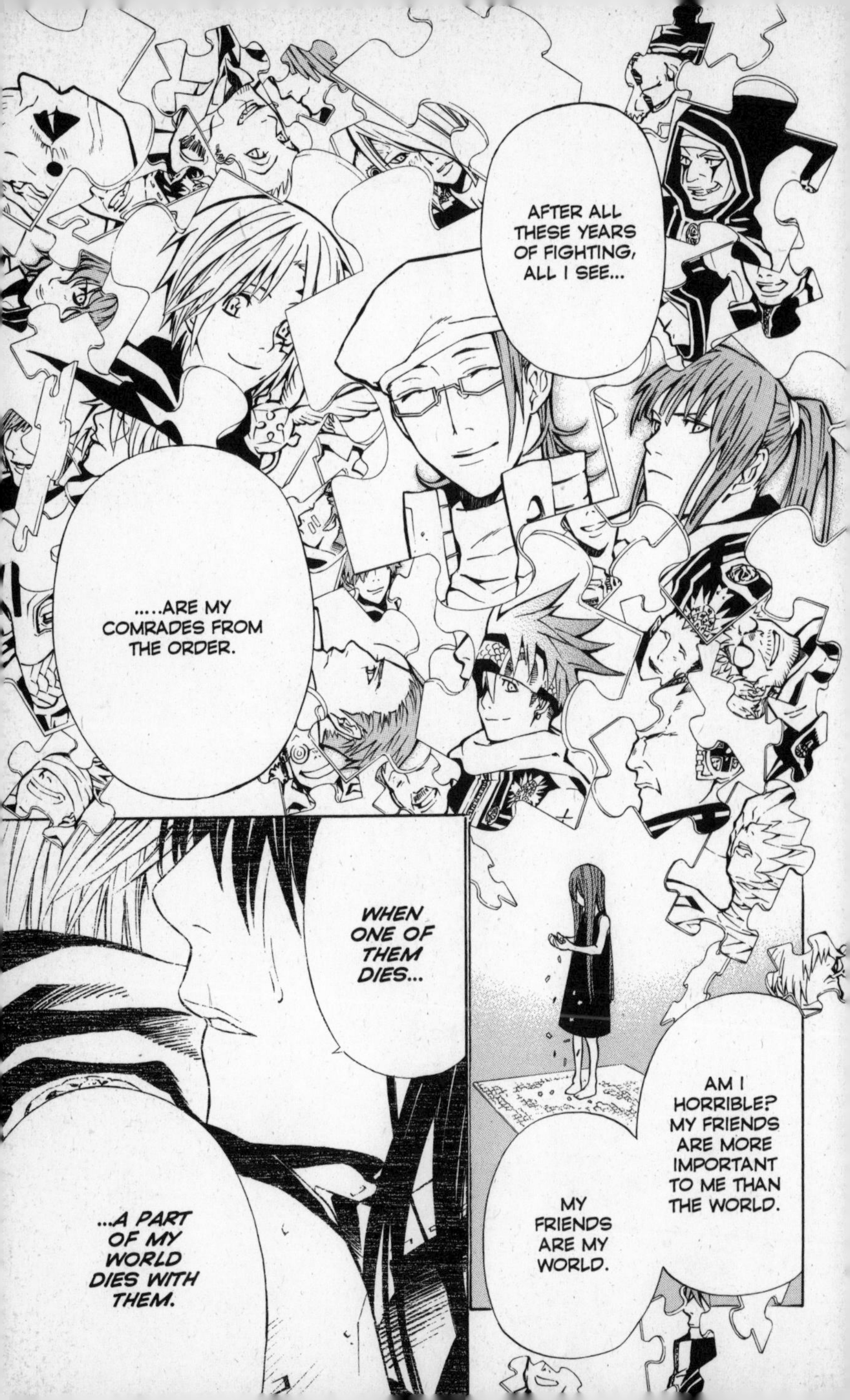
AFTER ALL THESE YEARS OF FIGHTING, ALL I SEE...
.....ARE MY COMRADES FROM THE ORDER.
AM I HORRIBLE? MY FRIENDS ARE MORE IMPORTANT TO ME THAN THE WORLD.
MY FRIENDS ARE MY WORLD.
WHEN ONE OF THEM DIES...
...A PART OF MY WORLD DIES WITH THEM.

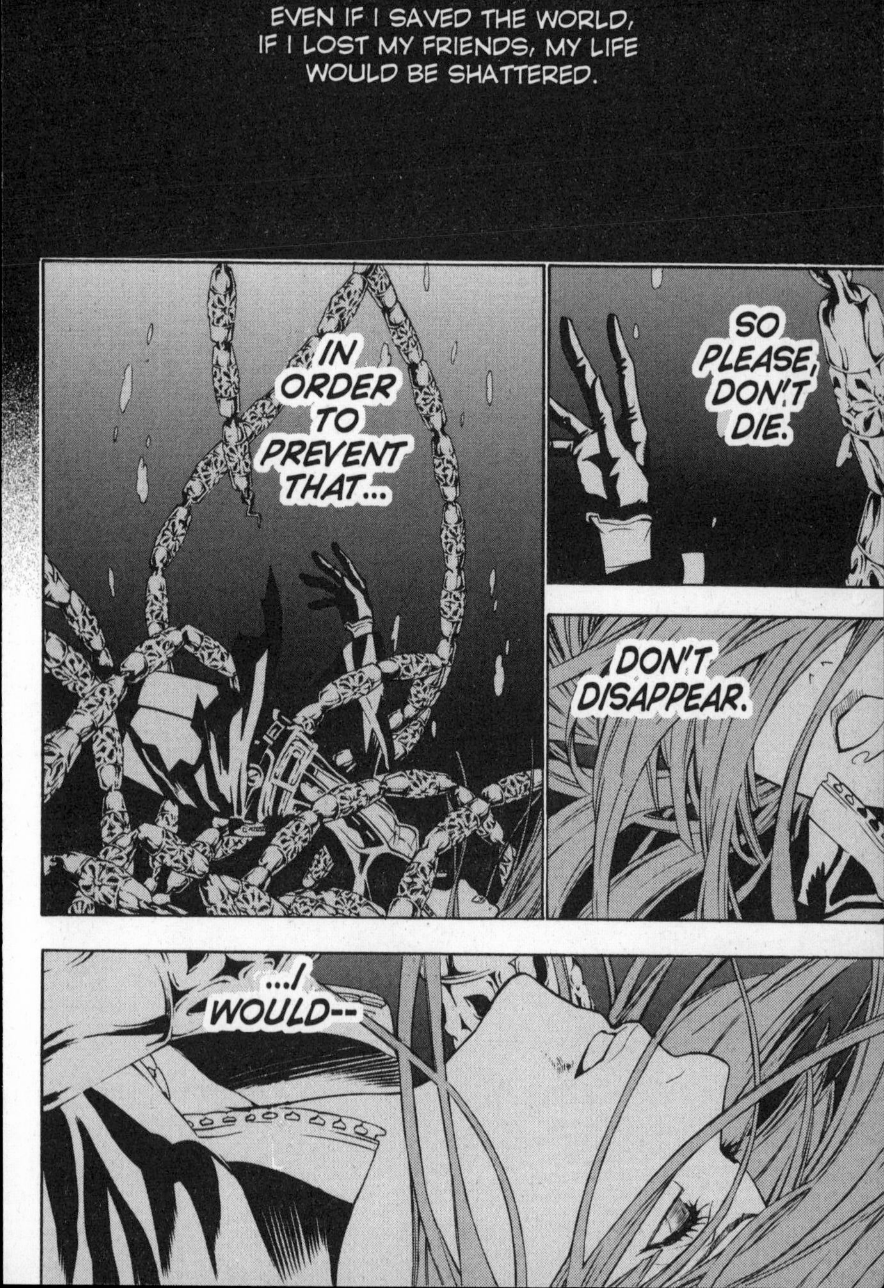
EVEN IF I SAVED THE WORLD, IF I LOST MY FRIENDS, MY LIFE WOULD BE SHATTERED.
SO PLEASE, DON'T DIE.
DON'T DISAPPEAR.
IN ORDER TO PREVENT THAT...
...I WOULD--

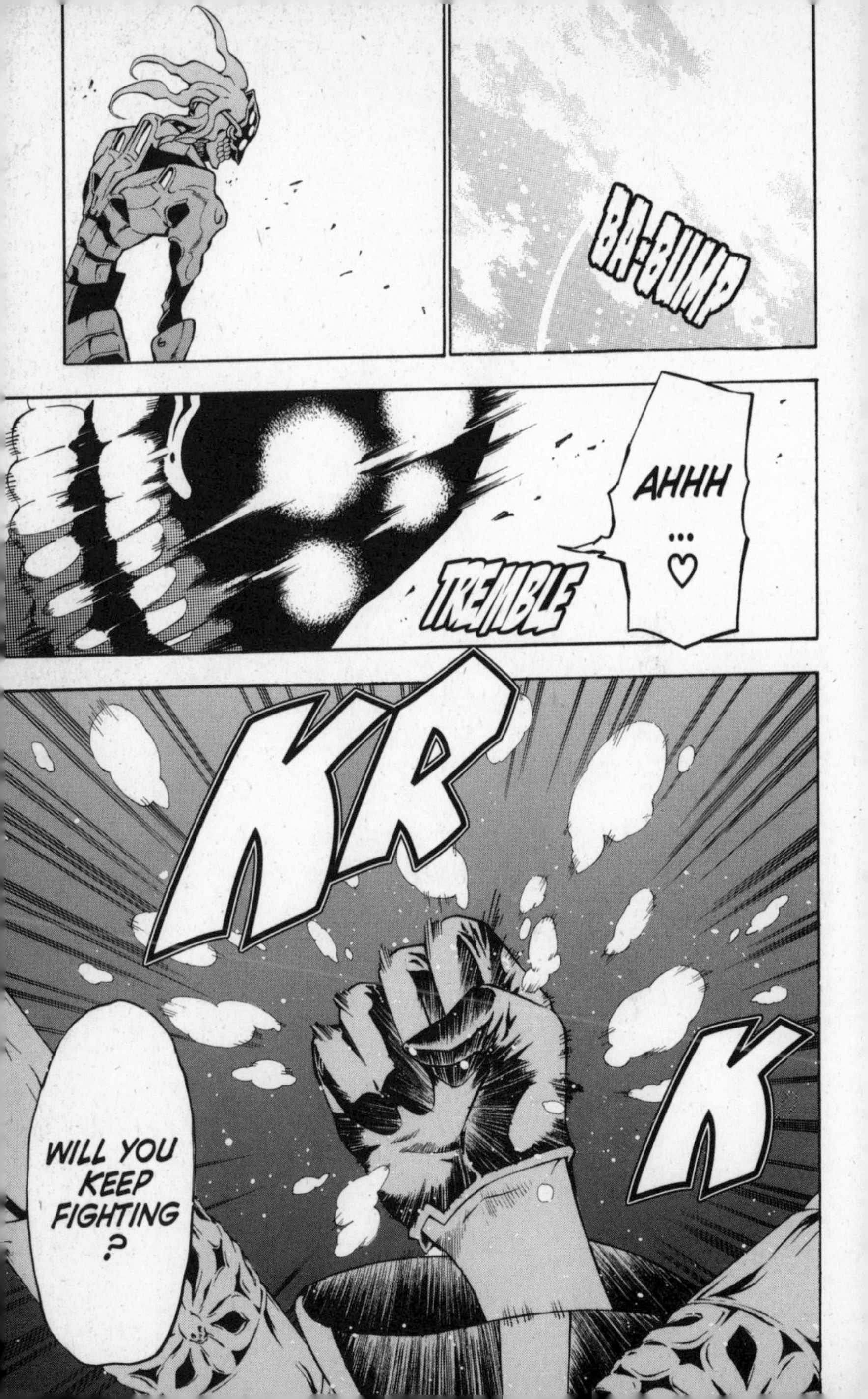
BA-BUMP
AHHH ... ♡
TREMBLE
KR
K
WILL YOU KEEP FIGHTING ?

KOMUI'S DISCUSSION ROOM, VOL. 2

∗∗∗

Q: WHAT HAPPENED TO KOMLIN II AFTER IT WAS DESTROYED BY LENALEE IN VOLUME 3?

(KANDA) KOMLIN?! THAT MONSTER IS STILL ALIVE?!

(ALLEN) WHAT? HOW DO YOU KNOW ABOUT KOMLIN, KANDA? I THOUGHT YOU WERE AWAY IN VOLUME 3.

(KANDA) WHAT? VOLUME 3? THE KOMLIN THAT I CUT DOWN WAS LONG BEFORE THAT.

(ALLEN) WAIT! ARE YOU TALKING ABOUT KOMLIN I? THE ONE IN VOLUME 3 WAS KOMLIN II. WHAT?! YOU CUT IT DOWN? YOU MEAN KOMLIN I WENT BERSERK AS WELL?!

(KANDA) IT ATE MY SOBA. (GRUMBLE)

(ALLEN) KANDA, LOOK OUT! YOU'RE SPILLING YOUR TEA. ANYWAY, I DON'T KNOW ANYTHING ABOUT KOMLIN I, BUT I HEARD THAT KOMLIN II WAS DISMANTLED BY REEVER AND THE SCIENCE TEAM. I UNDERSTAND THEY TOOK OUT THEIR FRUSTRATIONS ON IT.

BELOW IS A PICTURE THAT A TEARFUL KOMUI TOOK JUST BEFORE IT WENT INTO THE HYDRAULIC PRESS.

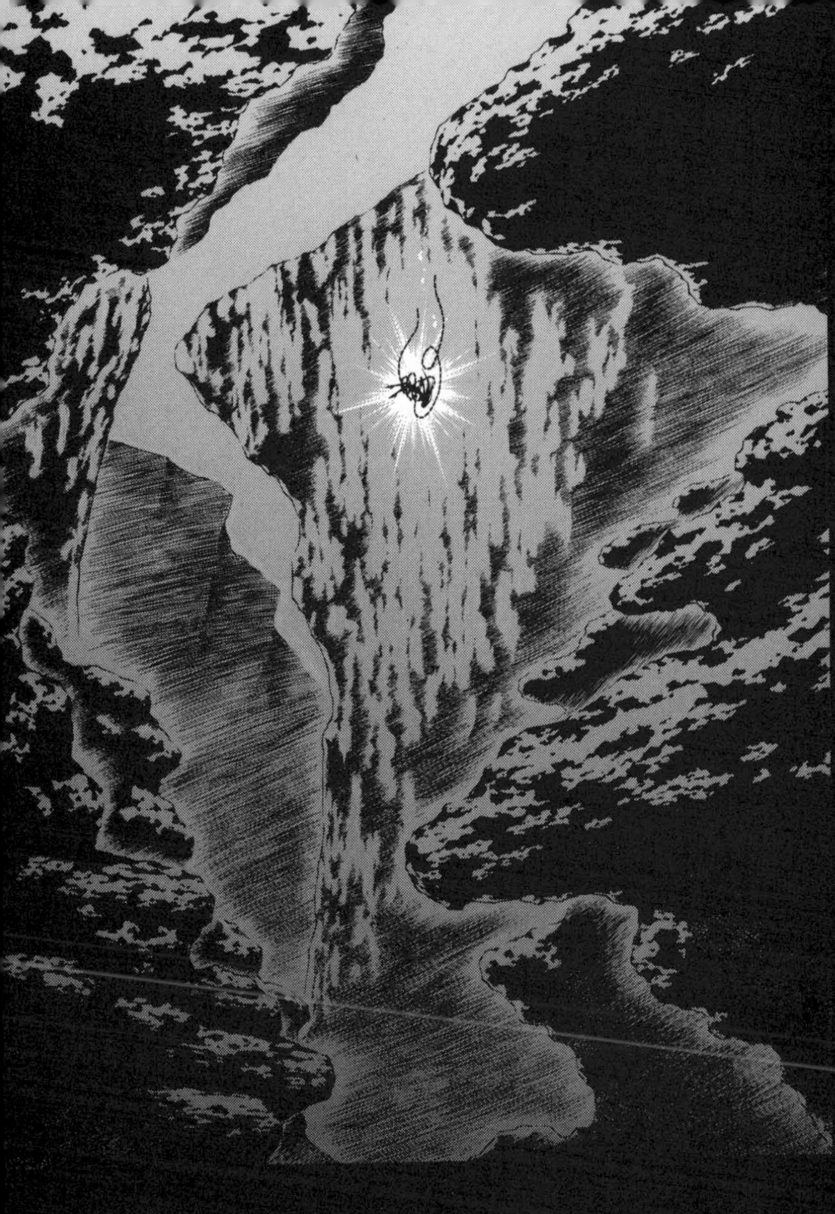

THE 70TH NIGHT: COUNTERATTACK

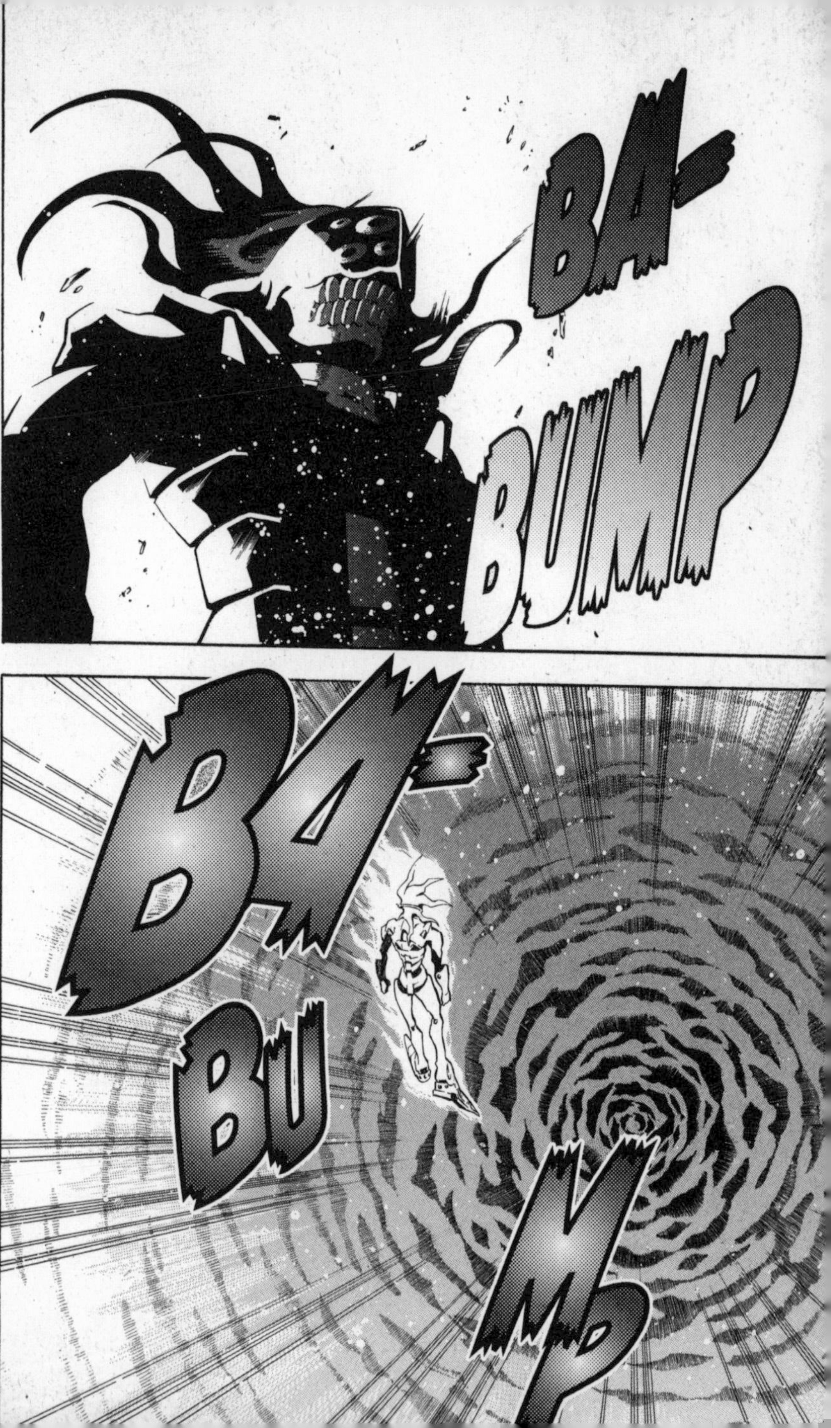
BA-
BUMP
BA-
BU
MP

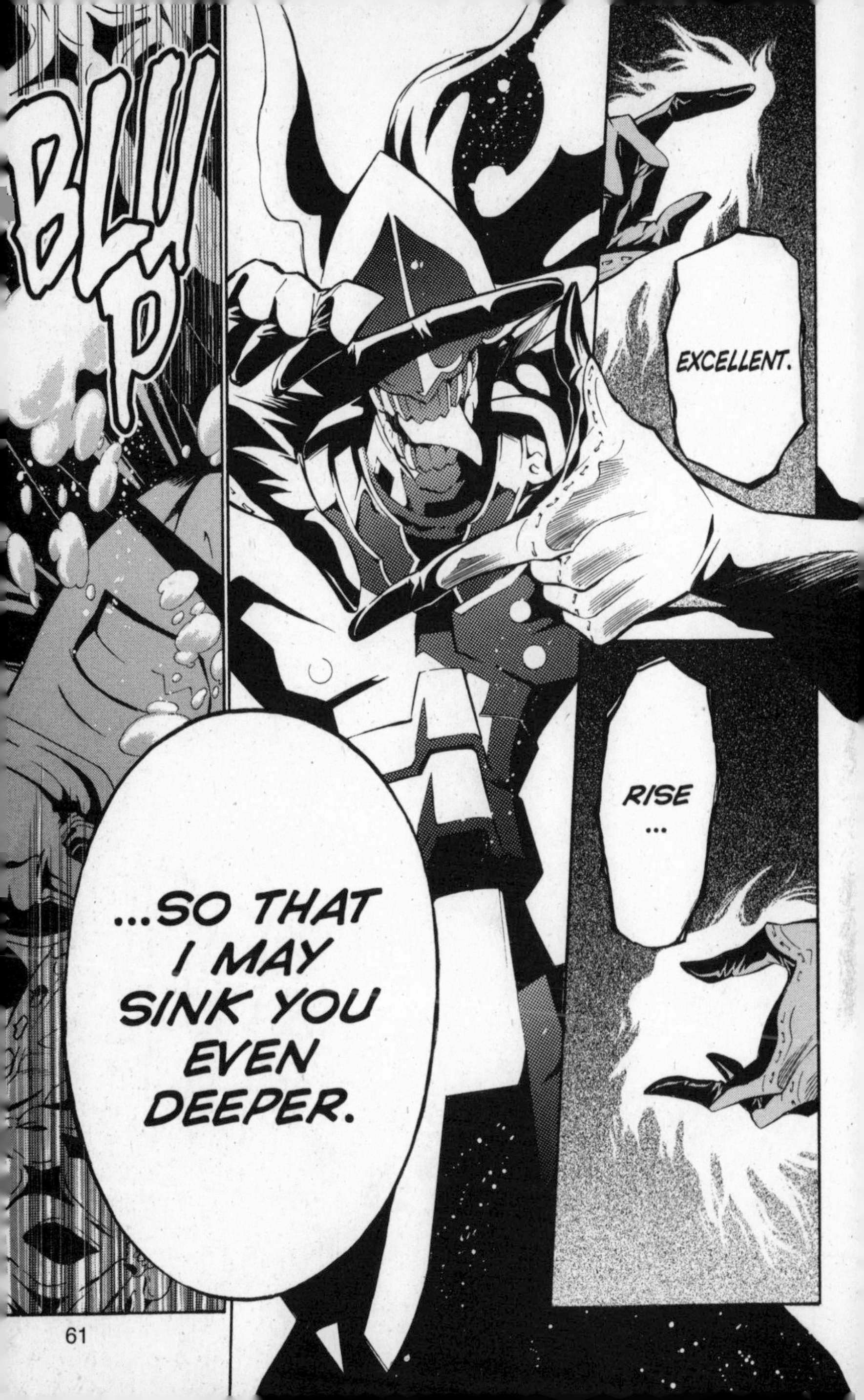
EXCELLENT.
RISE ...
...SO THAT I MAY SINK YOU EVEN DEEPER.
BLUP

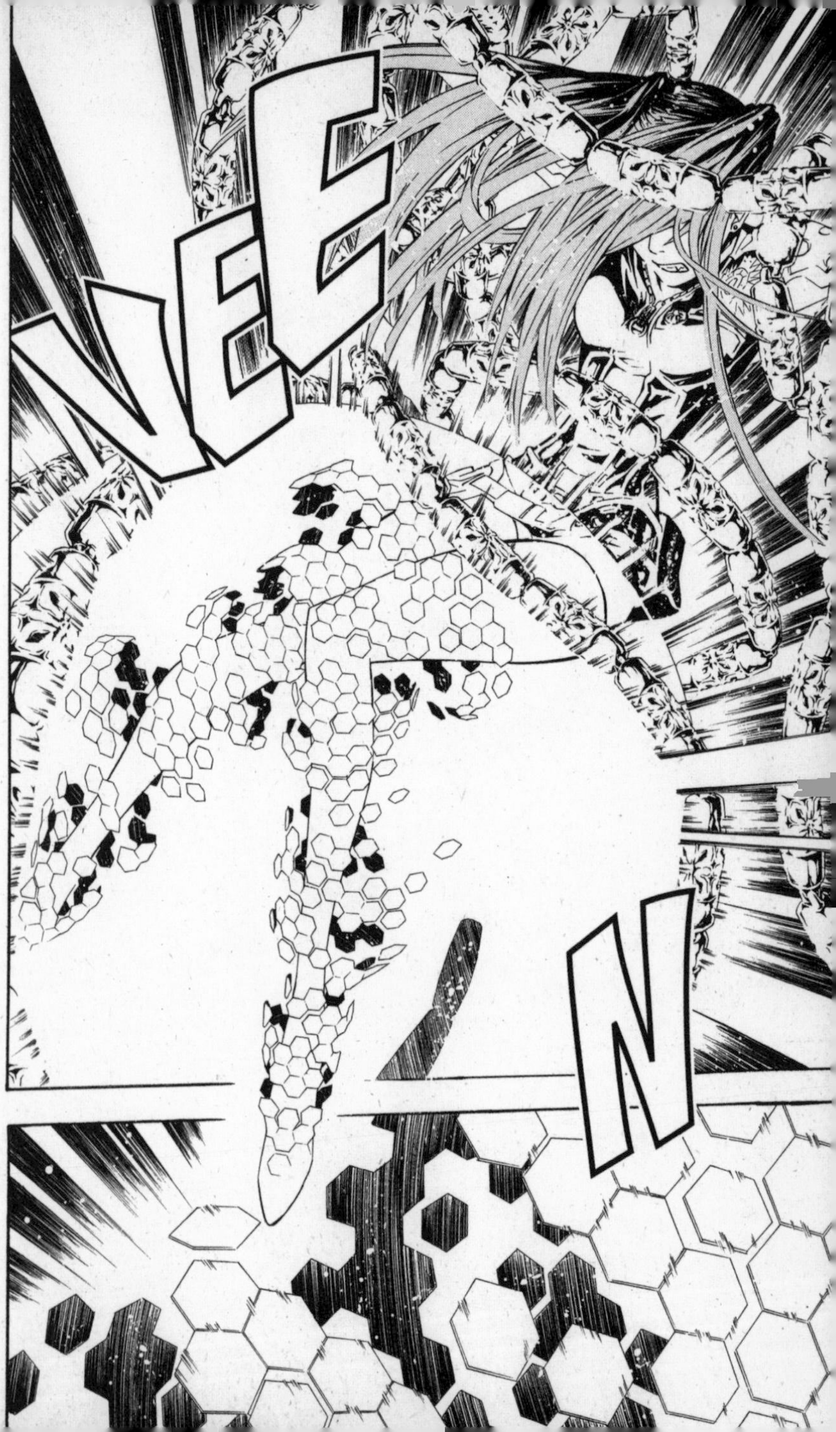
VEEN

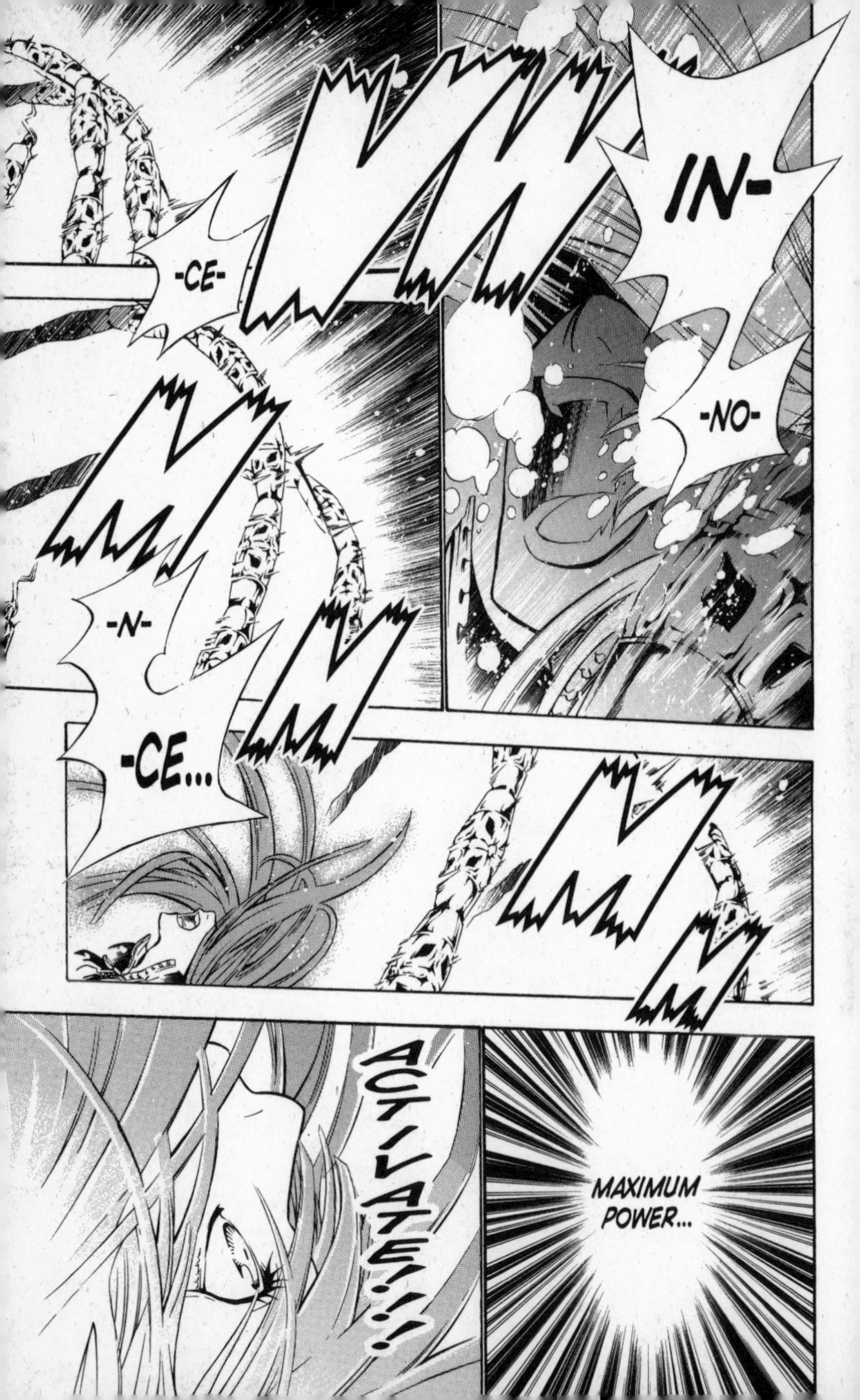
IN-
-NO-
-CE-
-N-
-CE...
MAXIMUM POWER...
ACTIVATE!!!

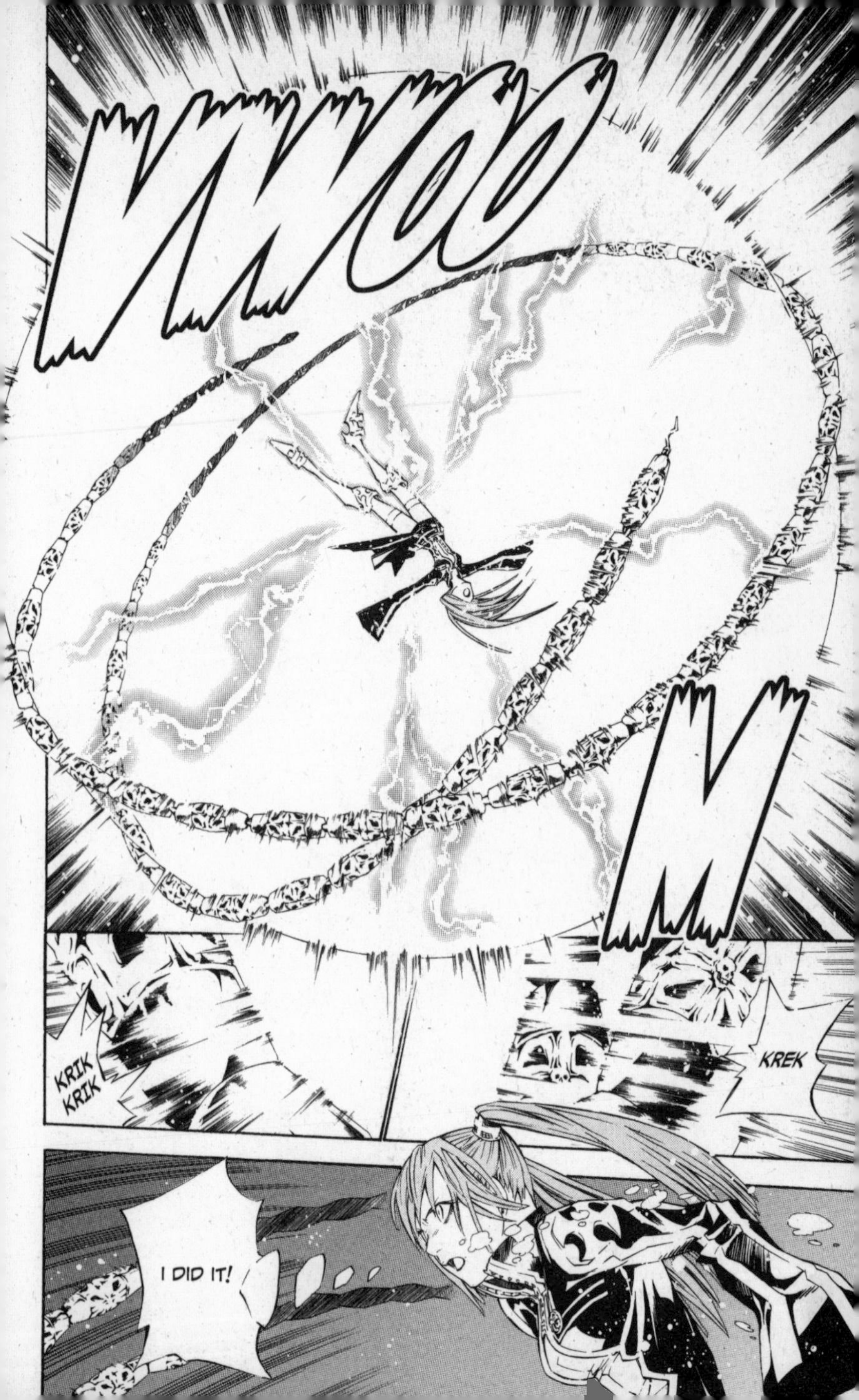
KREK
KRIK KRIK
I DID IT!

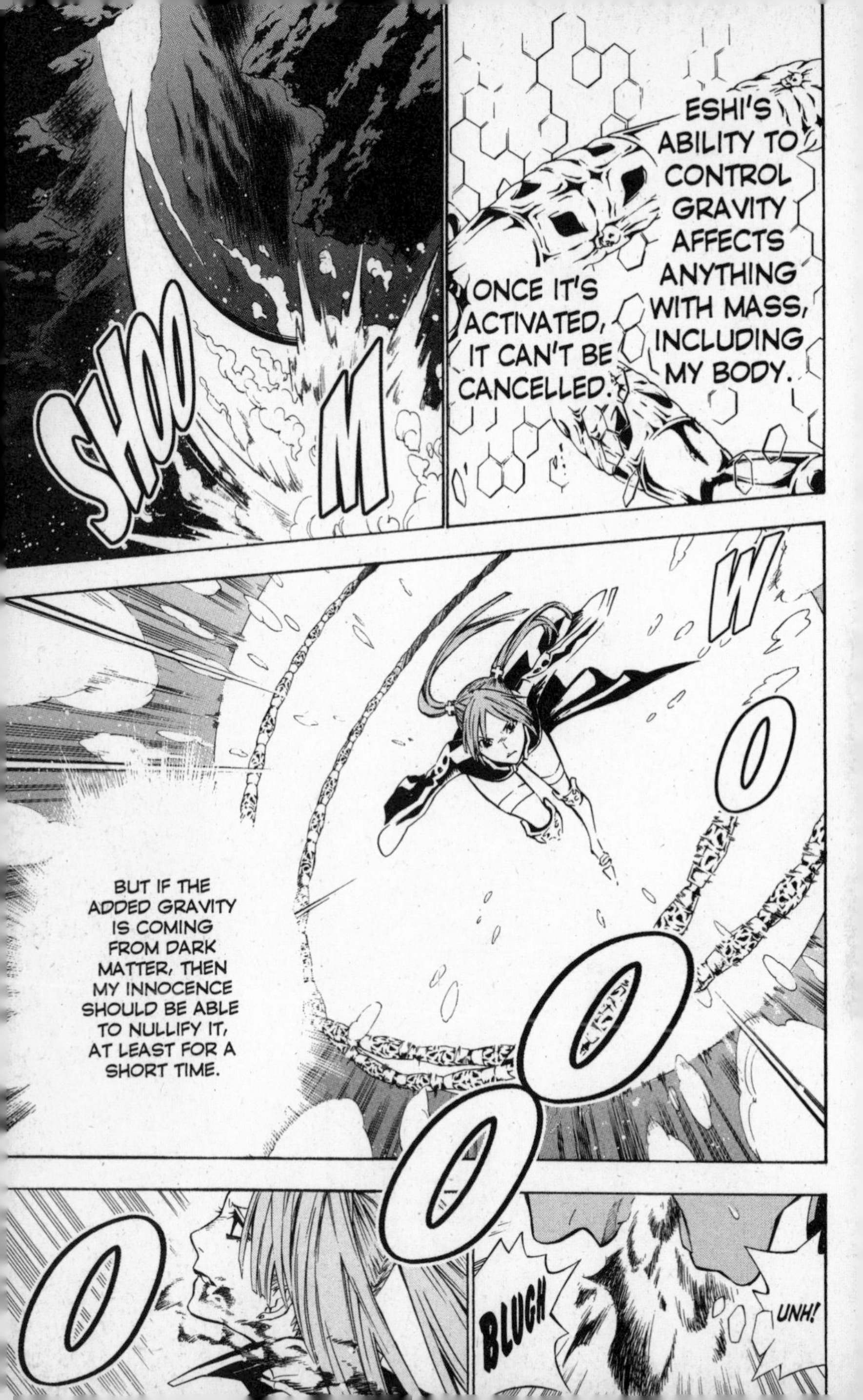
ESHI'S ABILITY TO CONTROL GRAVITY AFFECTS ANYTHING WITH MASS, INCLUDING MY BODY.
ONCE IT'S ACTIVATED, IT CAN'T BE CANCELLED.
SHOOM
WOOOOO
BUT IF THE ADDED GRAVITY IS COMING FROM DARK MATTER, THEN MY INNOCENCE SHOULD BE ABLE TO NULLIFY IT, AT LEAST FOR A SHORT TIME.
UNH!
BLUGH

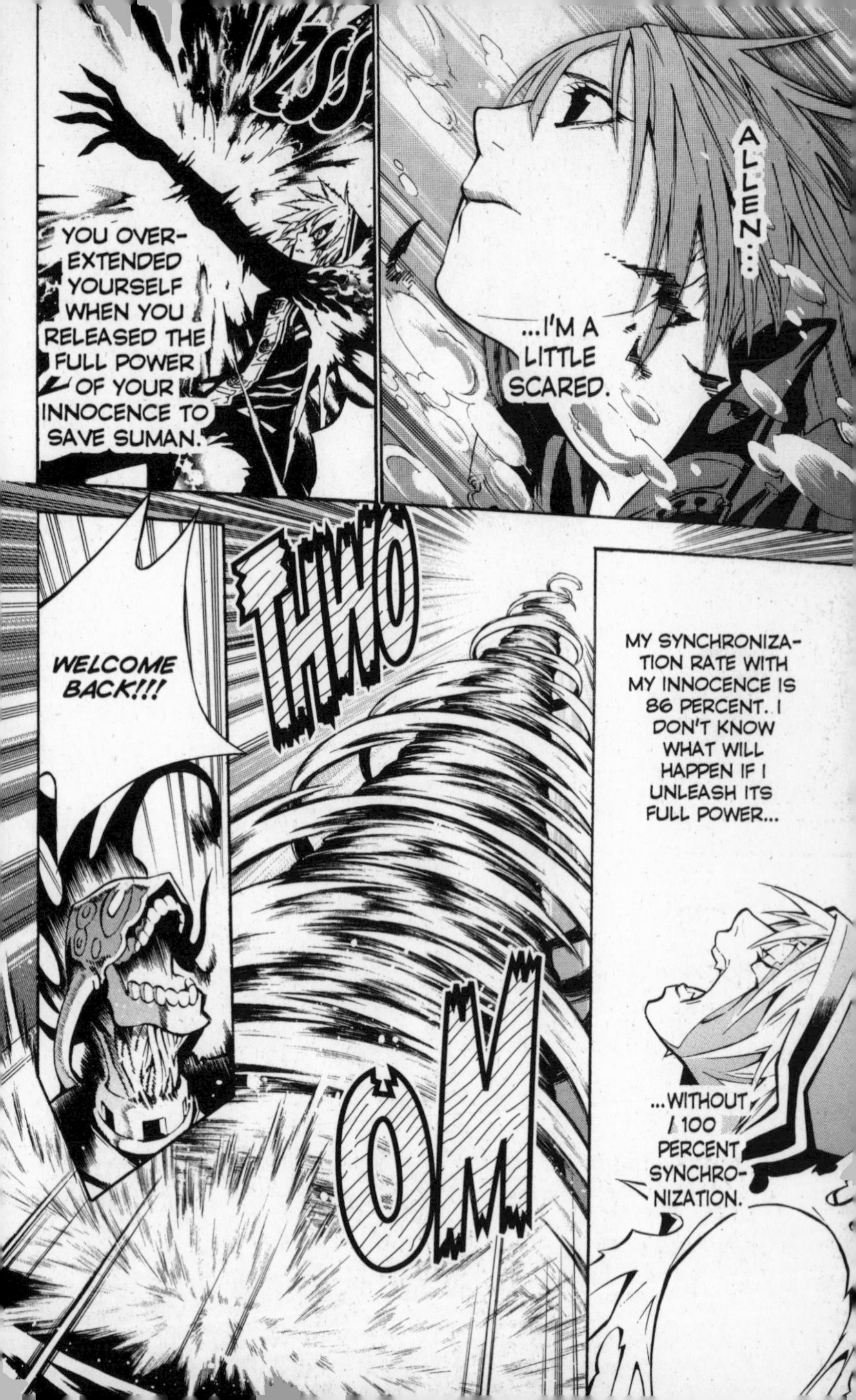
ALLEN...
...I'M A LITTLE SCARED.
ZSS
YOU OVER-EXTENDED YOURSELF WHEN YOU RELEASED THE FULL POWER OF YOUR INNOCENCE TO SAVE SUMAN.
MY SYNCHRONIZATION RATE WITH MY INNOCENCE IS 86 PERCENT. I DON'T KNOW WHAT WILL HAPPEN IF I UNLEASH ITS FULL POWER...
...WITHOUT 100 PERCENT SYNCHRONIZATION.
THWOOM
WELCOME BACK!!!

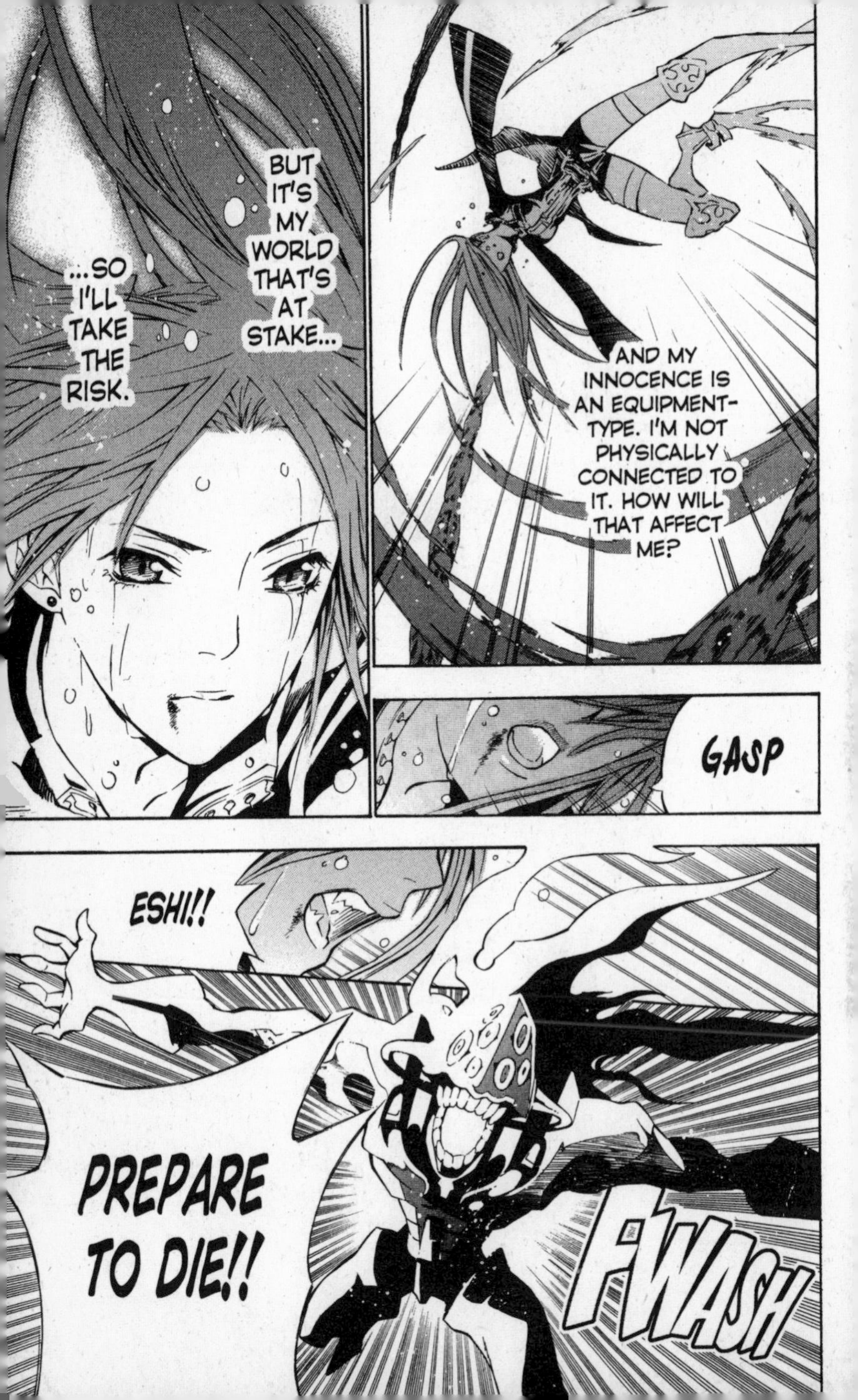
AND MY INNOCENCE IS AN EQUIPMENT-TYPE. I'M NOT PHYSICALLY CONNECTED TO IT. HOW WILL THAT AFFECT ME?
GASP
BUT IT'S MY WORLD THAT'S AT STAKE...
...SO I'LL TAKE THE RISK.
ESHI!!
F-WASH
PREPARE TO DIE!!

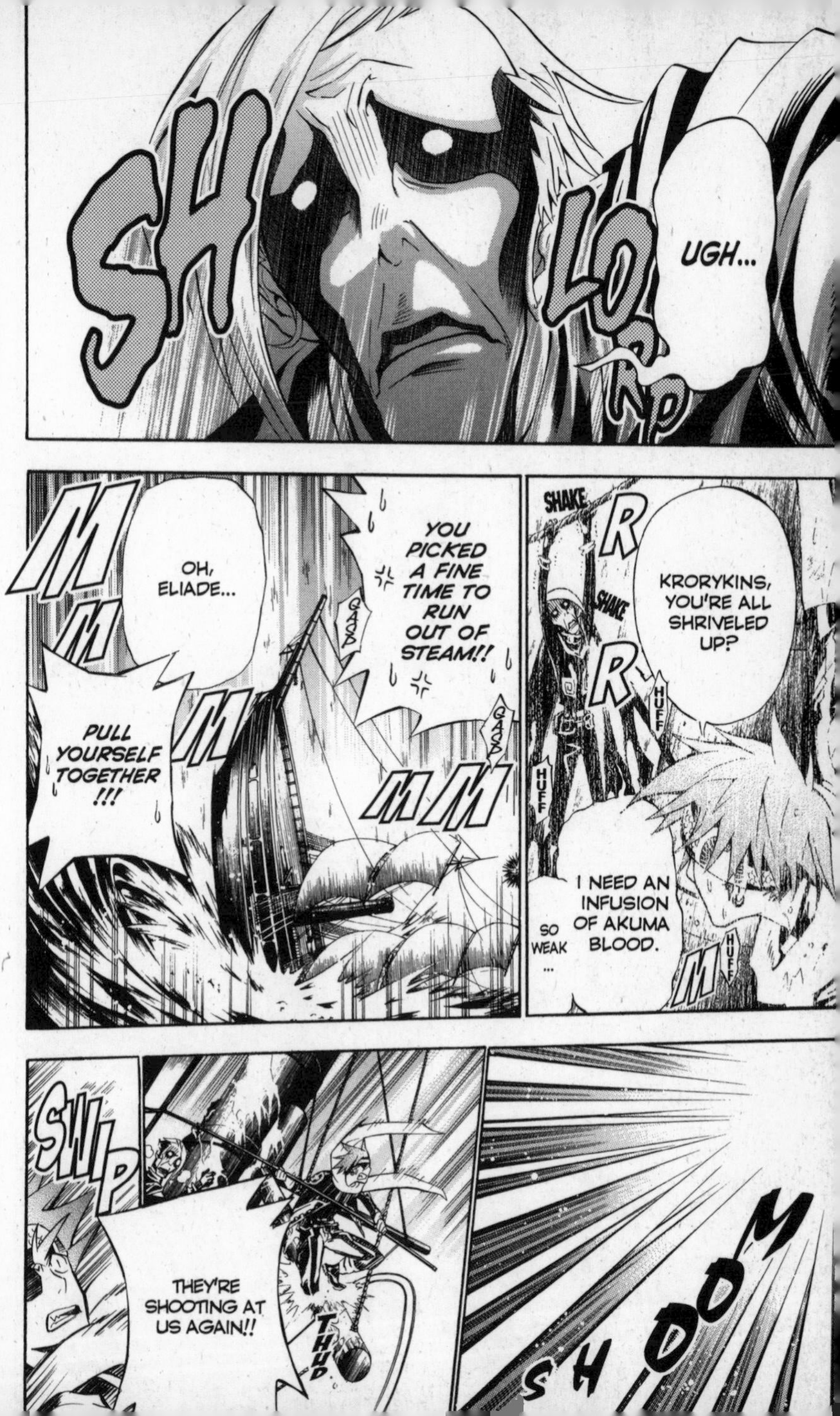
UGH...
SH
LOOP
SHAKE
SHAKE
RR
KRORYKINS, YOU'RE ALL SHRIVELED UP?
HUFF
HUFF
I NEED AN INFUSION OF AKUMA BLOOD.
SO WEAK...
HUFF
M
YOU PICKED A FINE TIME TO RUN OUT OF STEAM!!
GASP
GASP
OH, ELIADE...
MMMMMM
PULL YOURSELF TOGETHER!!!
SHDOOM
SWIP
THEY'RE SHOOTING AT US AGAIN!!
THUD

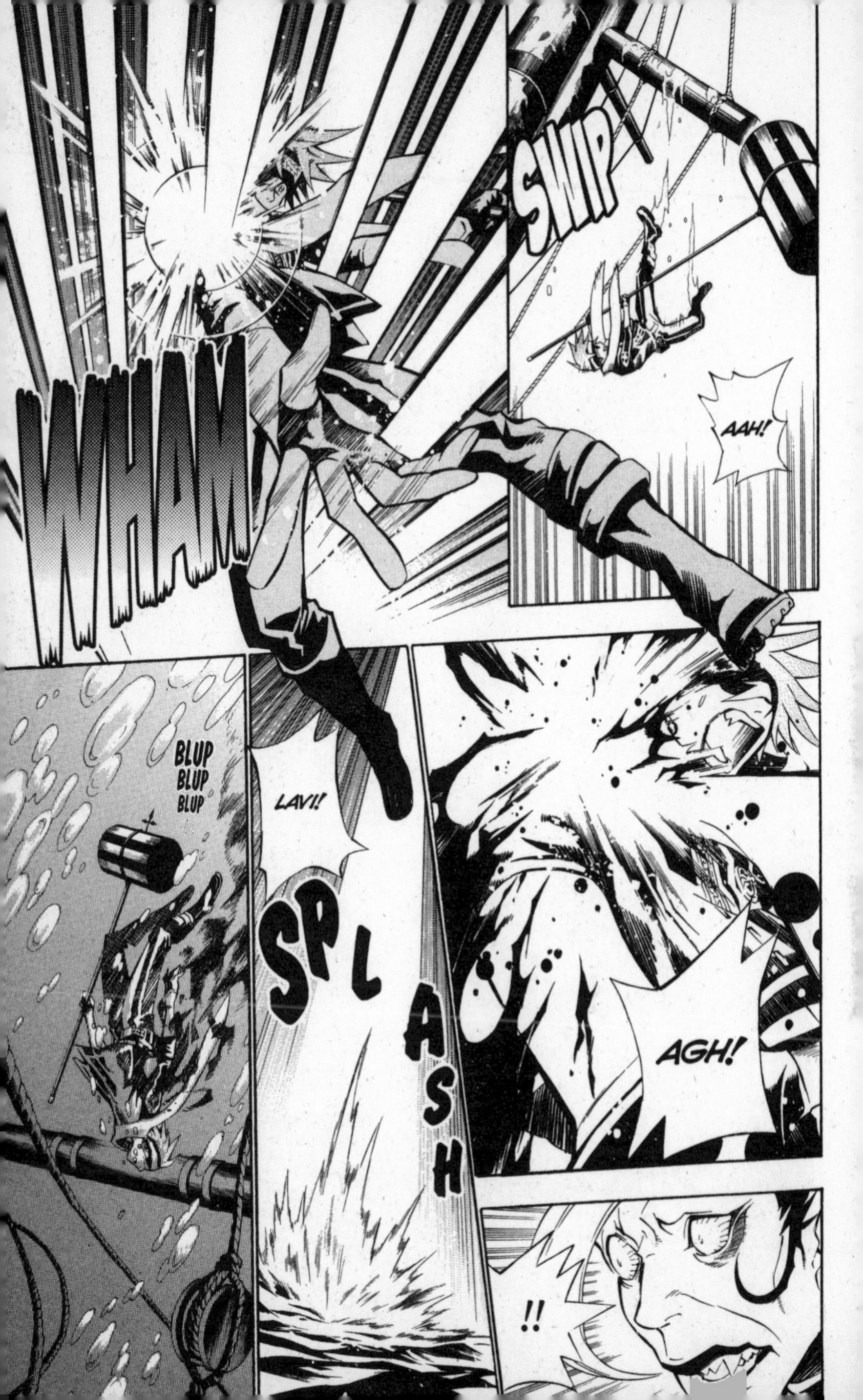
SWIP
AAH!
WHAM
AGH!
!!
LAVI!
SPLASH
BLUP
BLUP
BLUP

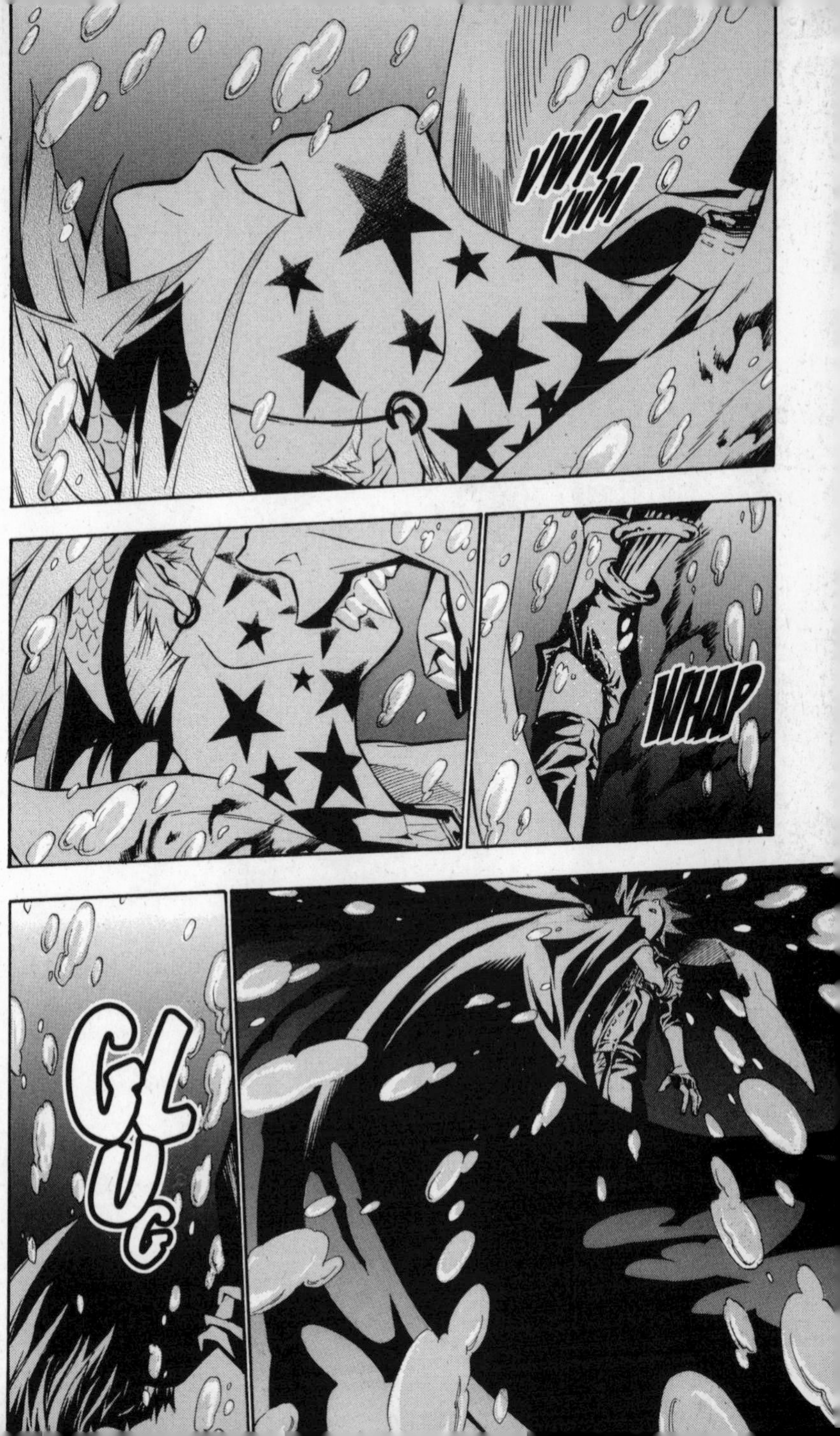
VWIM
VWIM
WHAP
GLUG

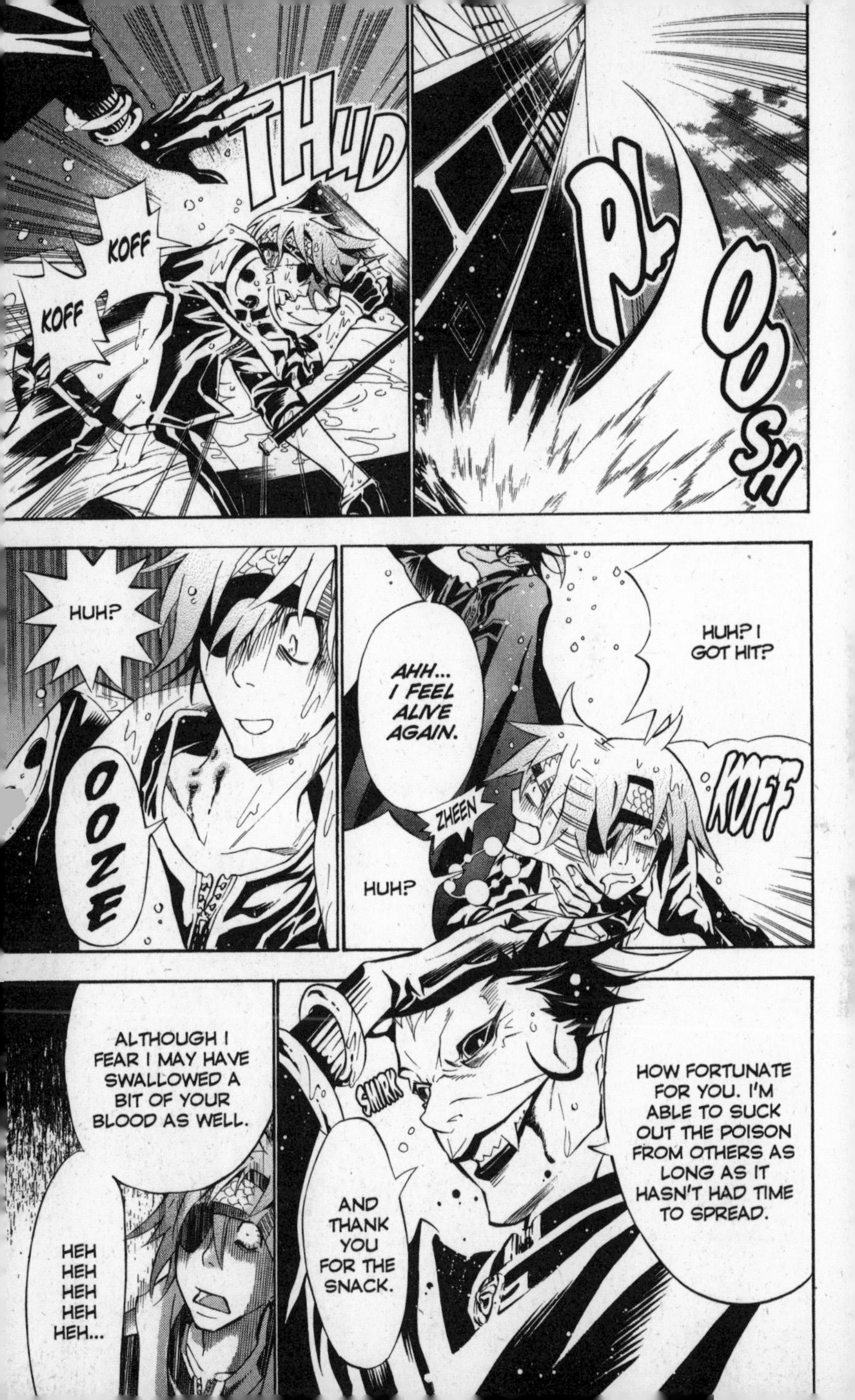
PLOOSH
THUD
KOFF
KOFF
HUH? I GOT HIT?
KOFF
AHH... I FEEL ALIVE AGAIN.
ZHEEN
HUH?
HUH?
OOZE
HOW FORTUNATE FOR YOU. I'M ABLE TO SUCK OUT THE POISON FROM OTHERS AS LONG AS IT HASN'T HAD TIME TO SPREAD.
SMIRK
AND THANK YOU FOR THE SNACK.
ALTHOUGH I FEAR I MAY HAVE SWALLOWED A BIT OF YOUR BLOOD AS WELL.
HEH HEH HEH HEH HEH...

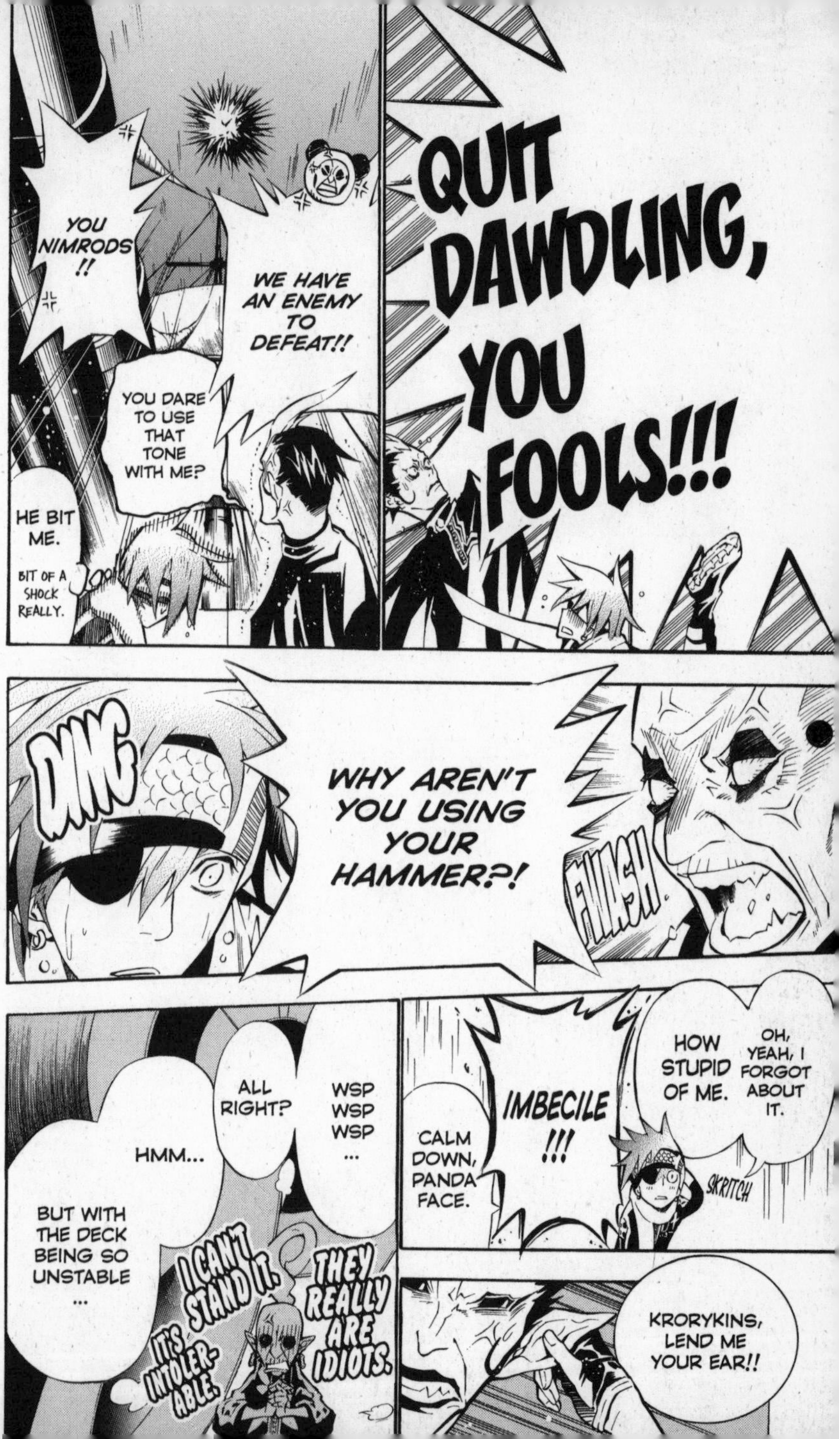
QUIT DAWDLING, YOU FOOLS!!!
WE HAVE AN ENEMY TO DEFEAT!!
YOU NIMRODS!!
YOU DARE TO USE THAT TONE WITH ME?
HE BIT ME.
BIT OF A SHOCK REALLY.
WHY AREN'T YOU USING YOUR HAMMER?!
FWASH
DING
OH, YEAH, I FORGOT ABOUT IT.
HOW STUPID OF ME.
SKRITCH
IMBECILE!!!
CALM DOWN, PANDA FACE.
KRORYKINS, LEND ME YOUR EAR!!
WSP WSP WSP...
ALL RIGHT?
HMM...
BUT WITH THE DECK BEING SO UNSTABLE...
THEY REALLY ARE IDIOTS.
I CAN'T STAND IT.
IT'S INTOLERABLE.

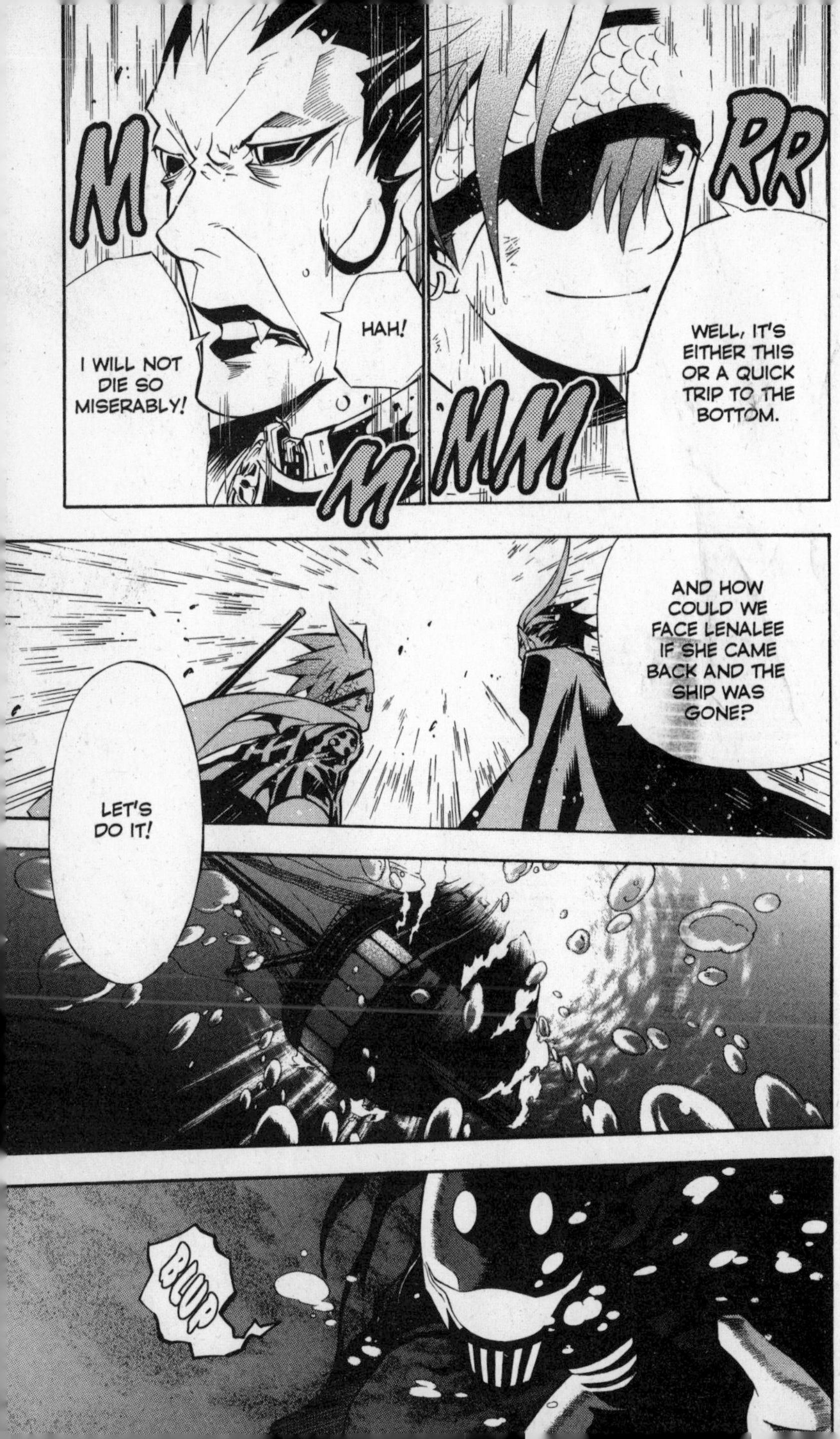
RR
WELL, IT'S EITHER THIS OR A QUICK TRIP TO THE BOTTOM.
MM
HAH!
M
I WILL NOT DIE SO MISERABLY!
M
AND HOW COULD WE FACE LENALEE IF SHE CAME BACK AND THE SHIP WAS GONE?
LET'S DO IT!
BLUP

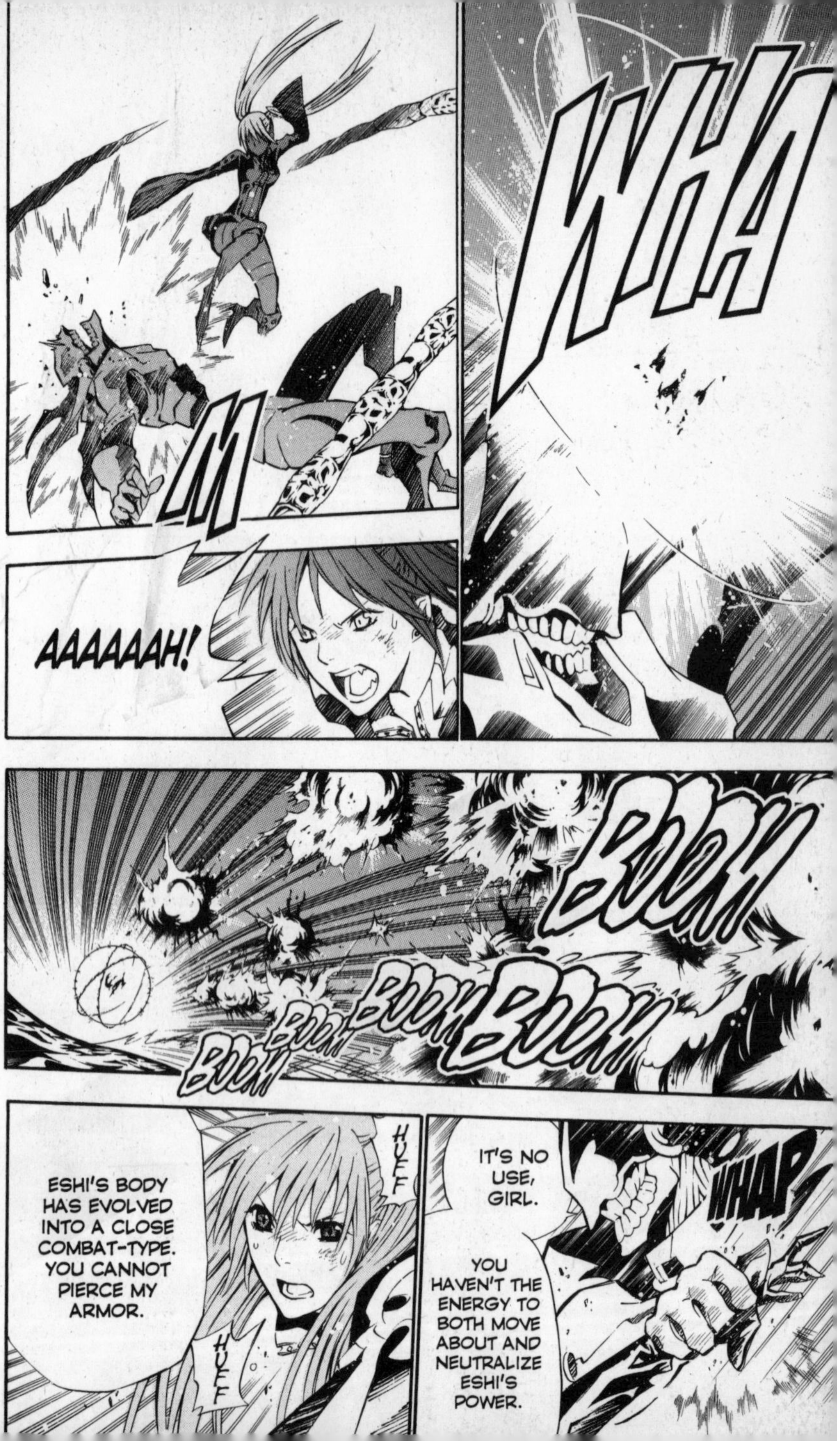
WHA
M
AAAAAAH!
BOOM
BOOM
BOOM
BOOM
BOOM
WHAP
IT'S NO USE, GIRL.
YOU HAVEN'T THE ENERGY TO BOTH MOVE ABOUT AND NEUTRALIZE ESHI'S POWER.
HUFF
ESHI'S BODY HAS EVOLVED INTO A CLOSE COMBAT-TYPE. YOU CANNOT PIERCE MY ARMOR.
HUFF

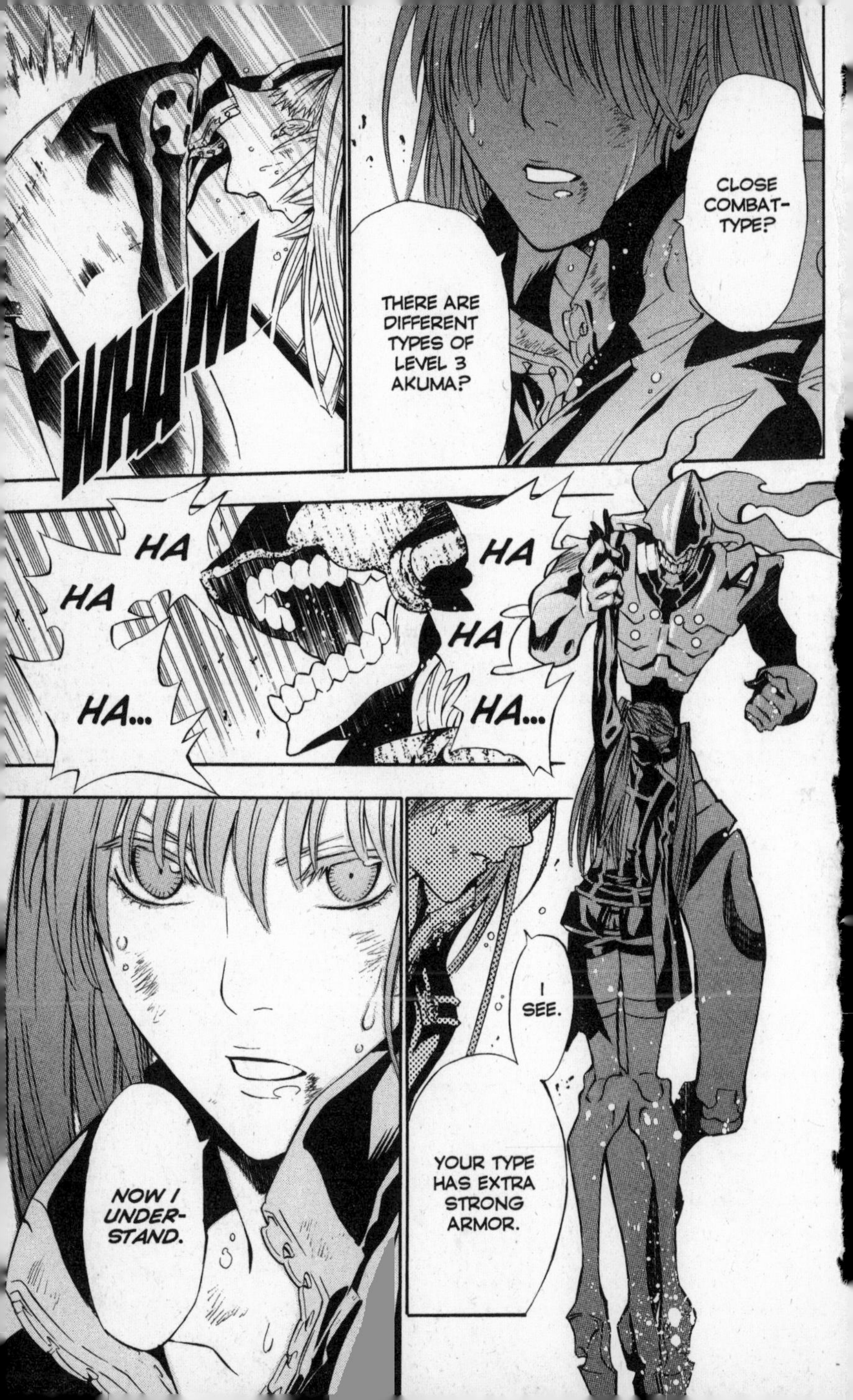

CLOSE COMBAT-TYPE?
THERE ARE DIFFERENT TYPES OF LEVEL 3 AKUMA?
WHAM
HA HA HA...
HA HA HA...
I SEE.
YOUR TYPE HAS EXTRA STRONG ARMOR.
NOW I UNDERSTAND.

KOMUI'S DISCUSSION ROOM, VOL. 3

Q: BESIDES PARASITE- AND EQUIPMENT-TYPES, WHAT TYPES OF WEAPONS DO EXORCISTS USE?
(ALLEN) THERE ARE ONLY THE TWO TYPES, BUT THERE ARE MANY MANIFESTATIONS OF EACH.
(KANDA) INNOCENCE IS VERY COMPLEX. NEW TYPES MAY YET EMERGE IN THE FUTURE.

Q: WHERE DOES THE FUNDING FOR THE BLACK ORDER COME FROM?
(ALLEN) FROM THE VATICAN, OR SO I'VE HEARD.

Q: IN VOLUME 7, FO MENTIONED THAT SOMEONE GOT LOST IN ASIA BRANCH'S BASEMENT. WHO WAS IT?
(ALLEN) I THINK IT WAS BAK CHAN. WONG LOOKED UNCOMFORTABLE WHEN IT WAS MENTIONED.
(KANDA) RIDICULOUS.

Q: HOW LONG HAS HEVLASKA BEEN IN ITS CURRENT FORM?
(ALLEN) A VERY LONG TIME, SO I'VE BEEN TOLD. HEVLASKA IS A MYSTERY TO ME. SHE APPEARS TO BE FEMALE, BUT I WONDER...
(KANDA) I HAVE NO IDEA.

Q: IS THE MILLENNIUM EARL HUMAN? I HOPE HE REMAINS A MYSTERY FOR A LONG TIME. I LOVE IT.
(KANDA) WELL, DO YOU WANT TO KNOW OR DON'T YOU?!
(ALLEN) DID KANDA JUST TRY TO BE FUNNY?

ZAK ZAK ZAK ZAK

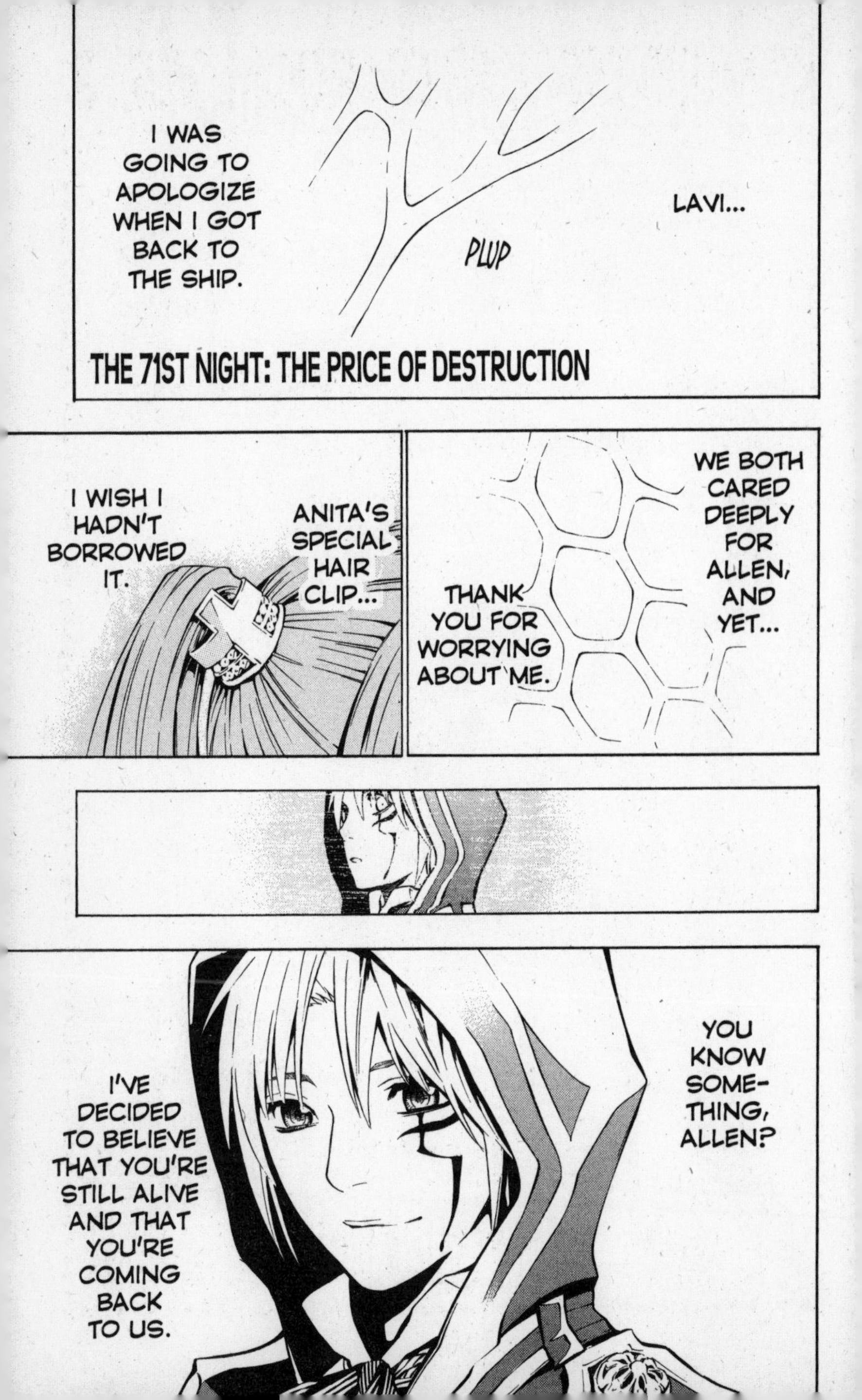
LAVI...
PLUP
I WAS GOING TO APOLOGIZE WHEN I GOT BACK TO THE SHIP.
THE 71ST NIGHT: THE PRICE OF DESTRUCTION
WE BOTH CARED DEEPLY FOR ALLEN, AND YET...
THANK YOU FOR WORRYING ABOUT ME.
ANITA'S SPECIAL HAIR CLIP...
I WISH I HADN'T BORROWED IT.
YOU KNOW SOME-THING, ALLEN?
I'VE DECIDED TO BELIEVE THAT YOU'RE STILL ALIVE AND THAT YOU'RE COMING BACK TO US.

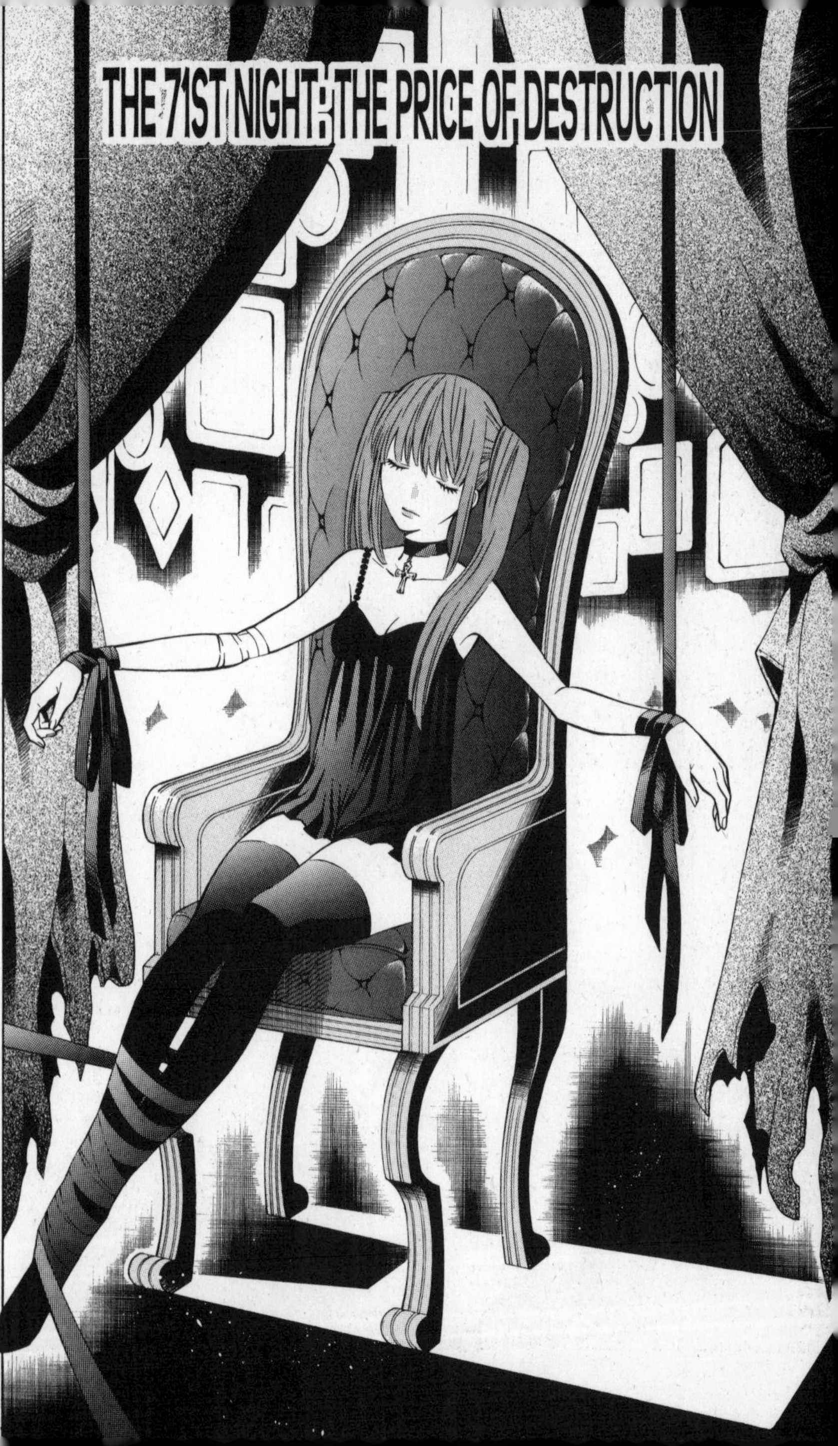
THE 71ST NIGHT: THE PRICE OF DESTRUCTION

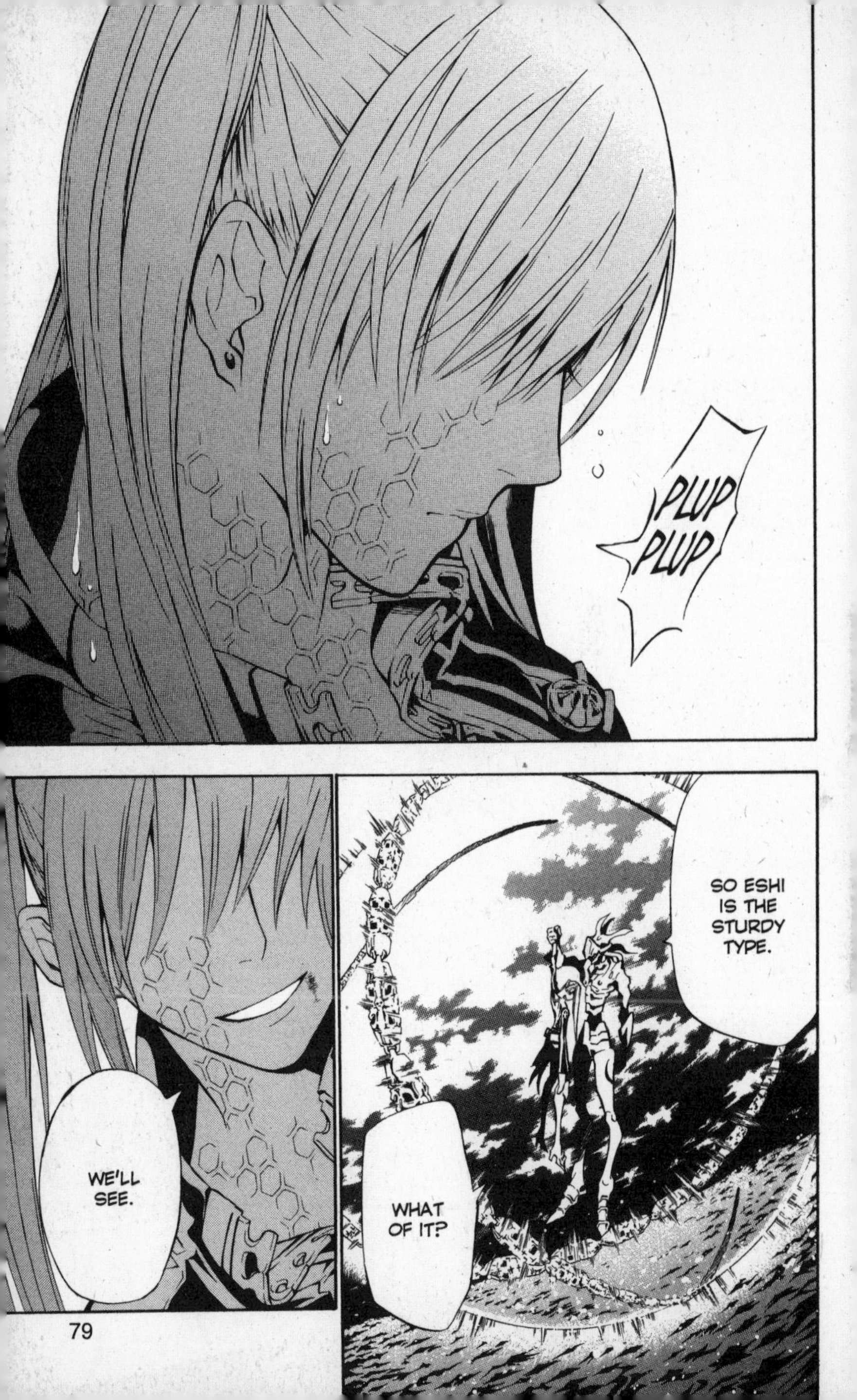
PLUP PLUP
SO ESHI IS THE STURDY TYPE.
WHAT OF IT?
WE'LL SEE.

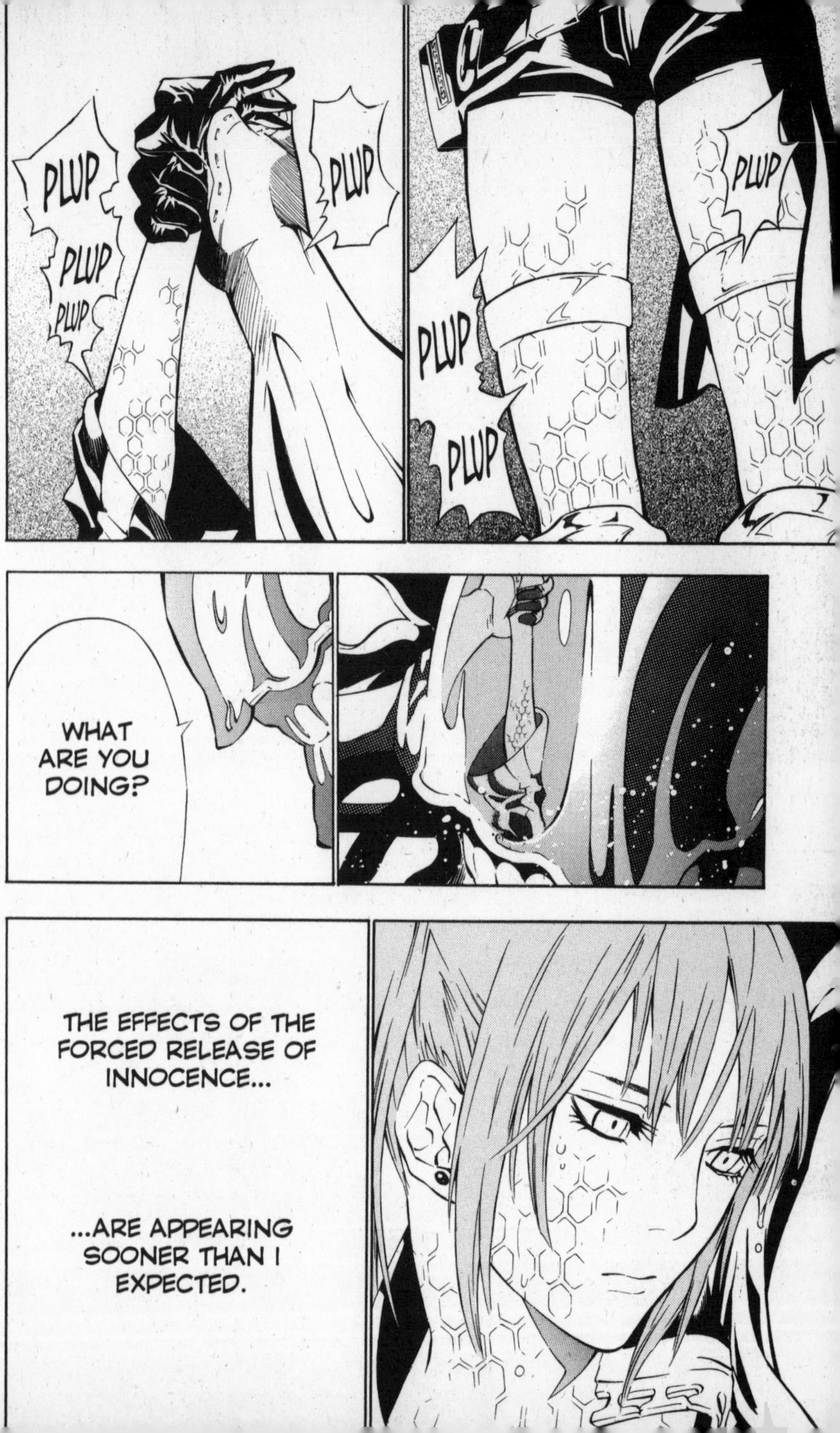
PLUP
PLUP
PLUP
PLUP
PLUP
PLUP
PLUP
WHAT ARE YOU DOING?
THE EFFECTS OF THE FORCED RELEASE OF INNOCENCE...
...ARE APPEARING SOONER THAN I EXPECTED.

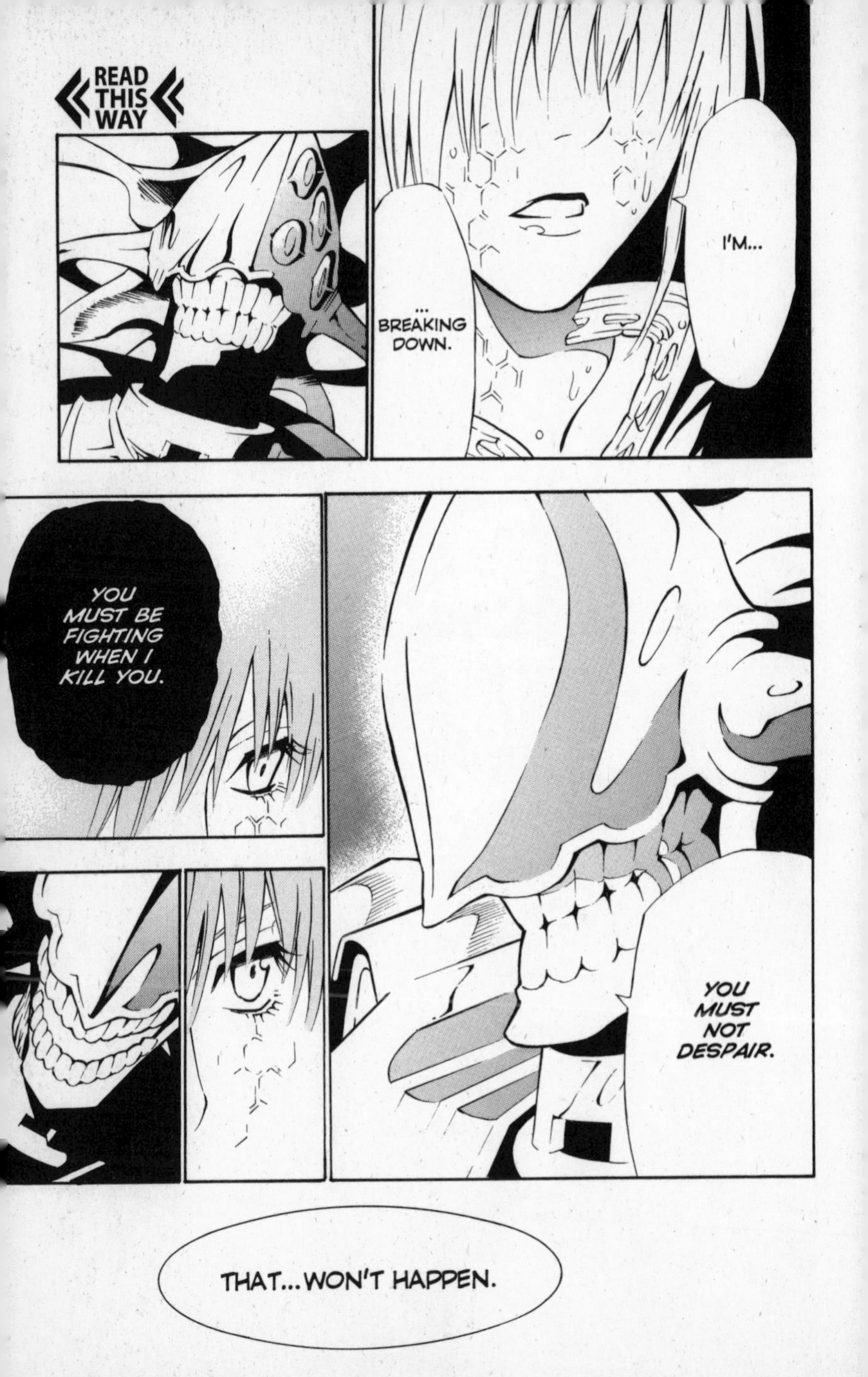
READ THIS WAY
I'M...
...BREAKING DOWN.
YOU MUST NOT DESPAIR.
YOU MUST BE FIGHTING WHEN I KILL YOU.
THAT...WON'T HAPPEN.

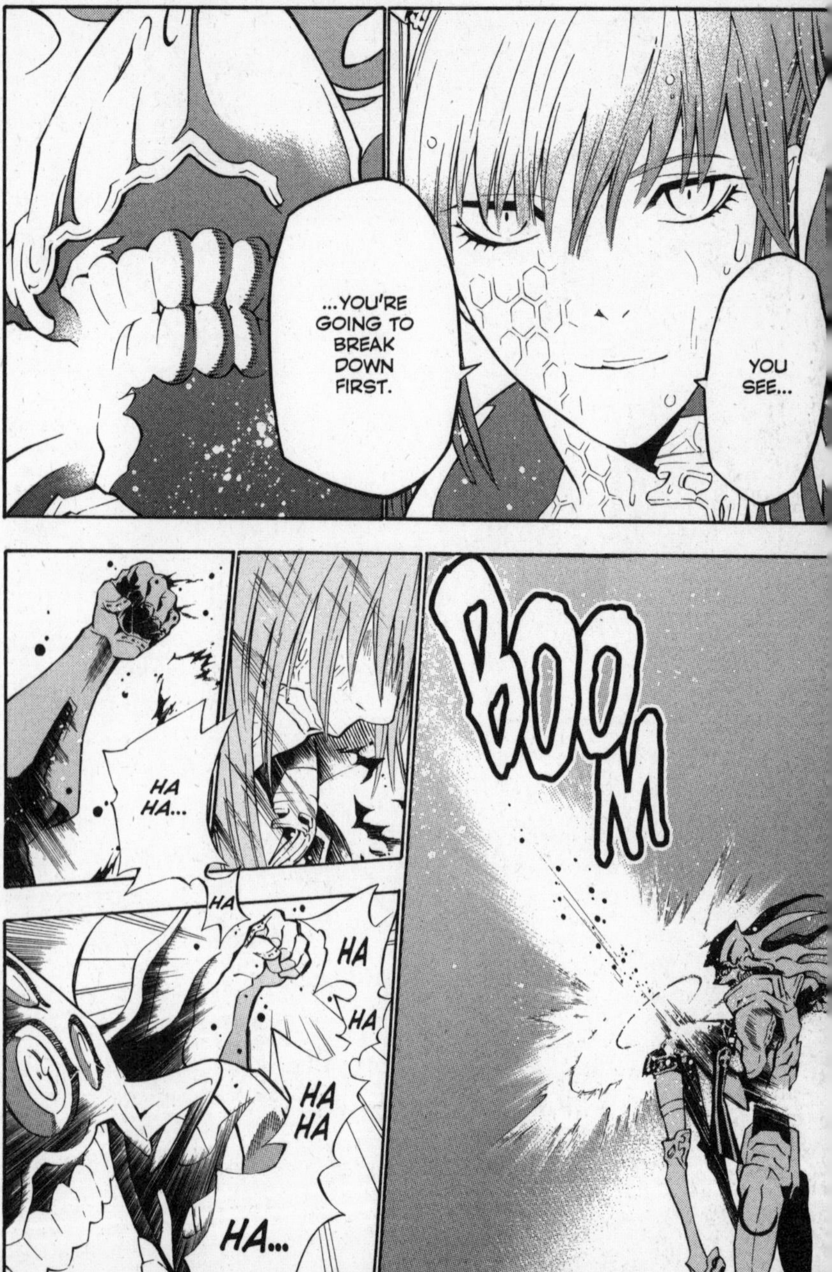
YOU SEE...
...YOU'RE GOING TO BREAK DOWN FIRST.
BOOM
HA HA...
HA
HA
HA
HA HA
HA...

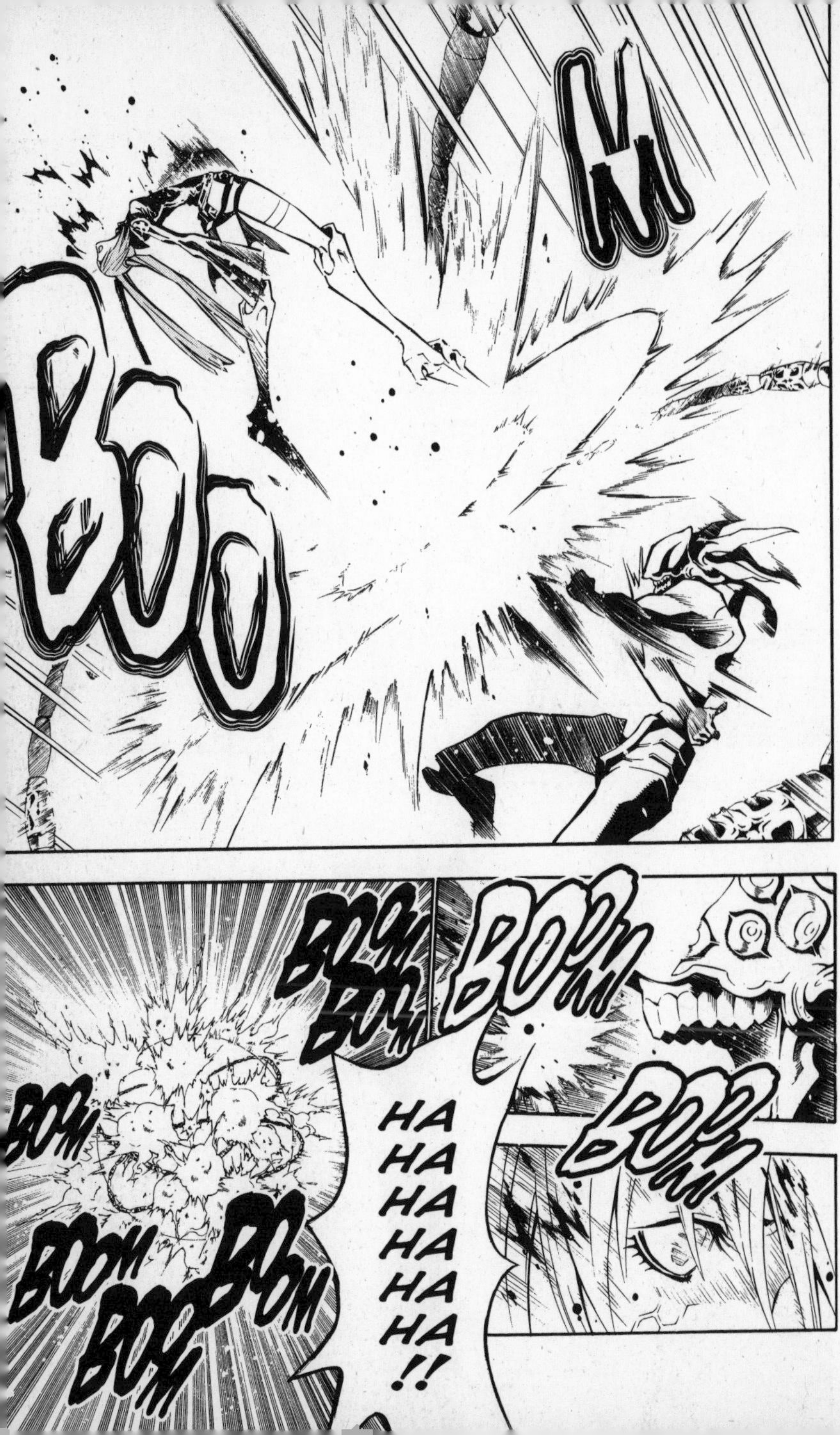
BOOM
BOOM
BOOM
BOOM
HA
HA
HA
HA
HA
HA!!
BOOM
BOOM
BOOM
BOOM

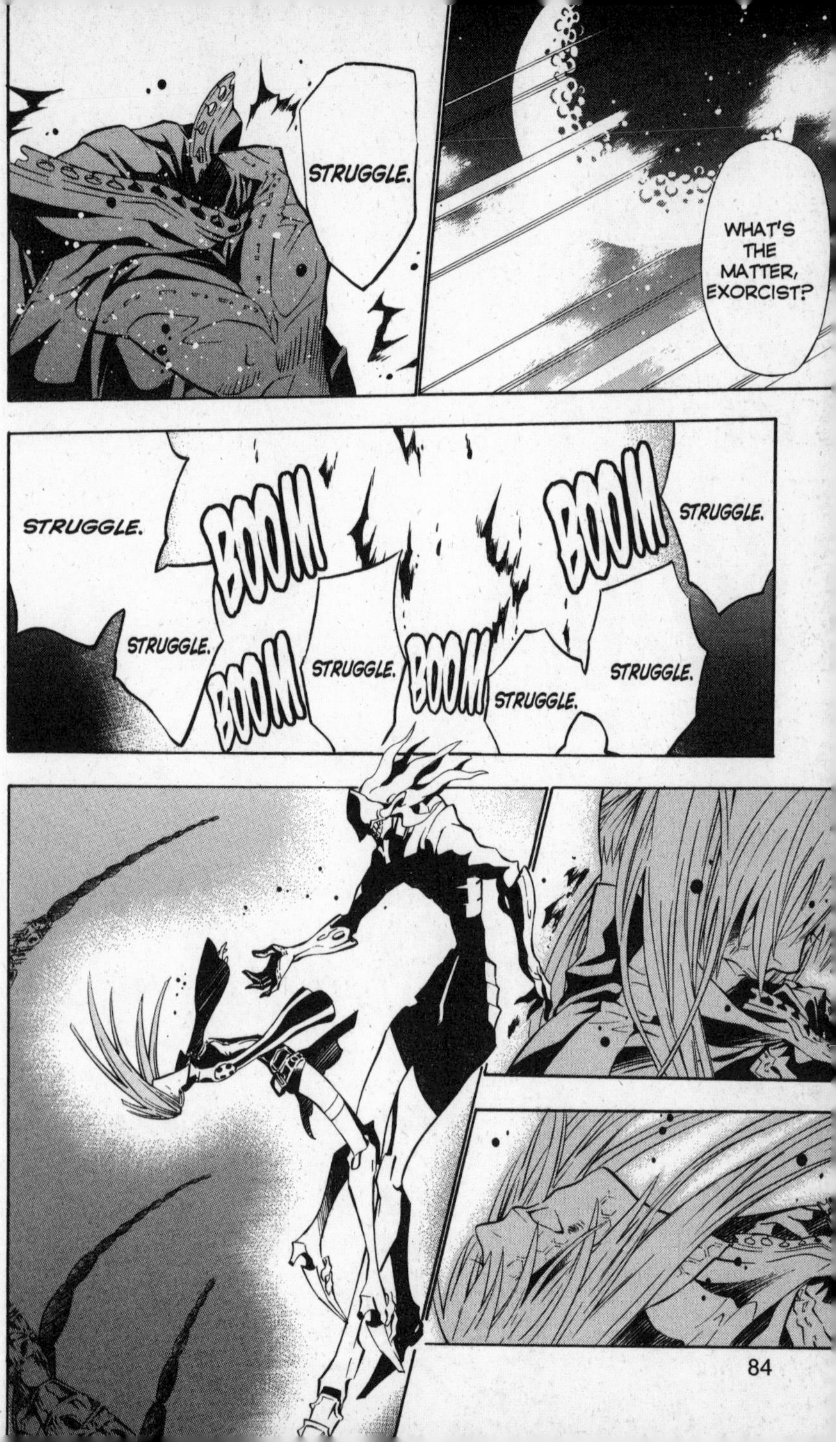
WHAT'S THE MATTER, EXORCIST?
STRUGGLE.
STRUGGLE.
BOOM
BOOM
STRUGGLE.
STRUGGLE.
STRUGGLE.
BOOM
STRUGGLE.
BOOM
STRUGGLE.

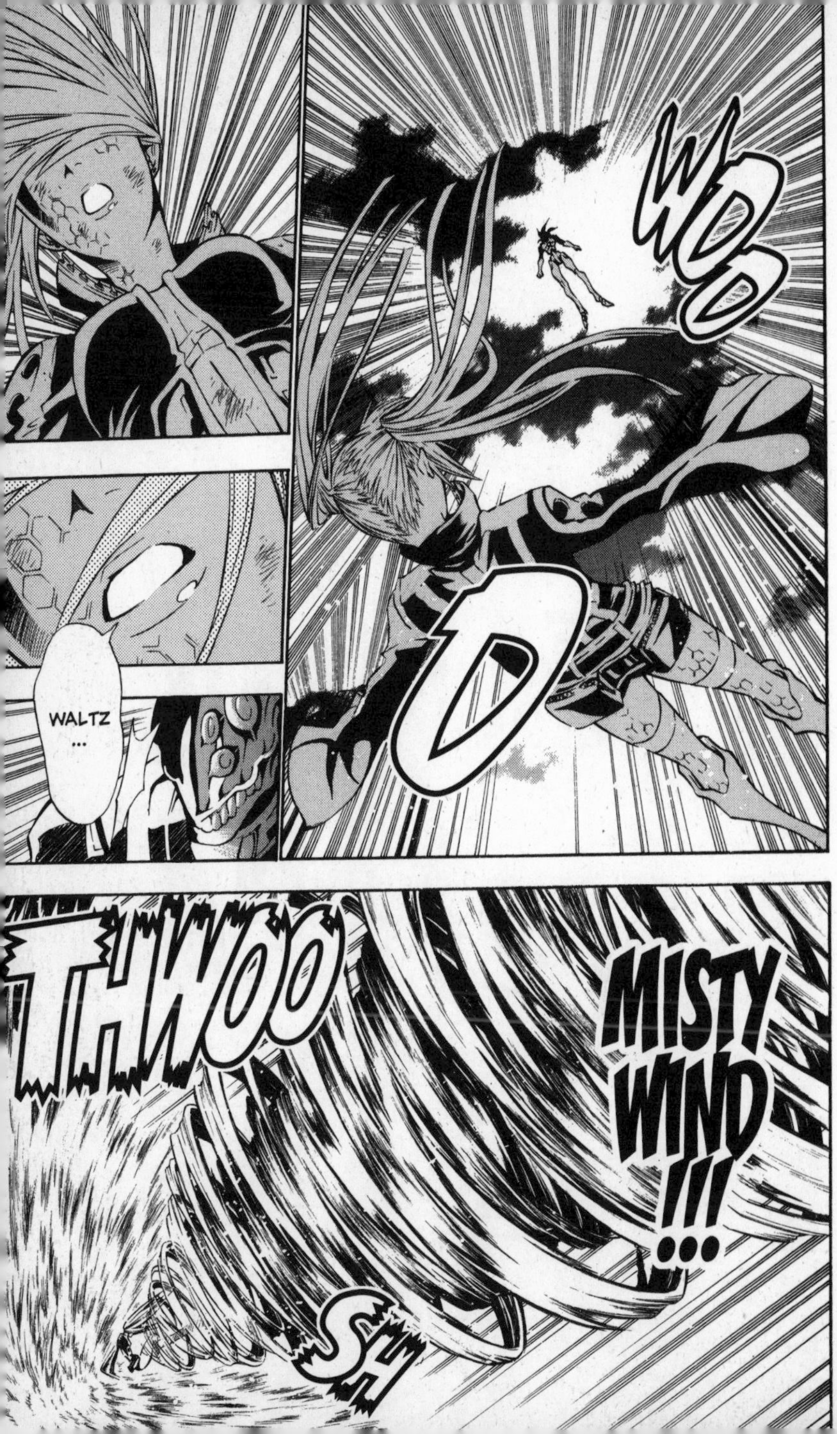
WOOD
D
WALTZ ...
MISTY WIND!!!...
THWOO
SH

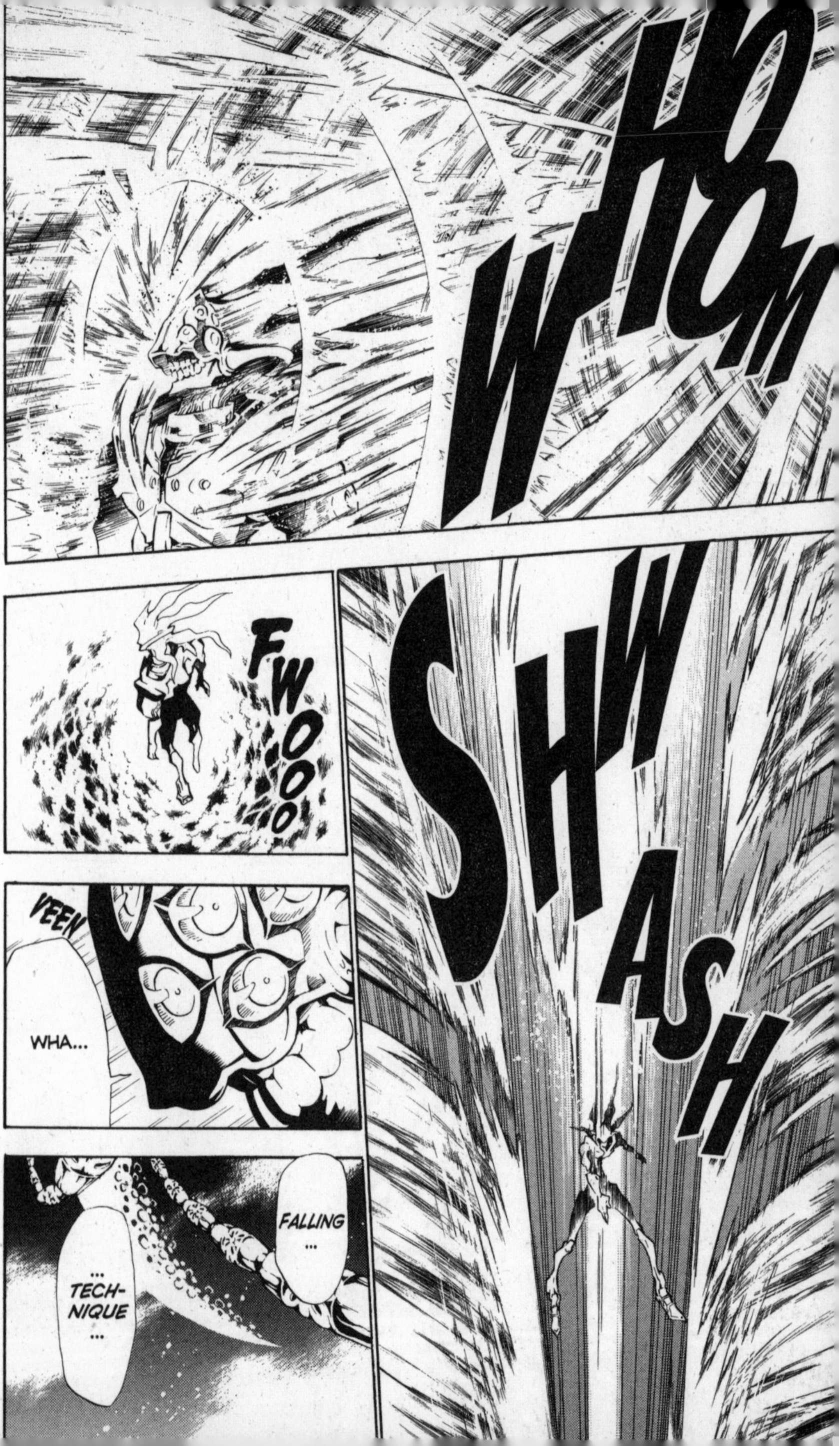
WHOOM
SHWASH
FWOOOO
VEEN
WHA...
FALLING ...
... TECH-NIQUE ...

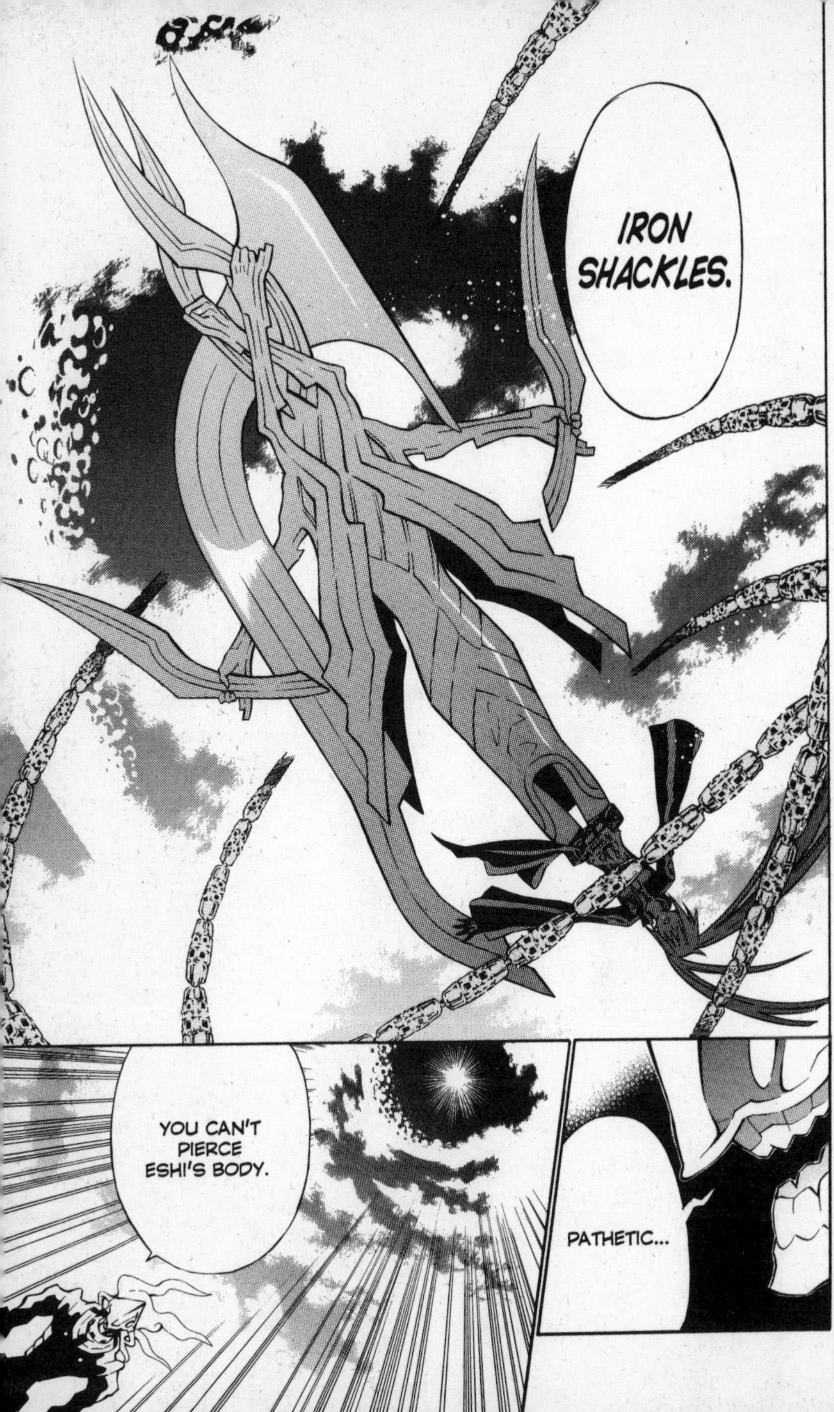
IRON SHACKLES.
PATHETIC...
YOU CAN'T PIERCE ESHI'S BODY.

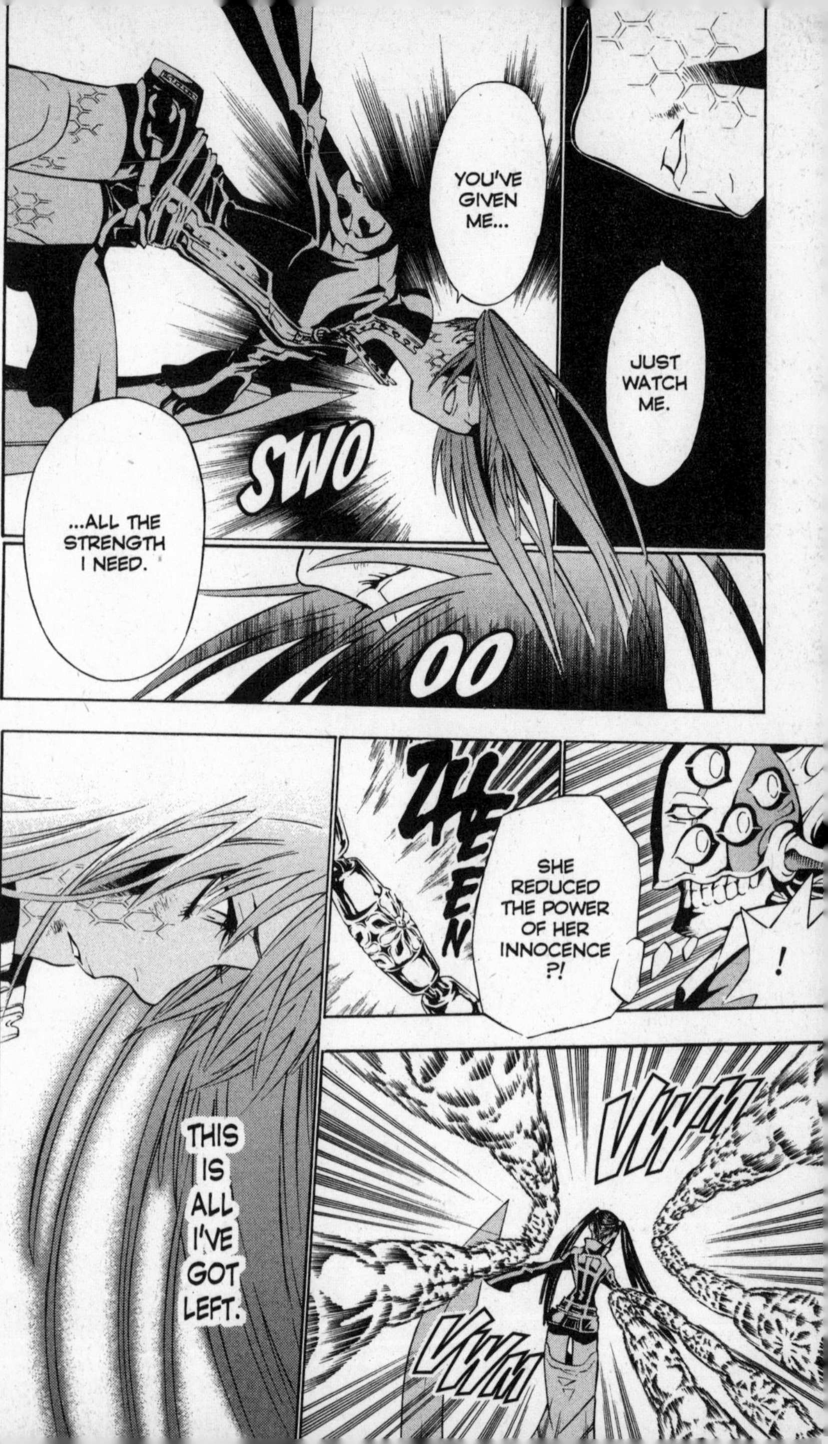
JUST WATCH ME.
YOU'VE GIVEN ME...
SWO
...ALL THE STRENGTH I NEED.
OO
!
SHE REDUCED THE POWER OF HER INNOCENCE?!
ZHEEN
VWM
VWM
THIS IS ALL I'VE GOT LEFT.

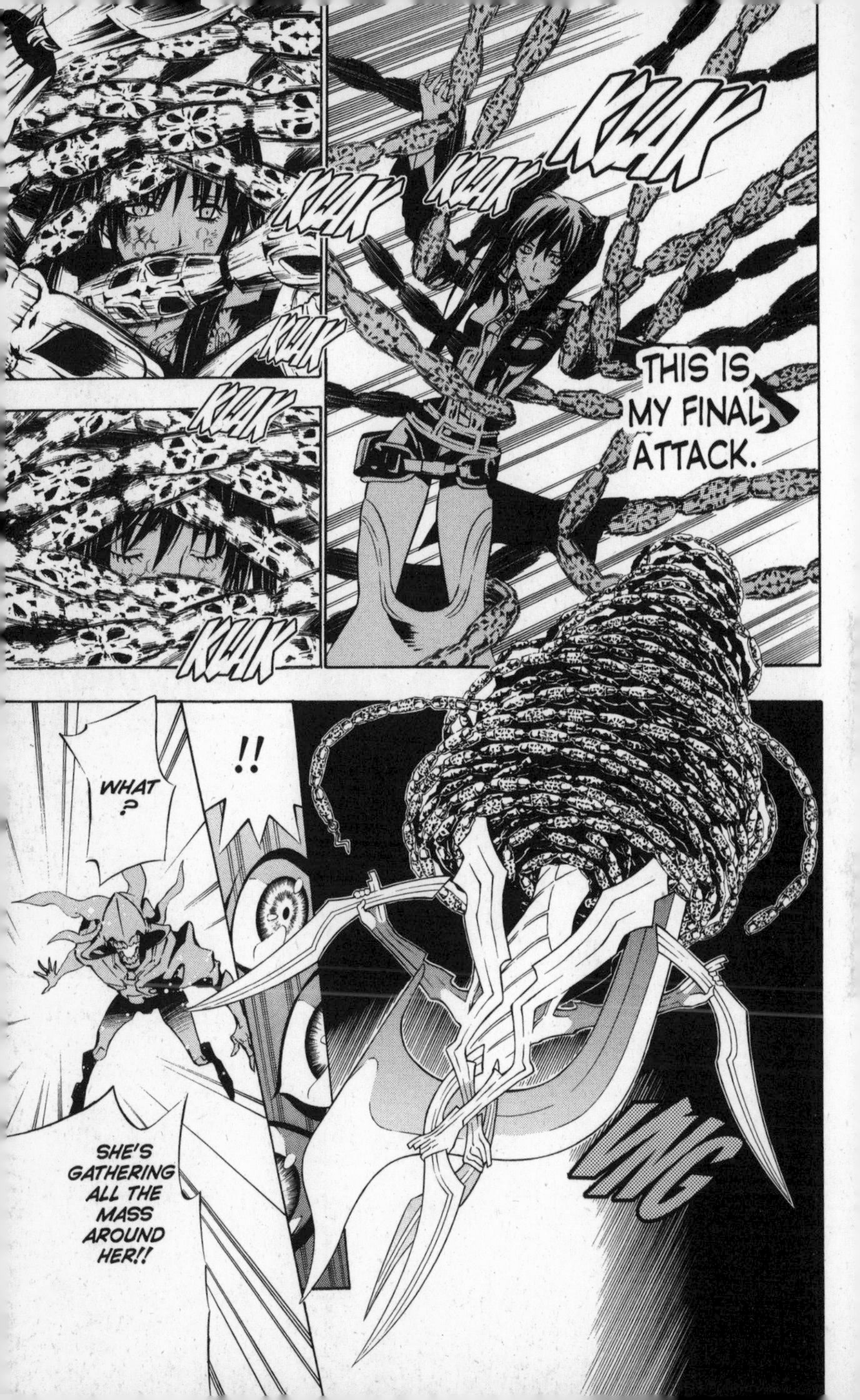
KLAK
KLAK
KLAK
THIS IS MY FINAL ATTACK.
KLAK
KLAK
KLAK
!!
WHAT?
SHE'S GATHERING ALL THE MASS AROUND HER!!
WNG

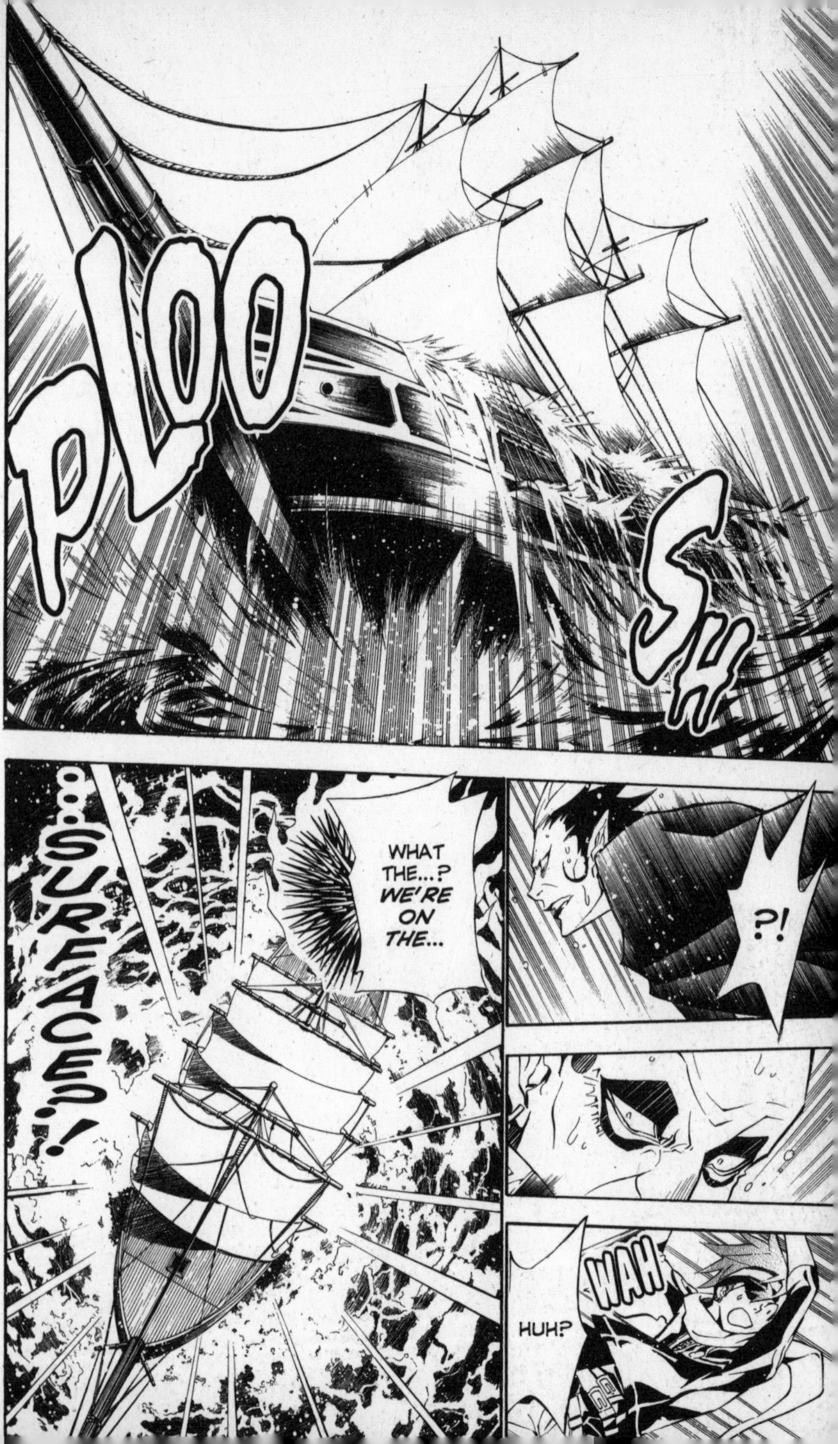
PLOOSH
?!
WAH
HUH?
WHAT THE...? WE'RE ON THE...
...SURFACE?!

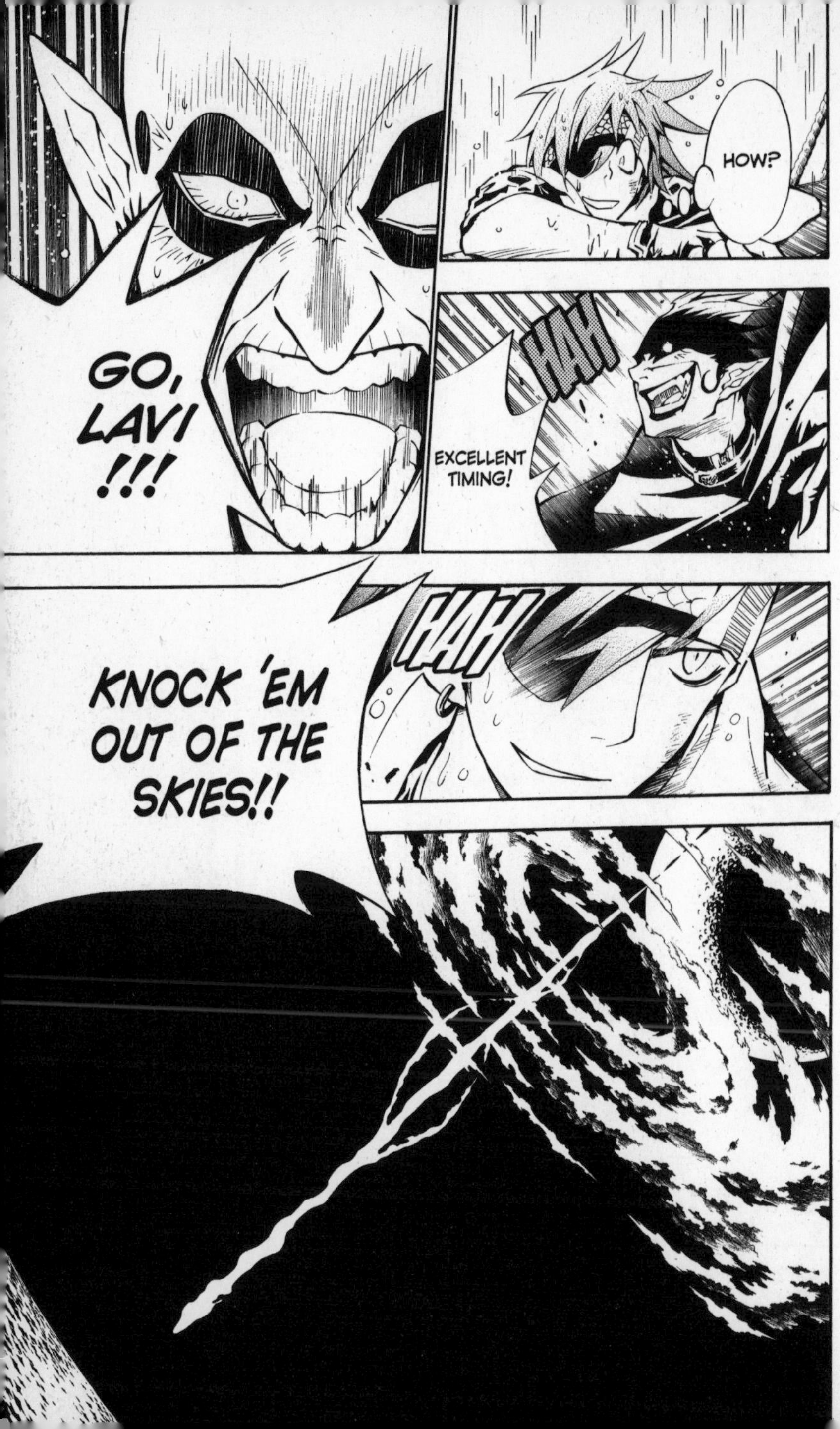
HOW?
HAH
EXCELLENT TIMING!
GO, LAVI!!!
HAH
KNOCK 'EM OUT OF THE SKIES!!

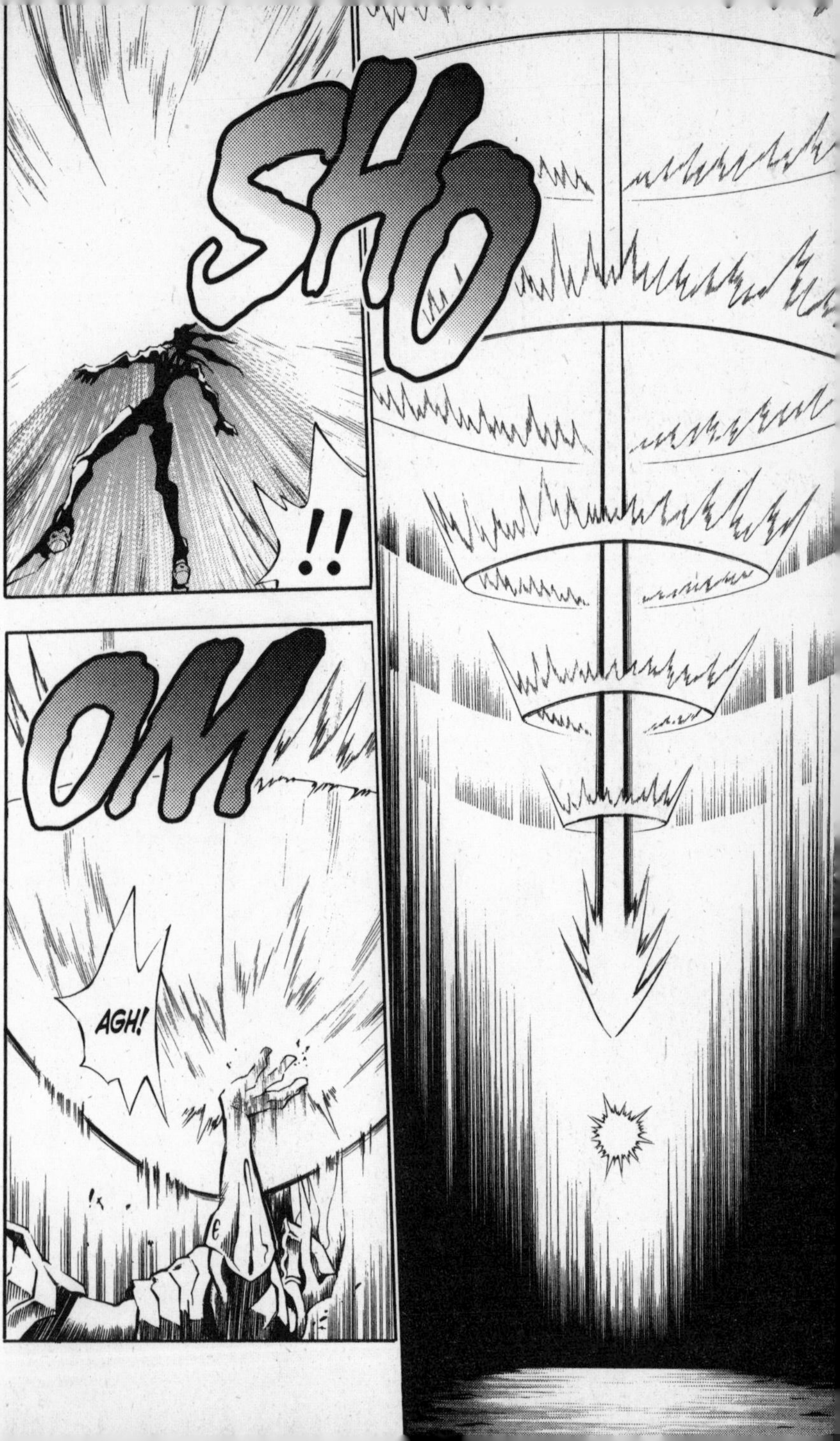
SHO
!!
OM
AGH!

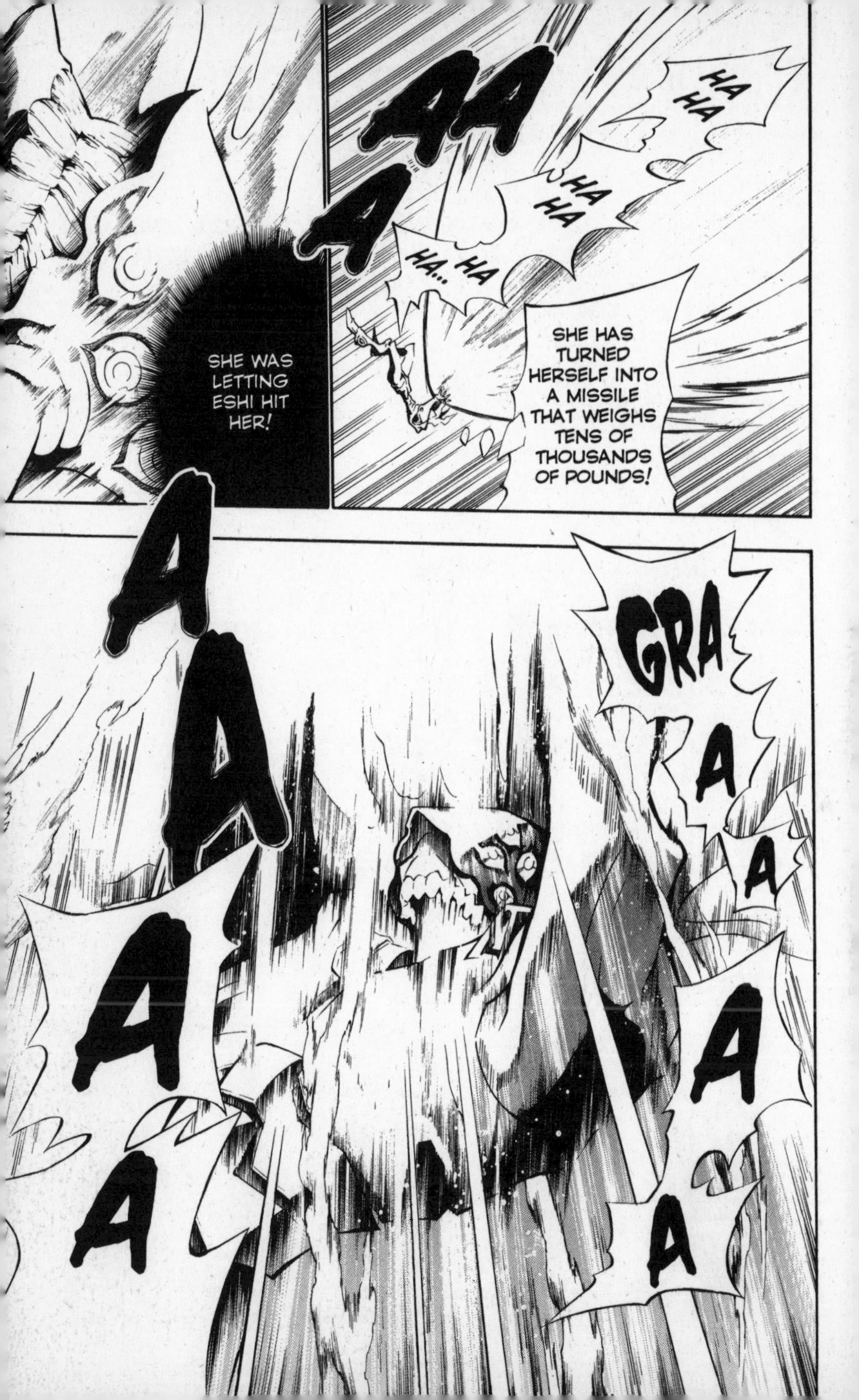
HA HA
HA HA
HA... HA
SHE HAS TURNED HERSELF INTO A MISSILE THAT WEIGHS TENS OF THOUSANDS OF POUNDS!
AAA A
SHE WAS LETTING ESHI HIT HER!
GRAAAAA
AAAAA

Komui's Discussion Room, Vol. 4

Q: THE OTHER DAY I WAS READING VOLUME 12 OF *GINTAMA*, AND I THOUGHT I WAS SEEING THINGS. I NOTICED A PICTURE OF LAVI FROM "THE 59TH NIGHT" IN THE LETTERS SECTION. THE ARTIST, SORACHI, SAID IT WAS JUST A MISUNDERSTANDING AND THAT "IT LOOKED LIKE LAVI HAD BEEN SUFFERING AND NEEDED A BREAK." HOW DO YOU FEEL ABOUT OTHER ARTISTS COMMENTING ON YOUR CHARACTERS?
(ALLEN) I HEARD THE STORY FROM ONE OF THE ASSISTANTS. I HAD A GOOD LAUGH ABOUT IT.
(KANDA) IT'S NOT UNUSUAL FOR POSTCARDS AND ILLUSTRATIONS TO GET MIXED UP.

Q: IS MAHOJA A MAN OR A WOMAN?
(ALLEN) SHE'S A WOMAN ALL RIGHT. SHE'S ALSO THE FIRST WOMAN EVER TO PICK ME UP AND CARRY ME LIKE THAT.
(KANDA) PATHETIC. (HEH)
(ALLEN) GRRR...

Q: IS BOOKMAN'S PANDA-LIKE MAKEUP PROTECTION AGAINST SOMETHING?
(ALLEN) HUH? I DON'T KNOW.
(KANDA) I DON'T KNOW AND I DON'T CARE.
(ALLEN) I'LL BE SURE TO ASK LAVI NEXT TIME I SEE HIM.

ZAK ZAK ZAK ZAK

THE 72ND NIGHT: DISAPPEARING FROM THE SEA

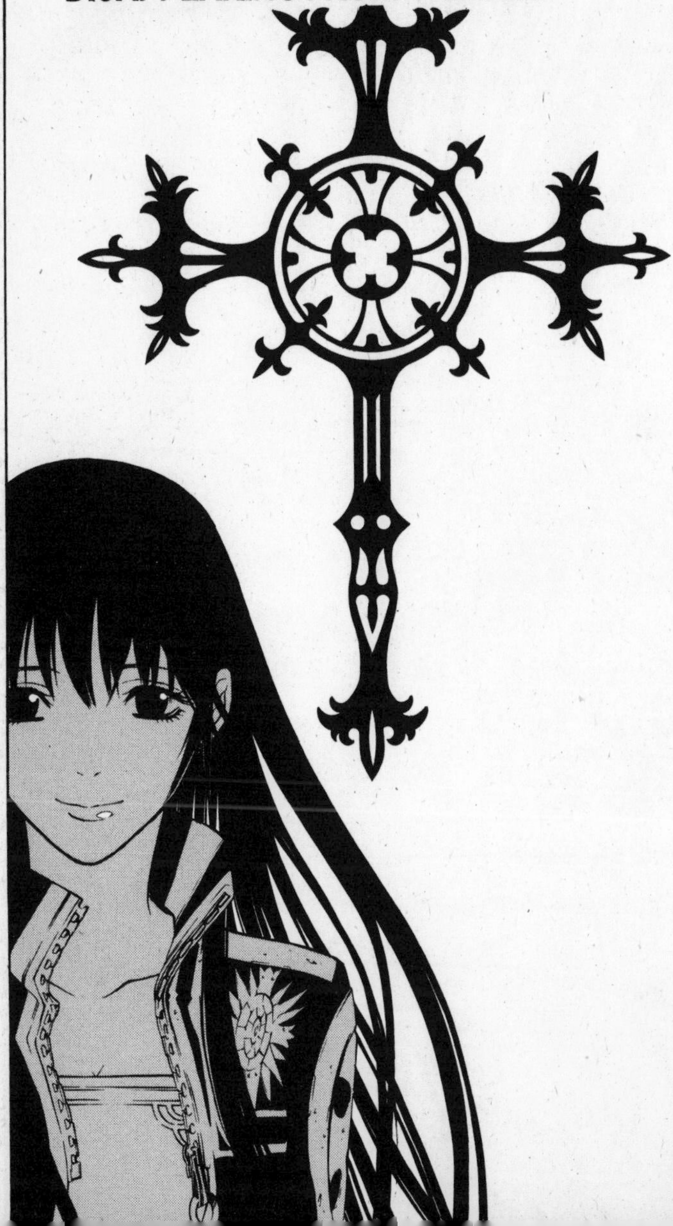

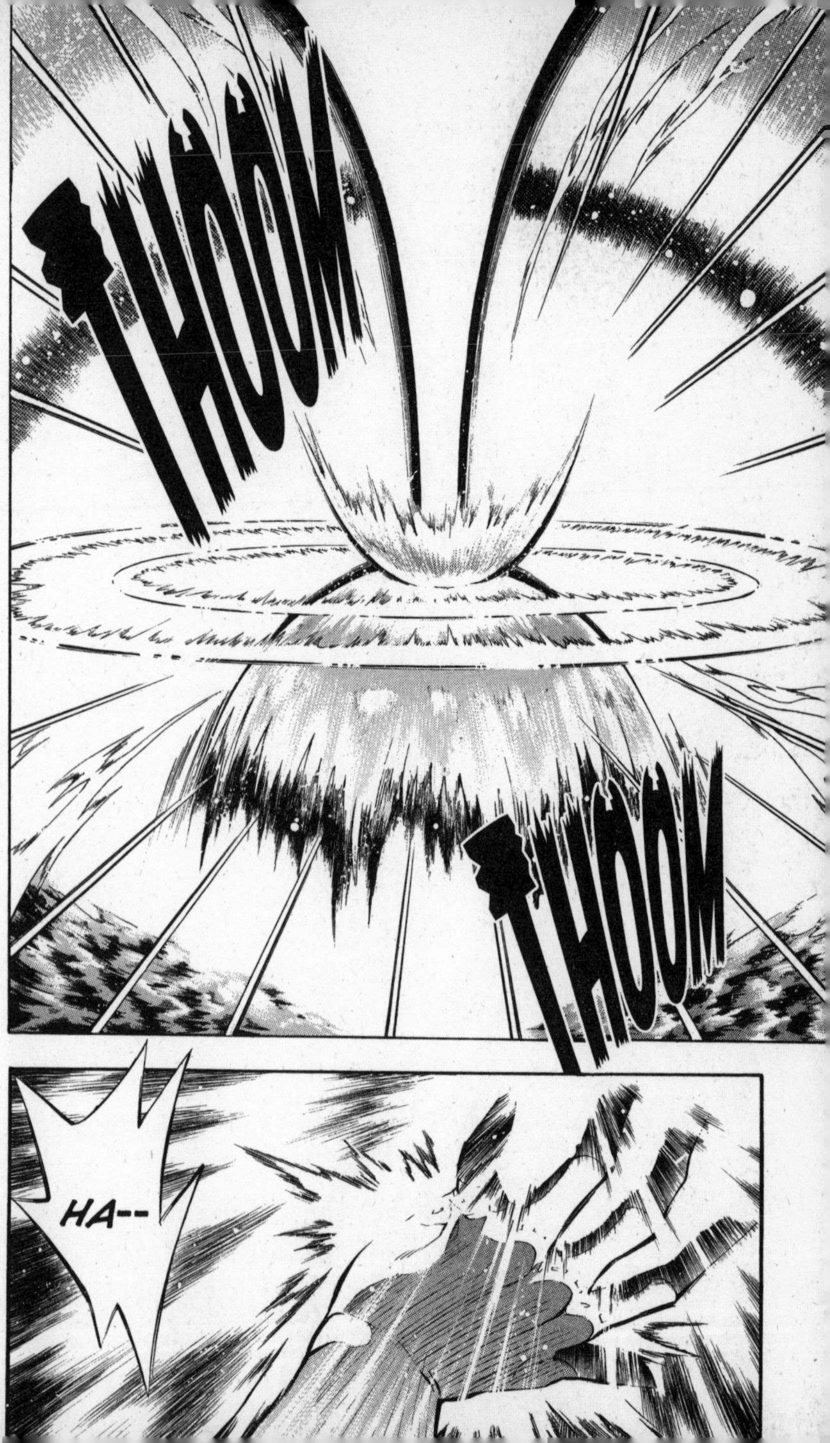
THOOM
THOOM
HA--

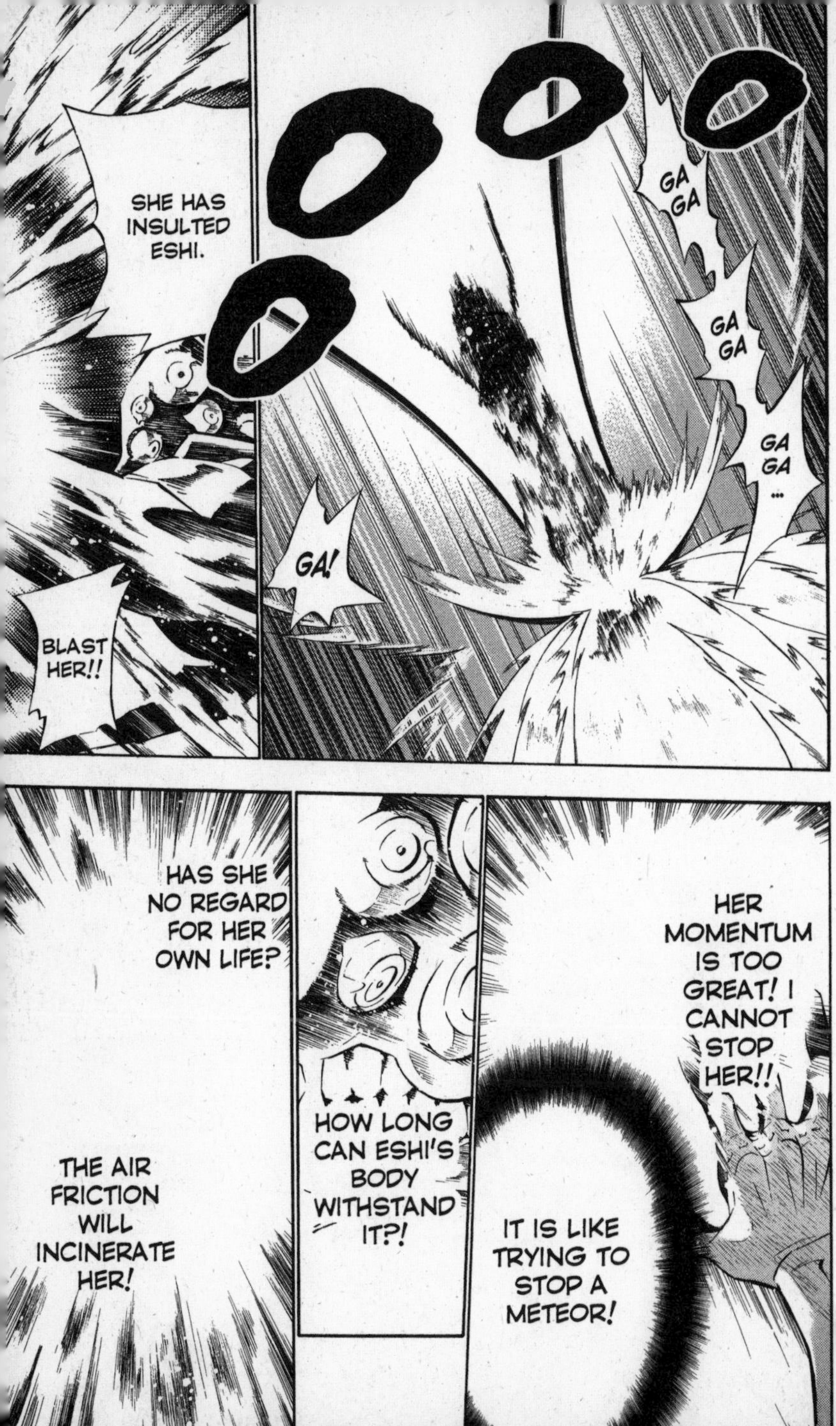
GA GA
GA GA
GA GA ...
GA!
SHE HAS INSULTED ESHI.
BLAST HER!!
HER MOMENTUM IS TOO GREAT! I CANNOT STOP HER!!
IT IS LIKE TRYING TO STOP A METEOR!
HOW LONG CAN ESHI'S BODY WITHSTAND IT?!
HAS SHE NO REGARD FOR HER OWN LIFE?
THE AIR FRICTION WILL INCINERATE HER!

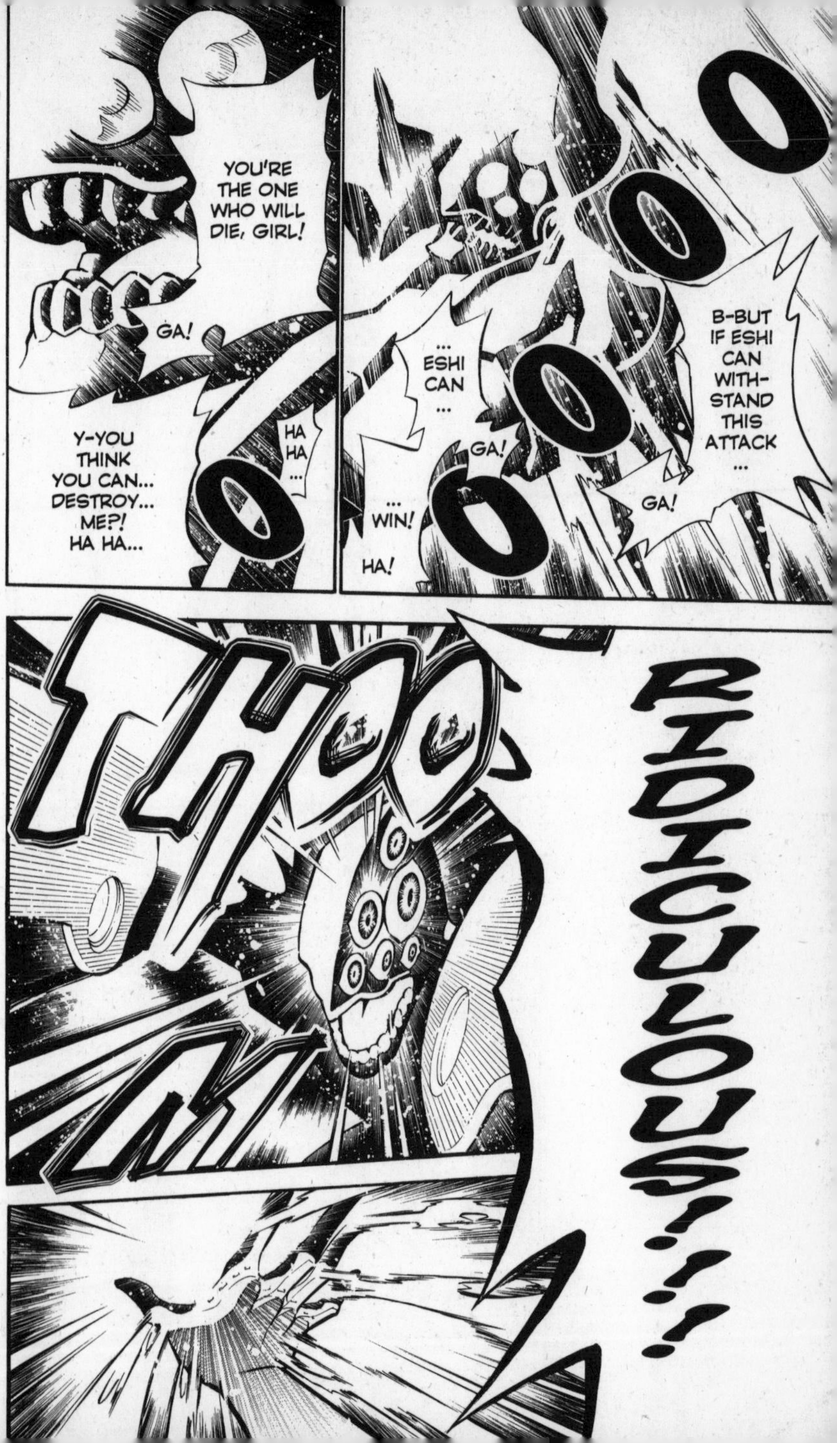
OOOOO
B-BUT IF ESHI CAN WITH-STAND THIS ATTACK ...
GA!
GA!
... ESHI CAN ...
... WIN!
HA!
YOU'RE THE ONE WHO WILL DIE, GIRL!
GA!
HA HA ...
Y-YOU THINK YOU CAN... DESTROY... ME?! HA HA...
RIDICULOUS!!!
THOOM

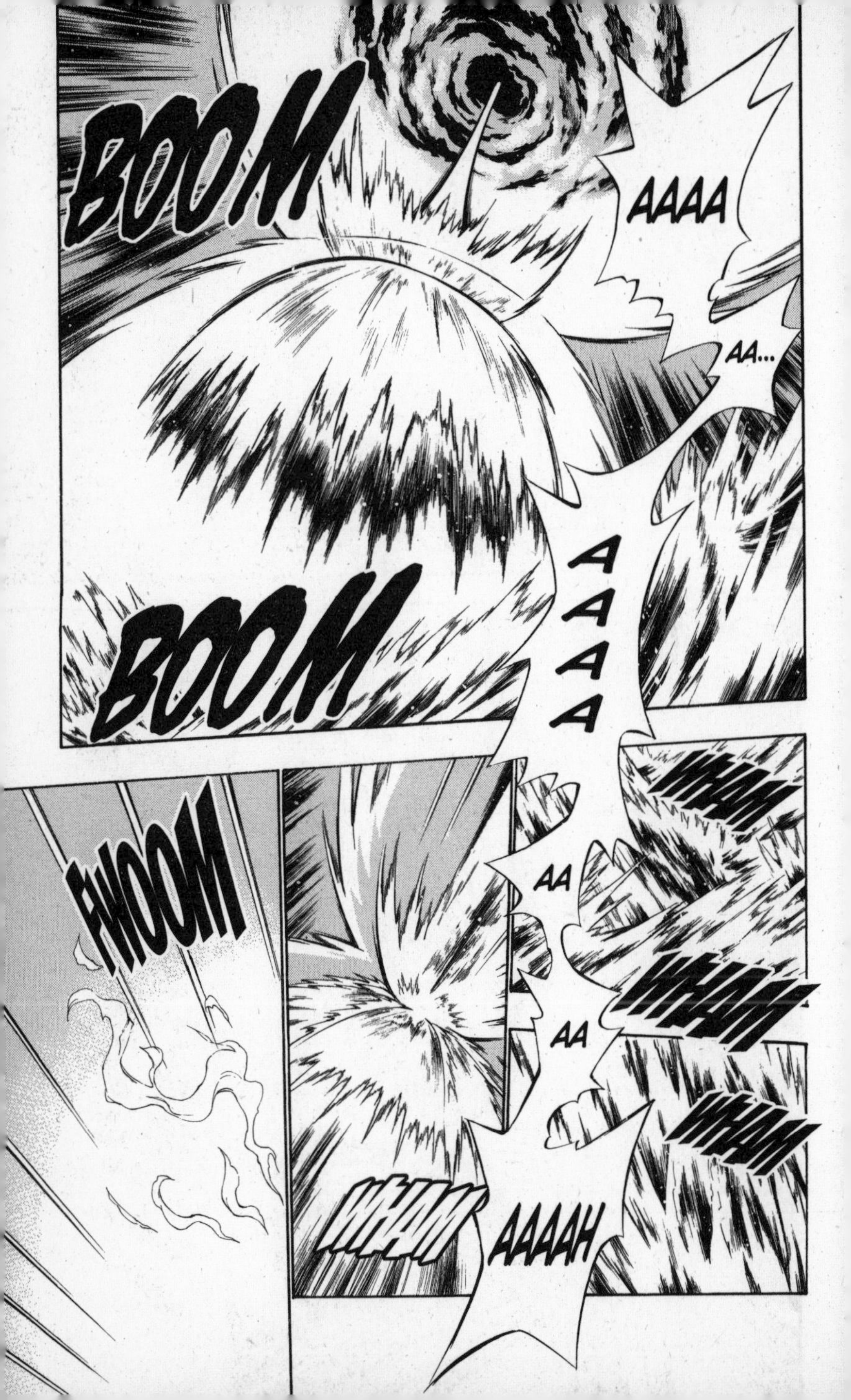
AAAA
BOOM
AA...
AAAA
BOOM
WHAM
AA
WHAM
AA
WHAM
WHAM
AAAAH
FWOOM

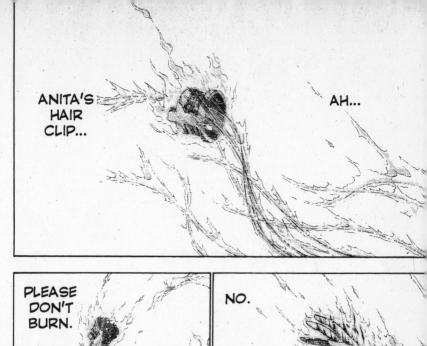

ANITA'S HAIR CLIP...

AH...

PLEASE DON'T BURN.

NO.

BOO

!!!

M

YOU'RE IMPORTANT TO ME.

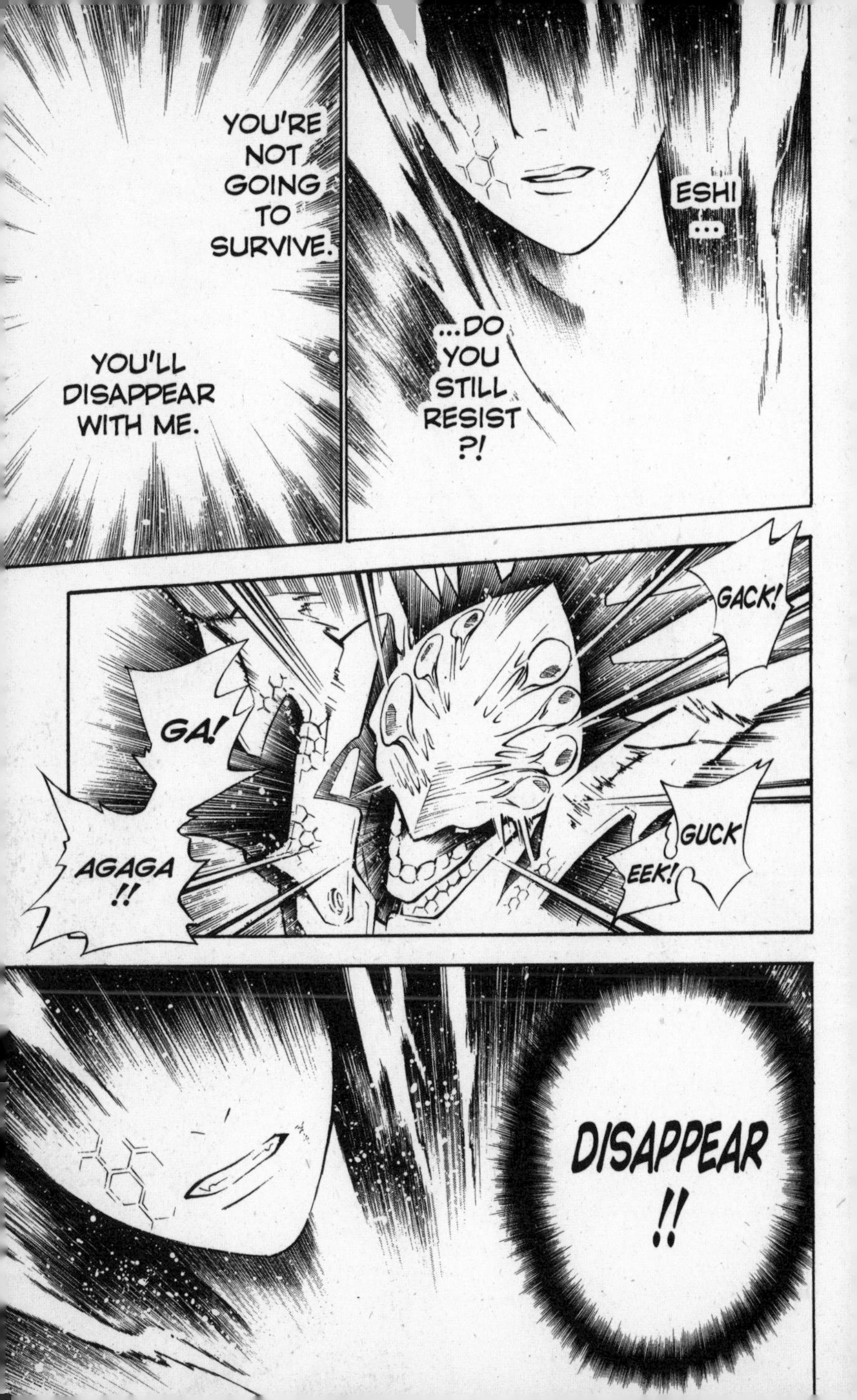
ESHI...
...DO YOU STILL RESIST?!
YOU'RE NOT GOING TO SURVIVE.
YOU'LL DISAPPEAR WITH ME.
GACK!
GUCK
EEK!
GA!
AGAGA!!
DISAPPEAR!!

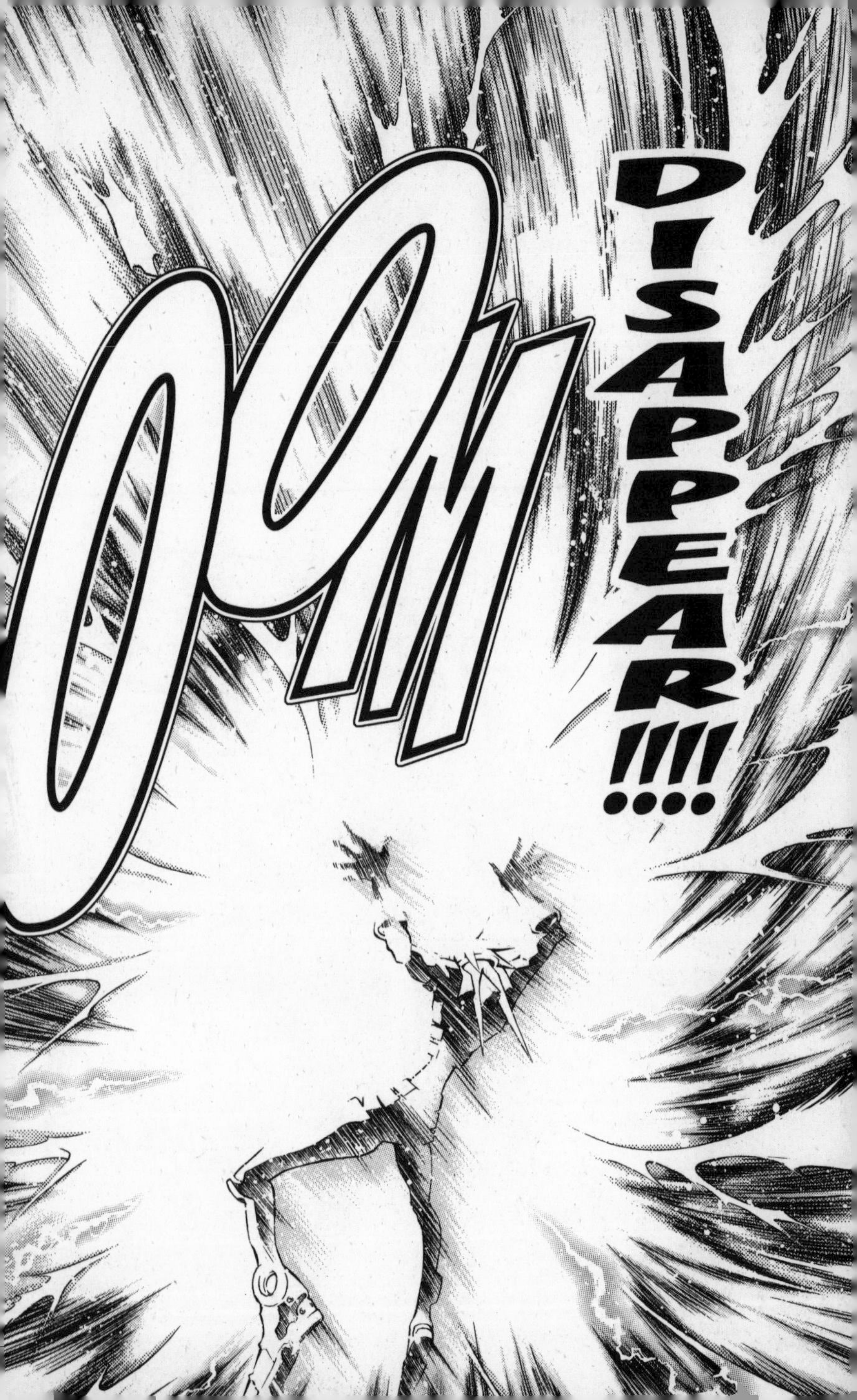
DISAPPEAR!!!!

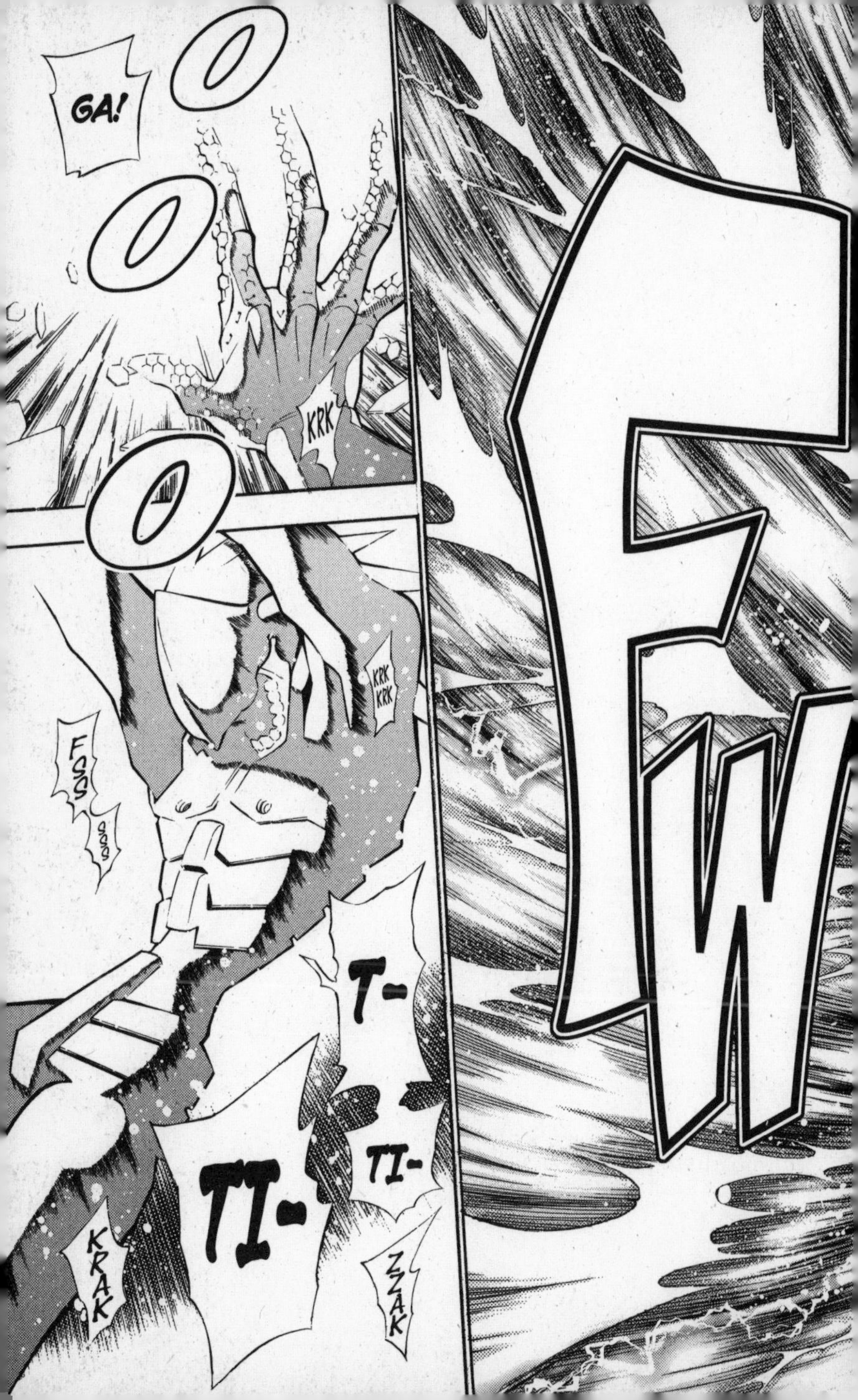
FW
O
GA!
O
KRK
O
KRK KRK
FSS
SSS
T-
TI-
TI-
ZZAK
KRAK

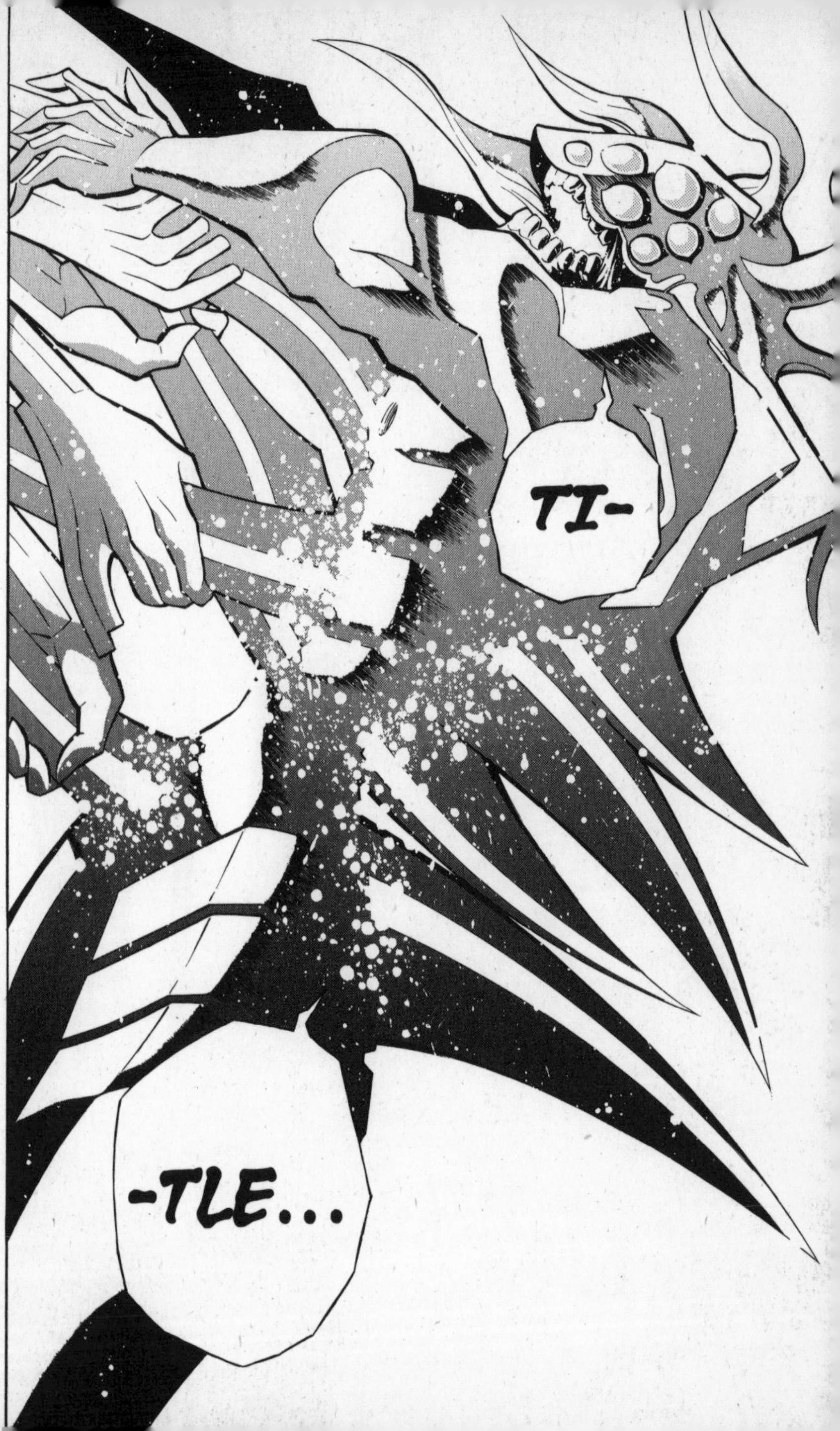
TI-
-TLE...

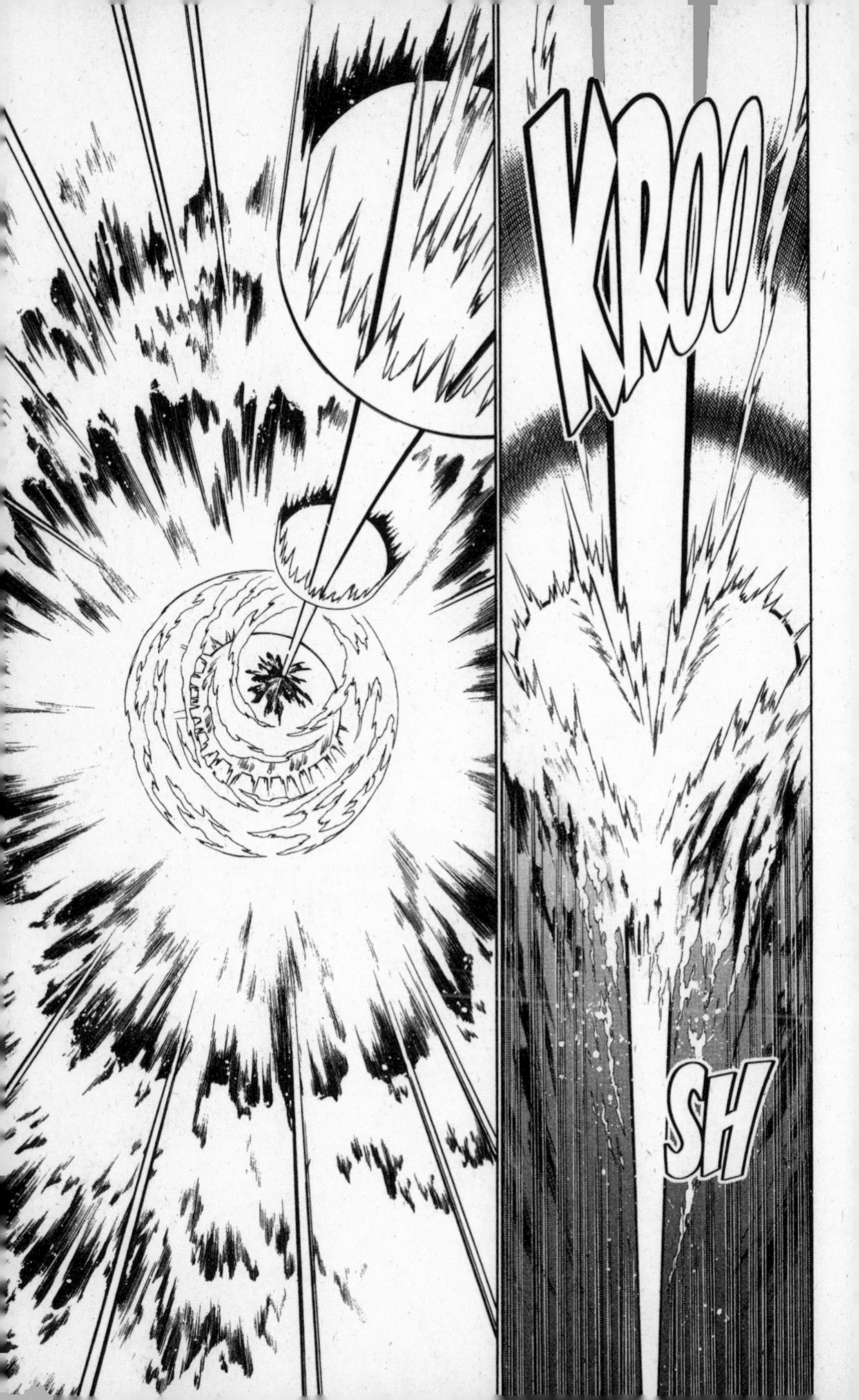
KROO
SH

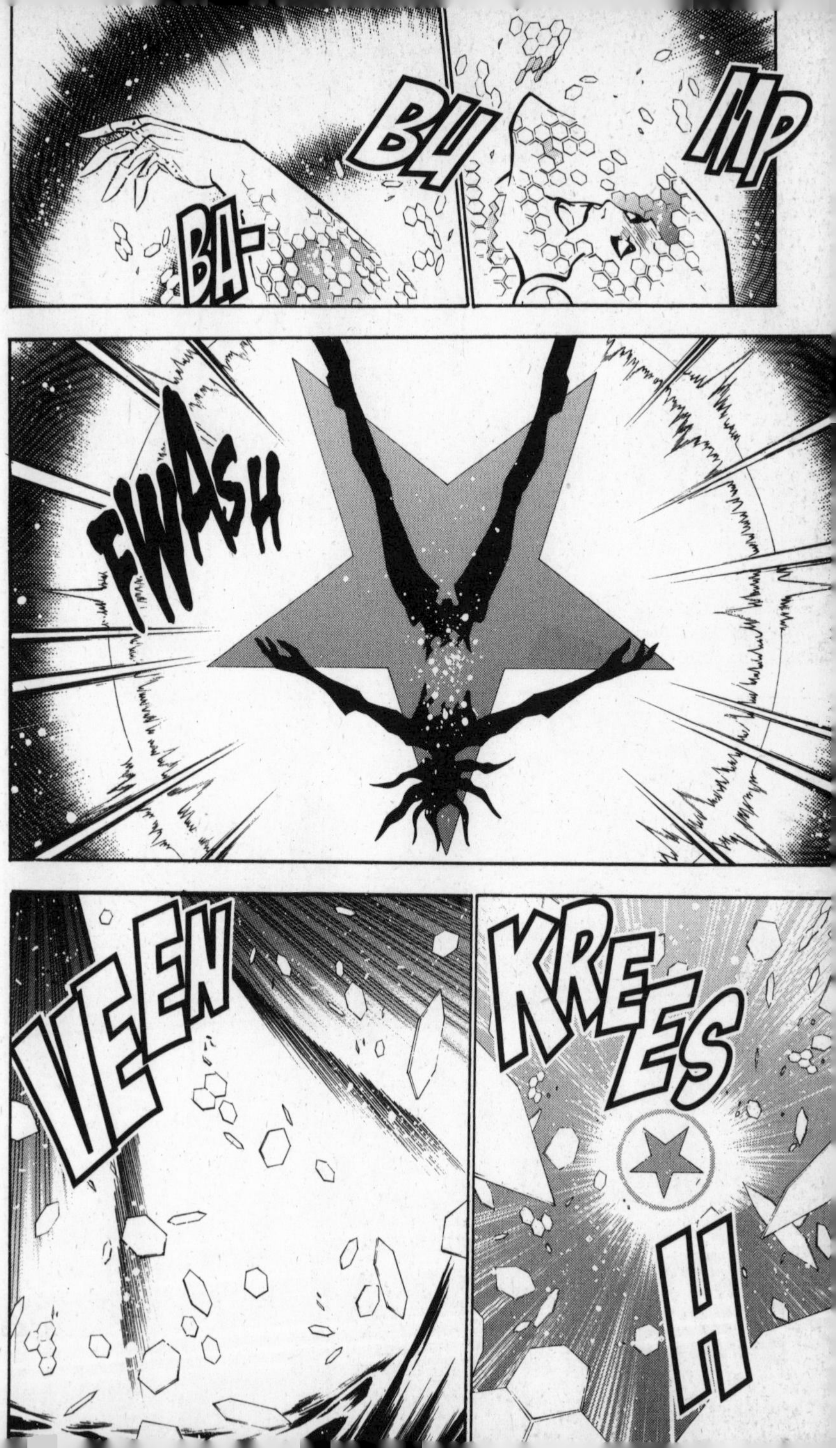
BA-BUMP
FWASH
KREESH
VEEN

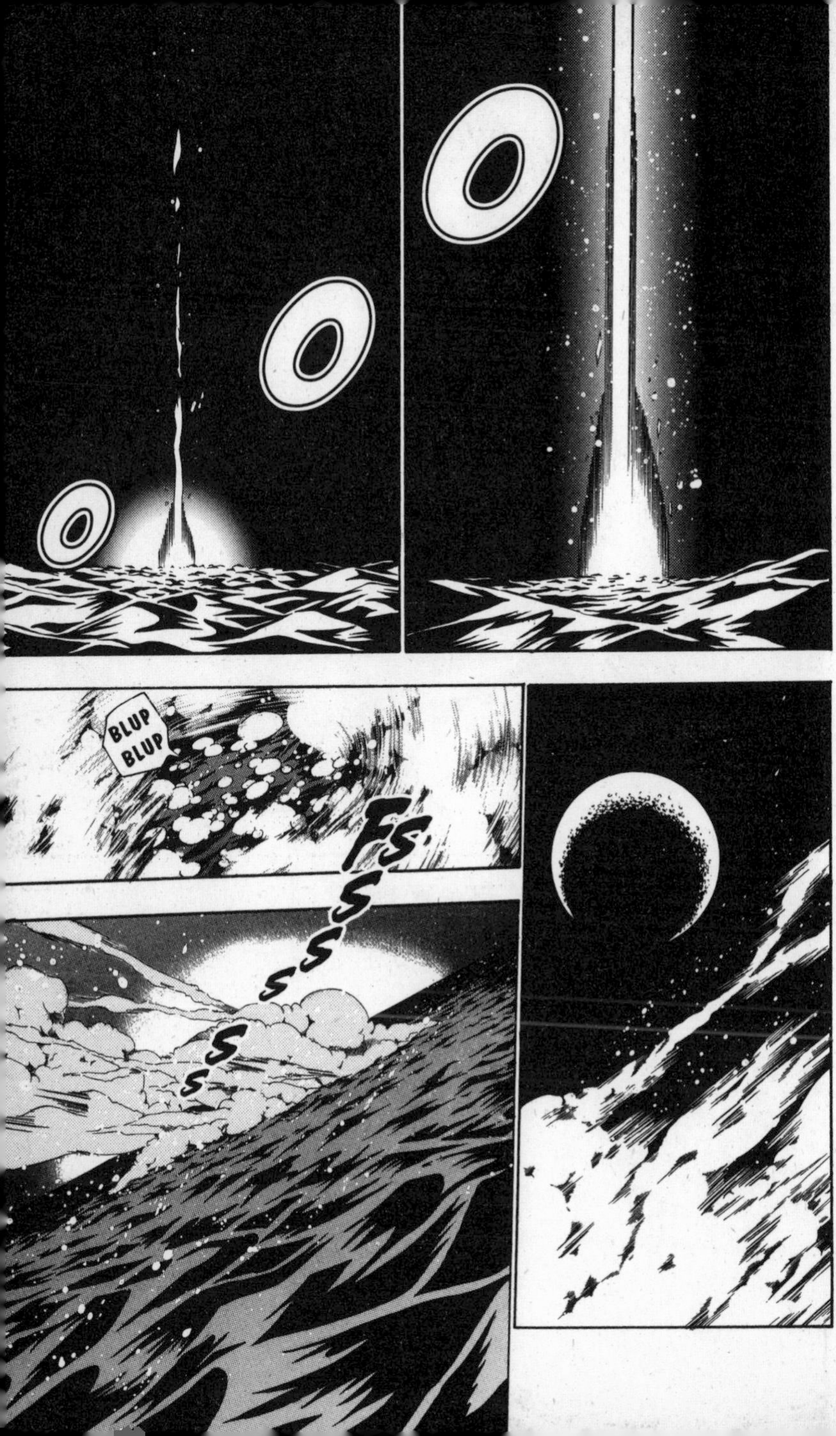
BLUP BLUP
FSSSSSSS

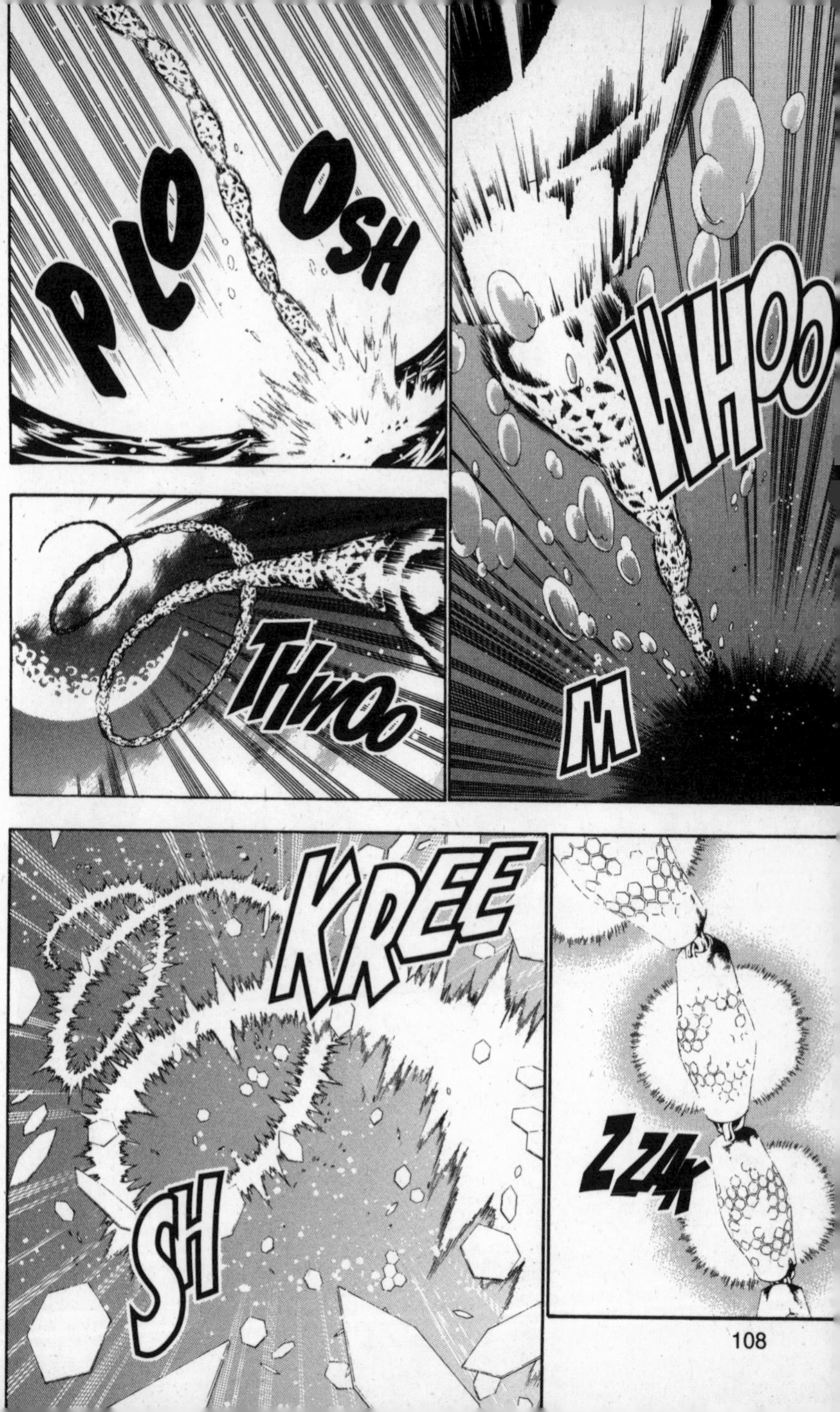
WHOOM
PLOOSH
THWOO
ZZAK
KREESH

KAMUI...

WOOO

BIG BROTHER ...

I'M SORRY.

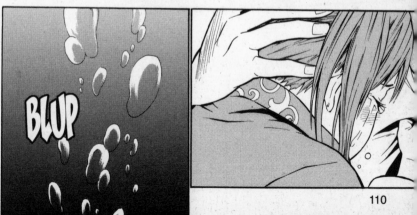

BLUP

KOMUI'S DISCUSSION ROOM, VOL. 5

Q: WHEN DID KOMUI DEVELOP THIS STRANGE ATTACHMENT TO HIS SISTER?
(ALLEN) HMM... I DON'T KNOW. MAYBE IT'S BECAUSE THE ORDER TOOK HER AWAY WHEN SHE WAS A CHILD. IF SO, THEN MAYBE IT'S NOT SO STRANGE AFTER ALL.
(KANDA) DON'T MAKE EXCUSES FOR HIS WEIRDNESS! HE'S SICK IN THE HEAD!

Q: WHO DO YOU THINK IS THE MOST POPULAR WITH THE OPPOSITE SEX?
(ALLEN) WELL, IT'S DEFINITELY NOT KANDA.
(KANDA) I PAY NO ATTENTION TO SUCH THINGS. THE BUSINESS OF THE BLACK ORDER IS WAR! THOSE WHO HAVE NO STOMACH FOR IT SHOULD GET OUT!
(ALLEN) OUCH! BE CAREFUL! YOU'RE SPILLING YOUR TEA ON ME!
(KANDA) HEY! THAT'S COLD! YOU STUPID BEAN SPROUT! HOW DARE YOU SPLASH THAT STICKY SLOP ON ME! I'LL CUT YOU DOWN!
(ALLEN) IT'S JUST MANGO JUICE!!

KA-POW!

(LAVI) WELL, THEY'VE STARTED FIGHTING SO THAT'S IT FOR THIS VOLUME...

ZAK ZAK ZAK ZAK

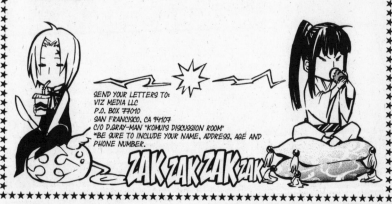

SEND YOUR LETTERS TO:
VIZ MEDIA LLC
P.O. BOX 77010
SAN FRANCISCO, CA 94107
C/O D.GRAY-MAN "KOMUI'S DISCUSSION ROOM"
*BE SURE TO INCLUDE YOUR NAME, ADDRESS, AGE AND PHONE NUMBER.

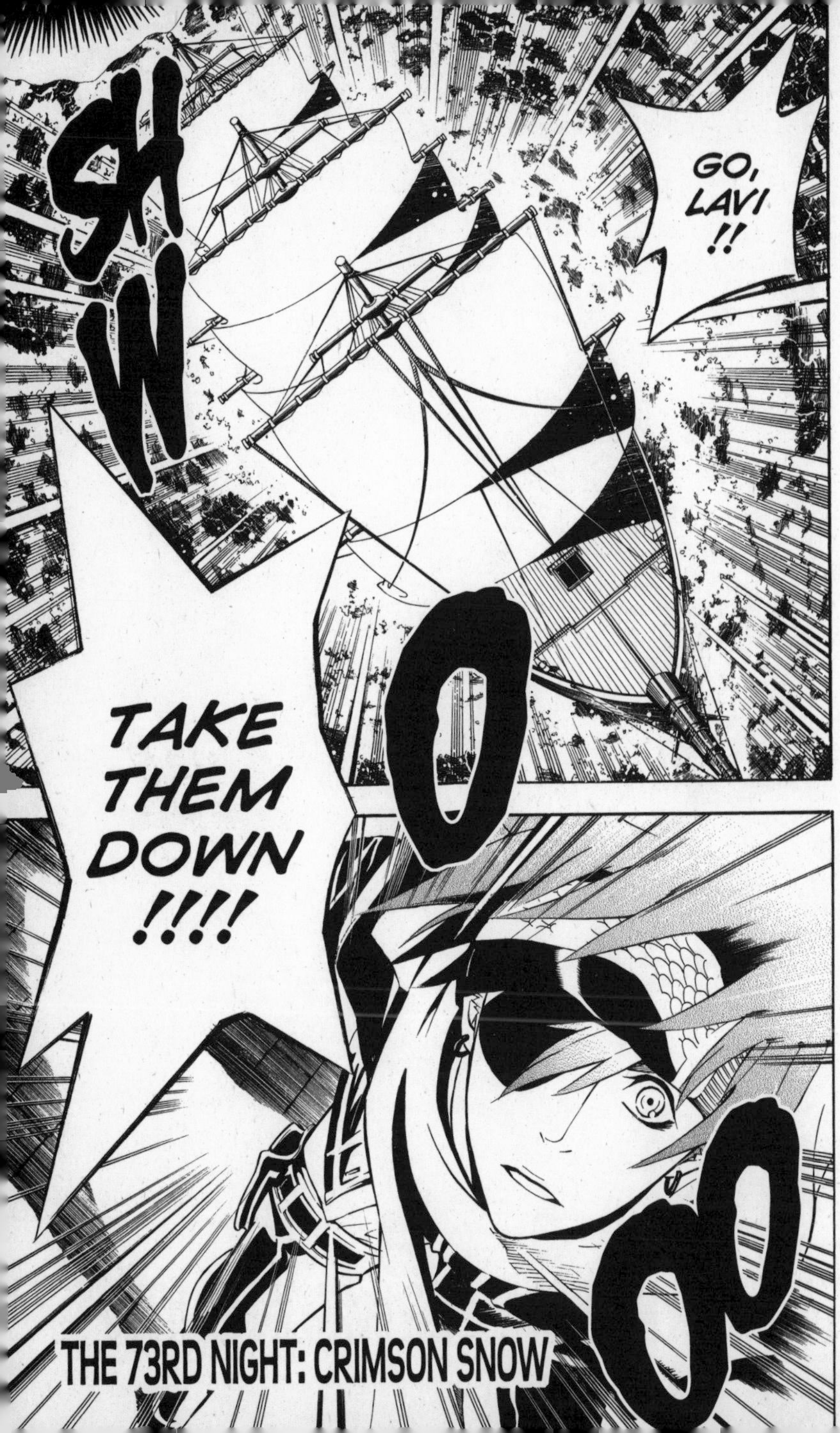
GO, LAVI!!
SHWOOO
TAKE THEM DOWN!!!!
THE 73RD NIGHT: CRIMSON SNOW

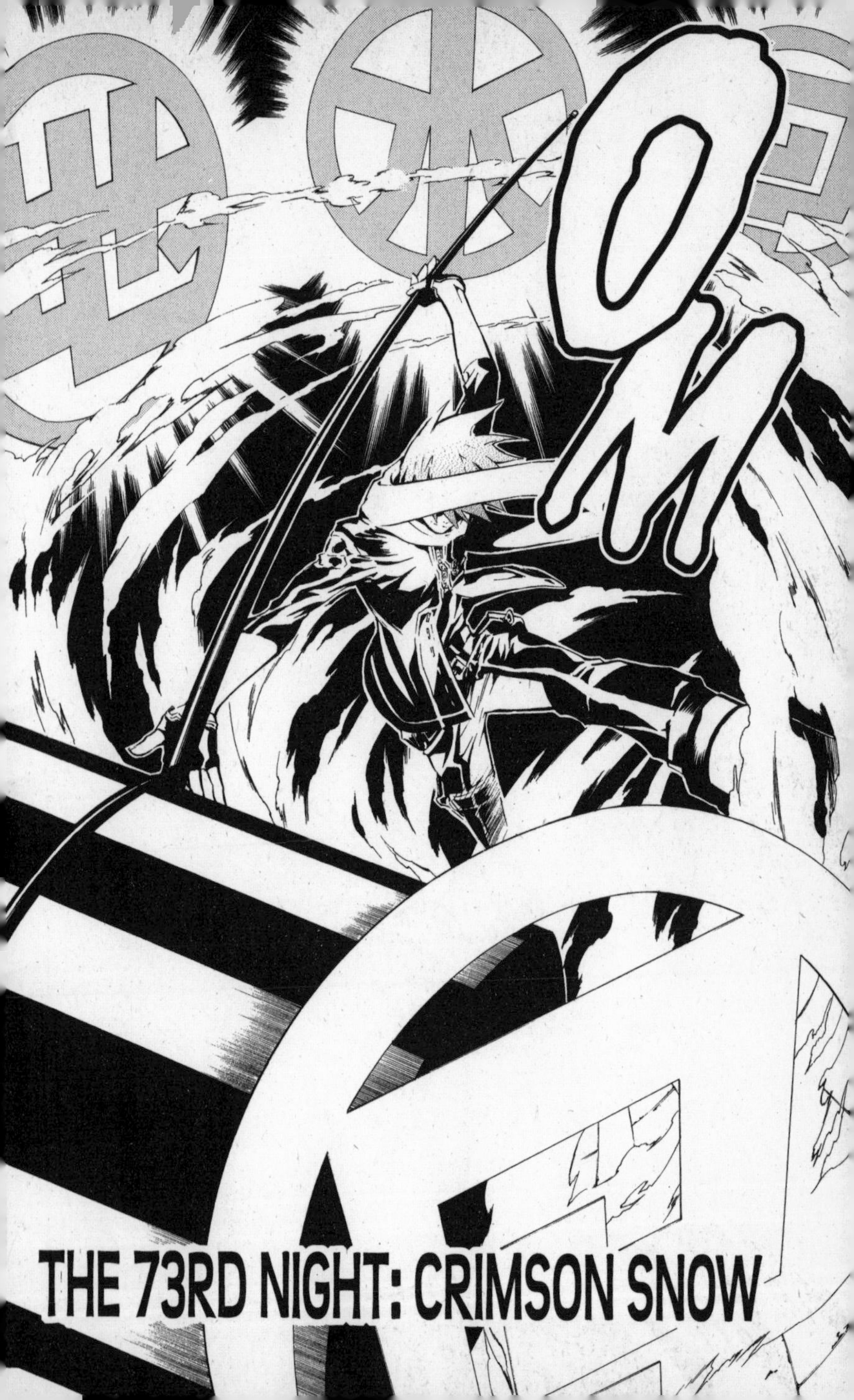
OM

THE 73RD NIGHT: CRIMSON SNOW

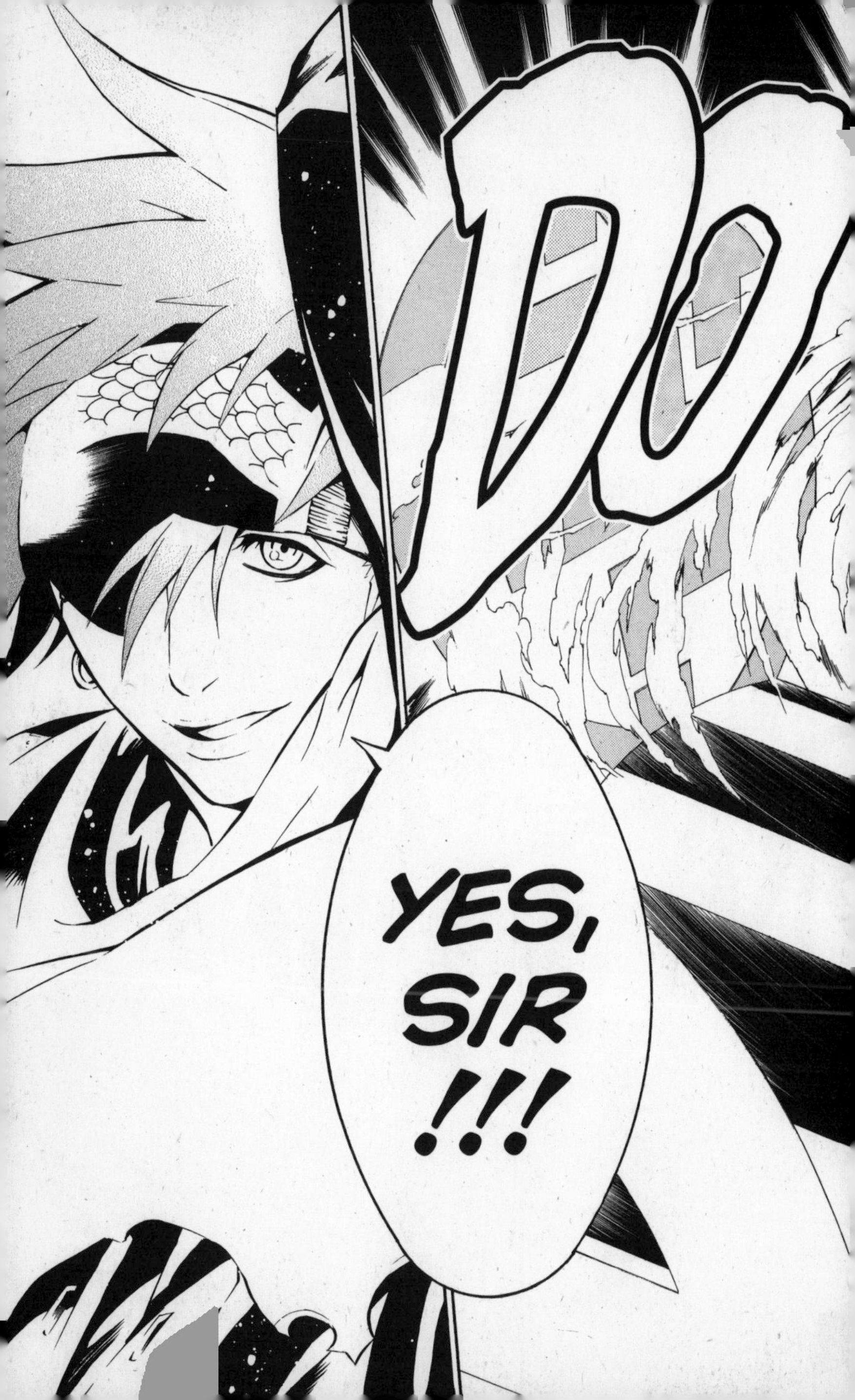
DO
YES, SIR!!!

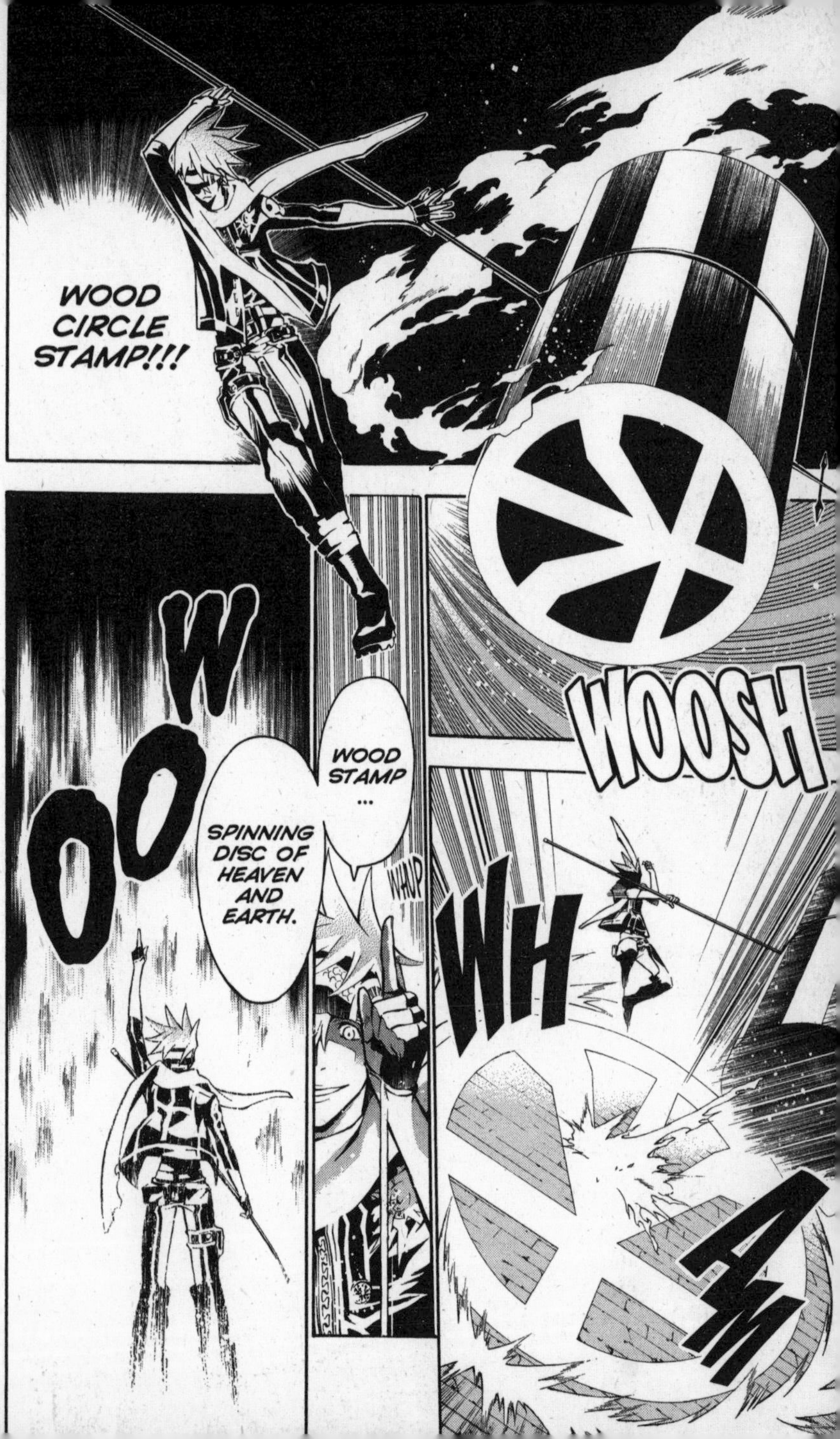

WOOD CIRCLE STAMP!!!
WOOSH
WHAM
WHUP
WOOD STAMP ...
SPINNING DISC OF HEAVEN AND EARTH.
OOW

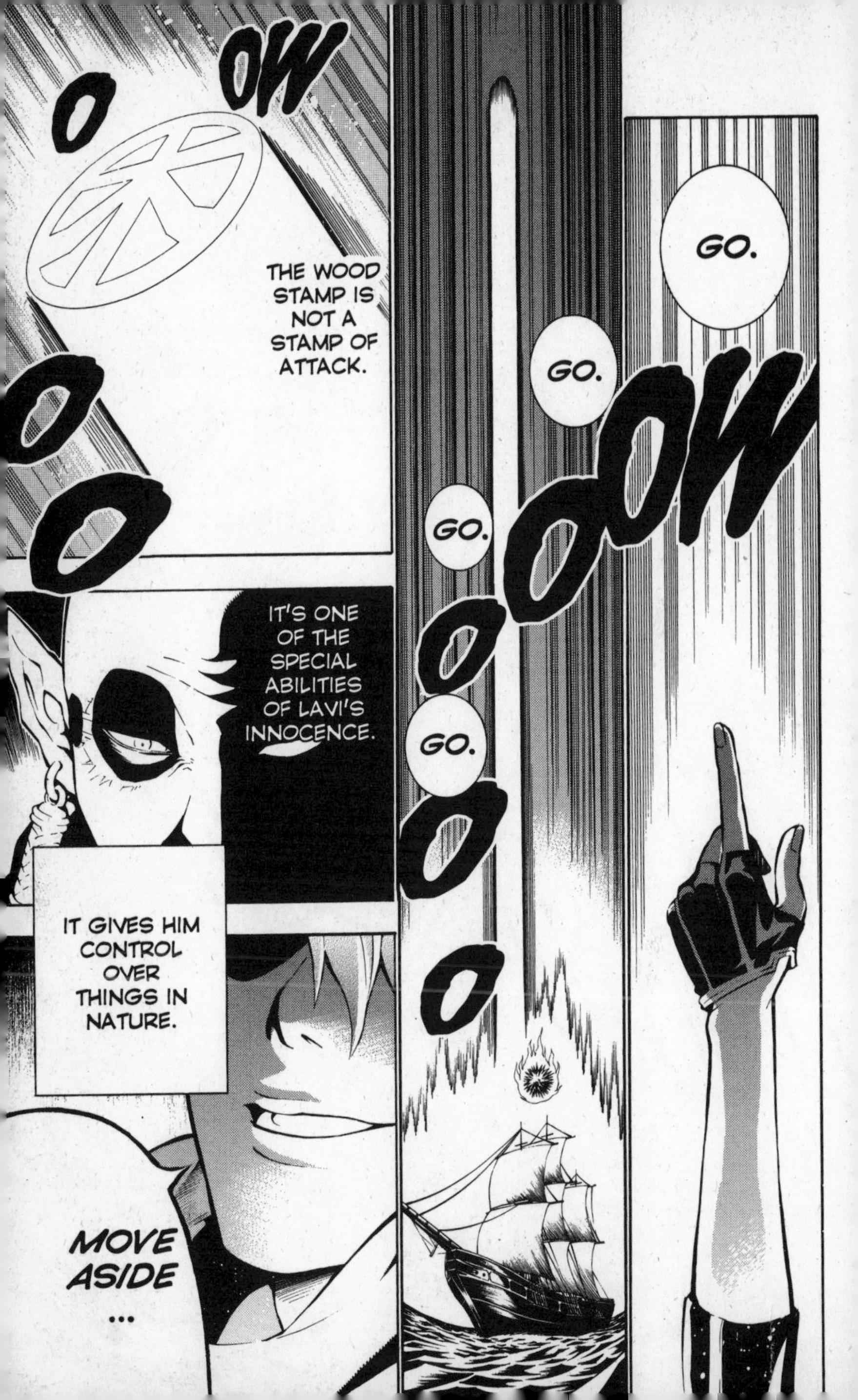
GO.
GO.
GO.
GO.
OOOOOOOW
O OW
OOO
THE WOOD STAMP IS NOT A STAMP OF ATTACK.
IT'S ONE OF THE SPECIAL ABILITIES OF LAVI'S INNOCENCE.
IT GIVES HIM CONTROL OVER THINGS IN NATURE.
MOVE ASIDE ...

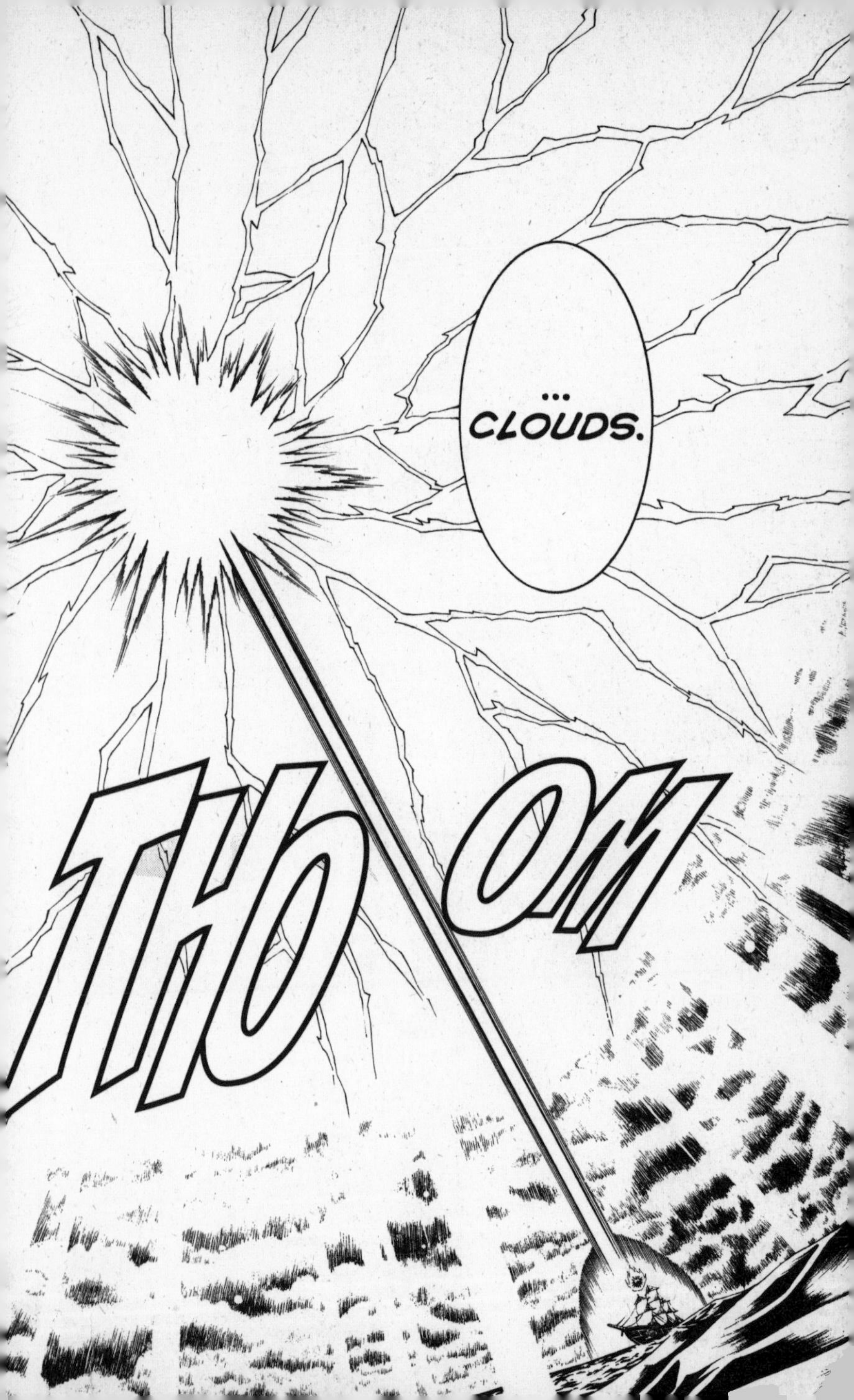
...CLOUDS.
THOOM

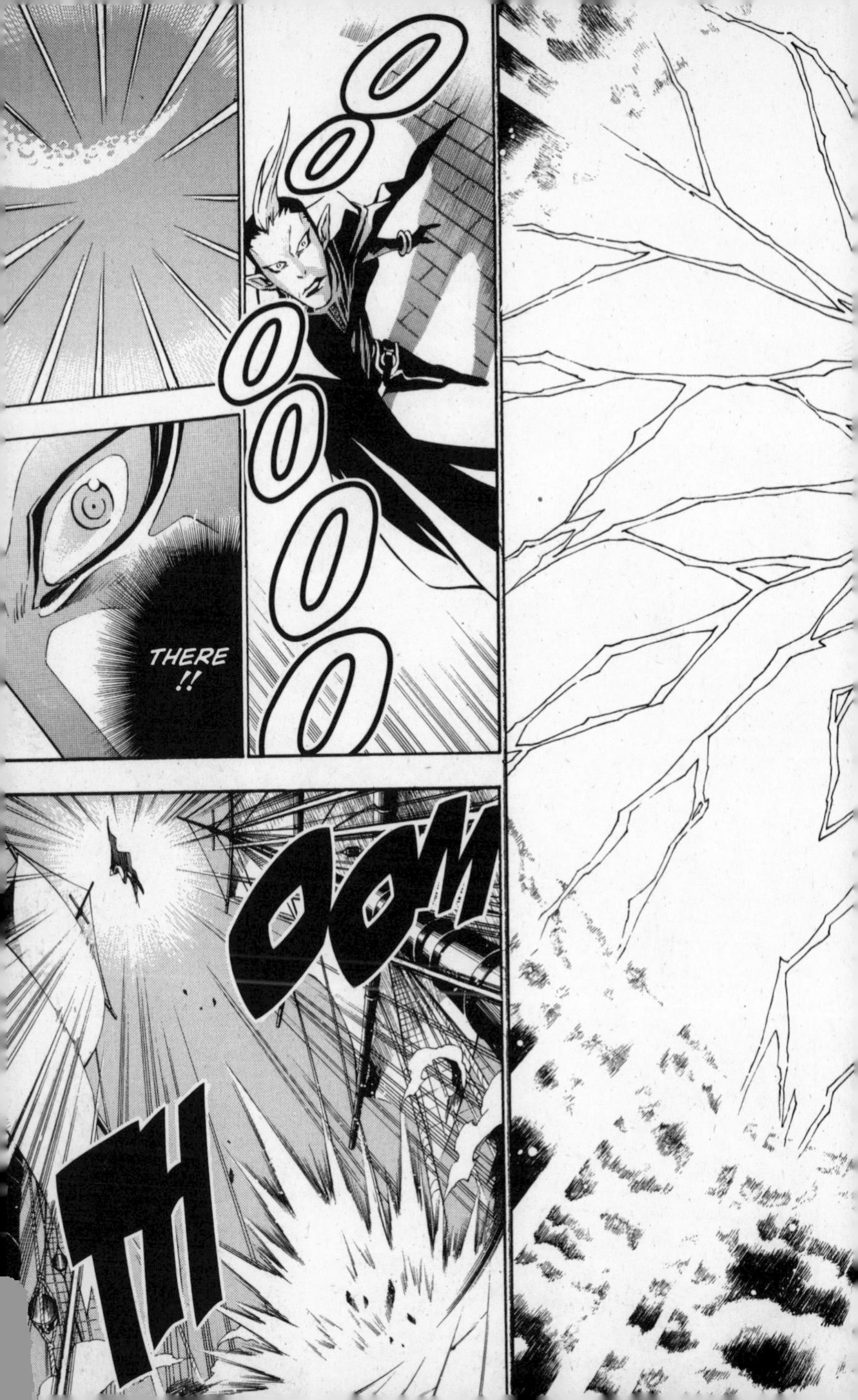
OOOOOO
THERE !!
THOOM

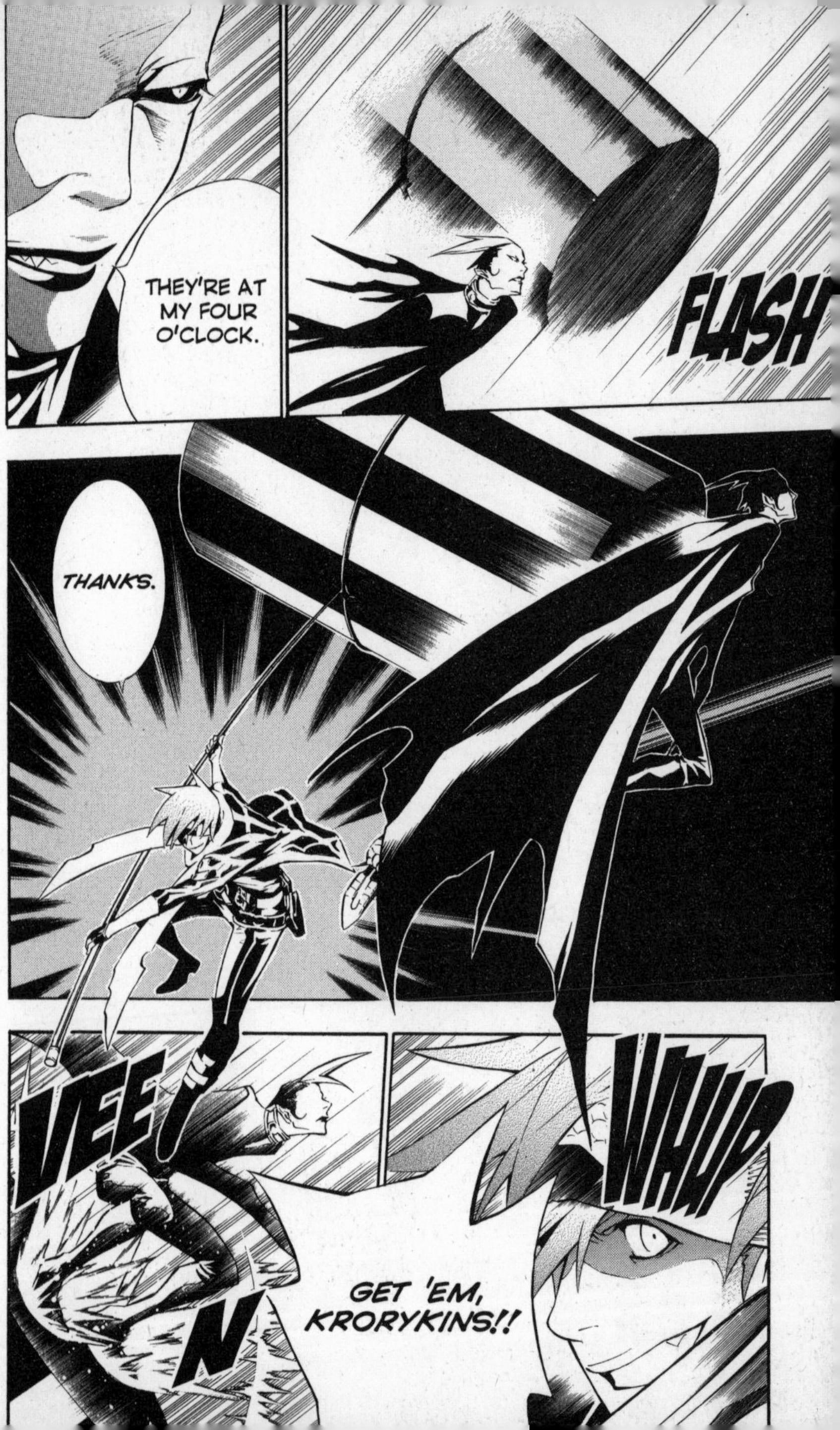
FLASH
THEY'RE AT MY FOUR O'CLOCK.
THANKS.
WHUP
GET 'EM, KRORYKINS!!
VEEN

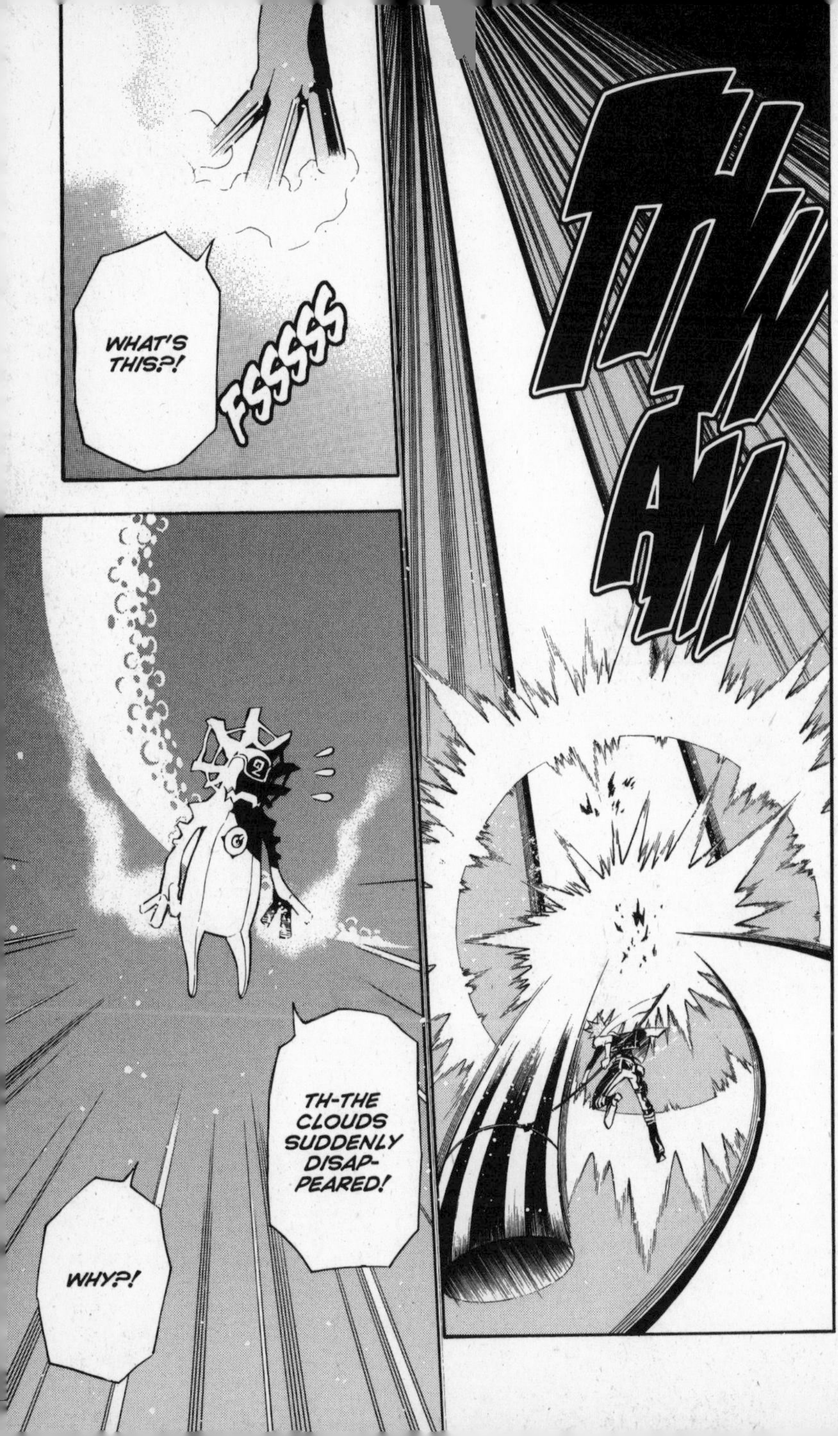
THWAM
WHAT'S THIS?!
FSSSSS
TH-THE CLOUDS SUDDENLY DISAP-PEARED!
WHY?!

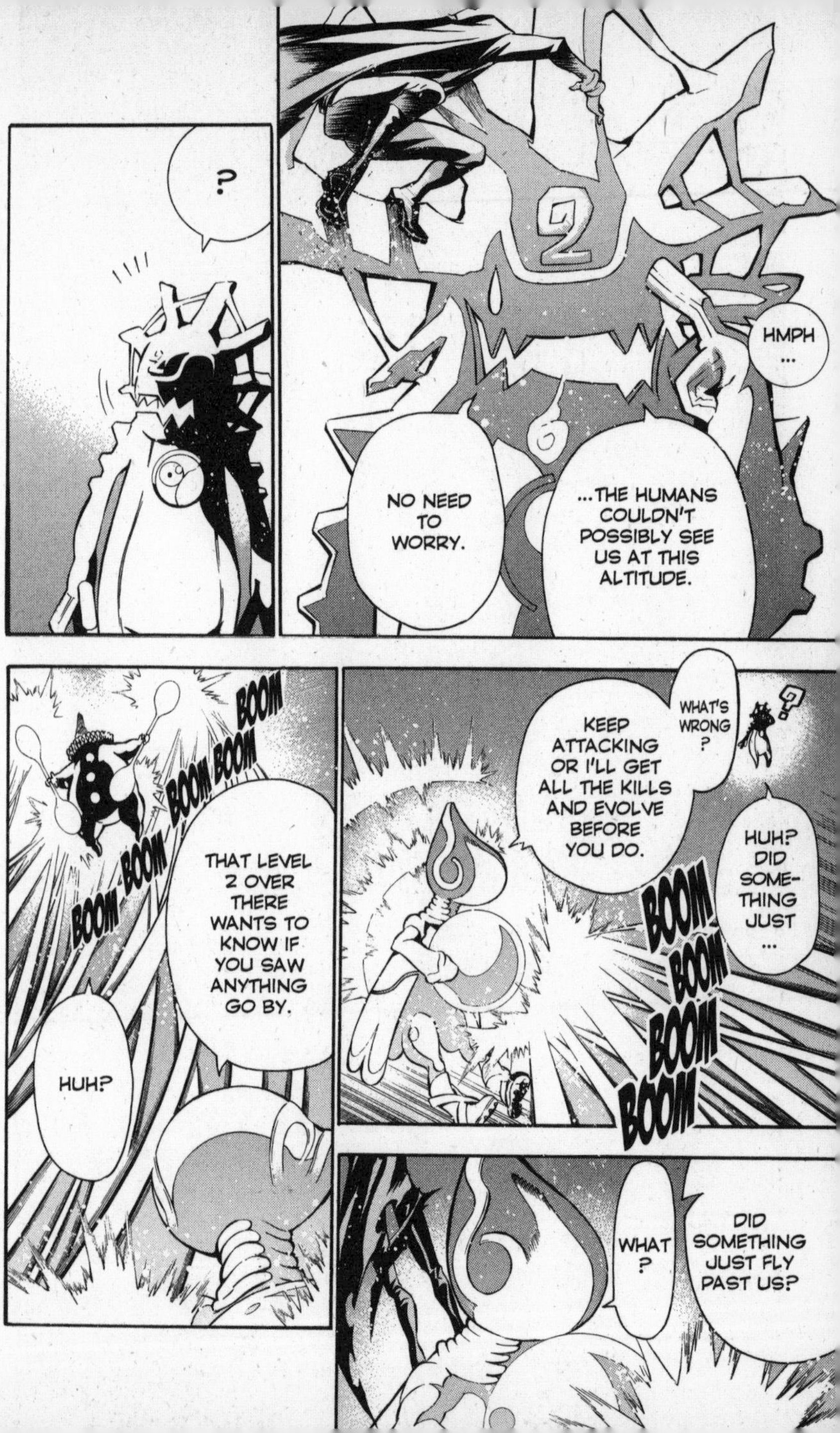
HMPH ...
...THE HUMANS COULDN'T POSSIBLY SEE US AT THIS ALTITUDE.
NO NEED TO WORRY.
?
WHAT'S WRONG ?
HUH? DID SOMETHING JUST ...
KEEP ATTACKING OR I'LL GET ALL THE KILLS AND EVOLVE BEFORE YOU DO.
BOOM BOOM BOOM BOOM
DID SOMETHING JUST FLY PAST US?
WHAT ?
BOOM BOOM BOOM BOOM BOOM BOOM
THAT LEVEL 2 OVER THERE WANTS TO KNOW IF YOU SAW ANYTHING GO BY.
HUH?

READ THIS WAY

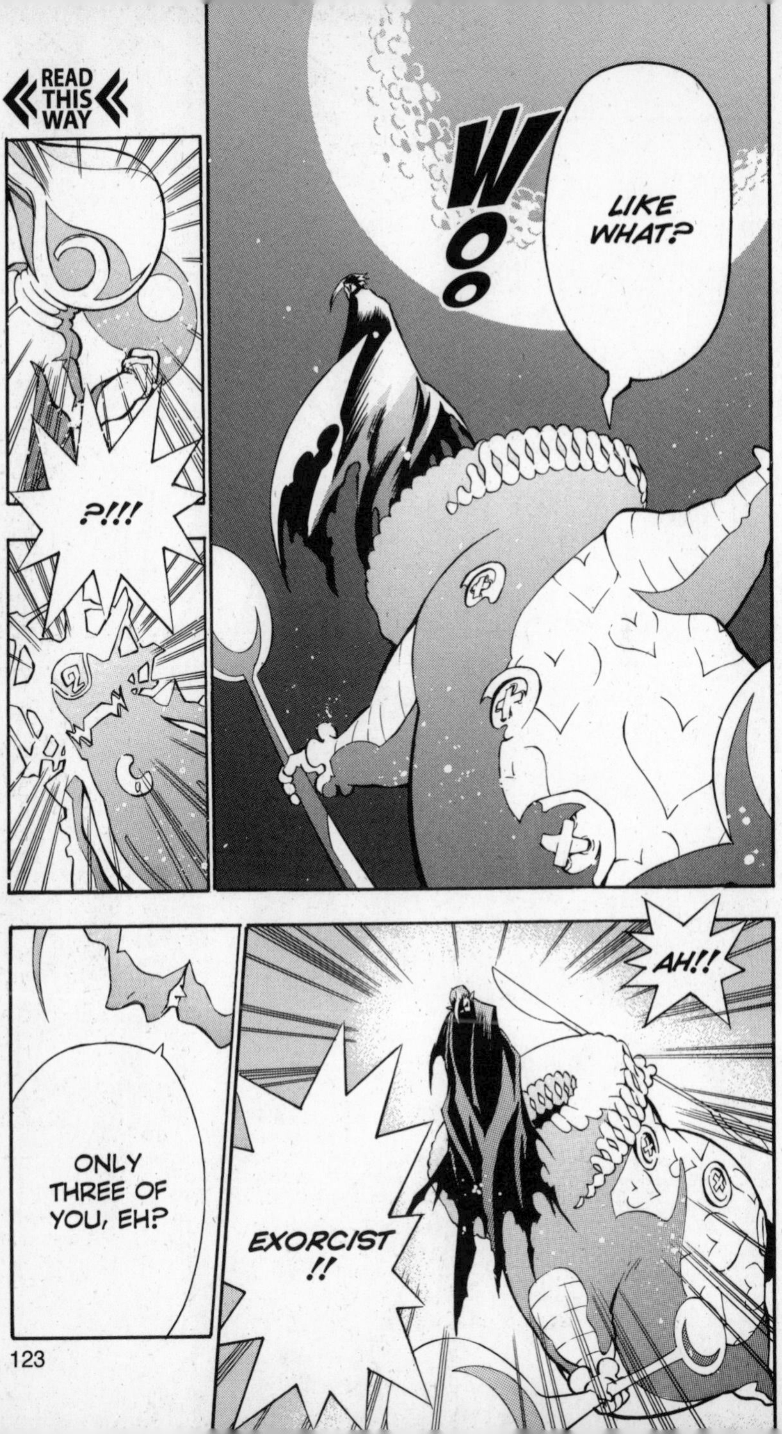
LIKE WHAT?
WOO
?!!!
AH!!
EXORCIST !!
ONLY THREE OF YOU, EH?

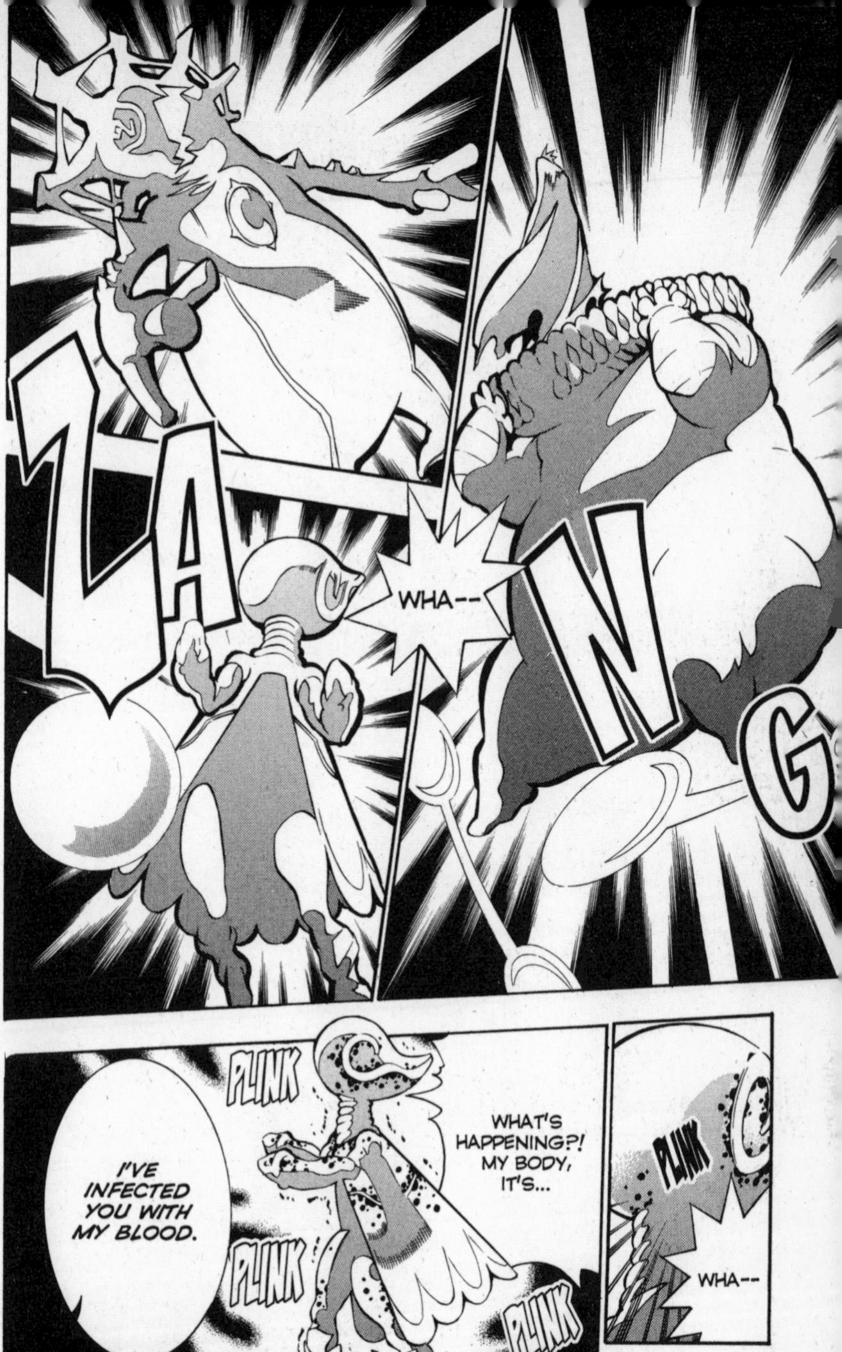
ZANG
WHA--
PLINK
WHA--
WHAT'S HAPPENING?! MY BODY, IT'S...
PLINK
I'VE INFECTED YOU WITH MY BLOOD.
PLINK
PLINK

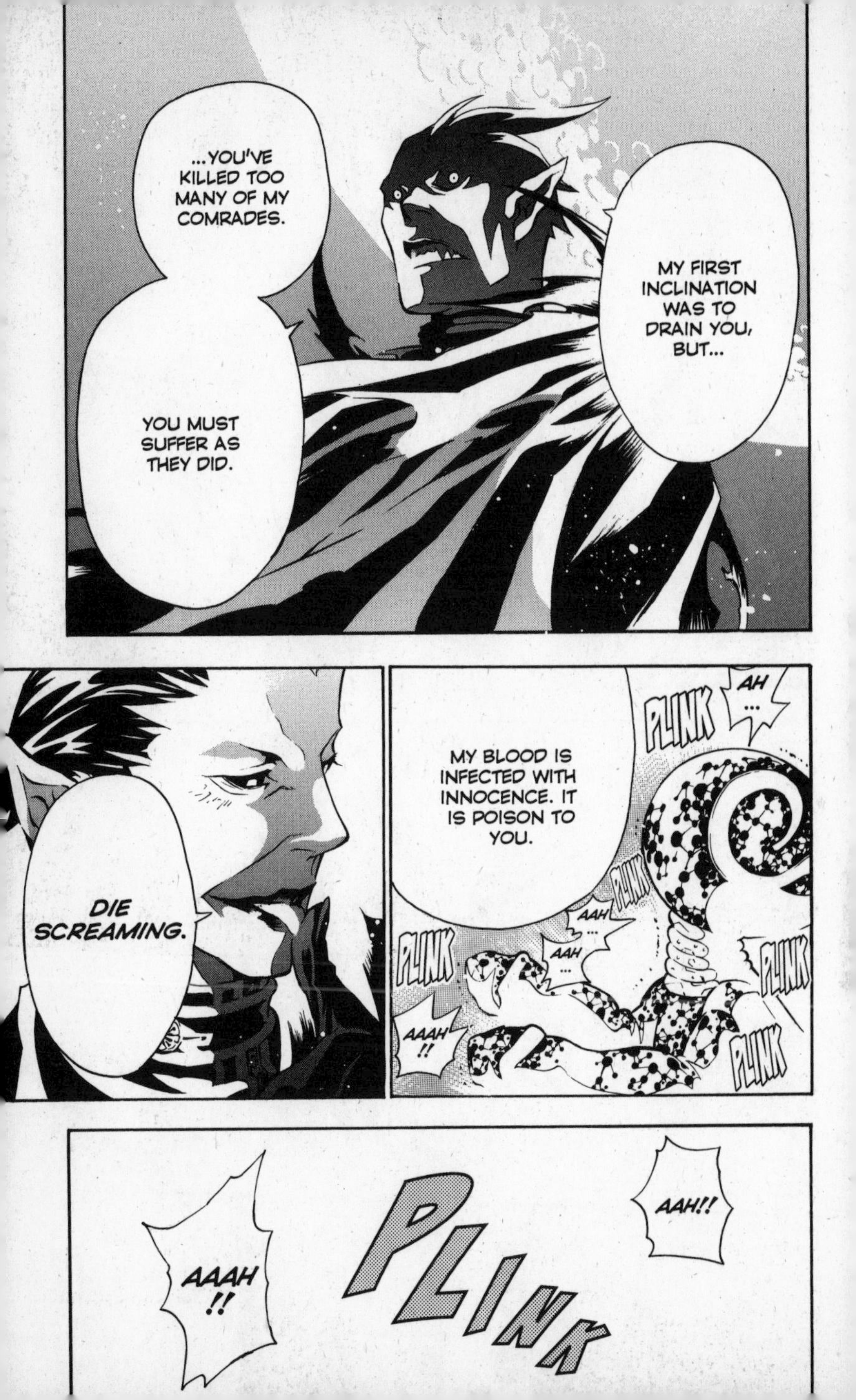
MY FIRST INCLINATION WAS TO DRAIN YOU, BUT...
...YOU'VE KILLED TOO MANY OF MY COMRADES.
YOU MUST SUFFER AS THEY DID.
AH ...
PLINK
MY BLOOD IS INFECTED WITH INNOCENCE. IT IS POISON TO YOU.
PLINK
PLINK
AAH ...
AAH ...
PLINK
PLINK
AAAH !!
DIE SCREAMING.
AAH!!
PLINK
AAAH !!

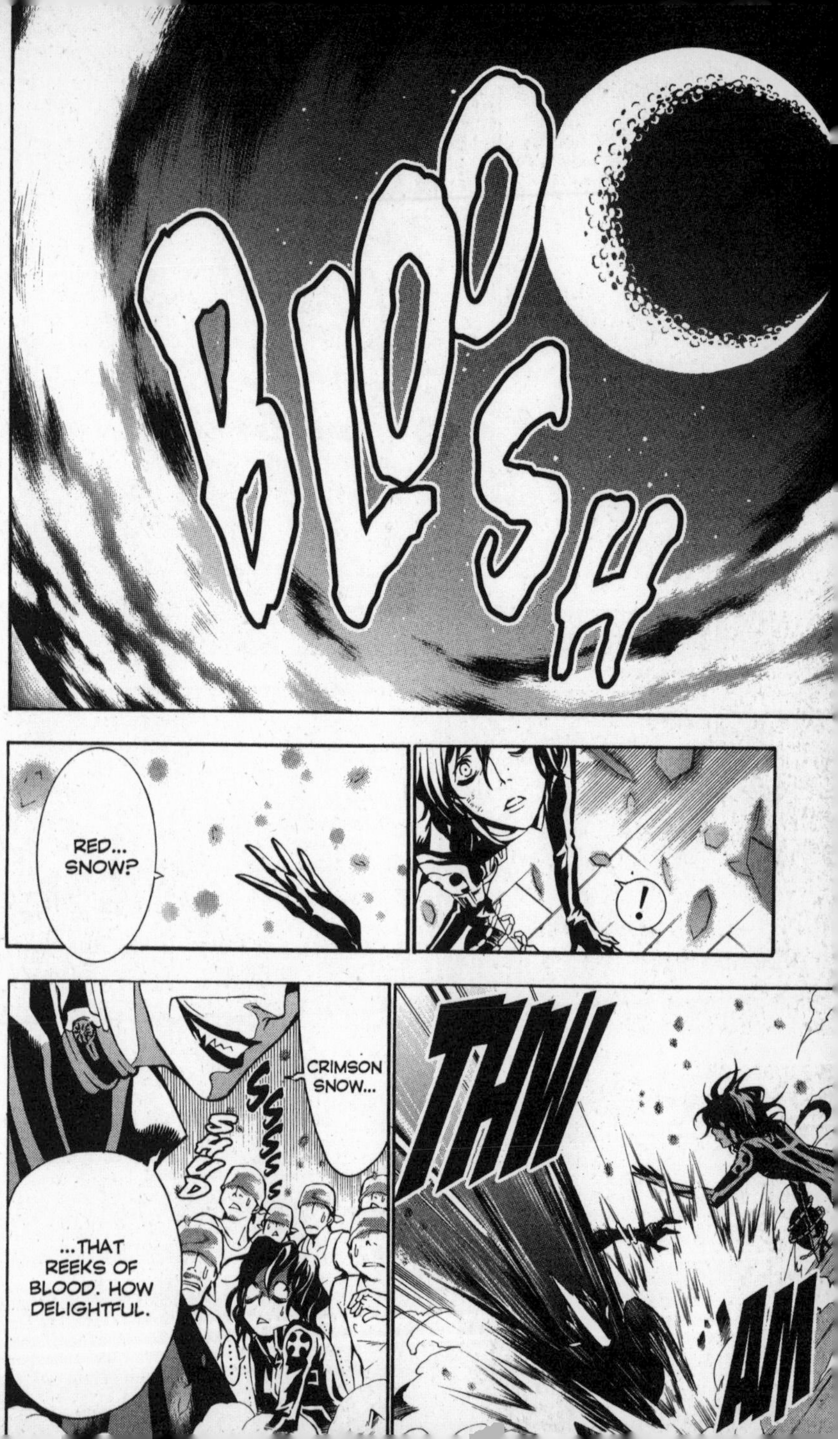
BLOOSH
!
RED... SNOW?
THWAM
CRIMSON SNOW...
SSSSSS
SHUD
...THAT REEKS OF BLOOD. HOW DELIGHTFUL.

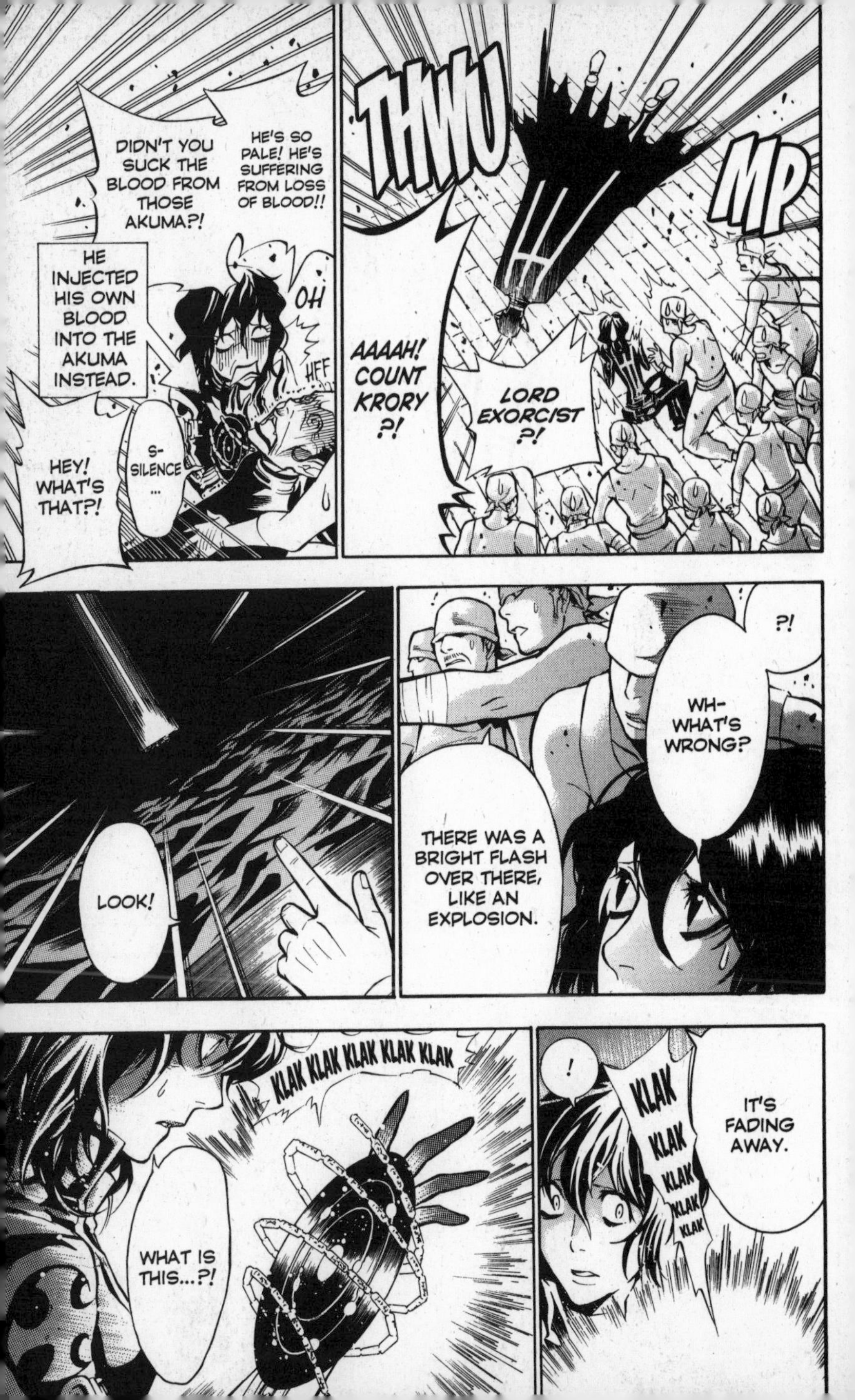
THWUMP
LORD EXORCIST?!
AAAAH! COUNT KRORY?!
HE'S SO PALE! HE'S SUFFERING FROM LOSS OF BLOOD!!
DIDN'T YOU SUCK THE BLOOD FROM THOSE AKUMA?!
HE INJECTED HIS OWN BLOOD INTO THE AKUMA INSTEAD.
OH
HFF
S-SILENCE...
HEY! WHAT'S THAT?!
?!
WH-WHAT'S WRONG?
THERE WAS A BRIGHT FLASH OVER THERE, LIKE AN EXPLOSION.
LOOK!
!
IT'S FADING AWAY.
KLAK KLAK KLAK KLAK KLAK
KLAK KLAK KLAK KLAK KLAK KLAK
WHAT IS THIS...?!

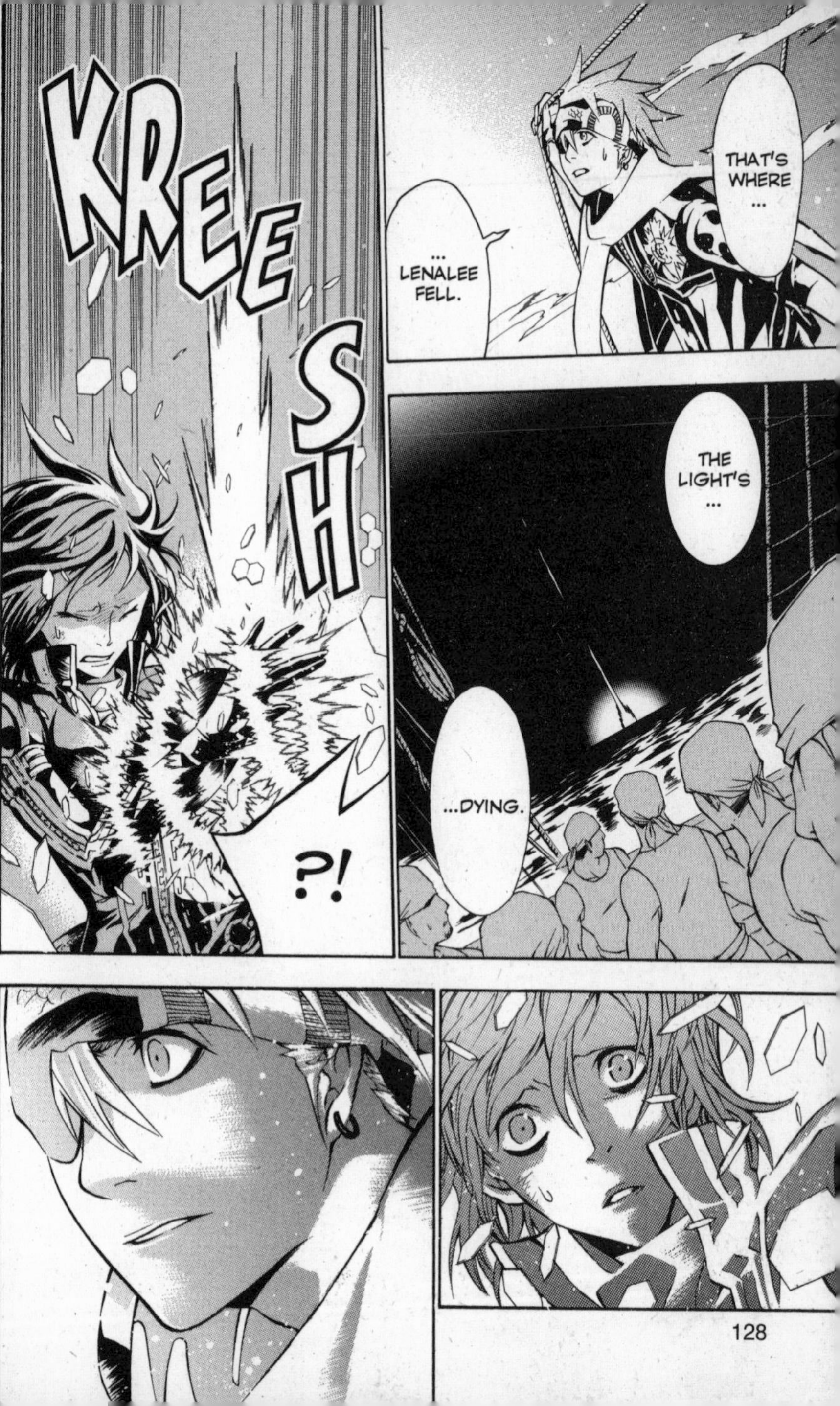
THAT'S WHERE ...
... LENALEE FELL.
THE LIGHT'S ...
...DYING.
KREESH
?!

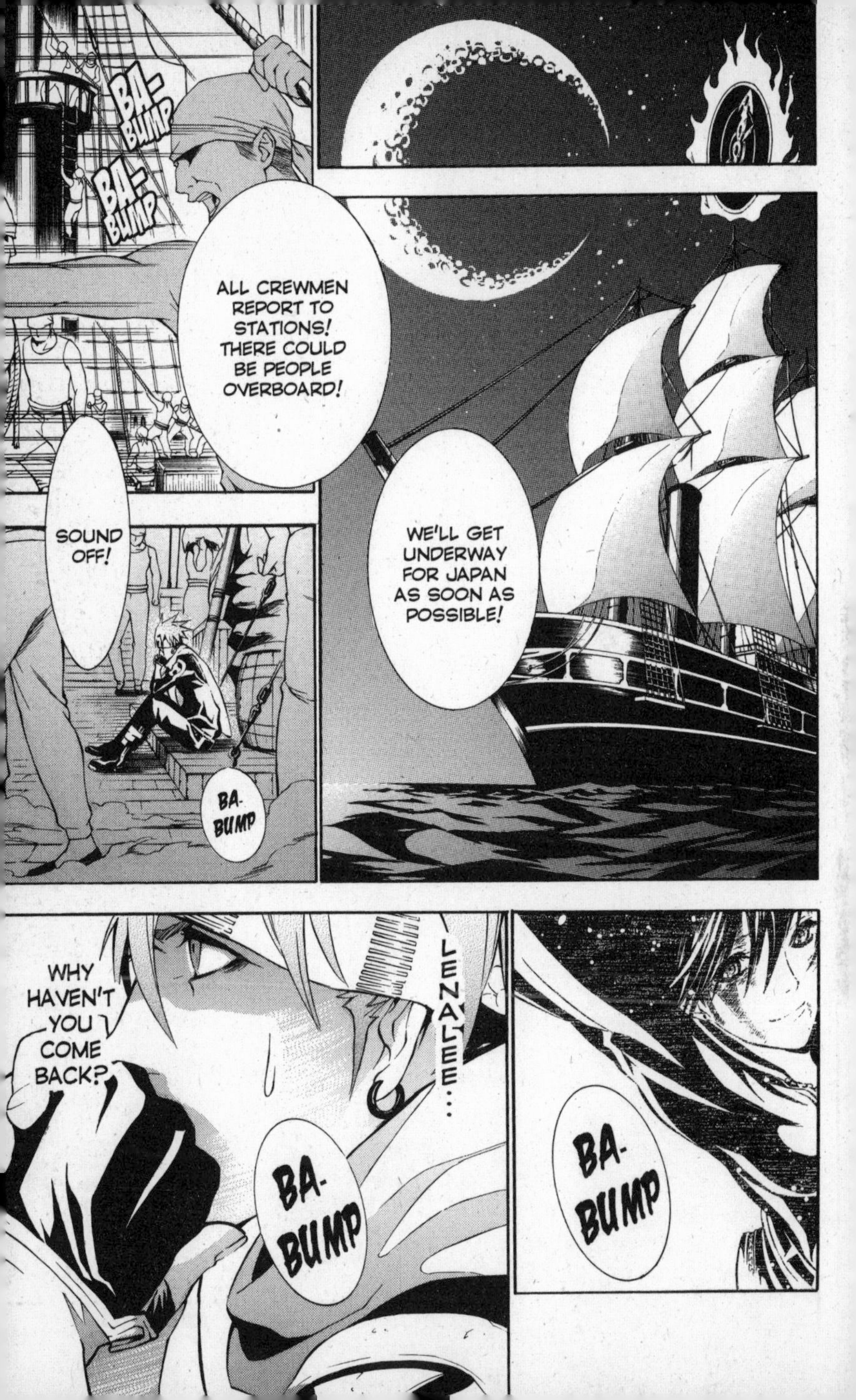
WE'LL GET UNDERWAY FOR JAPAN AS SOON AS POSSIBLE!
BA-BUMP
BA-BUMP
ALL CREWMEN REPORT TO STATIONS! THERE COULD BE PEOPLE OVERBOARD!
SOUND OFF!
BA-BUMP
BA-BUMP
LENALEE...
WHY HAVEN'T YOU COME BACK?
BA-BUMP

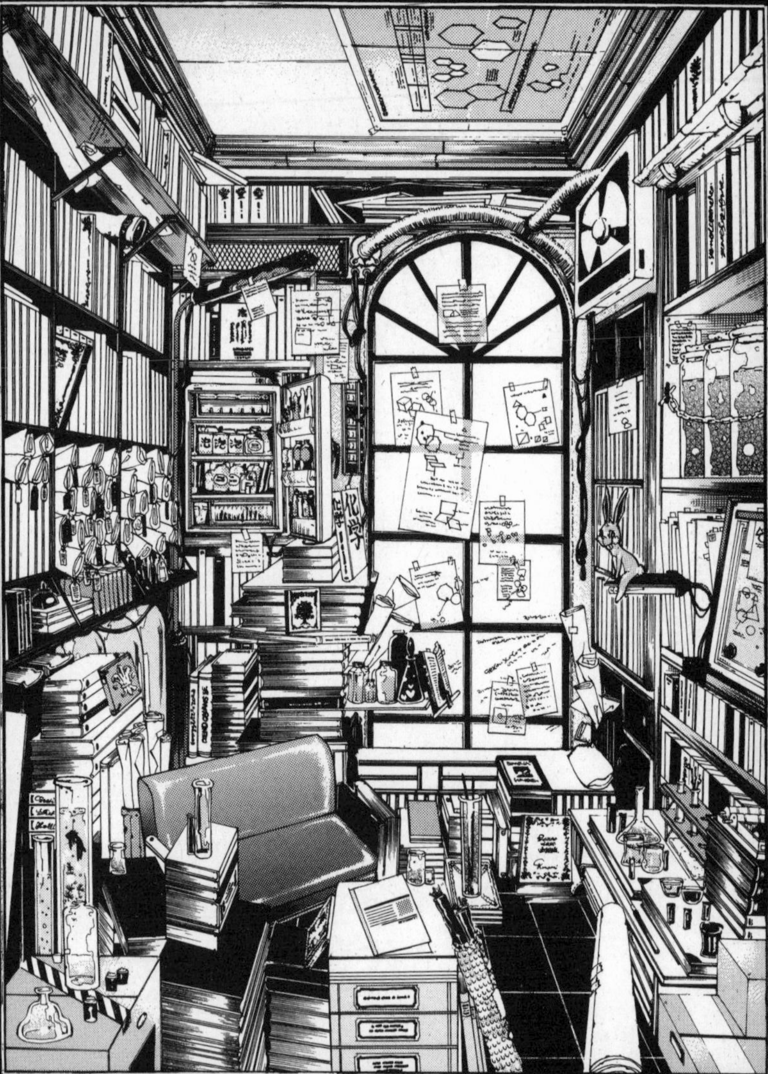
化学

REEVER'S ROOM

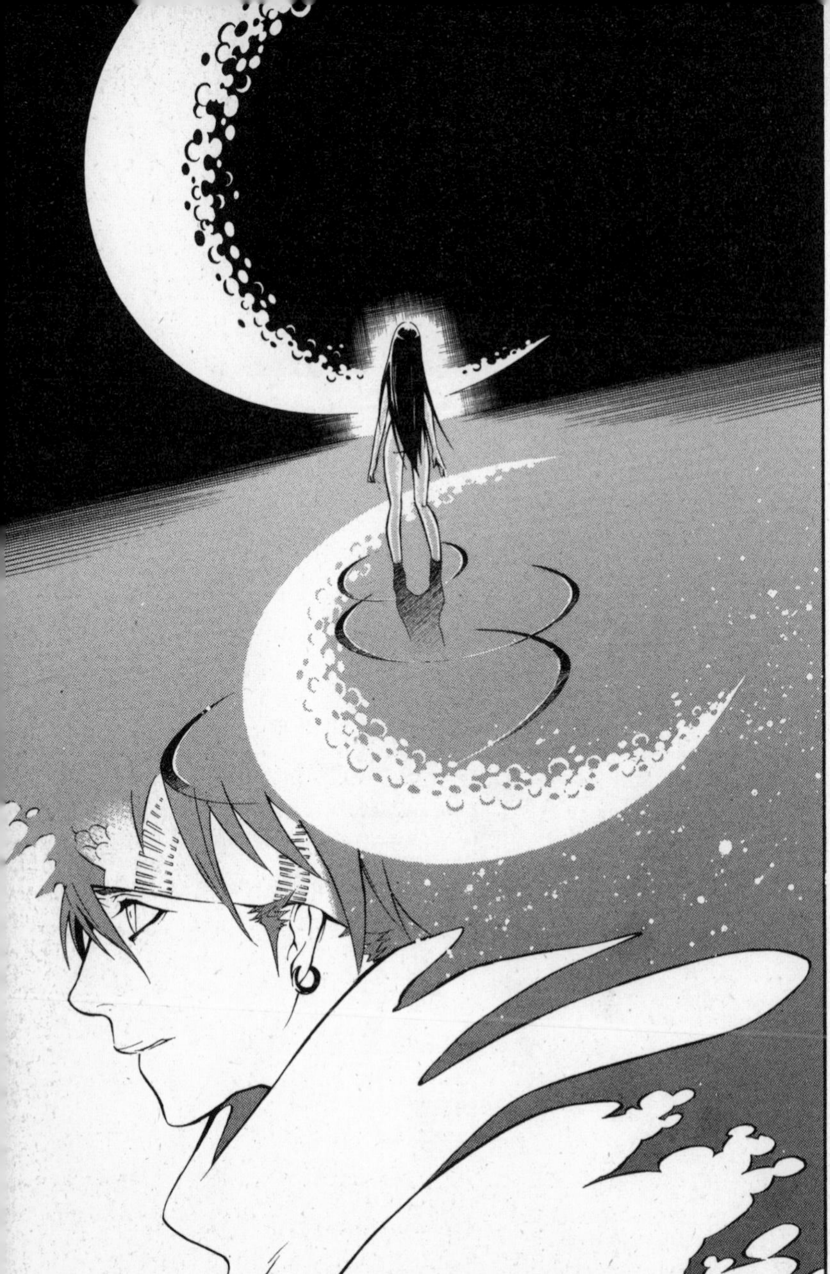

THE 74TH NIGHT: SHIP IN RUINS, GIRL MISSING

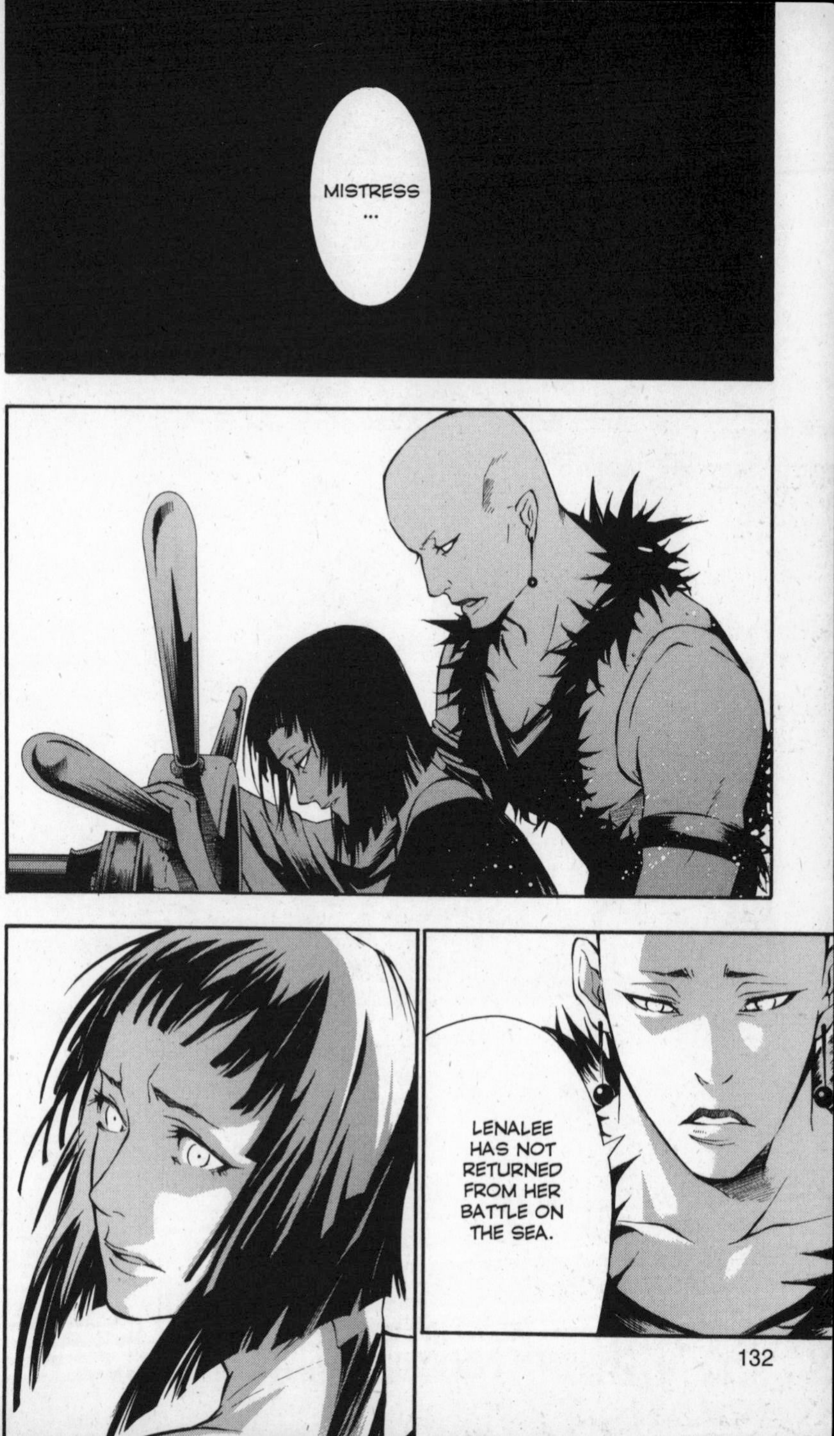
MISTRESS ...
LENALEE HAS NOT RETURNED FROM HER BATTLE ON THE SEA.

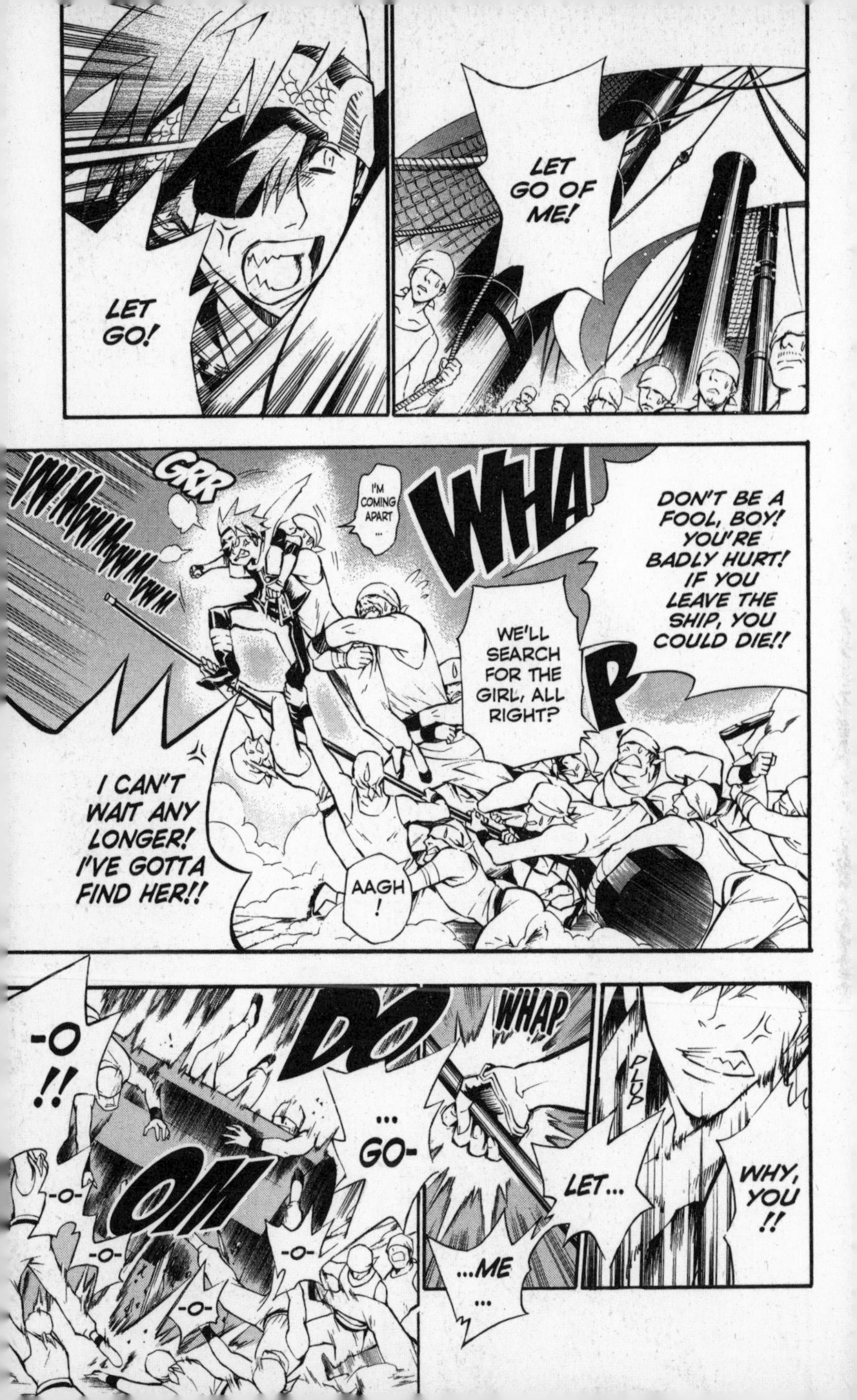

LET GO OF ME!
LET GO!
DON'T BE A FOOL, BOY! YOU'RE BADLY HURT! IF YOU LEAVE THE SHIP, YOU COULD DIE!!
WHAP
WE'LL SEARCH FOR THE GIRL, ALL RIGHT?
I'M COMING APART ...
GRR
VWMMVWMMVWMMVWM
I CAN'T WAIT ANY LONGER! I'VE GOTTA FIND HER!!
AAGH!
WHY, YOU !!
PLUP
WHAP
DO
LET...
... GO-
...ME ...
-O !!
-O-
-O-
-O-
-O-
OM

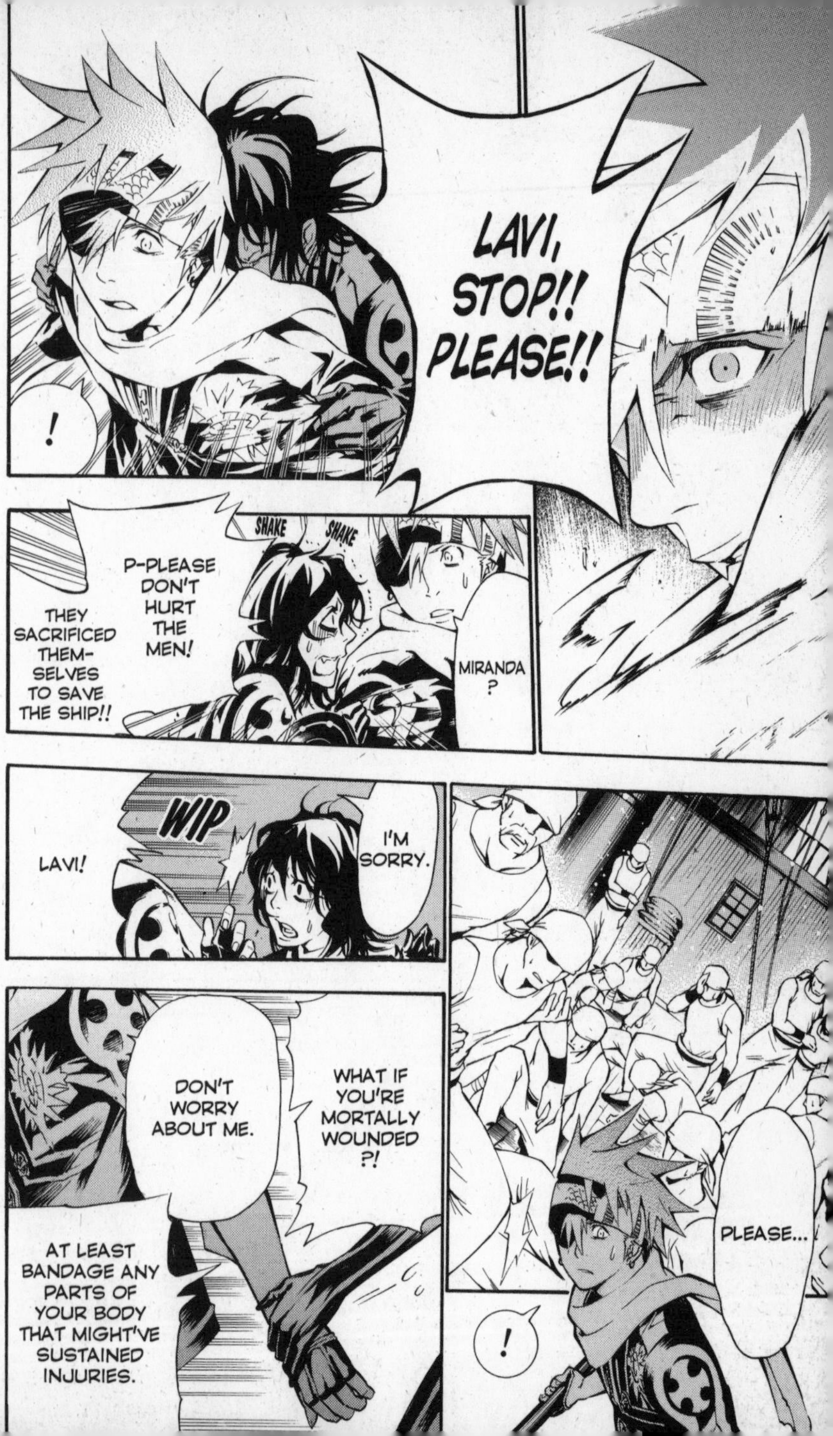
LAVI, STOP!! PLEASE!!
!
MIRANDA?
SHAKE
SHAKE
P-PLEASE DON'T HURT THE MEN!
THEY SACRIFICED THEM-SELVES TO SAVE THE SHIP!!
PLEASE...
!
I'M SORRY.
WIP
LAVI!
WHAT IF YOU'RE MORTALLY WOUNDED?!
DON'T WORRY ABOUT ME.
AT LEAST BANDAGE ANY PARTS OF YOUR BODY THAT MIGHT'VE SUSTAINED INJURIES.

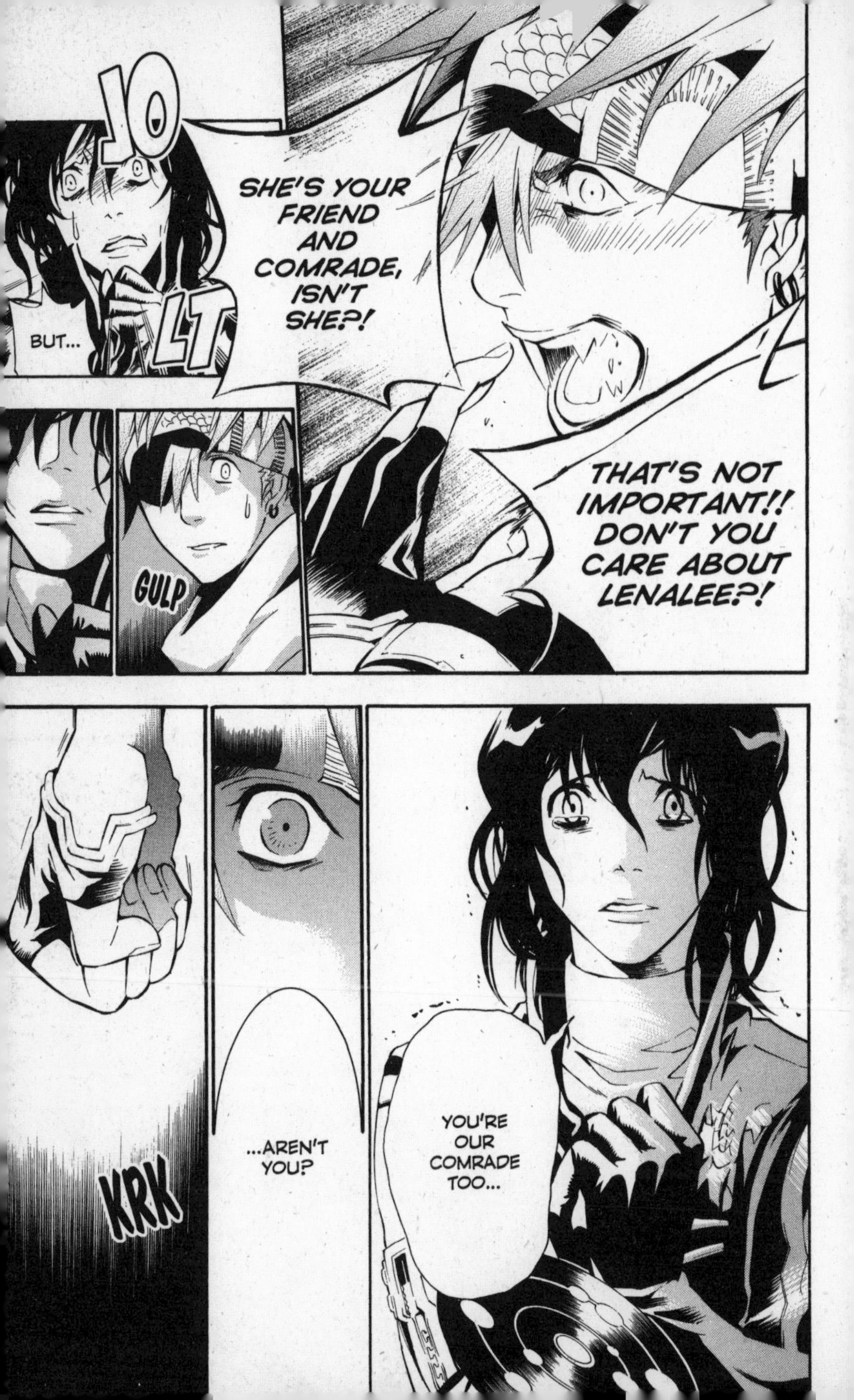
SHE'S YOUR FRIEND AND COMRADE, ISN'T SHE?!
THAT'S NOT IMPORTANT!! DON'T YOU CARE ABOUT LENALEE?!
JOLT
BUT...
GULP
YOU'RE OUR COMRADE TOO...
...AREN'T YOU?
KRK

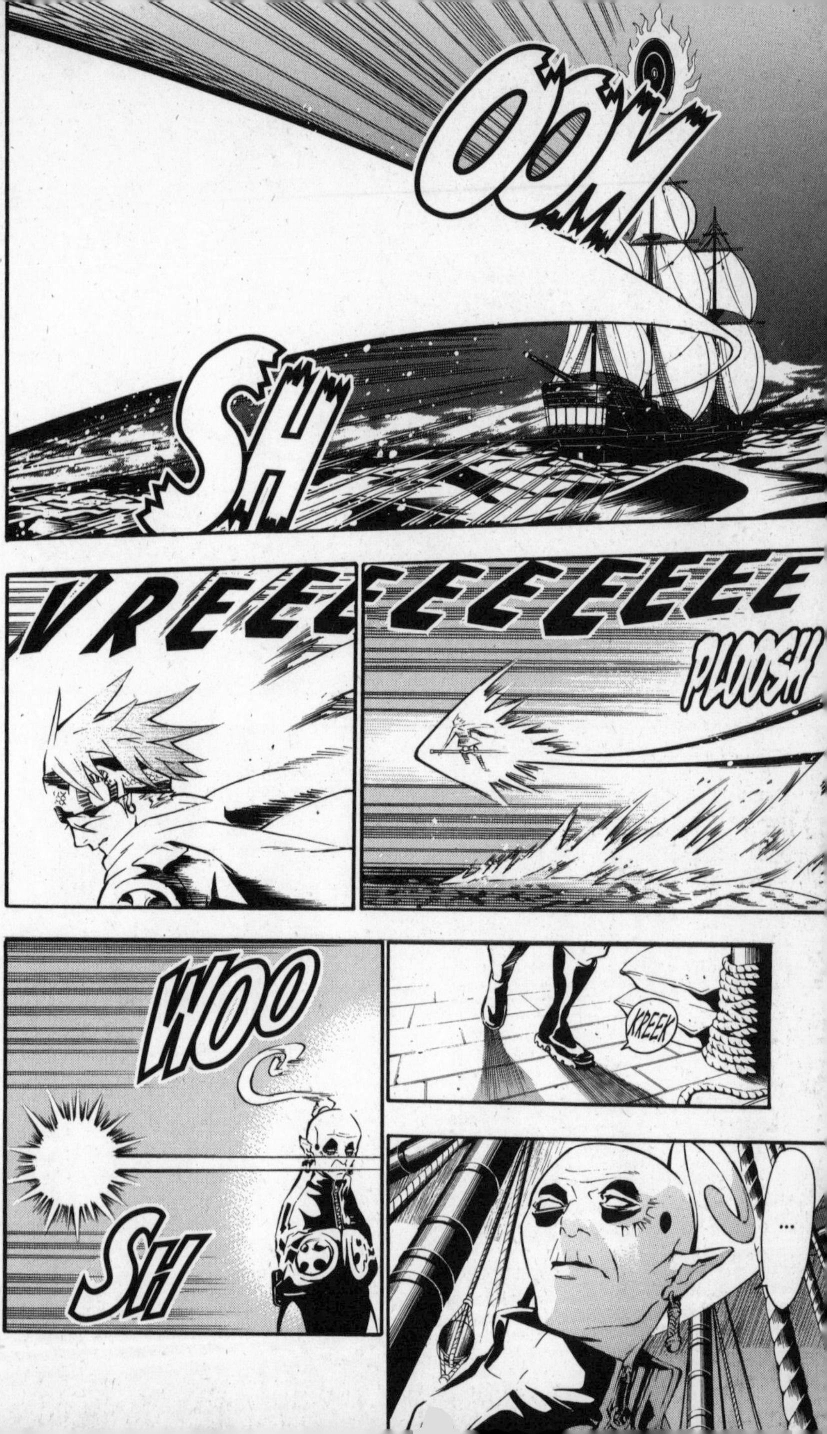
OOM
SH
VREEEEEEEEEE
PLOOSH
KREEK
...
WOO
SH

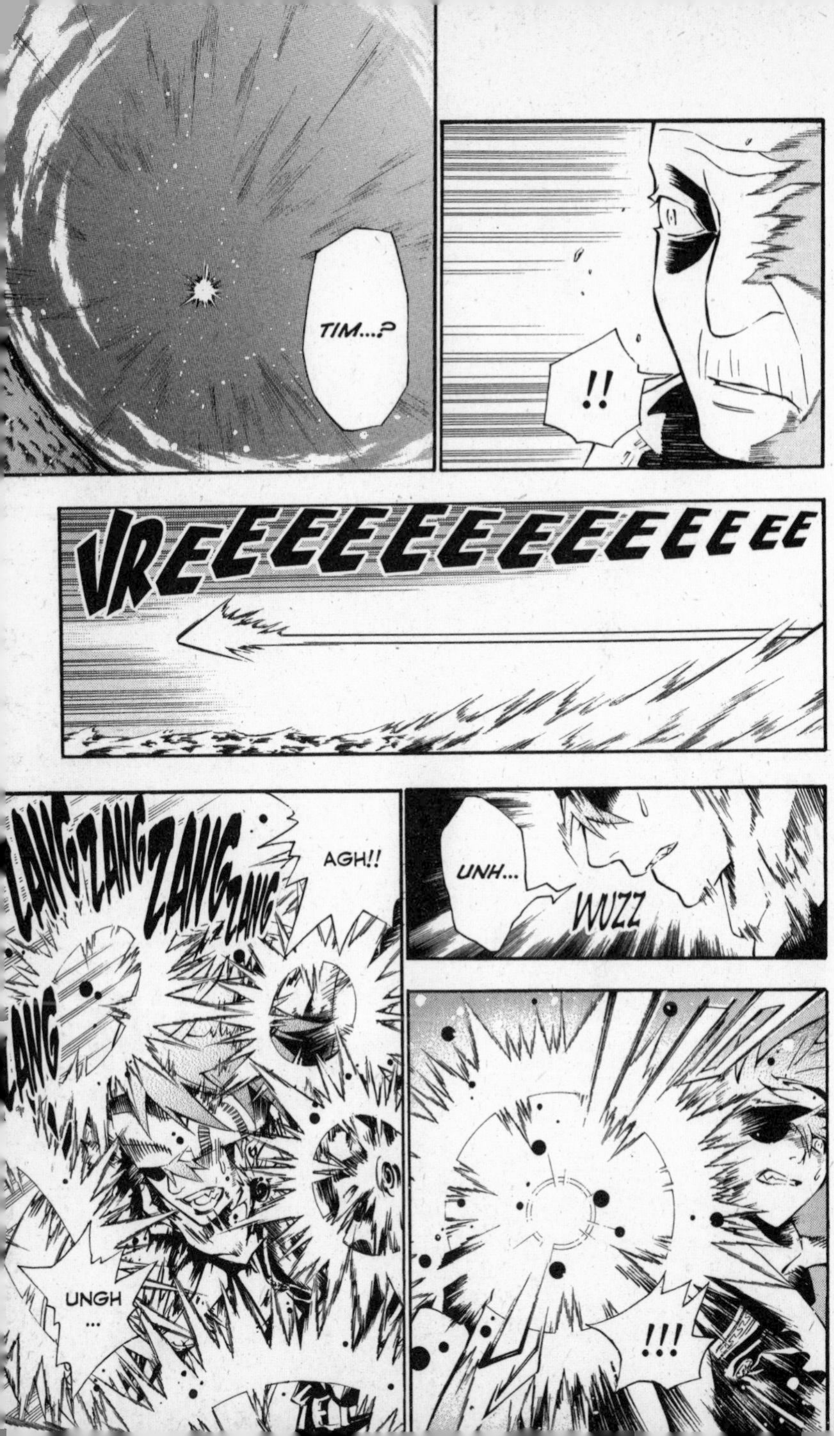
!!
TIM...?
VREEEEEEEEEEEE
UNH...
WUZZ
!!!
ZANG ZANG ZANG ZANG
AGH!!
UNGH ...

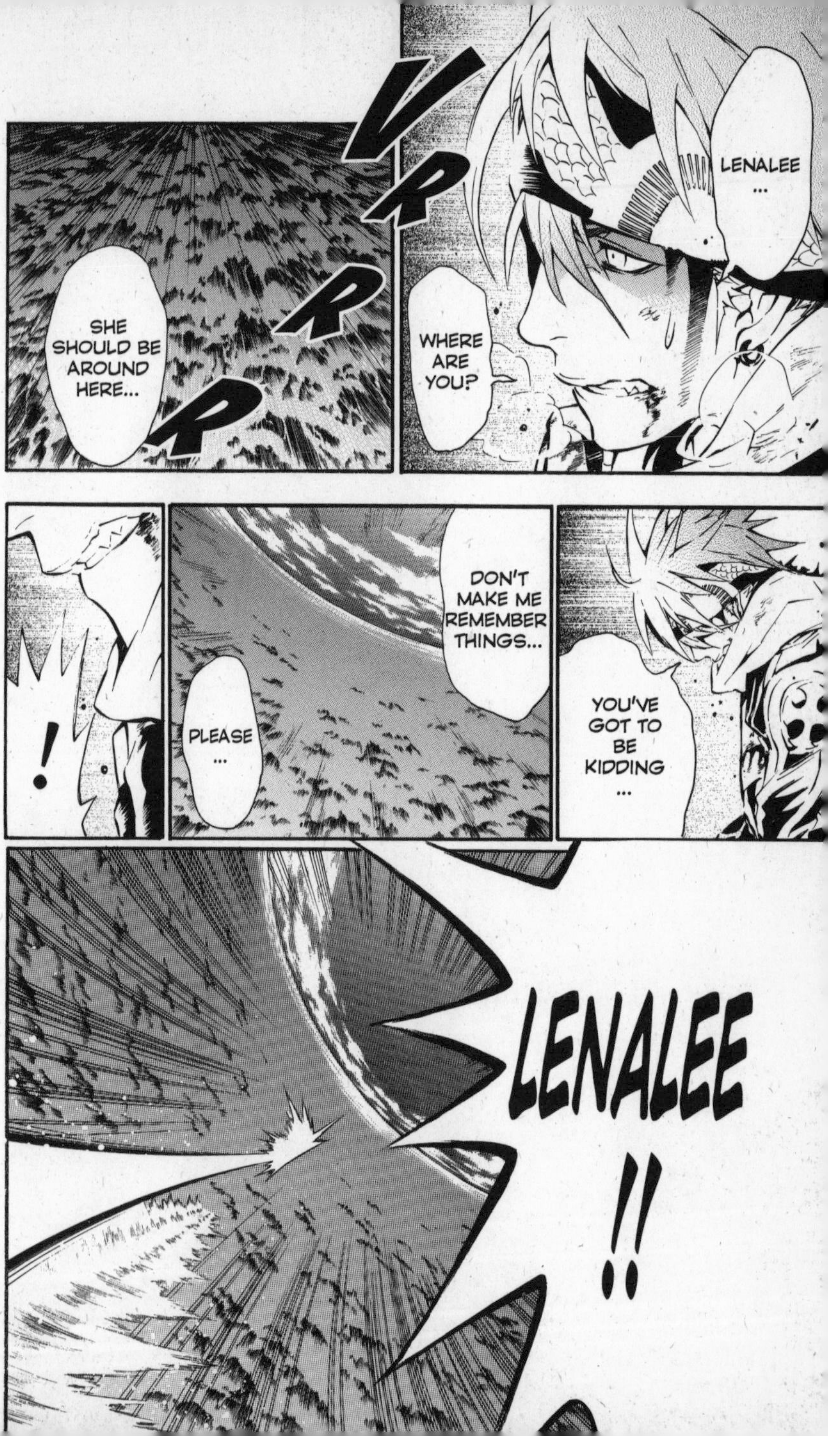
LENALEE ...
WHERE ARE YOU?
VRRR
SHE SHOULD BE AROUND HERE...
YOU'VE GOT TO BE KIDDING ...
DON'T MAKE ME REMEMBER THINGS...
PLEASE ...
!
LENALEE !!

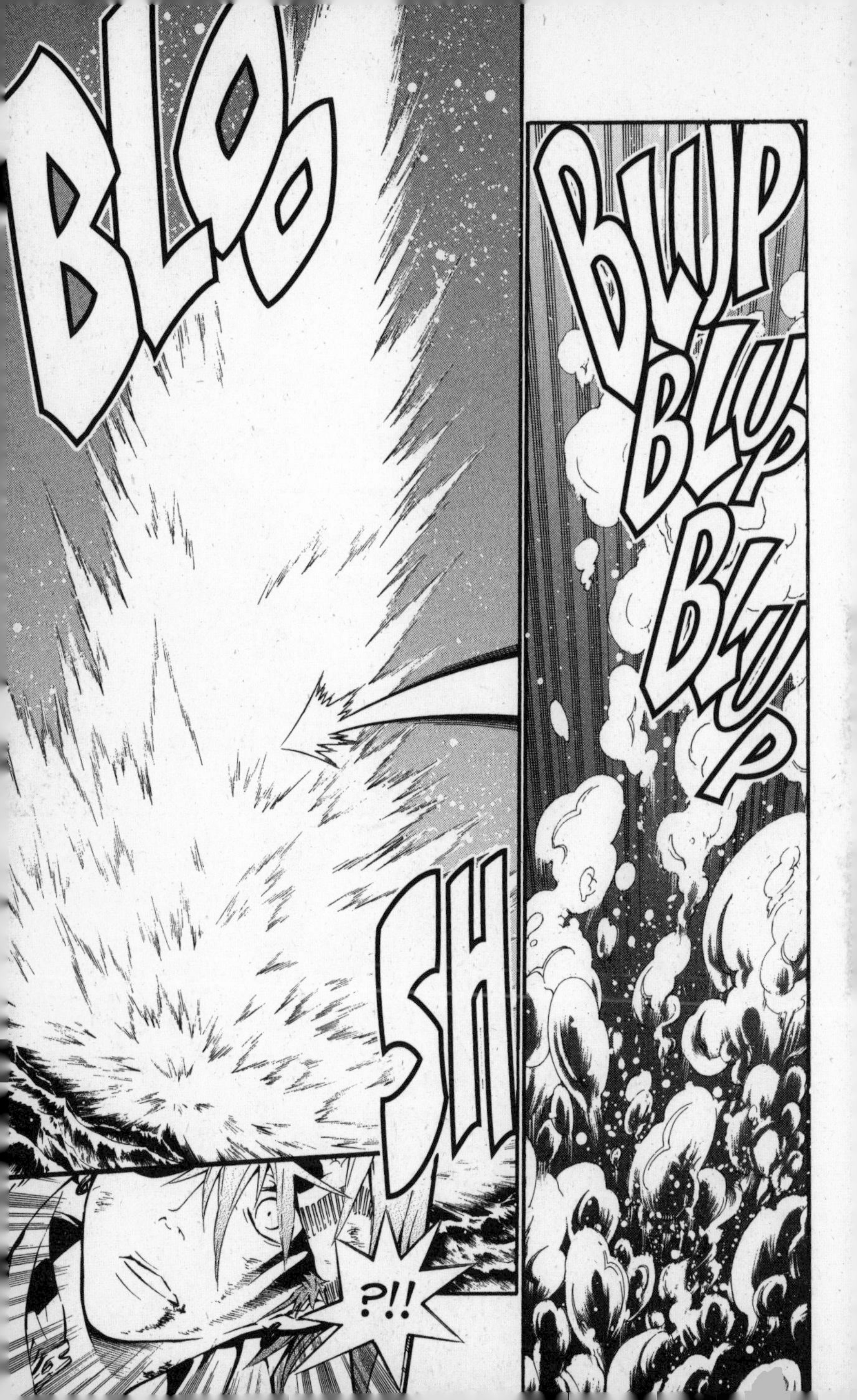
BLUP
BLUP
BLUP
BLOO
SH
?!!

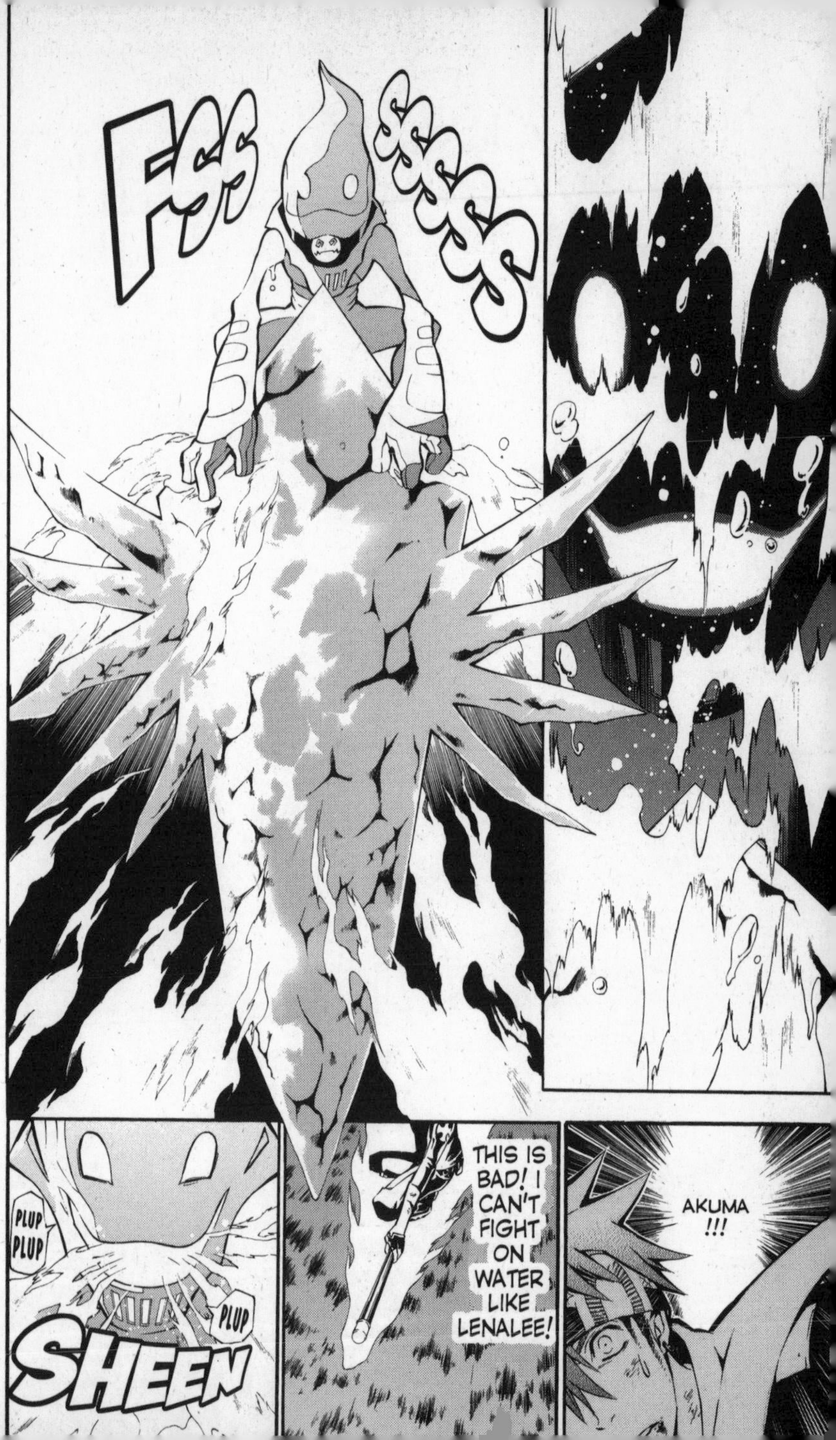
FSS
SSSSS
AKUMA !!!
THIS IS BAD! I CAN'T FIGHT ON WATER LIKE LENALEE!
PLUP PLUP
PLUP
SHEEN

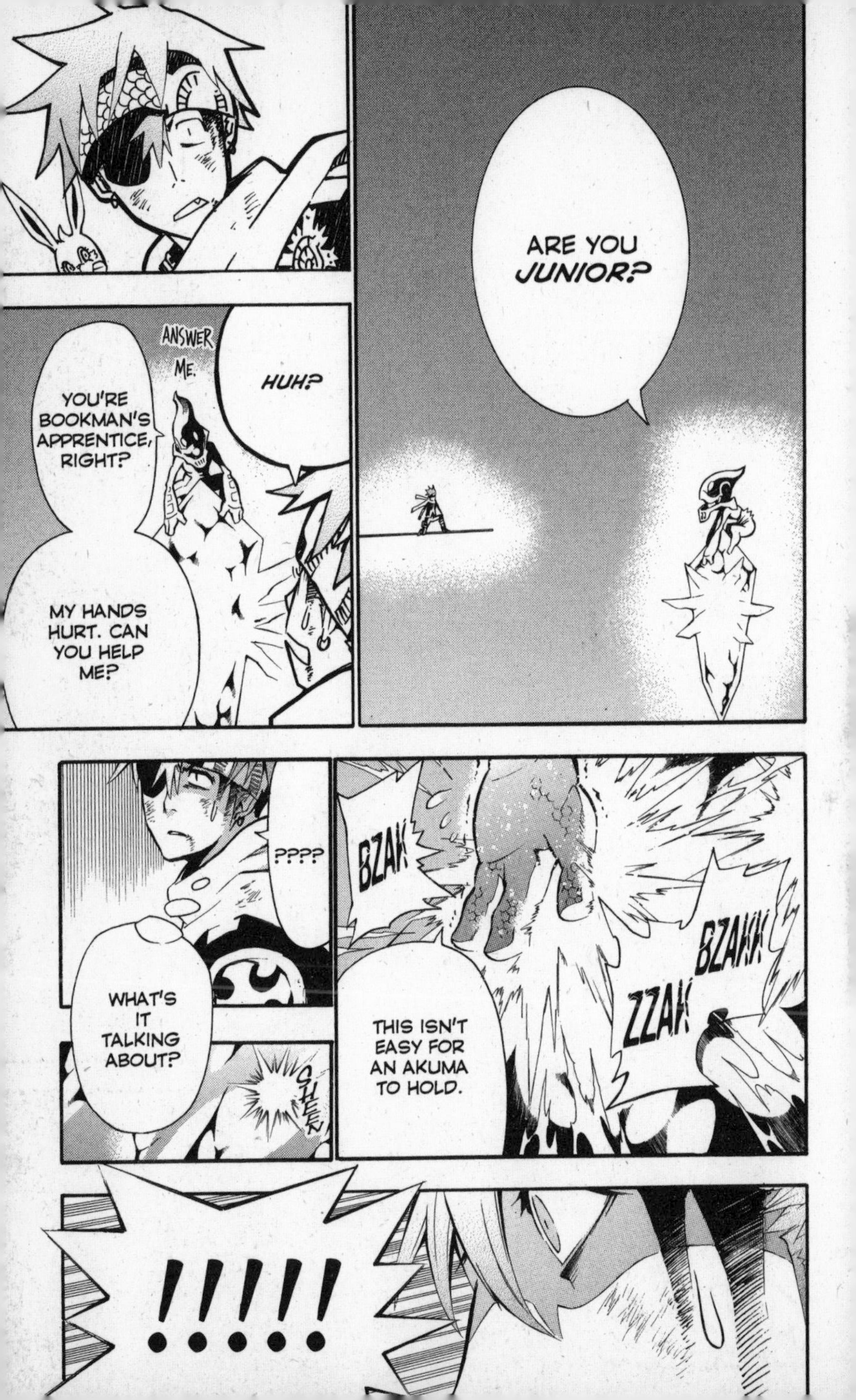
ARE YOU JUNIOR?
HUH?
ANSWER ME.
YOU'RE BOOKMAN'S APPRENTICE, RIGHT?
MY HANDS HURT. CAN YOU HELP ME?
BZAK!
BZAKK!
ZZAK!
THIS ISN'T EASY FOR AN AKUMA TO HOLD.
????
WHAT'S IT TALKING ABOUT?
SHEEN
!!!!!

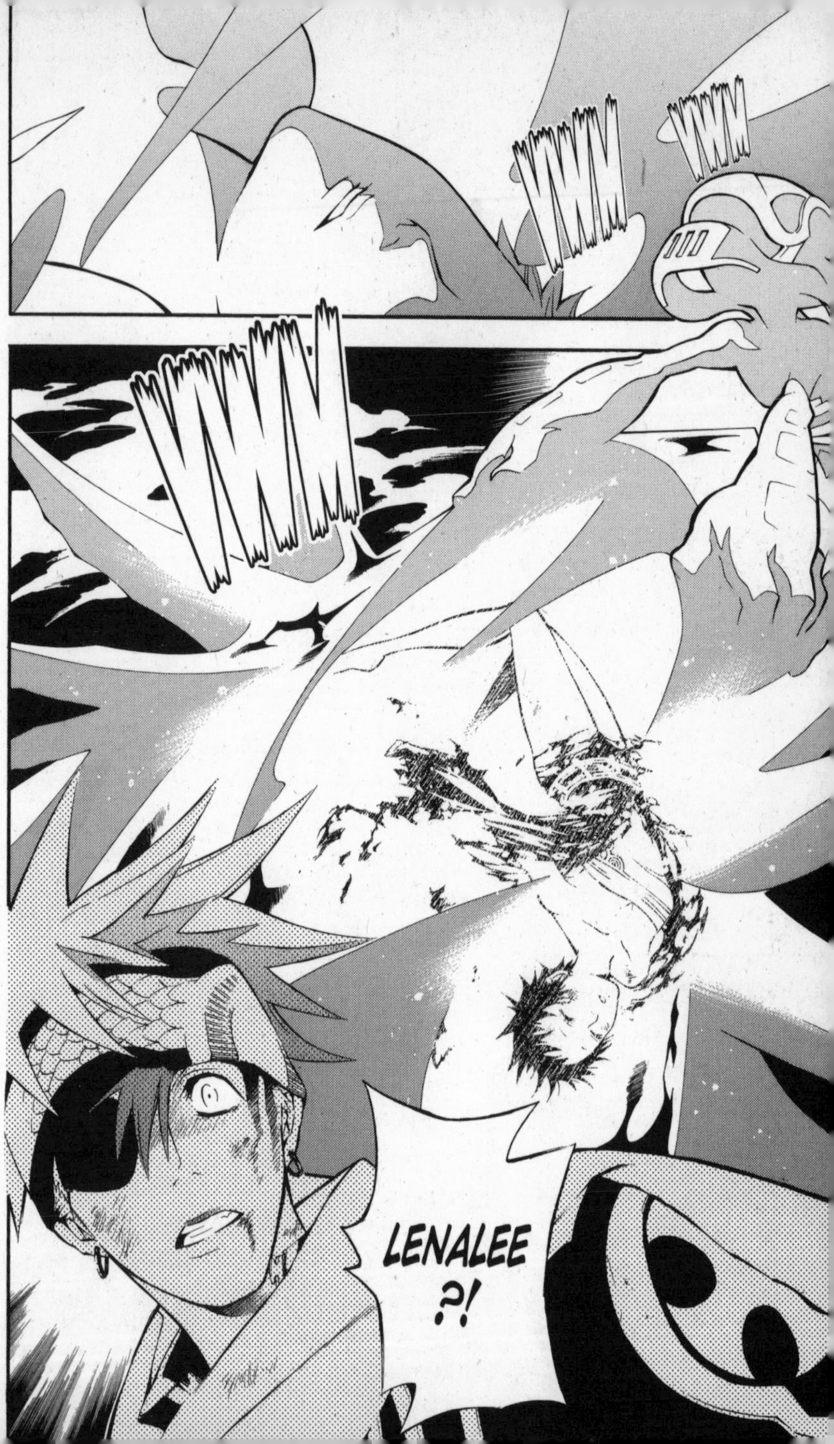
VWVM
VWVM
VWVM
LENALEE ?!

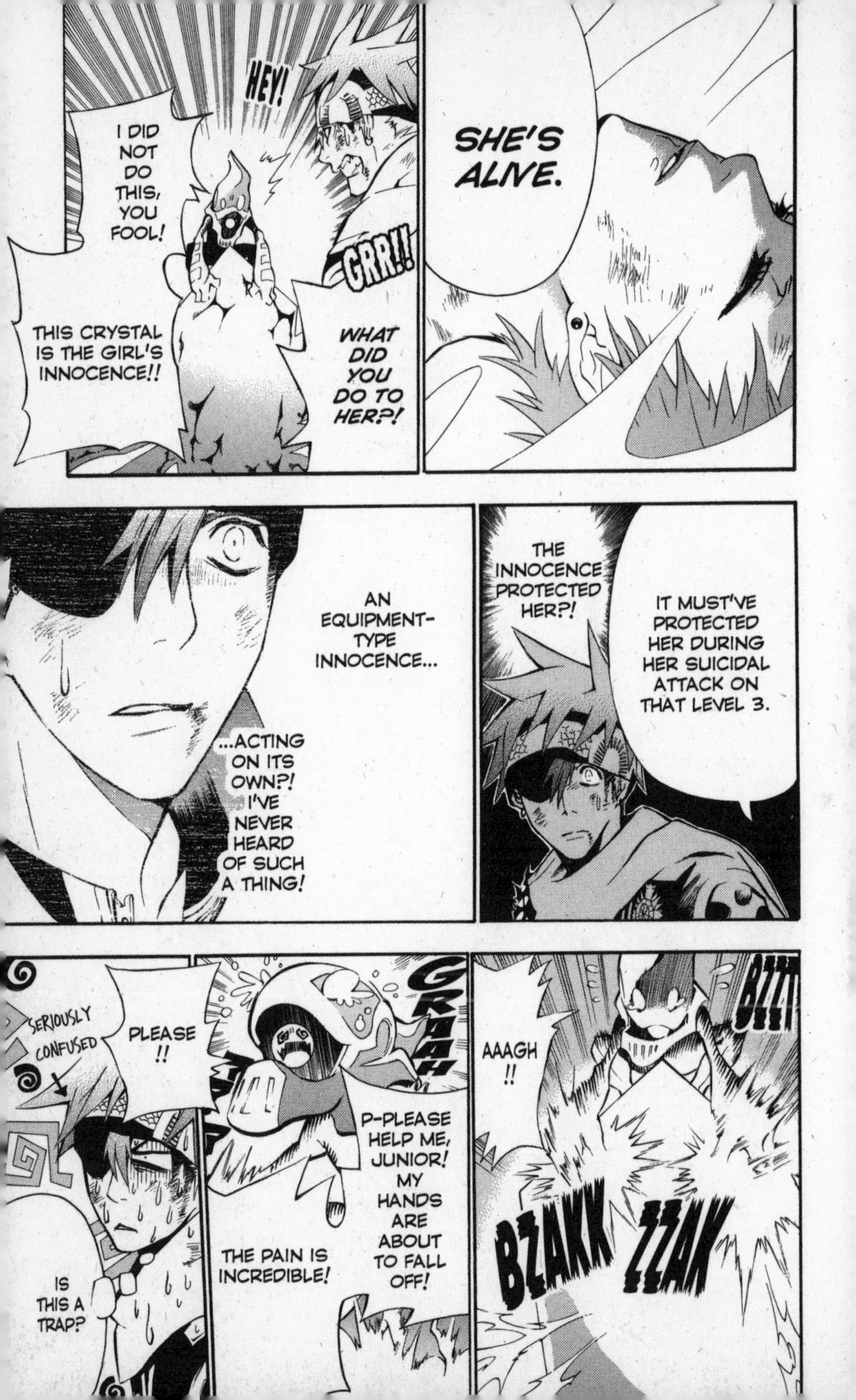
SHE'S ALIVE.
HEY!
GRR!!
WHAT DID YOU DO TO HER?!
I DID NOT DO THIS, YOU FOOL!
THIS CRYSTAL IS THE GIRL'S INNOCENCE!!
IT MUST'VE PROTECTED HER DURING HER SUICIDAL ATTACK ON THAT LEVEL 3.
THE INNOCENCE PROTECTED HER?!
AN EQUIPMENT-TYPE INNOCENCE...
...ACTING ON ITS OWN?! I'VE NEVER HEARD OF SUCH A THING!
BZZT
AAAGH !!
BZAKK
ZZAK
GRAAH
P-PLEASE HELP ME, JUNIOR! MY HANDS ARE ABOUT TO FALL OFF!
THE PAIN IS INCREDIBLE!
PLEASE !!
SERIOUSLY CONFUSED
IS THIS A TRAP?

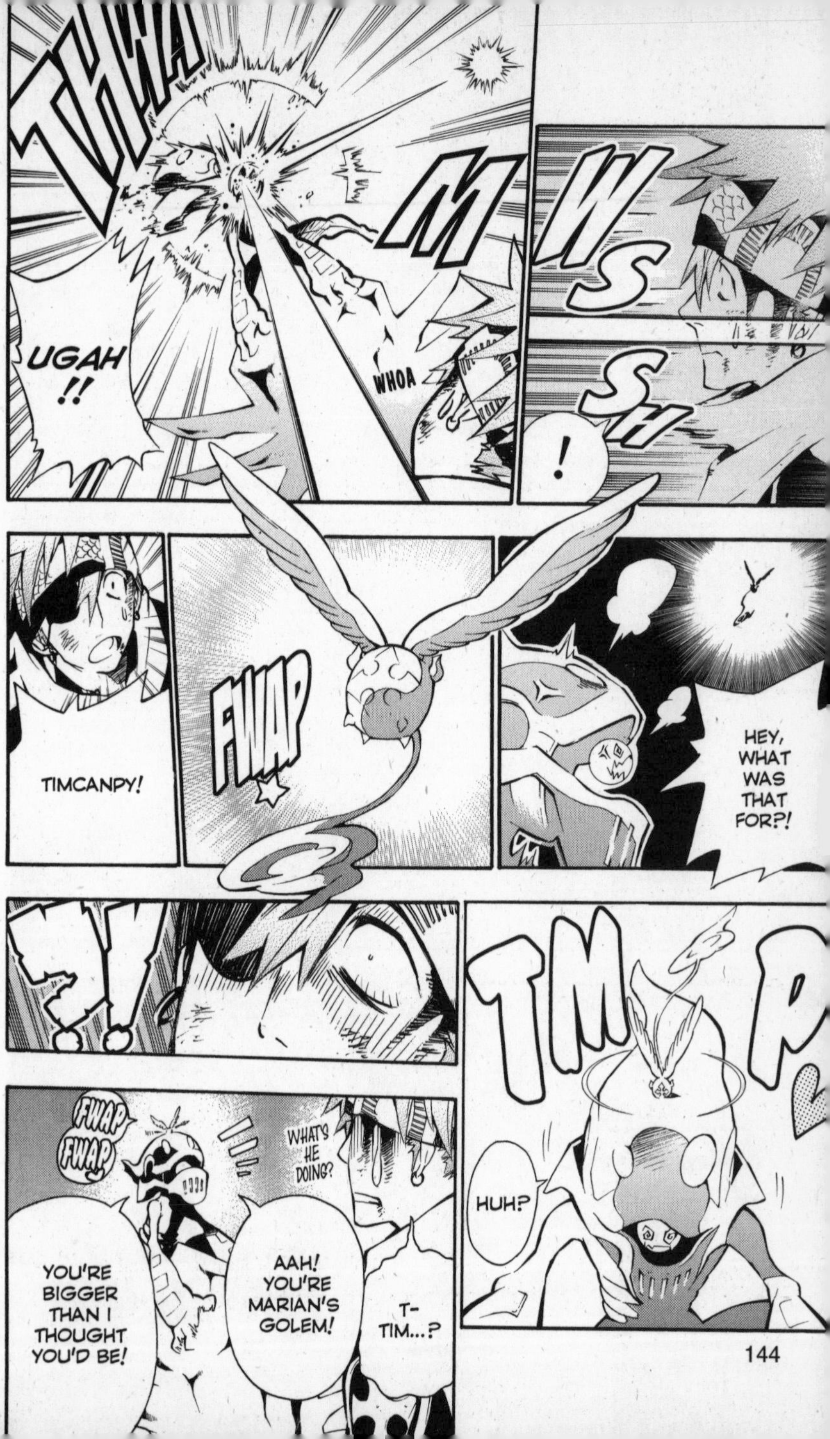
!
UGAH!!
WHOA
HEY, WHAT WAS THAT FOR?!
FWAP
TIMCANPY!
HUH?
WHAT'S HE DOING?
T-TIM...?
AAH! YOU'RE MARIAN'S GOLEM!
FWAP FWAP
YOU'RE BIGGER THAN I THOUGHT YOU'D BE!

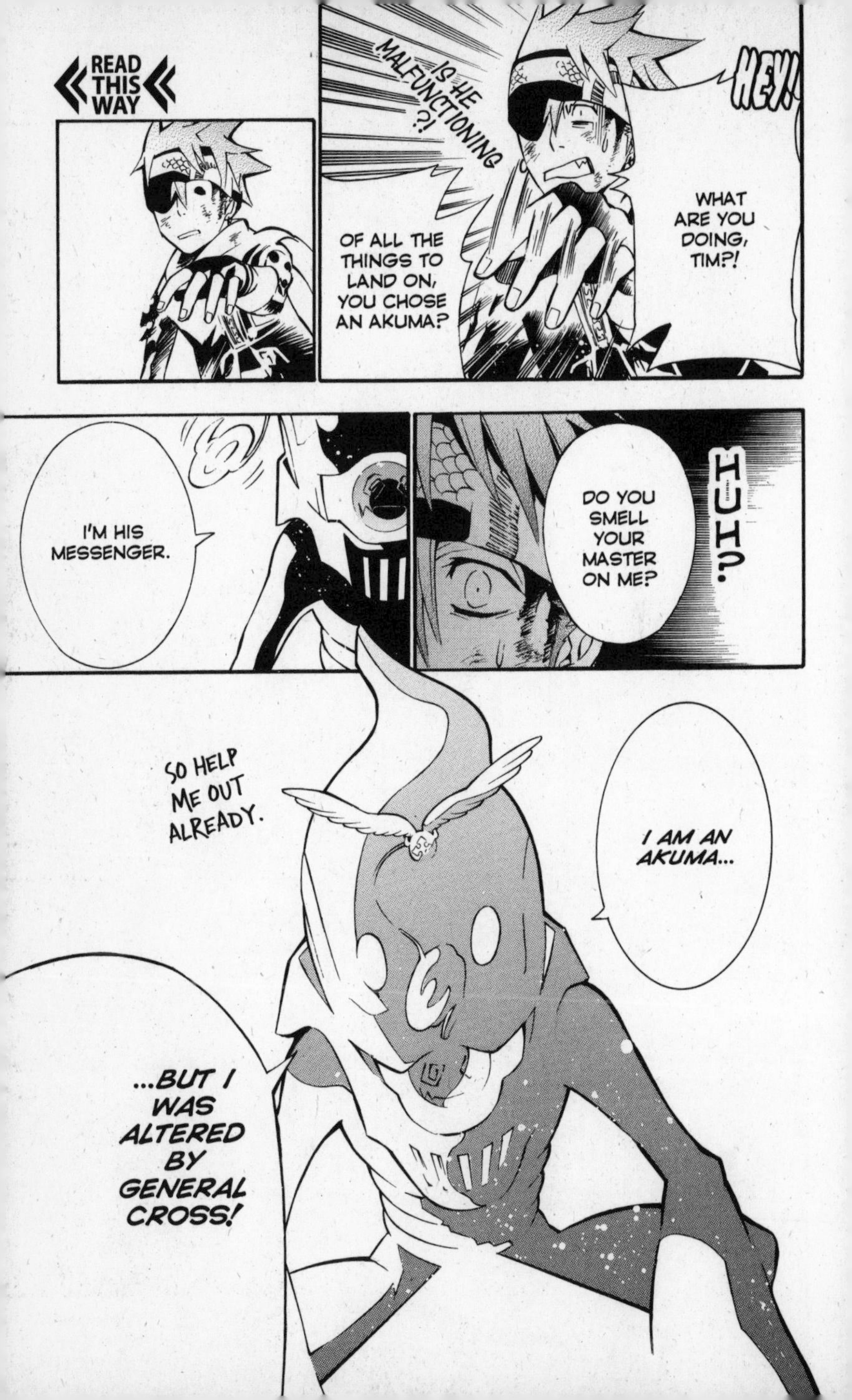
READ THIS WAY
HEY!!
WHAT ARE YOU DOING, TIM?!
OF ALL THE THINGS TO LAND ON, YOU CHOSE AN AKUMA?
IS HE MALFUNCTIONING ?!
HUH?
DO YOU SMELL YOUR MASTER ON ME?
I'M HIS MESSENGER.
I AM AN AKUMA...
SO HELP ME OUT ALREADY.
...BUT I WAS ALTERED BY GENERAL CROSS!

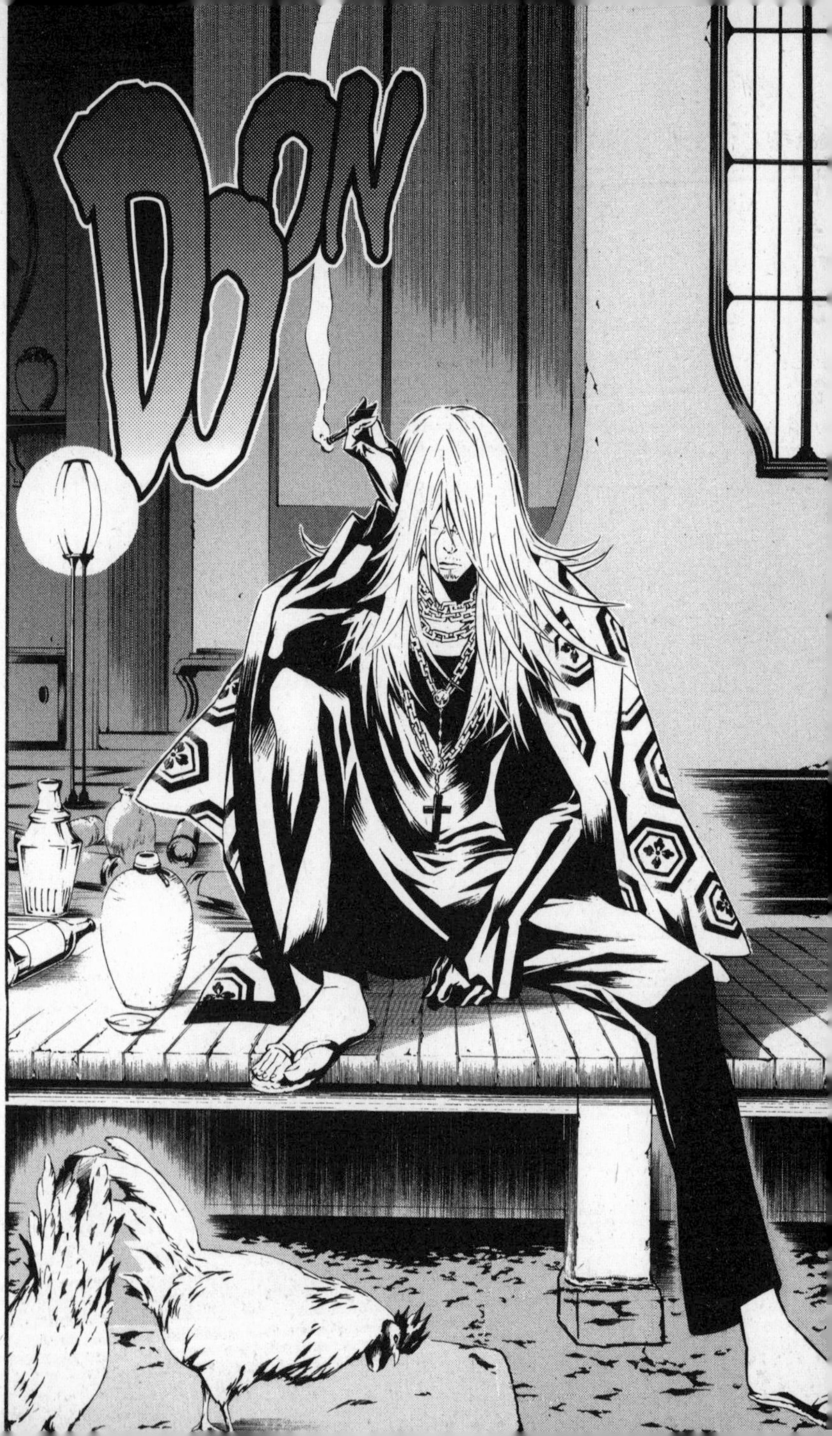
DOON

READ THIS WAY

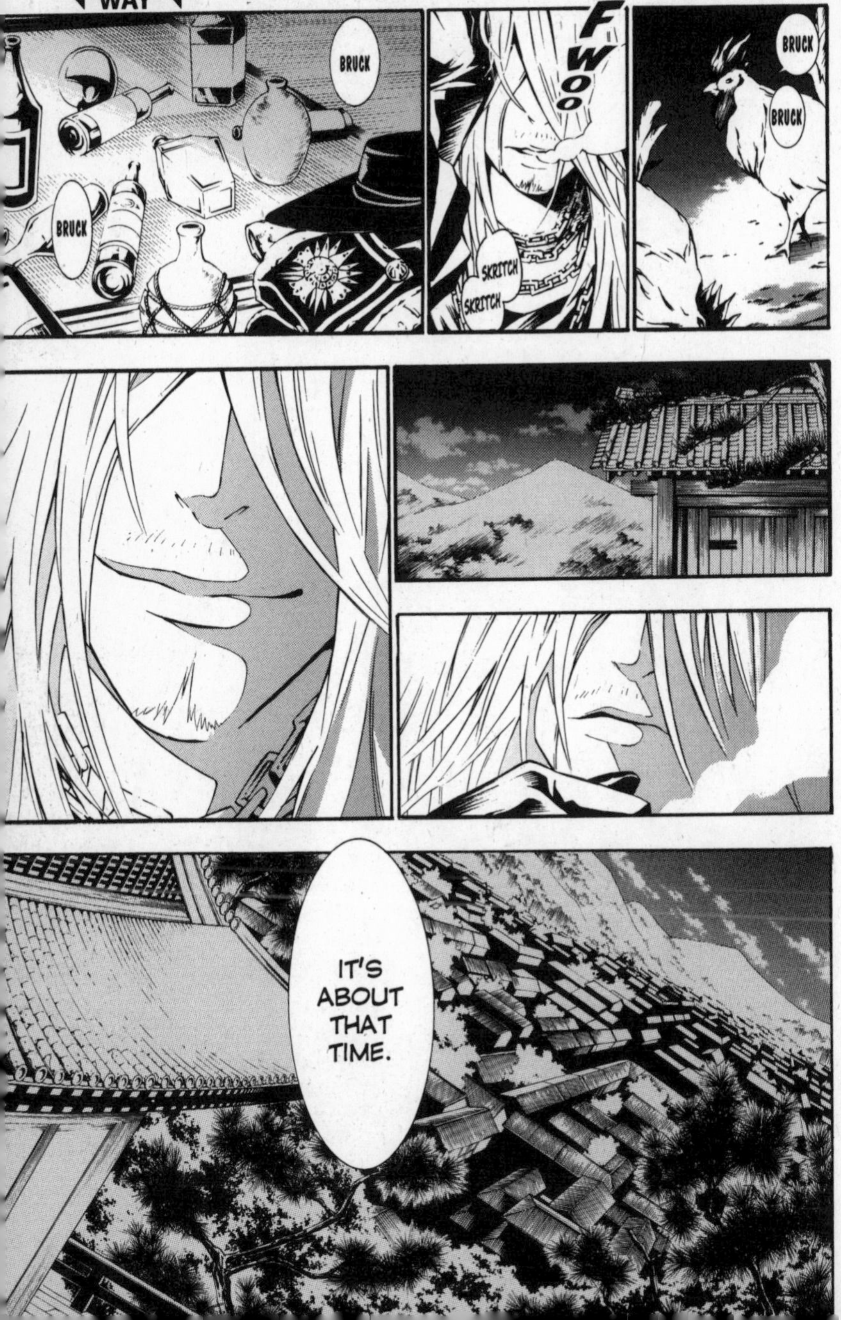

BRUCK
BRUCK
FWOO
SKRITCH
SKRITCH
BRUCK
BRUCK
IT'S ABOUT THAT TIME.

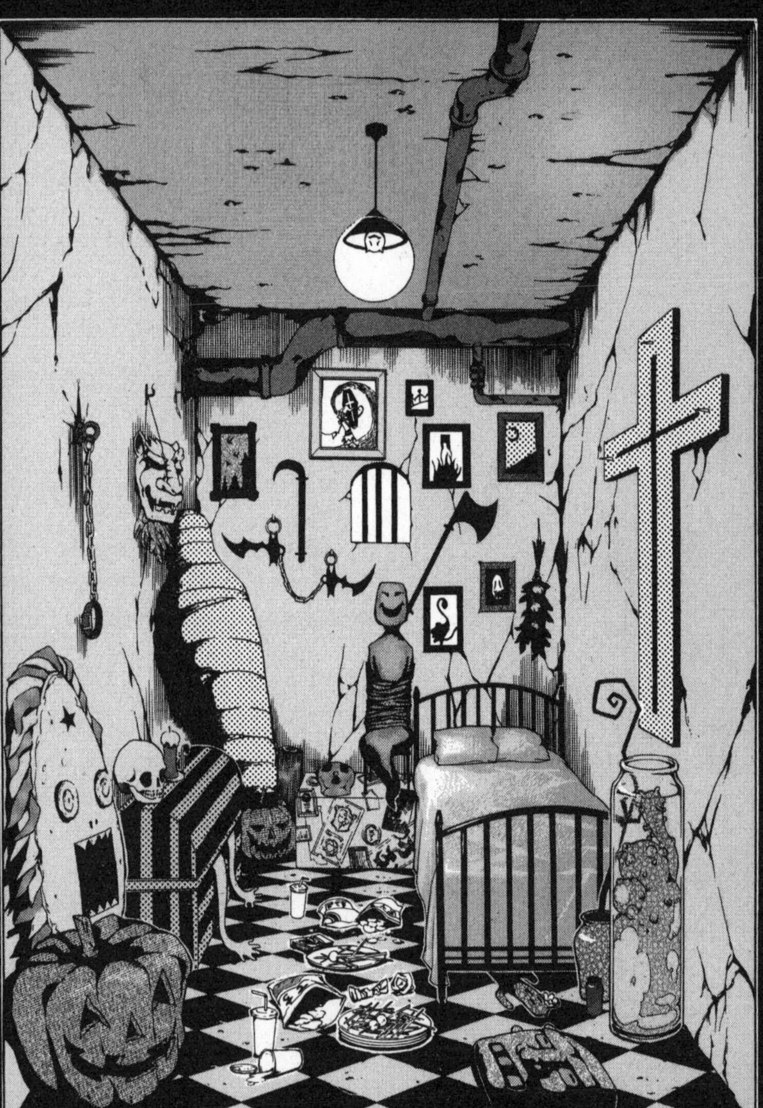

ALLEN'S ROOM
CURRENTLY UNOCCUPIED

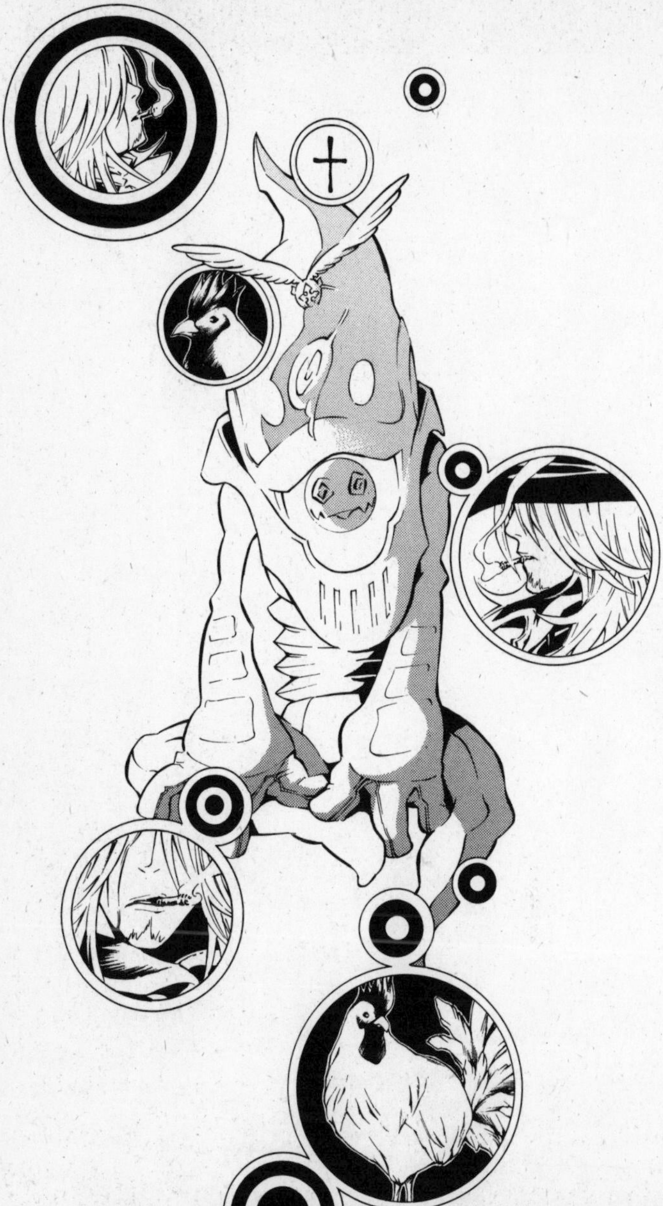

THE 75TH NIGHT: THE MESSAGE

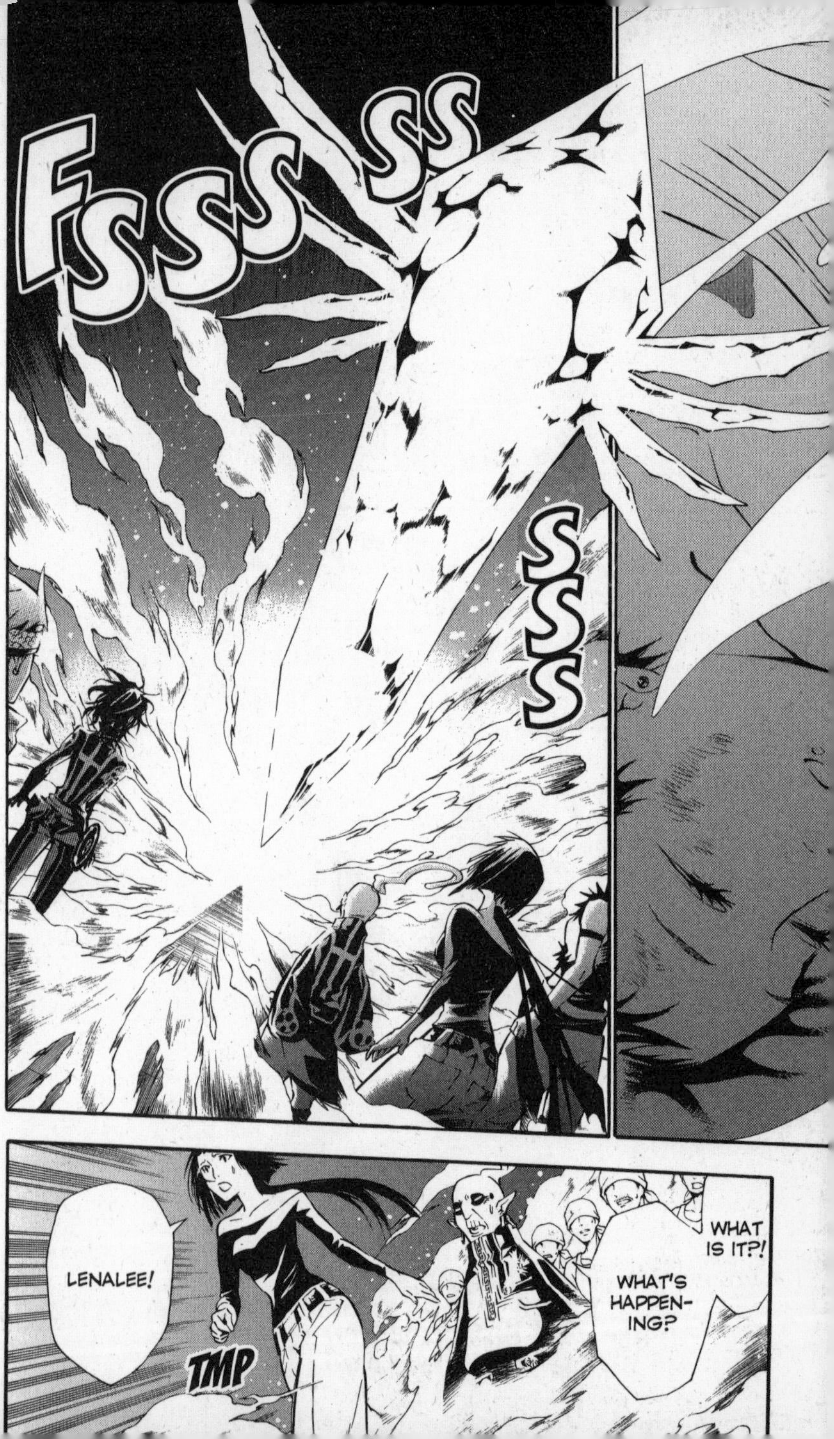
FSSSSS
SSSS
WHAT IS IT?!
WHAT'S HAPPEN-ING?
LENALEE!
TMP

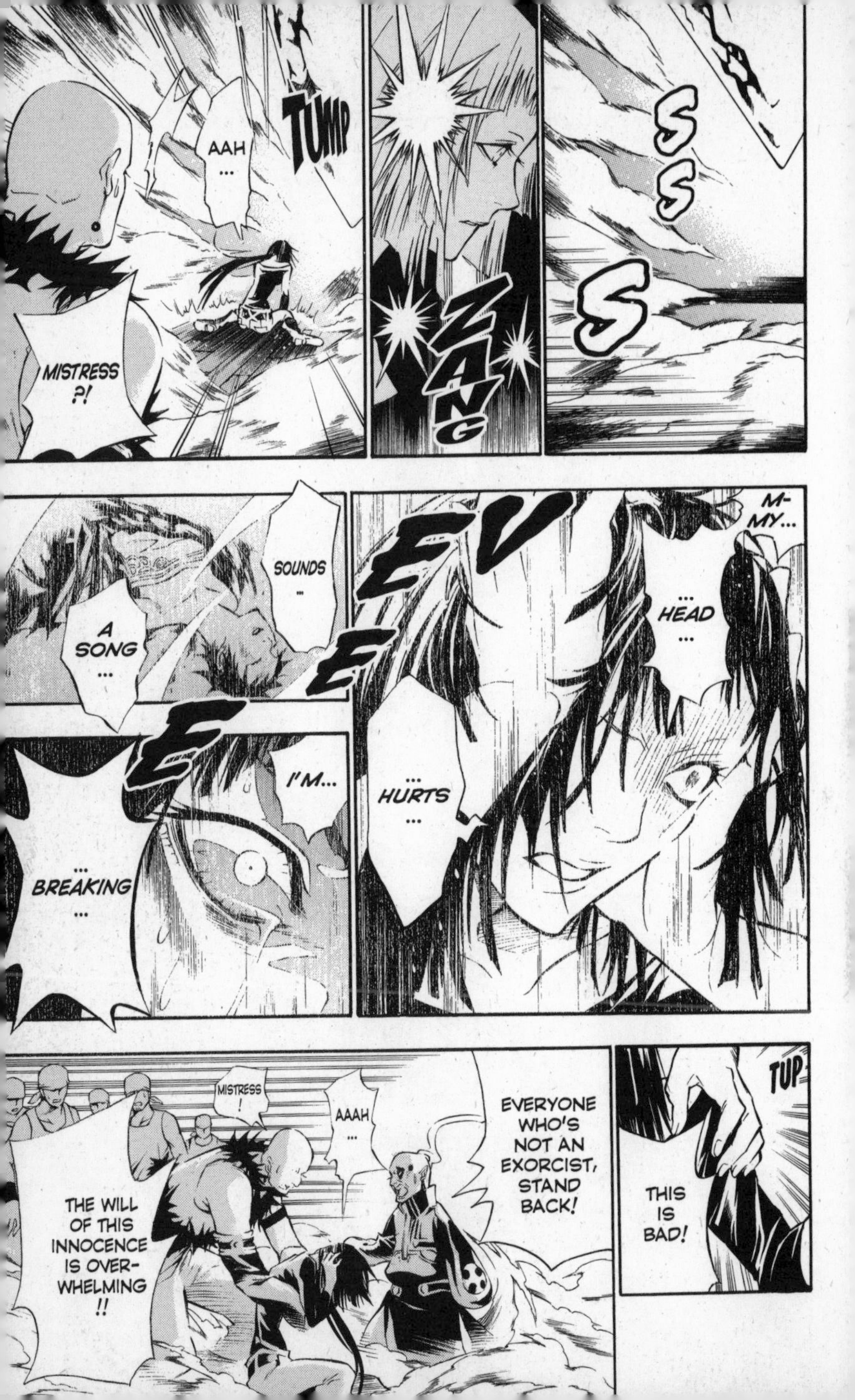
SSSS
ZANG
TUMP
AAH...
MISTRESS?!
M-MY...
...HEAD...
...HURTS...
EEEV
SOUNDS...
A SONG...
I'M...
...BREAKING...
TUP
THIS IS BAD!
EVERYONE WHO'S NOT AN EXORCIST, STAND BACK!
AAAH...
MISTRESS!
THE WILL OF THIS INNOCENCE IS OVER-WHELMING!!

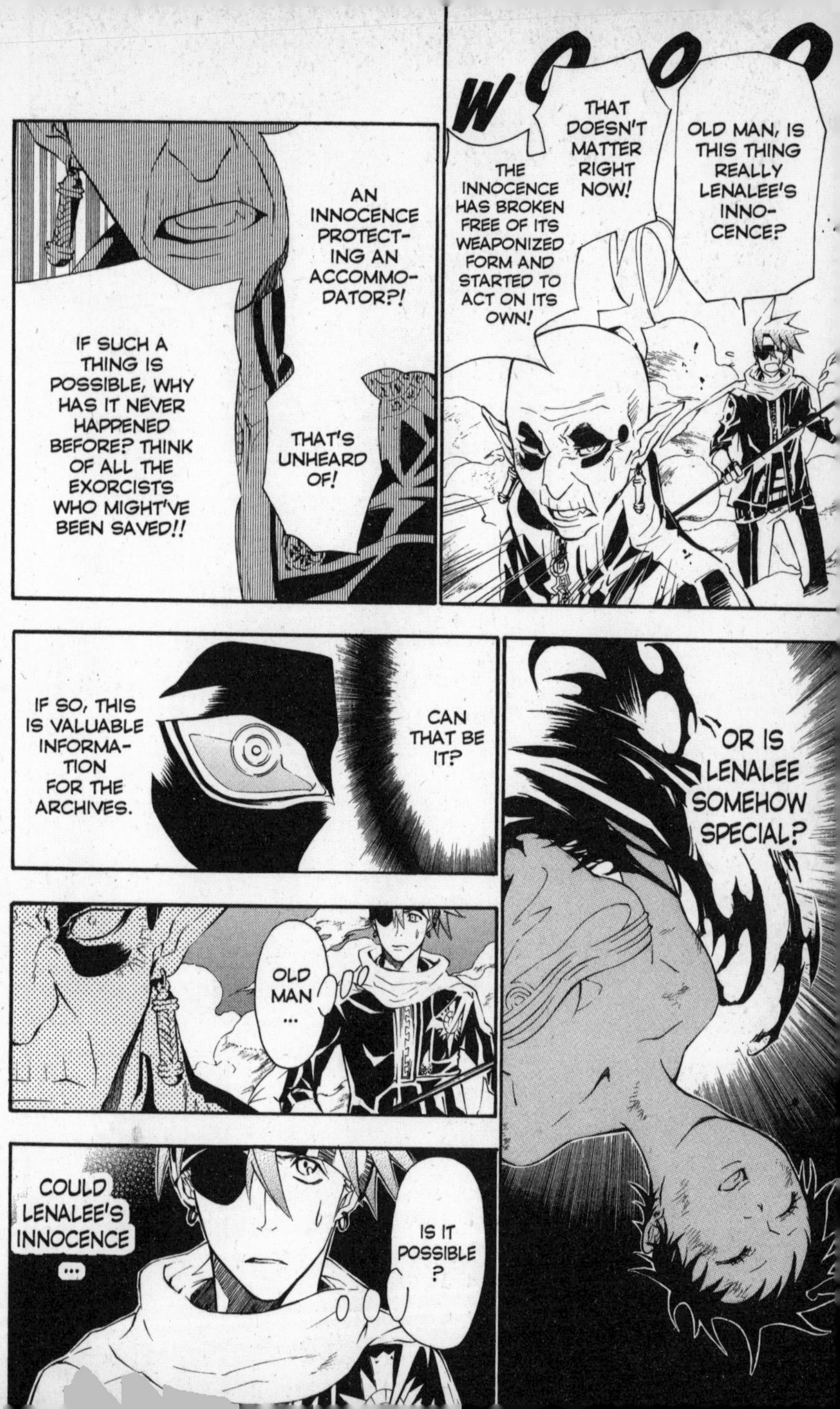
WOOO
OLD MAN, IS THIS THING REALLY LENALEE'S INNO-CENCE?
THAT DOESN'T MATTER RIGHT NOW!
THE INNOCENCE HAS BROKEN FREE OF ITS WEAPONIZED FORM AND STARTED TO ACT ON ITS OWN!
AN INNOCENCE PROTECT-ING AN ACCOMMO-DATOR?!
THAT'S UNHEARD OF!
IF SUCH A THING IS POSSIBLE, WHY HAS IT NEVER HAPPENED BEFORE? THINK OF ALL THE EXORCISTS WHO MIGHT'VE BEEN SAVED!!
OR IS LENALEE SOMEHOW SPECIAL?
CAN THAT BE IT?
IF SO, THIS IS VALUABLE INFORMA-TION FOR THE ARCHIVES.
OLD MAN ...
IS IT POSSIBLE ?
COULD LENALEE'S INNOCENCE ...

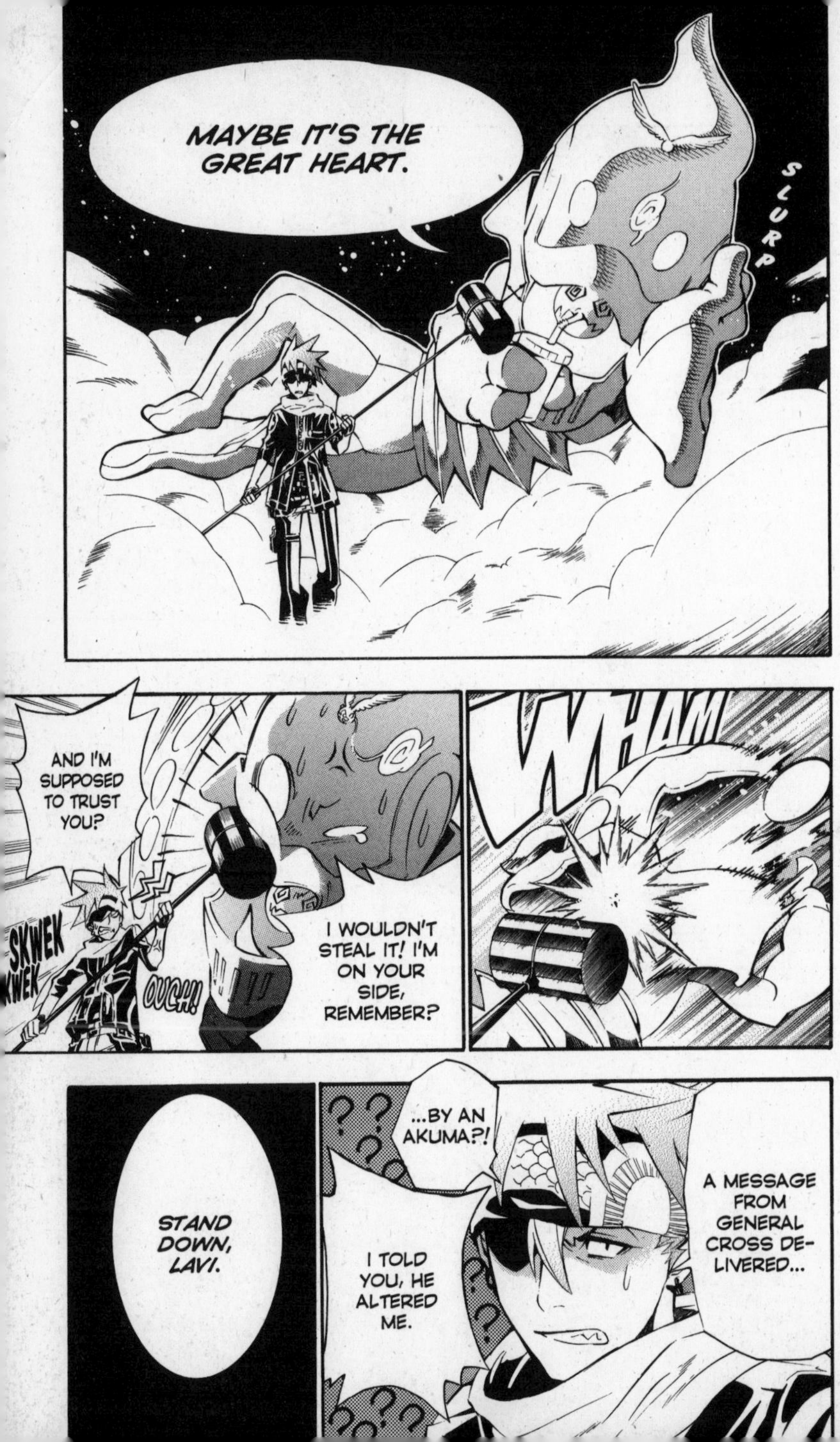
MAYBE IT'S THE GREAT HEART.
SLURP
WHAM
AND I'M SUPPOSED TO TRUST YOU?
SKWEK SKWEK
OUCH!
I WOULDN'T STEAL IT! I'M ON YOUR SIDE, REMEMBER?
A MESSAGE FROM GENERAL CROSS DE-LIVERED...
...BY AN AKUMA?!
I TOLD YOU, HE ALTERED ME.
STAND DOWN, LAVI.

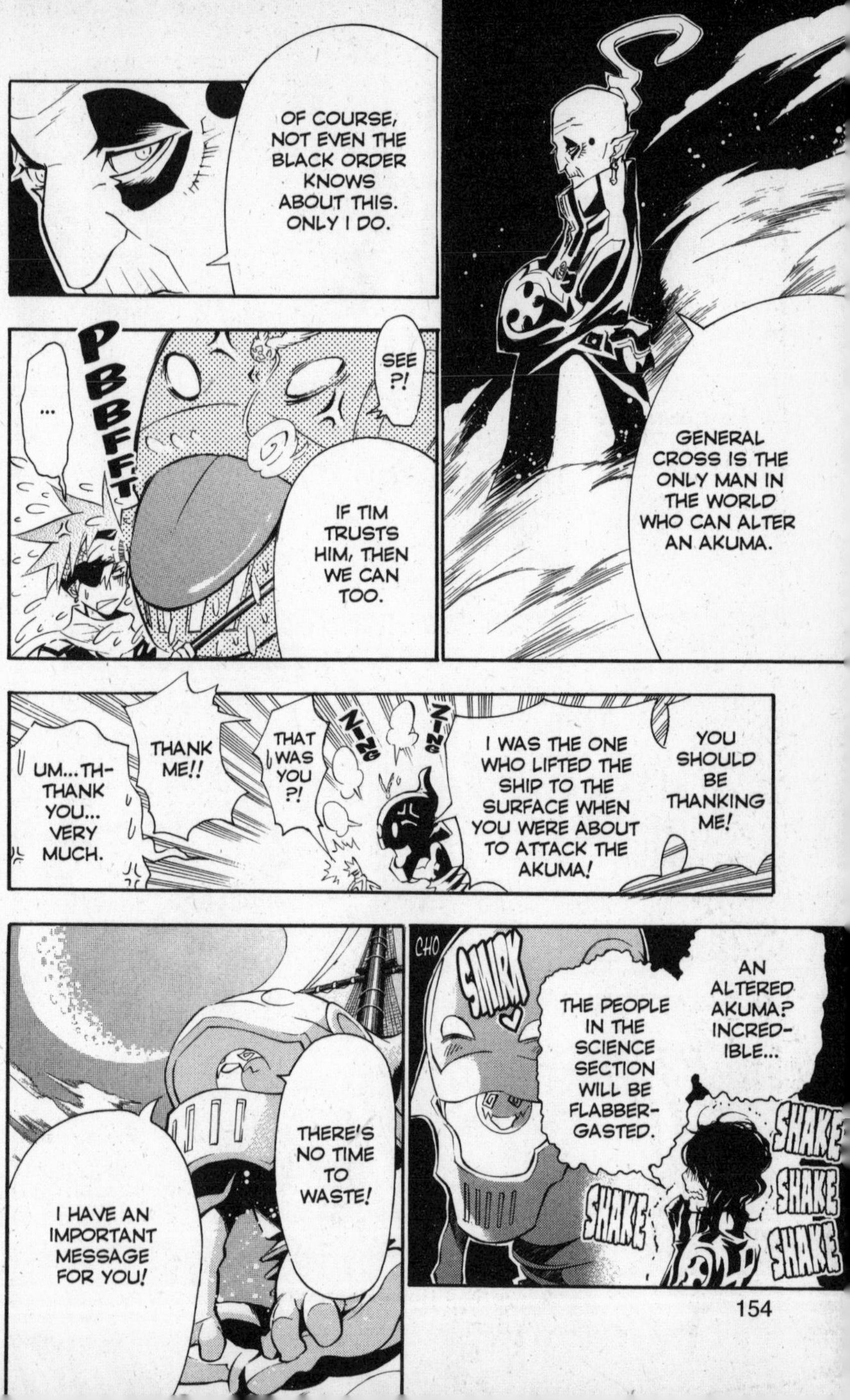

GENERAL CROSS IS THE ONLY MAN IN THE WORLD WHO CAN ALTER AN AKUMA.
OF COURSE, NOT EVEN THE BLACK ORDER KNOWS ABOUT THIS. ONLY I DO.
SEE?!
IF TIM TRUSTS HIM, THEN WE CAN TOO.
PBBFFT
...
YOU SHOULD BE THANKING ME!
I WAS THE ONE WHO LIFTED THE SHIP TO THE SURFACE WHEN YOU WERE ABOUT TO ATTACK THE AKUMA!
ZING
ZING
THAT WAS YOU?!
THANK ME!!
UM...TH-THANK YOU... VERY MUCH.
AN ALTERED AKUMA? INCREDIBLE...
CHO
SMIRK
THE PEOPLE IN THE SCIENCE SECTION WILL BE FLABBERGASTED.
SHAKE
SHAKE
SHAKE
SHAKE
THERE'S NO TIME TO WASTE!
I HAVE AN IMPORTANT MESSAGE FOR YOU!

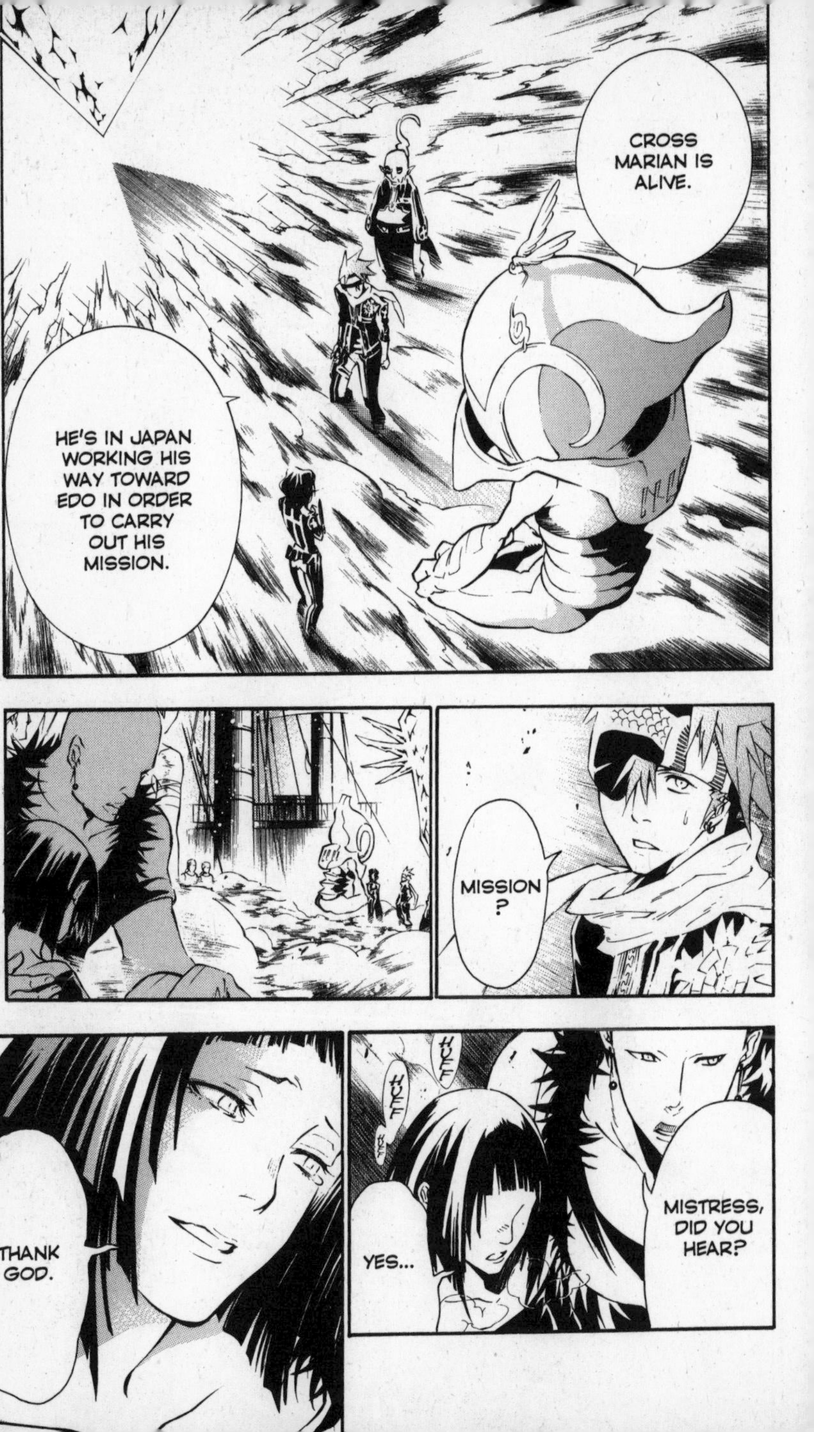
CROSS MARIAN IS ALIVE.
HE'S IN JAPAN WORKING HIS WAY TOWARD EDO IN ORDER TO CARRY OUT HIS MISSION.
MISSION ?
HUFF
HUFF
HUFF
MISTRESS, DID YOU HEAR?
YES...
THANK GOD.

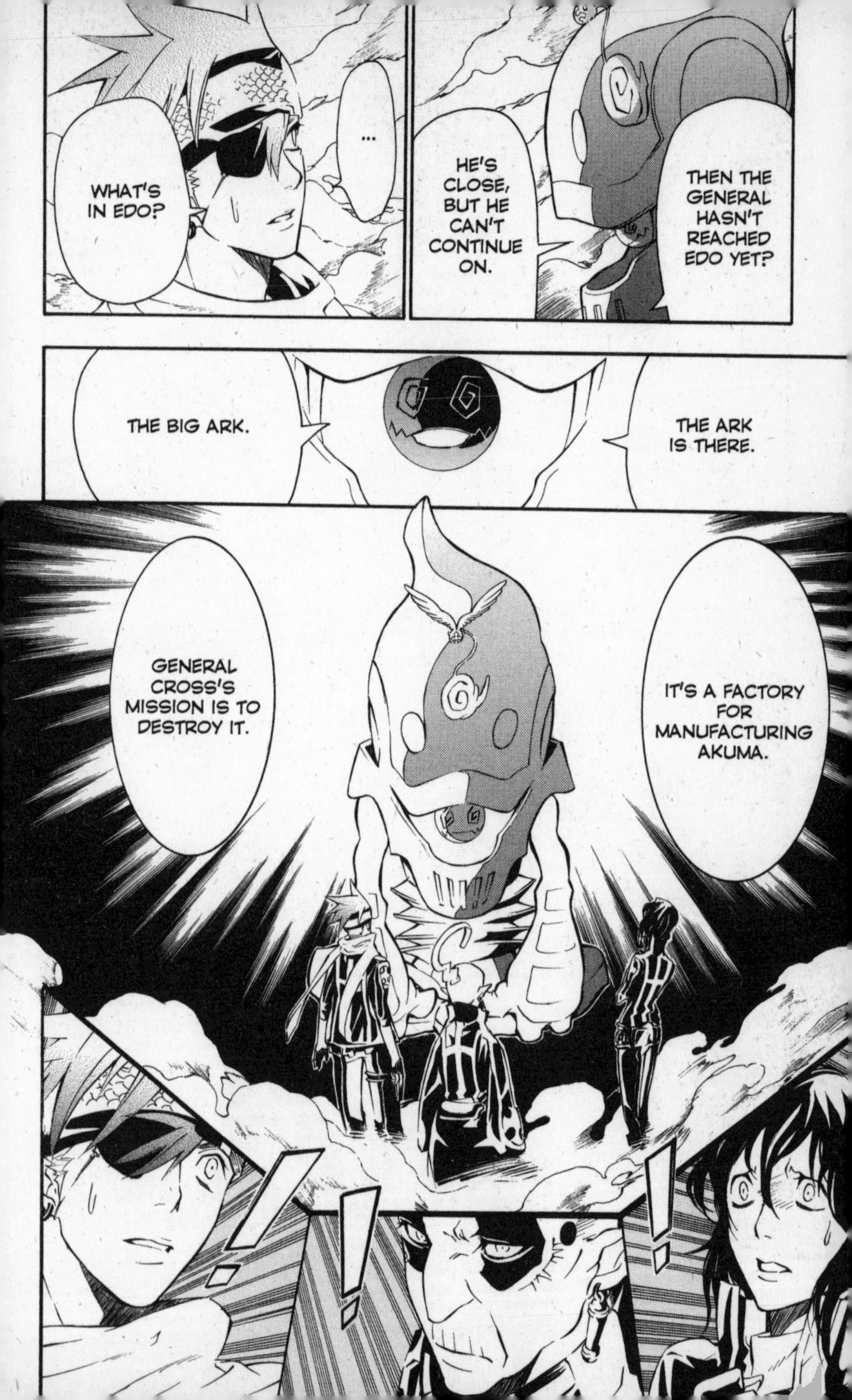
THEN THE GENERAL HASN'T REACHED EDO YET?
HE'S CLOSE, BUT HE CAN'T CONTINUE ON.
...
WHAT'S IN EDO?
THE ARK IS THERE.
THE BIG ARK.
IT'S A FACTORY FOR MANUFACTURING AKUMA.
GENERAL CROSS'S MISSION IS TO DESTROY IT.
!
!
!

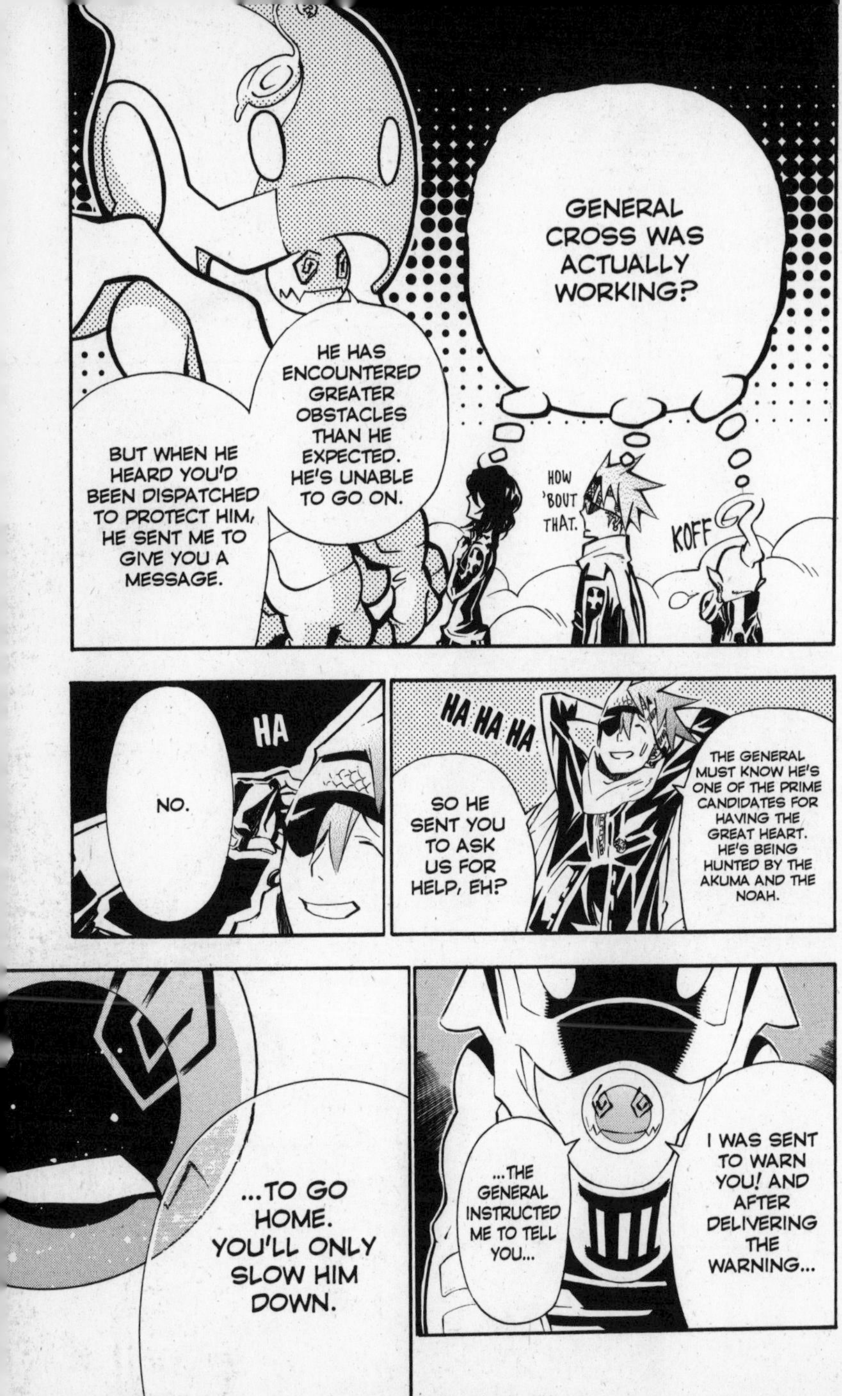
GENERAL CROSS WAS ACTUALLY WORKING?
HOW 'BOUT THAT.
KOFF
HE HAS ENCOUNTERED GREATER OBSTACLES THAN HE EXPECTED. HE'S UNABLE TO GO ON.
BUT WHEN HE HEARD YOU'D BEEN DISPATCHED TO PROTECT HIM, HE SENT ME TO GIVE YOU A MESSAGE.
HA HA HA
THE GENERAL MUST KNOW HE'S ONE OF THE PRIME CANDIDATES FOR HAVING THE GREAT HEART. HE'S BEING HUNTED BY THE AKUMA AND THE NOAH.
SO HE SENT YOU TO ASK US FOR HELP, EH?
HA
NO.
I WAS SENT TO WARN YOU! AND AFTER DELIVERING THE WARNING...
...THE GENERAL INSTRUCTED ME TO TELL YOU...
...TO GO HOME. YOU'LL ONLY SLOW HIM DOWN.

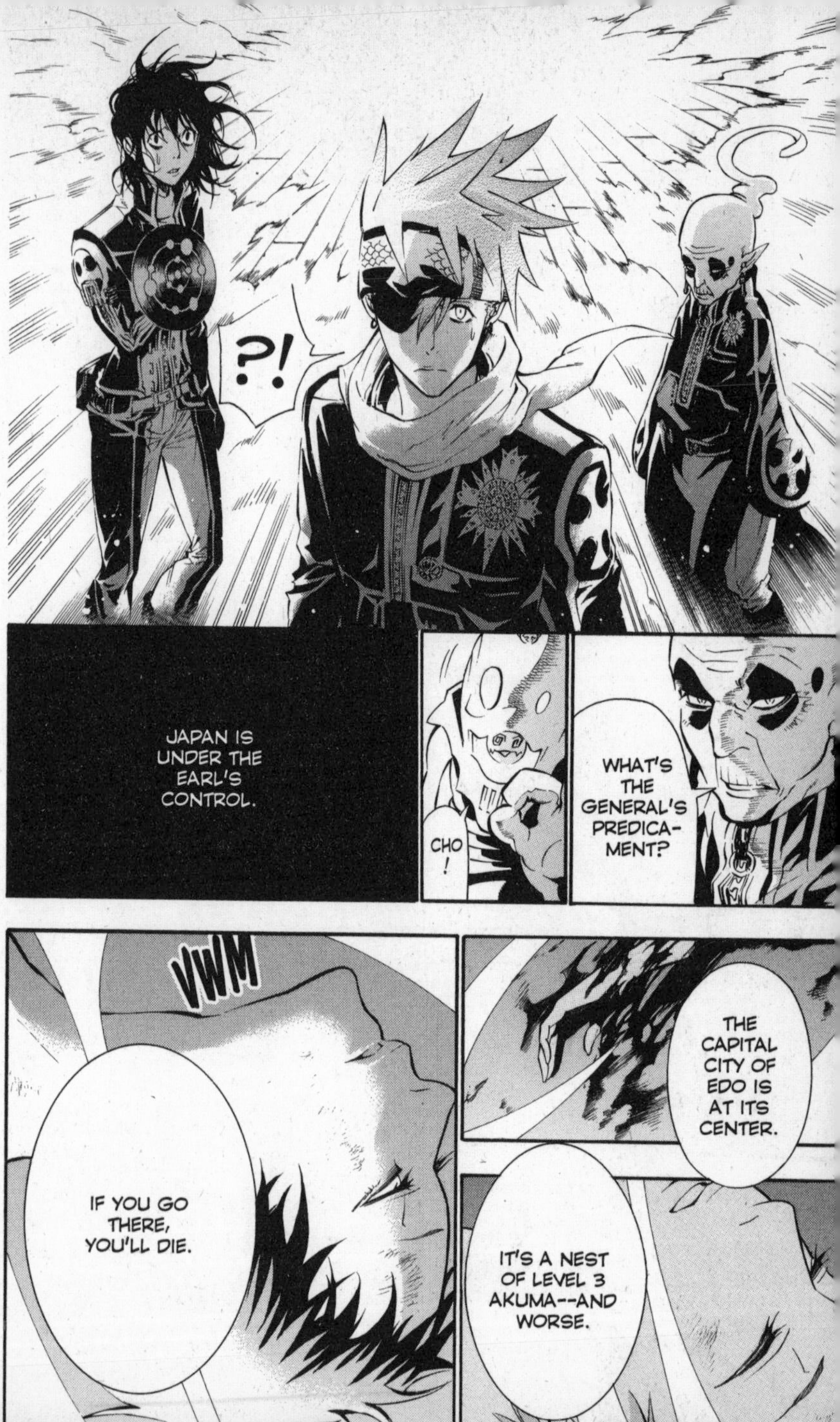
?!
WHAT'S THE GENERAL'S PREDICAMENT?
CHO!
JAPAN IS UNDER THE EARL'S CONTROL.
THE CAPITAL CITY OF EDO IS AT ITS CENTER.
IT'S A NEST OF LEVEL 3 AKUMA--AND WORSE.
VWM
IF YOU GO THERE, YOU'LL DIE.

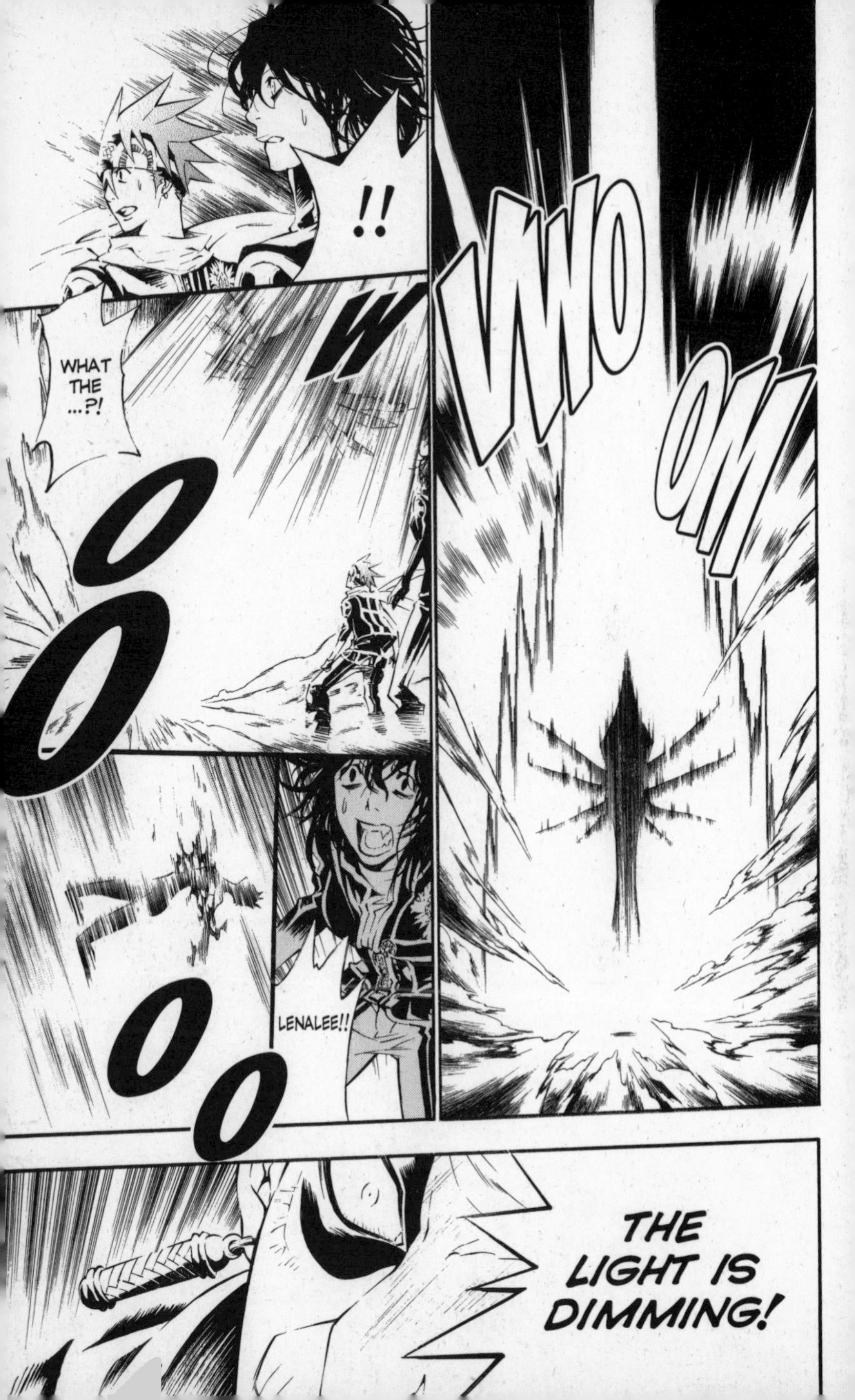
VWOOOM
!!
WHAT THE ...?!
WOOOOO
LENALEE!!
THE LIGHT IS DIMMING!

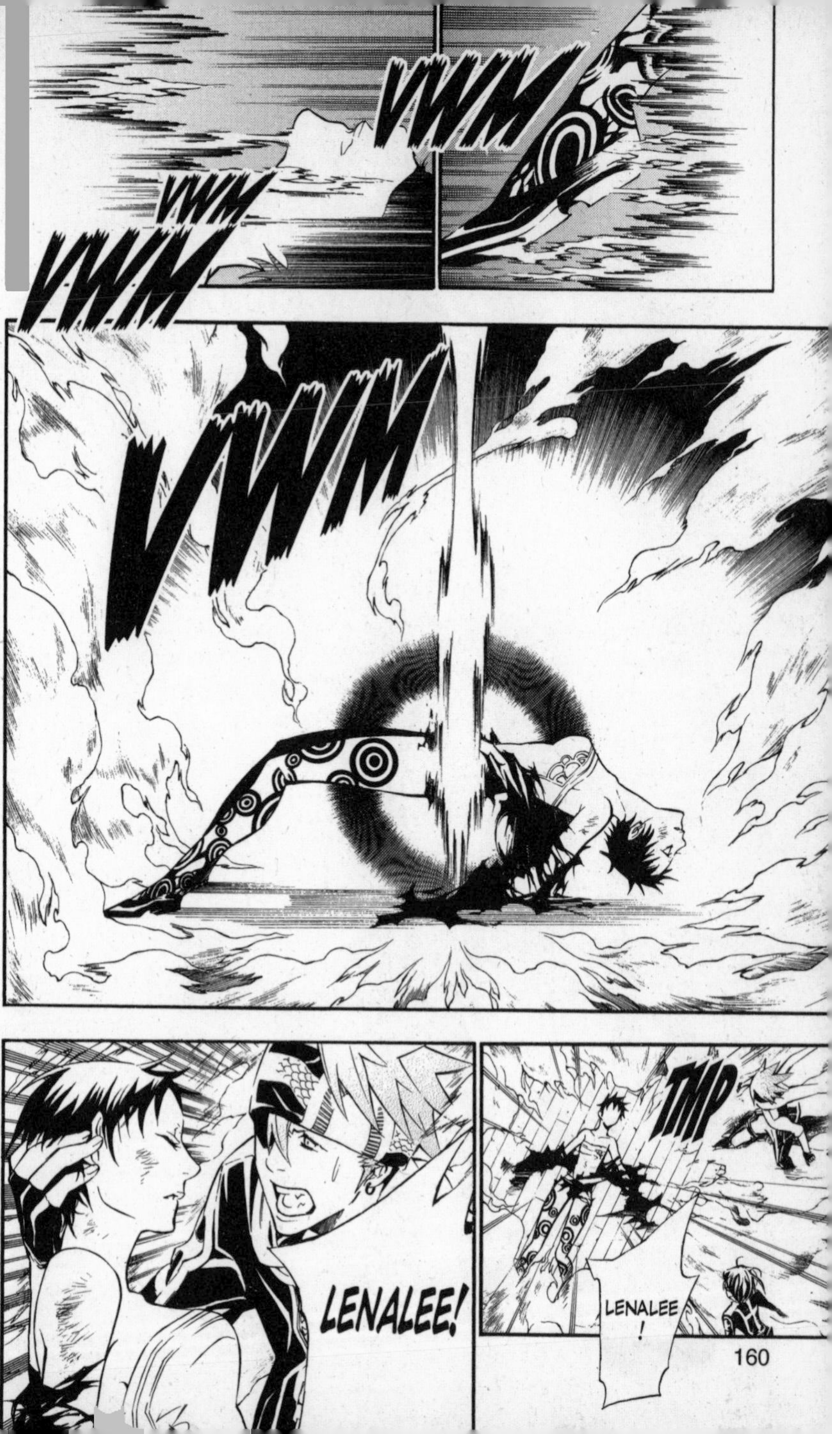
VWM
VWM
VWM
VWM
TMP
LENALEE
!
LENALEE!

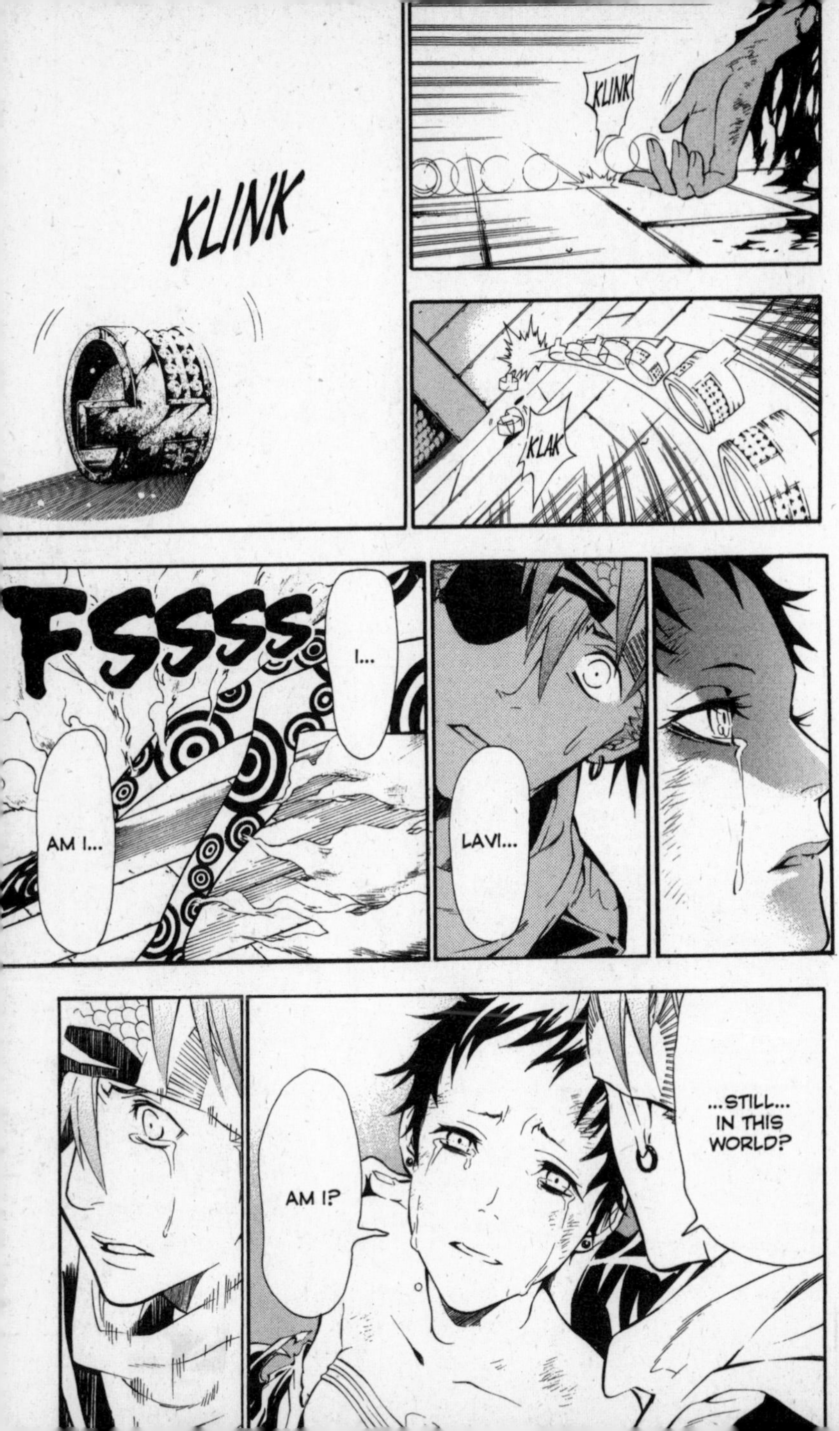
KLINK
KLAK
KLINK
LAVI...
I...
FSSSSS
AM I...
...STILL... IN THIS WORLD?
AM I?

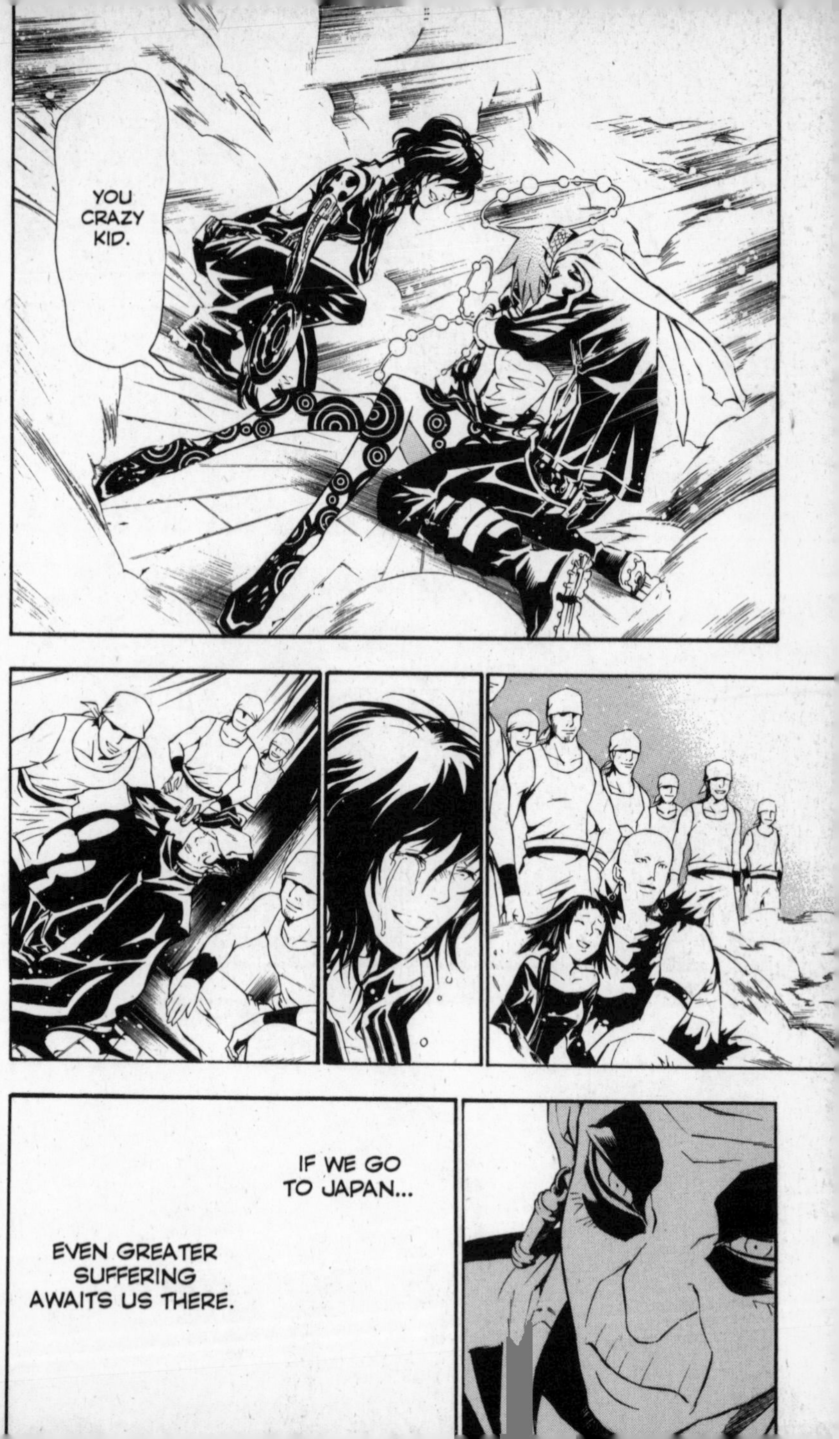
YOU CRAZY KID.
IF WE GO TO JAPAN...
EVEN GREATER SUFFERING AWAITS US THERE.

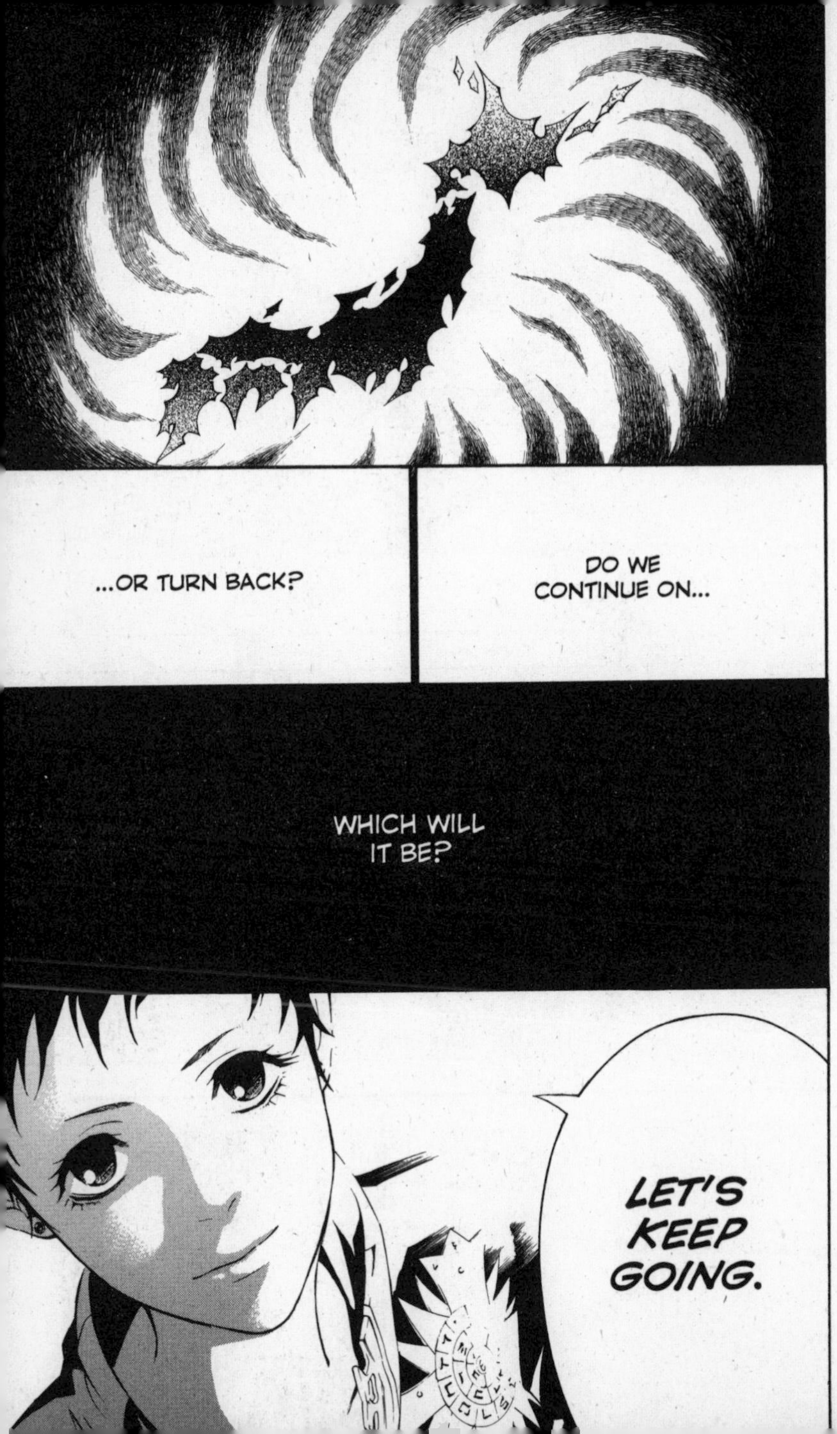
DO WE CONTINUE ON...
...OR TURN BACK?
WHICH WILL IT BE?
LET'S KEEP GOING.

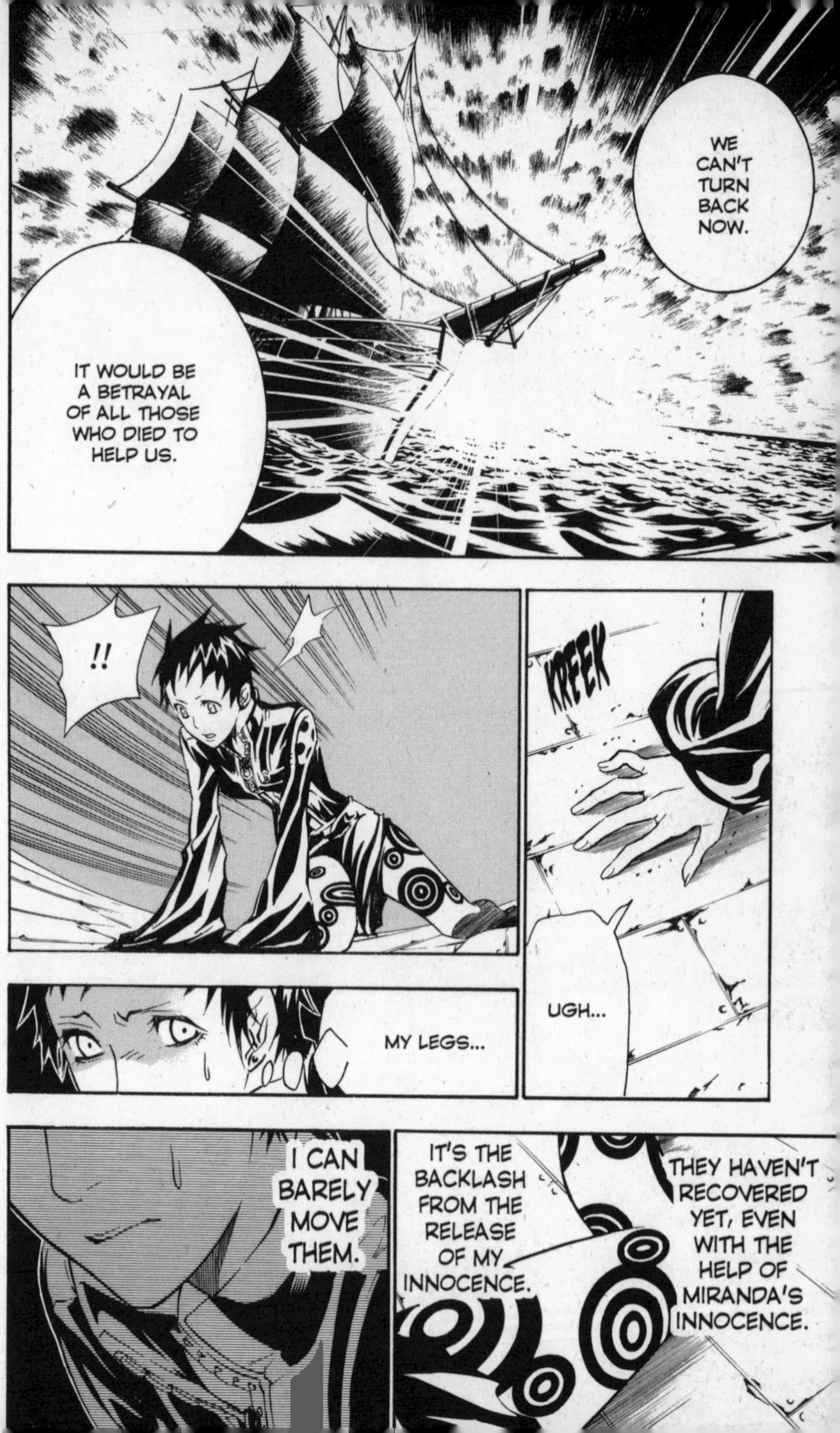
WE CAN'T TURN BACK NOW.
IT WOULD BE A BETRAYAL OF ALL THOSE WHO DIED TO HELP US.
KREEK
UGH...
!!
MY LEGS...
THEY HAVEN'T RECOVERED YET, EVEN WITH THE HELP OF MIRANDA'S INNOCENCE.
IT'S THE BACKLASH FROM THE RELEASE OF MY INNOCENCE.
I CAN BARELY MOVE THEM.

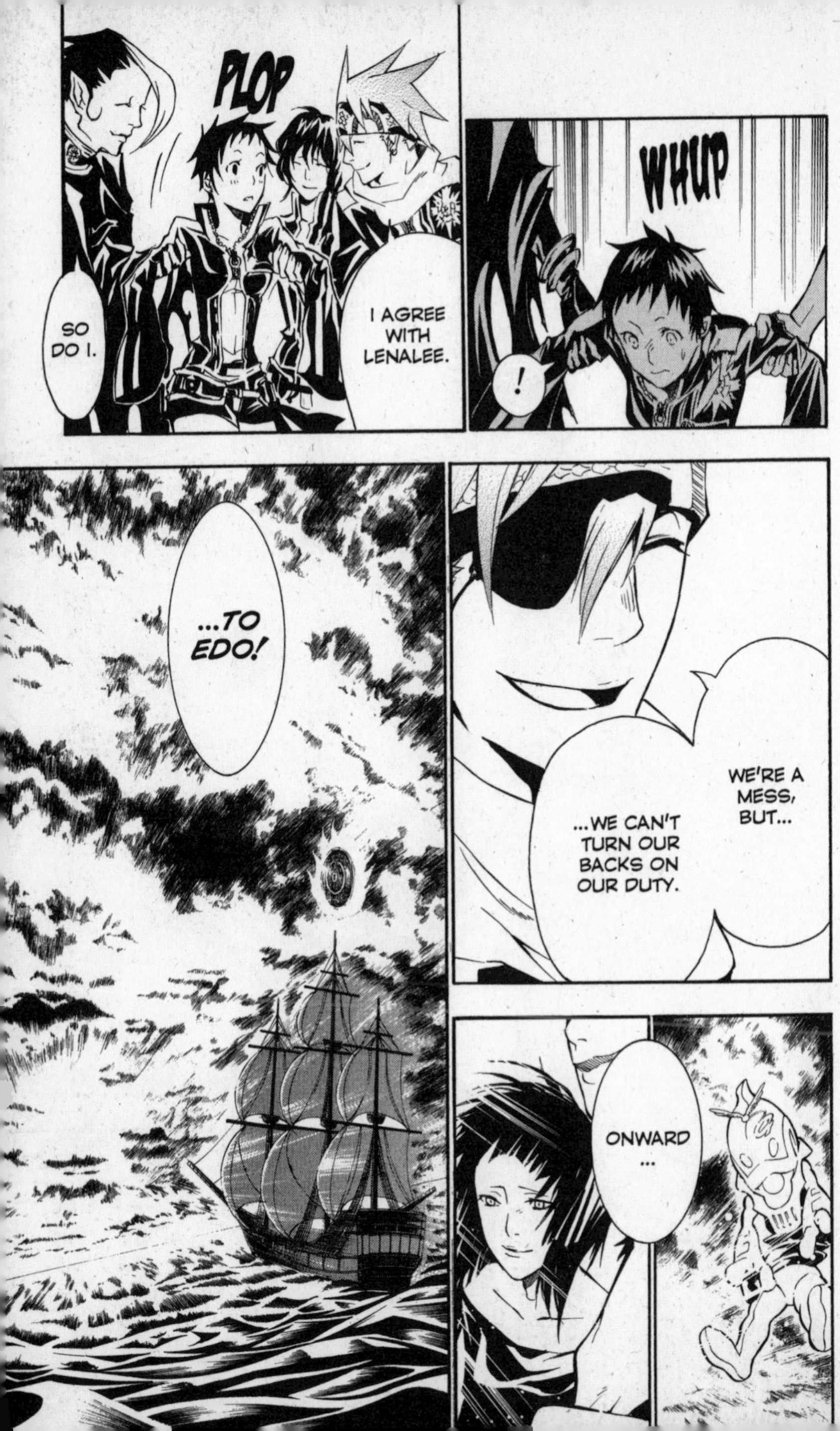
WHUP
!
PLOP
I AGREE WITH LENALEE.
SO DO I.
WE'RE A MESS, BUT...
...WE CAN'T TURN OUR BACKS ON OUR DUTY.
ONWARD ...
...TO EDO!

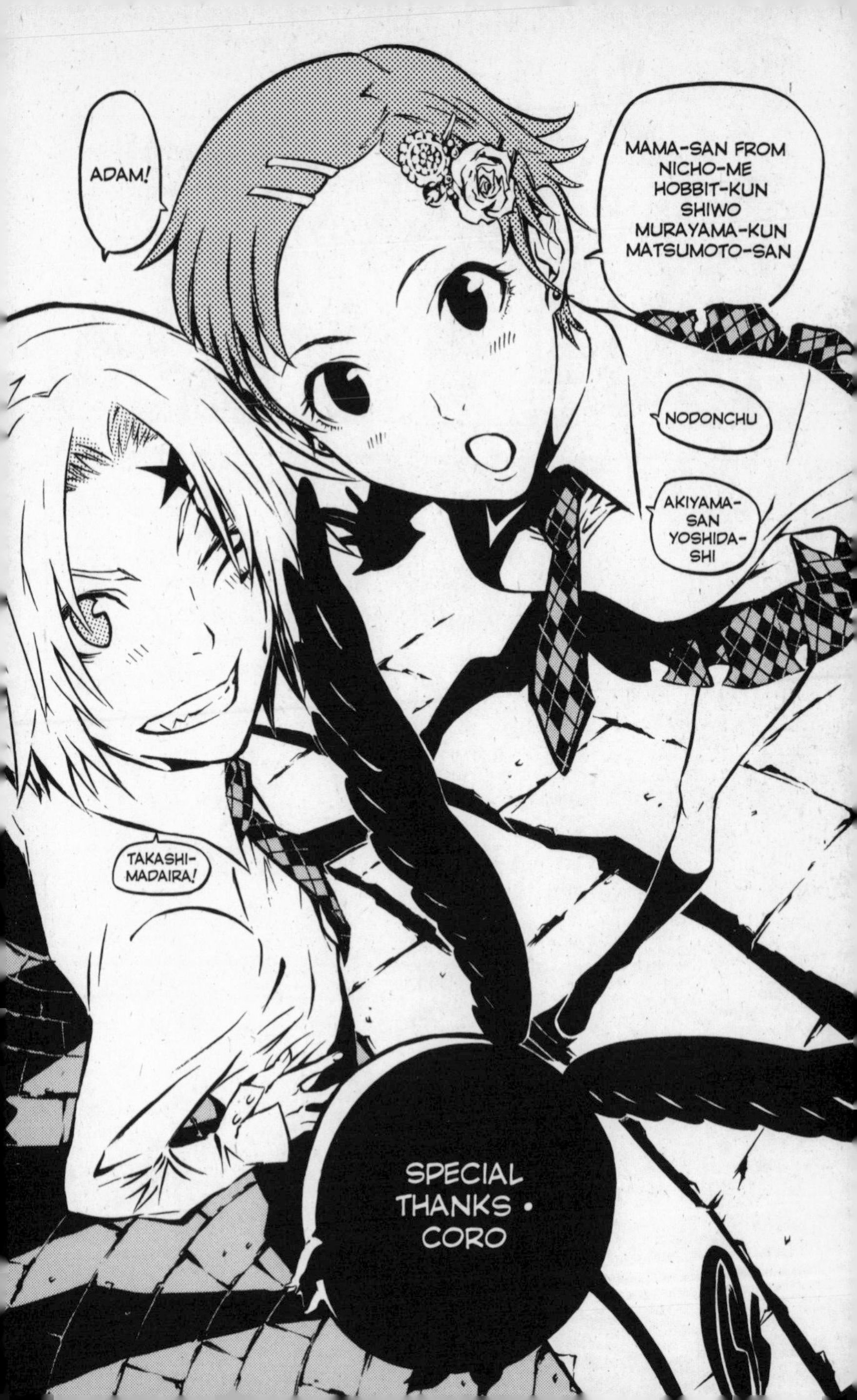
MAMA-SAN FROM NICHO-ME HOBBIT-KUN SHIWO MURAYAMA-KUN MATSUMOTO-SAN
ADAM!
NODONCHU
AKIYAMA-SAN YOSHIDA-SHI
TAKASHI-MADAIRA!
SPECIAL THANKS • CORO

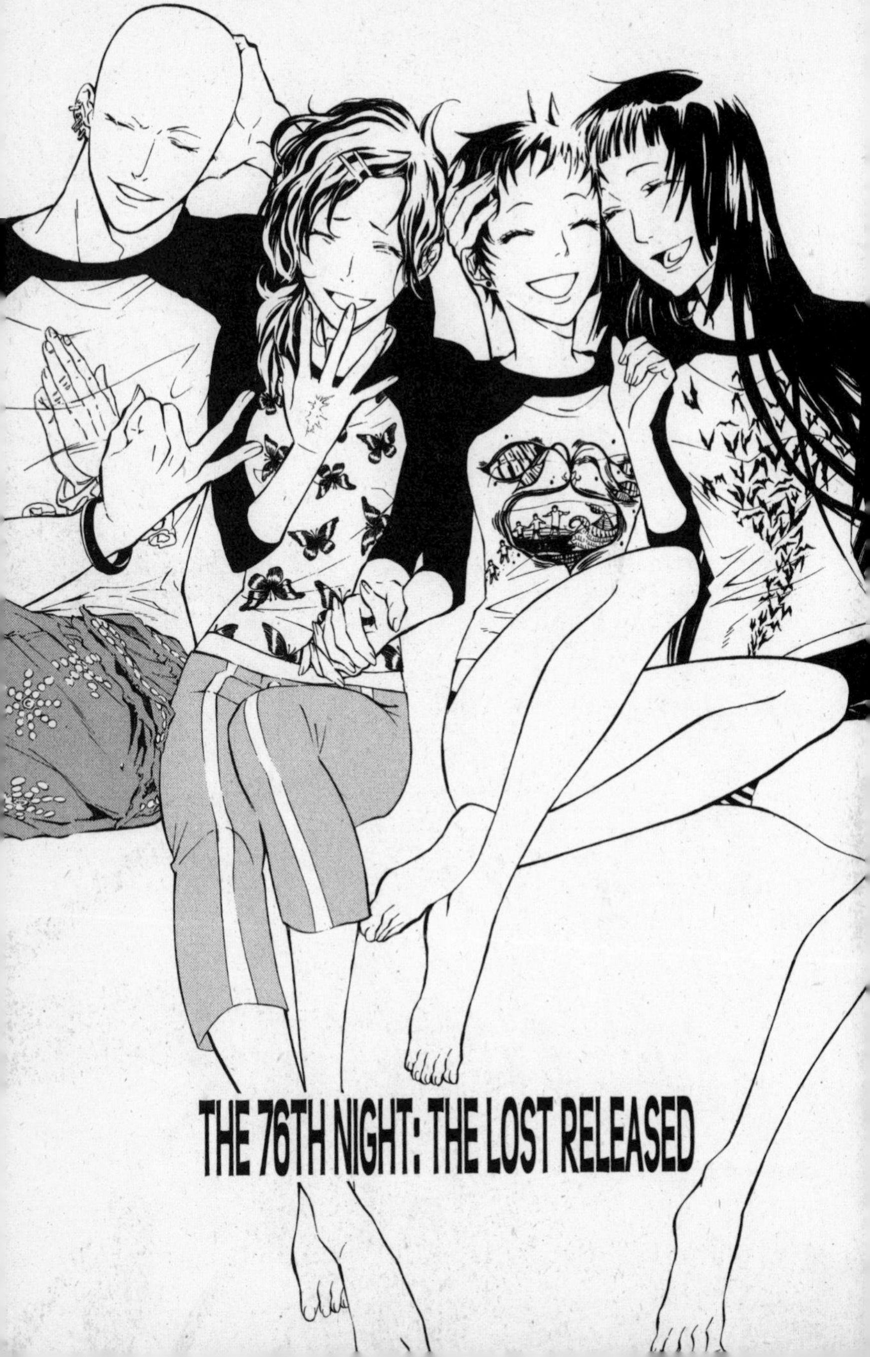

THE 76TH NIGHT: THE LOST RELEASED

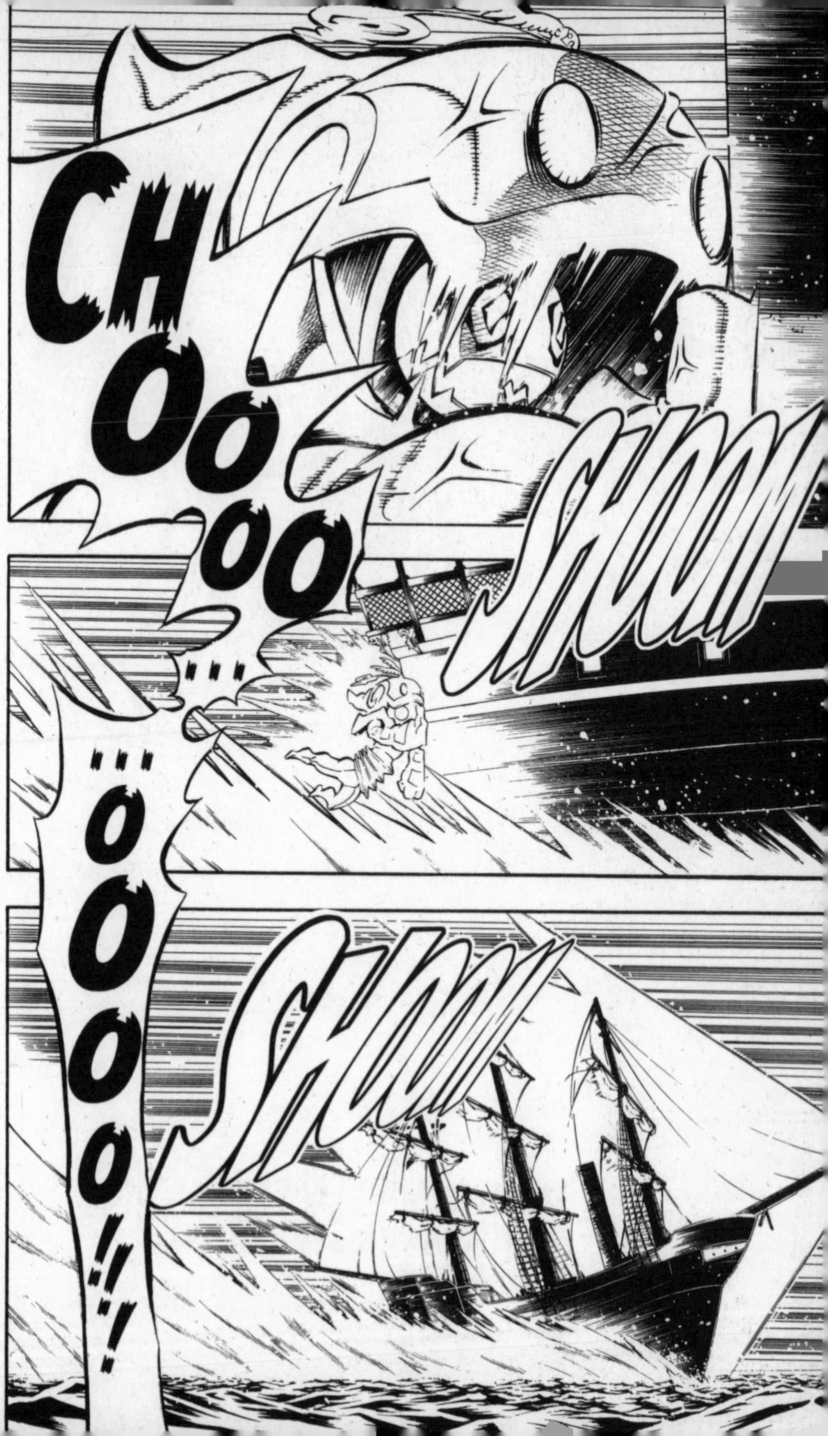
CHOOOO...
SHOOM
...OOOOO!!!
SHOOM

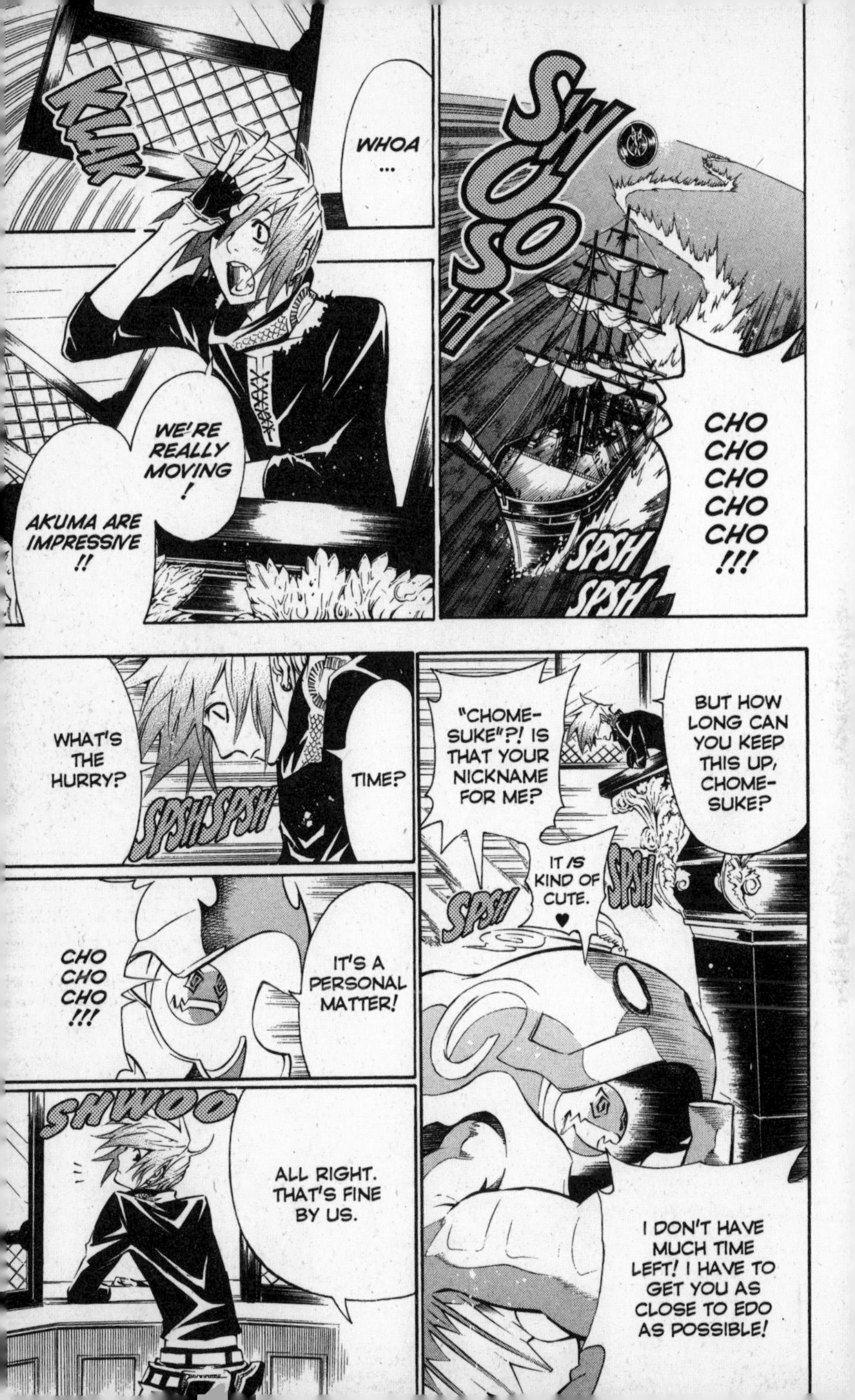
SWOOSH
CHO CHO CHO CHO CHO!!!
SPSH SPSH
KWAK
WHOA...
WE'RE REALLY MOVING!
AKUMA ARE IMPRESSIVE!!
BUT HOW LONG CAN YOU KEEP THIS UP, CHOME-SUKE?
"CHOME-SUKE"?! IS THAT YOUR NICKNAME FOR ME?
SPSH
IT IS KIND OF CUTE. ♥
SPSH
I DON'T HAVE MUCH TIME LEFT! I HAVE TO GET YOU AS CLOSE TO EDO AS POSSIBLE!
TIME?
WHAT'S THE HURRY?
SPSH SPSH
IT'S A PERSONAL MATTER!
CHO CHO CHO!!!
SHWOO
ALL RIGHT. THAT'S FINE BY US.

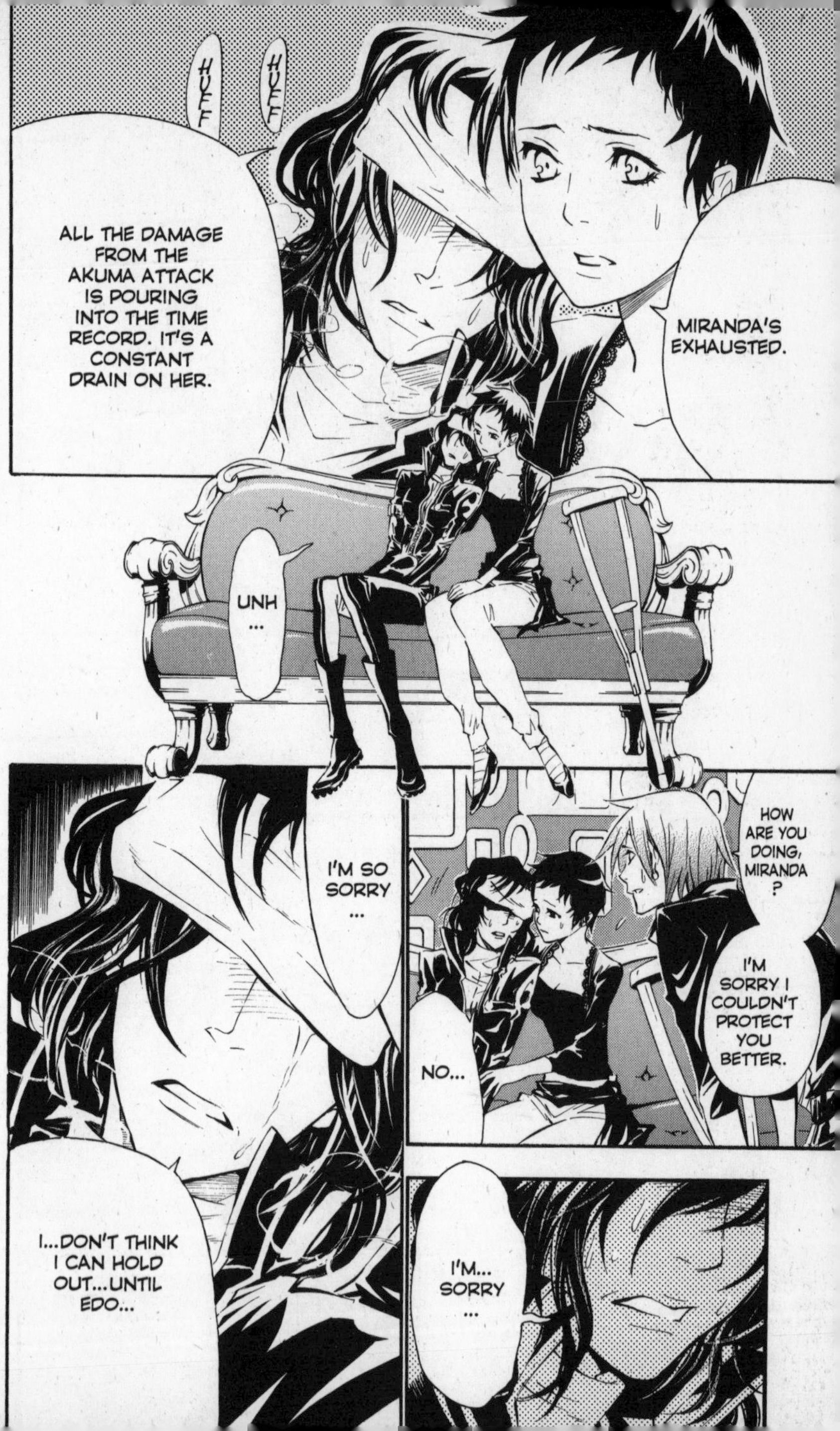
HUFF
HUFF
MIRANDA'S EXHAUSTED.
ALL THE DAMAGE FROM THE AKUMA ATTACK IS POURING INTO THE TIME RECORD. IT'S A CONSTANT DRAIN ON HER.
UNH...
HOW ARE YOU DOING, MIRANDA?
I'M SORRY I COULDN'T PROTECT YOU BETTER.
NO...
I'M... SORRY...
I'M SO SORRY...
I...DON'T THINK I CAN HOLD OUT...UNTIL EDO...

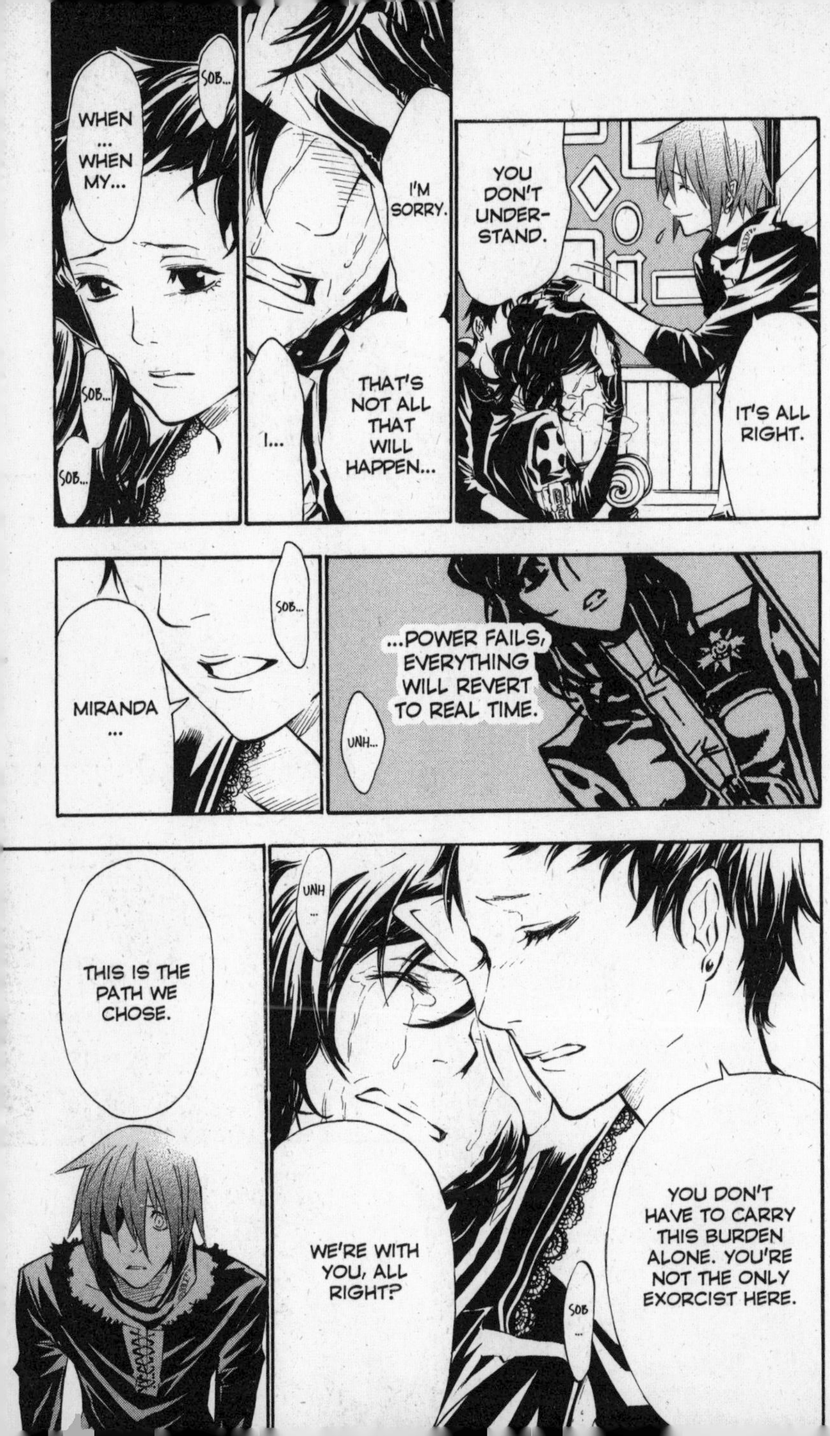
YOU DON'T UNDER-STAND.
IT'S ALL RIGHT.
I'M SORRY.
THAT'S NOT ALL THAT WILL HAPPEN...
I...
SOB...
WHEN ... WHEN MY...
SOB...
SOB...
...POWER FAILS, EVERYTHING WILL REVERT TO REAL TIME.
UNH...
SOB...
MIRANDA ...
UNH ...
YOU DON'T HAVE TO CARRY THIS BURDEN ALONE. YOU'RE NOT THE ONLY EXORCIST HERE.
SOB ...
WE'RE WITH YOU, ALL RIGHT?
THIS IS THE PATH WE CHOSE.

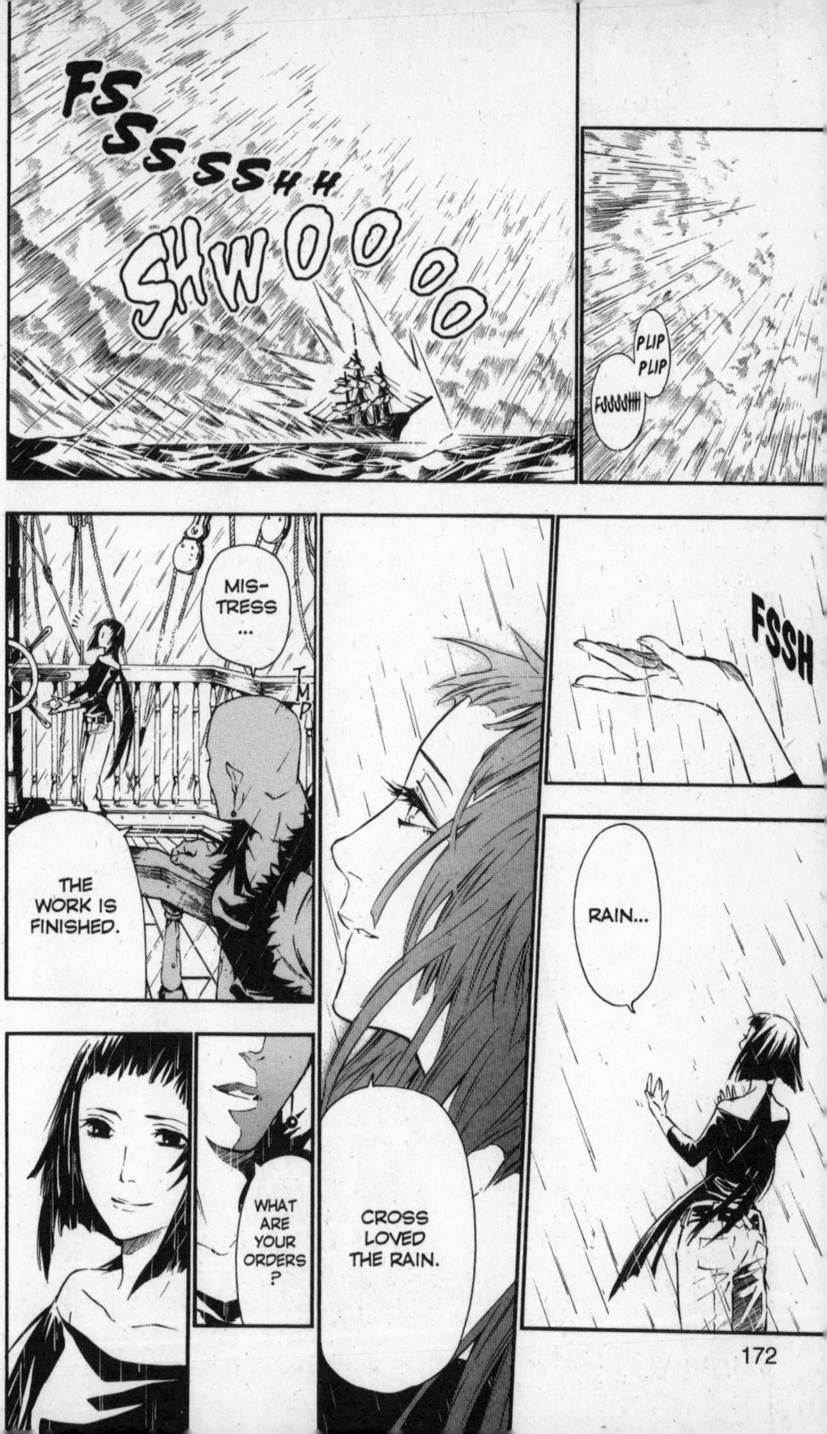
PLIP PLIP
FSSSSHH
FSSSSSHH
SHWOOOO
FSSH
RAIN...
CROSS LOVED THE RAIN.
MIS-TRESS...
TMP
THE WORK IS FINISHED.
WHAT ARE YOUR ORDERS?

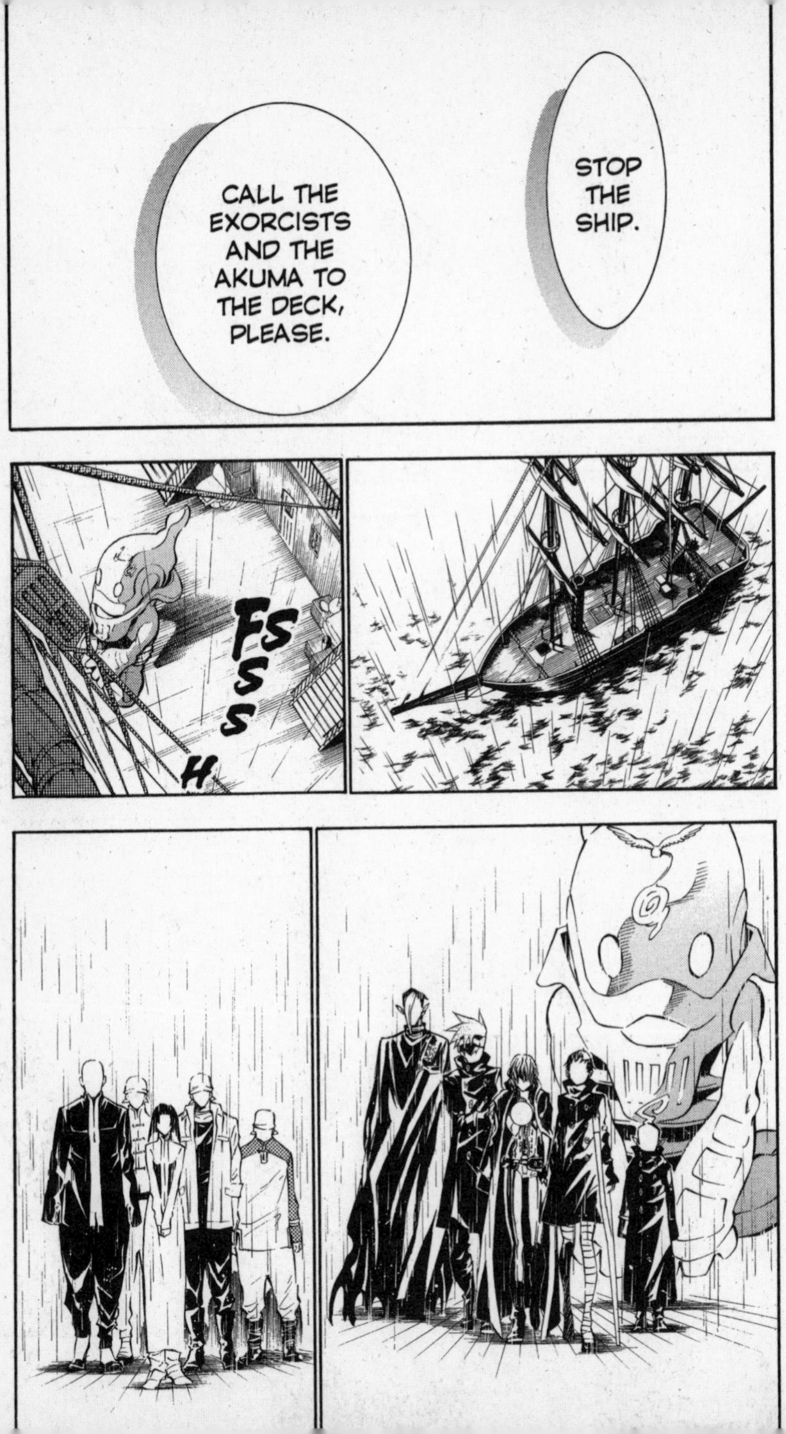
STOP THE SHIP.
CALL THE EXORCISTS AND THE AKUMA TO THE DECK, PLEASE.
FSSSH

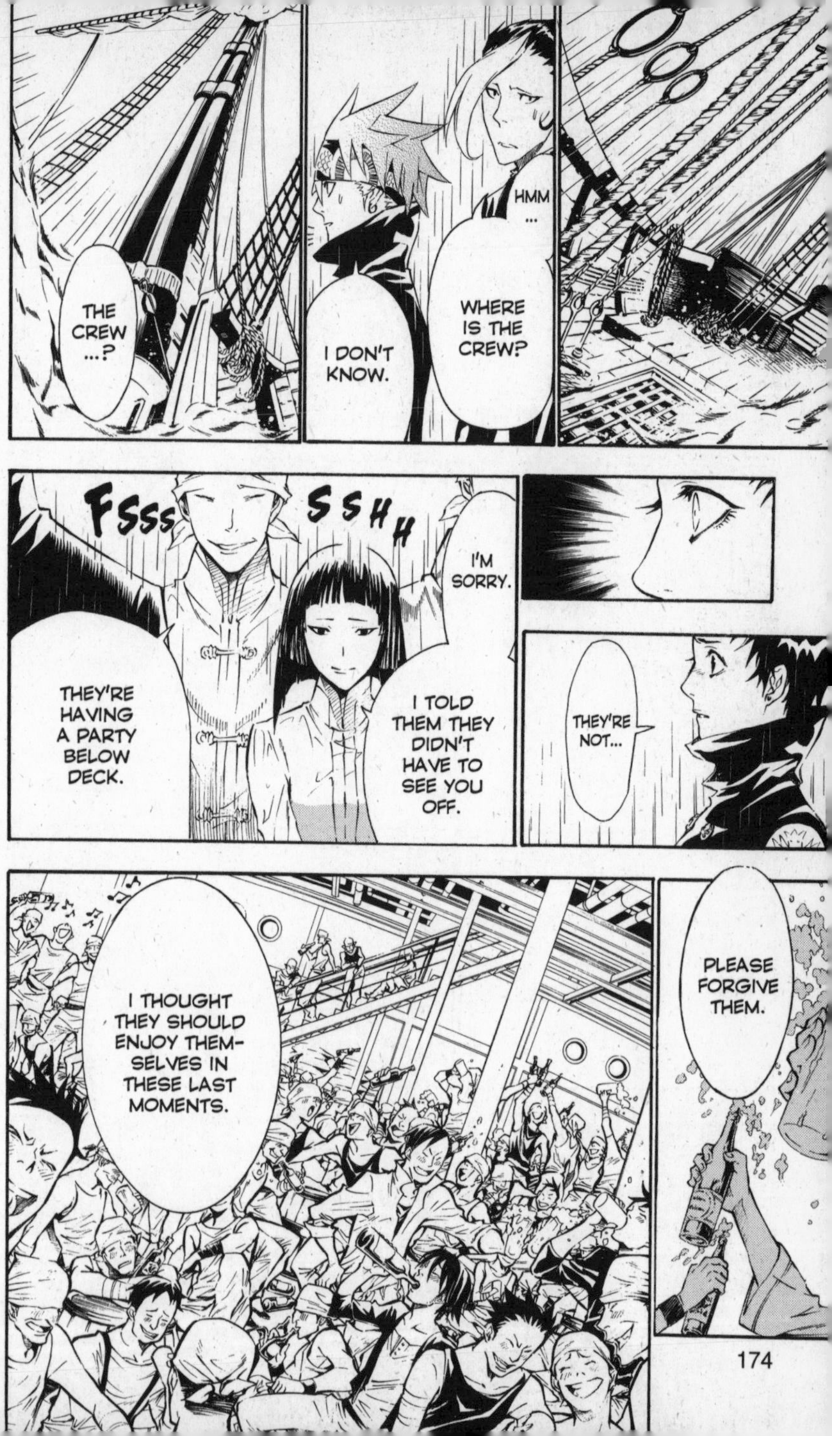

HMM ...
WHERE IS THE CREW?
I DON'T KNOW.
THE CREW ...?
THEY'RE NOT...
FSSS SSHH
I'M SORRY.
I TOLD THEM THEY DIDN'T HAVE TO SEE YOU OFF.
THEY'RE HAVING A PARTY BELOW DECK.
PLEASE FORGIVE THEM.
I THOUGHT THEY SHOULD ENJOY THEM-SELVES IN THESE LAST MOMENTS.

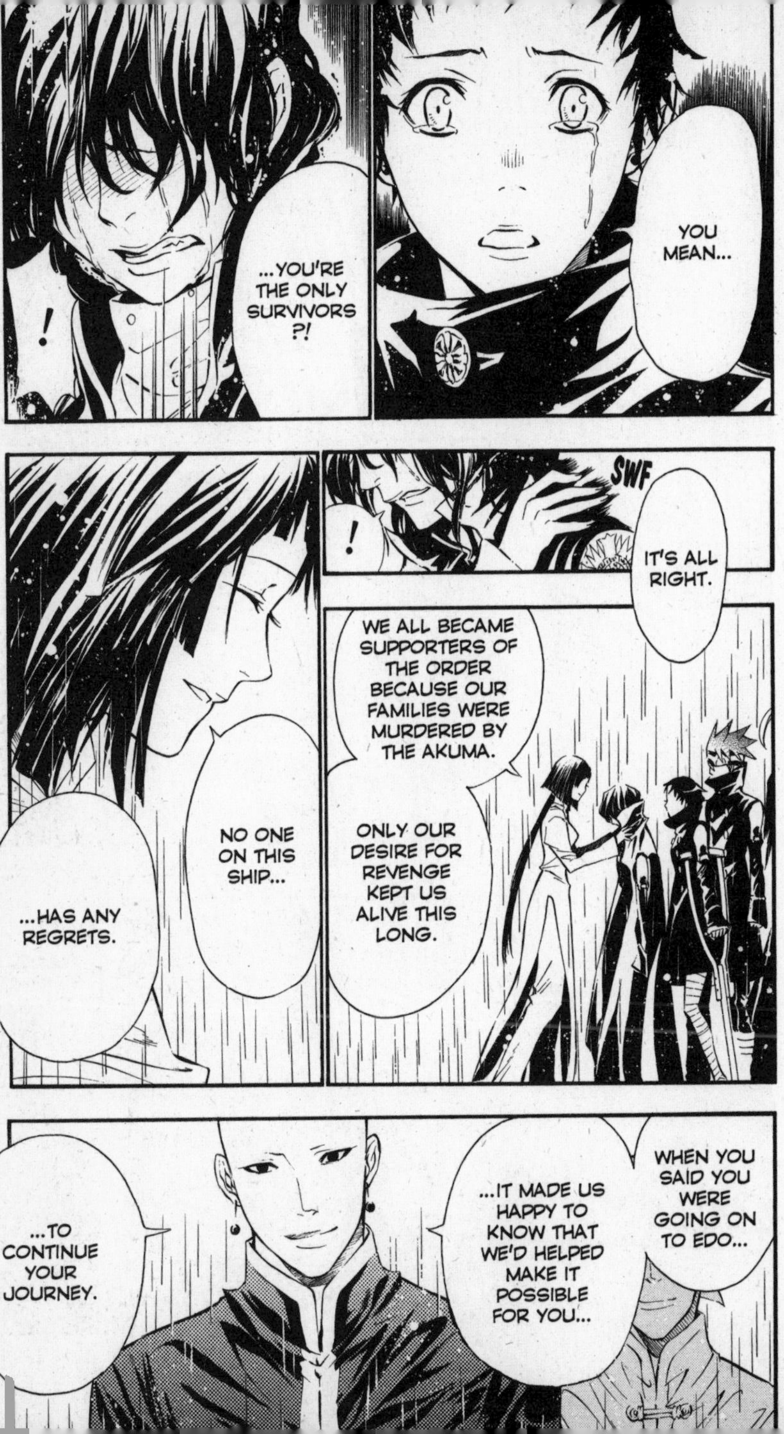
YOU MEAN...
...YOU'RE THE ONLY SURVIVORS ?!
!
SWF
!
IT'S ALL RIGHT.
WE ALL BECAME SUPPORTERS OF THE ORDER BECAUSE OUR FAMILIES WERE MURDERED BY THE AKUMA.
ONLY OUR DESIRE FOR REVENGE KEPT US ALIVE THIS LONG.
NO ONE ON THIS SHIP...
...HAS ANY REGRETS.
WHEN YOU SAID YOU WERE GOING ON TO EDO...
...IT MADE US HAPPY TO KNOW THAT WE'D HELPED MAKE IT POSSIBLE FOR YOU...
...TO CONTINUE YOUR JOURNEY.

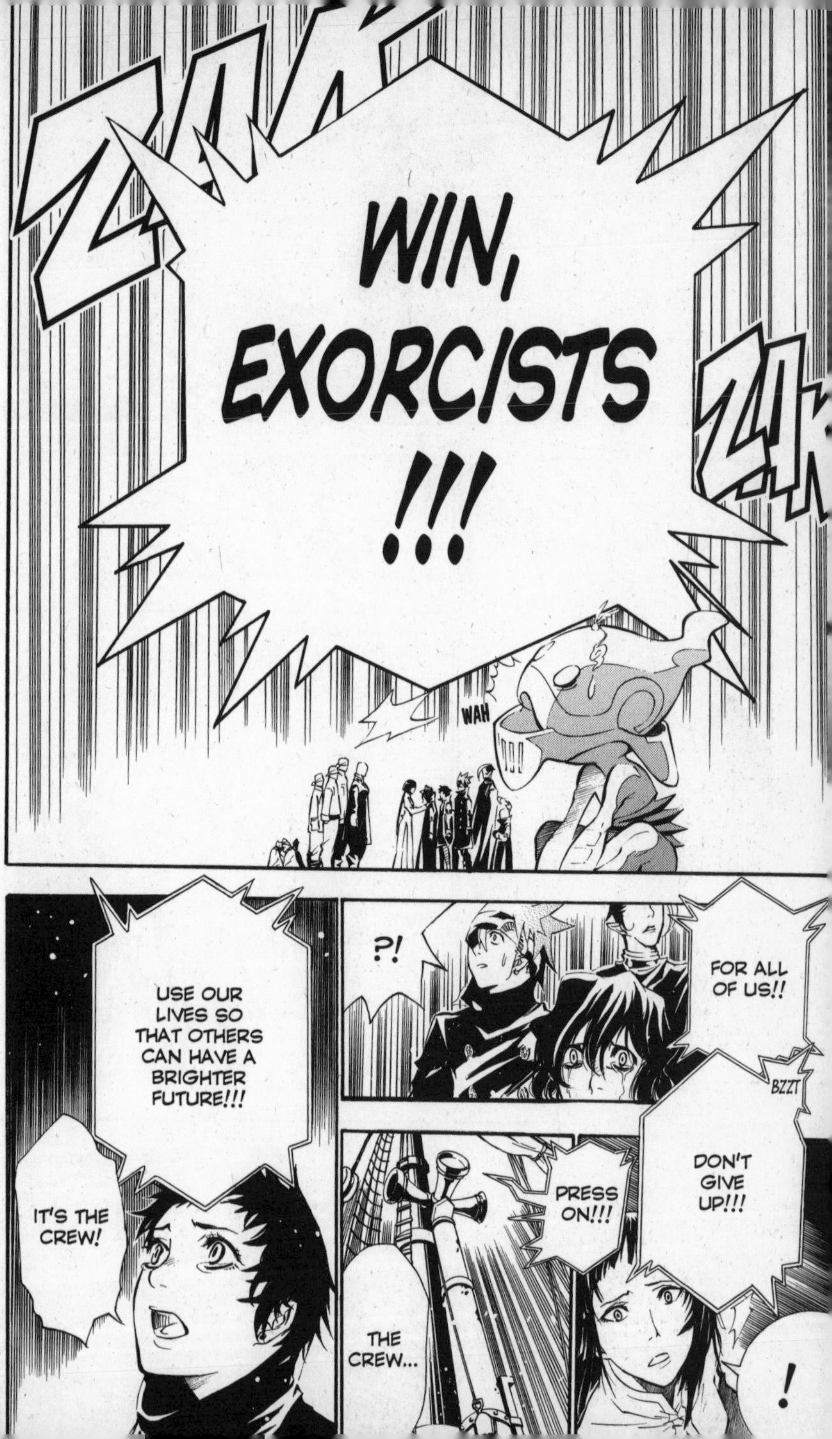
WIN, EXORCISTS!!!
WAH
FOR ALL OF US!!
?!
BZZT
DON'T GIVE UP!!!
PRESS ON!!!
!
THE CREW...
USE OUR LIVES SO THAT OTHERS CAN HAVE A BRIGHTER FUTURE!!!
IT'S THE CREW!

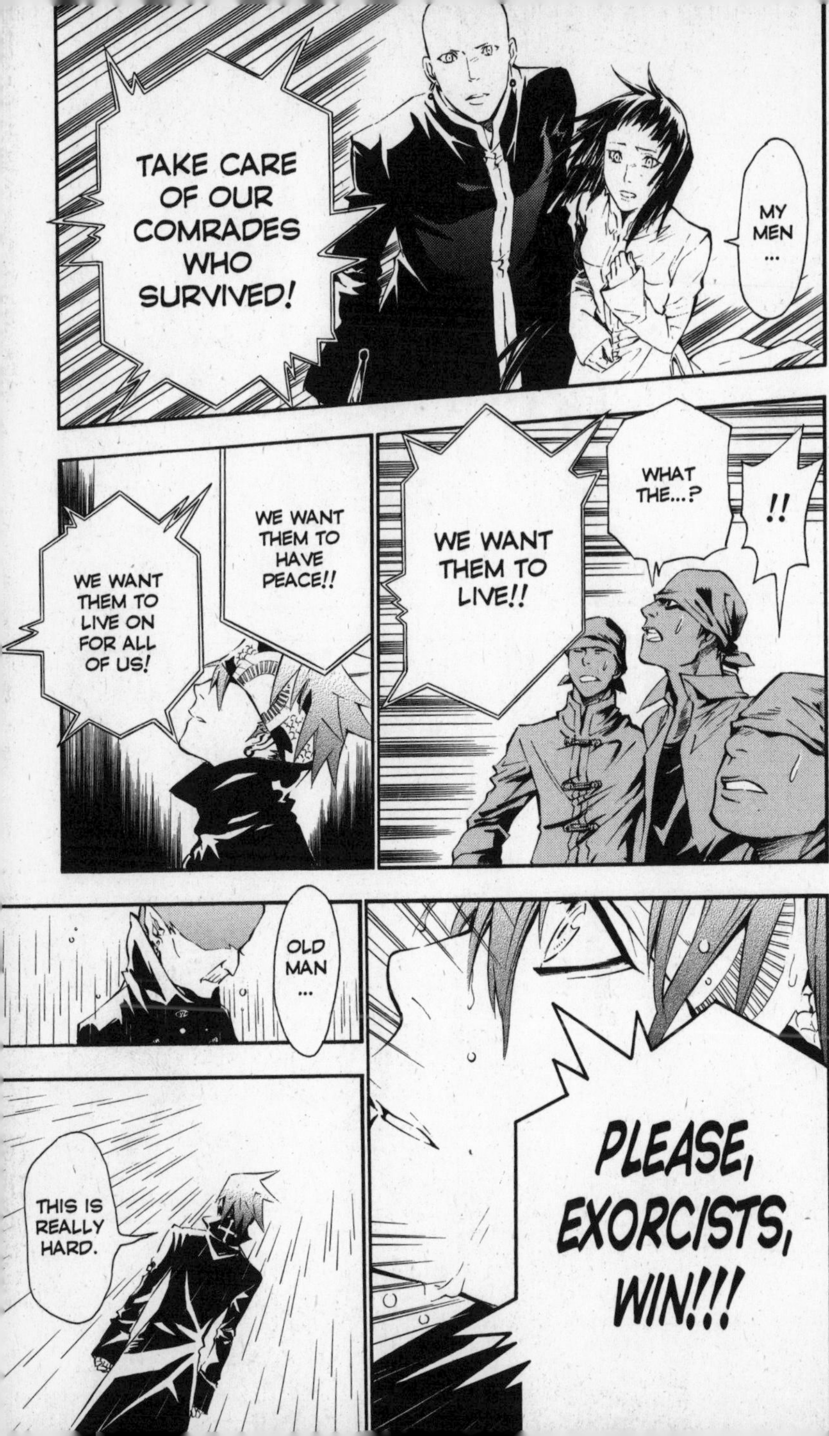
TAKE CARE OF OUR COMRADES WHO SURVIVED!
MY MEN...
!!
WHAT THE...?
WE WANT THEM TO LIVE!!
WE WANT THEM TO HAVE PEACE!!
WE WANT THEM TO LIVE ON FOR ALL OF US!
PLEASE, EXORCISTS, WIN!!!
OLD MAN...
THIS IS REALLY HARD.

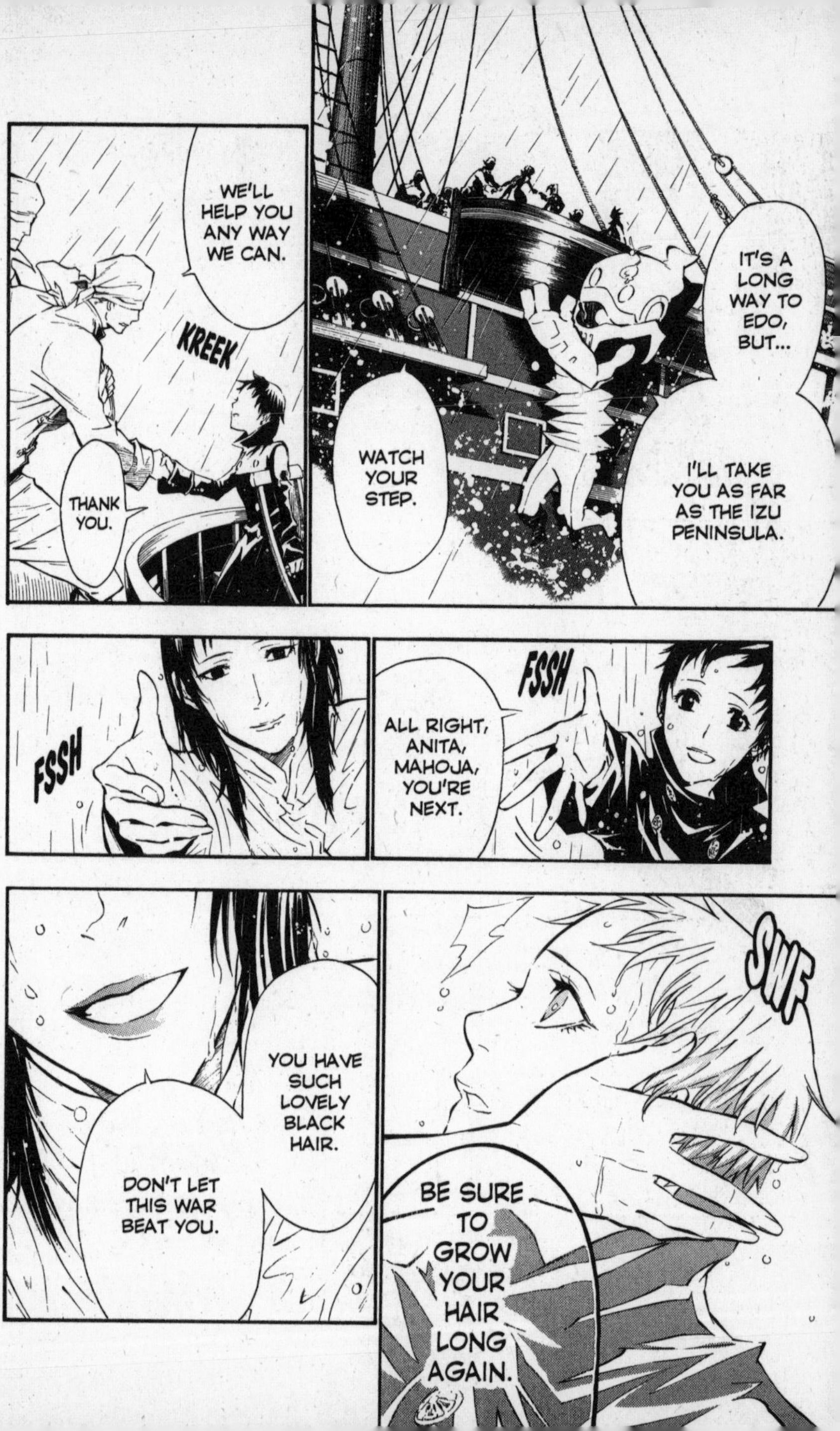
IT'S A LONG WAY TO EDO, BUT...
I'LL TAKE YOU AS FAR AS THE IZU PENINSULA.
WATCH YOUR STEP.
WE'LL HELP YOU ANY WAY WE CAN.
KREEK
THANK YOU.
FSSH
ALL RIGHT, ANITA, MAHOJA, YOU'RE NEXT.
FSSH
SNIF
BE SURE TO GROW YOUR HAIR LONG AGAIN.
YOU HAVE SUCH LOVELY BLACK HAIR.
DON'T LET THIS WAR BEAT YOU.

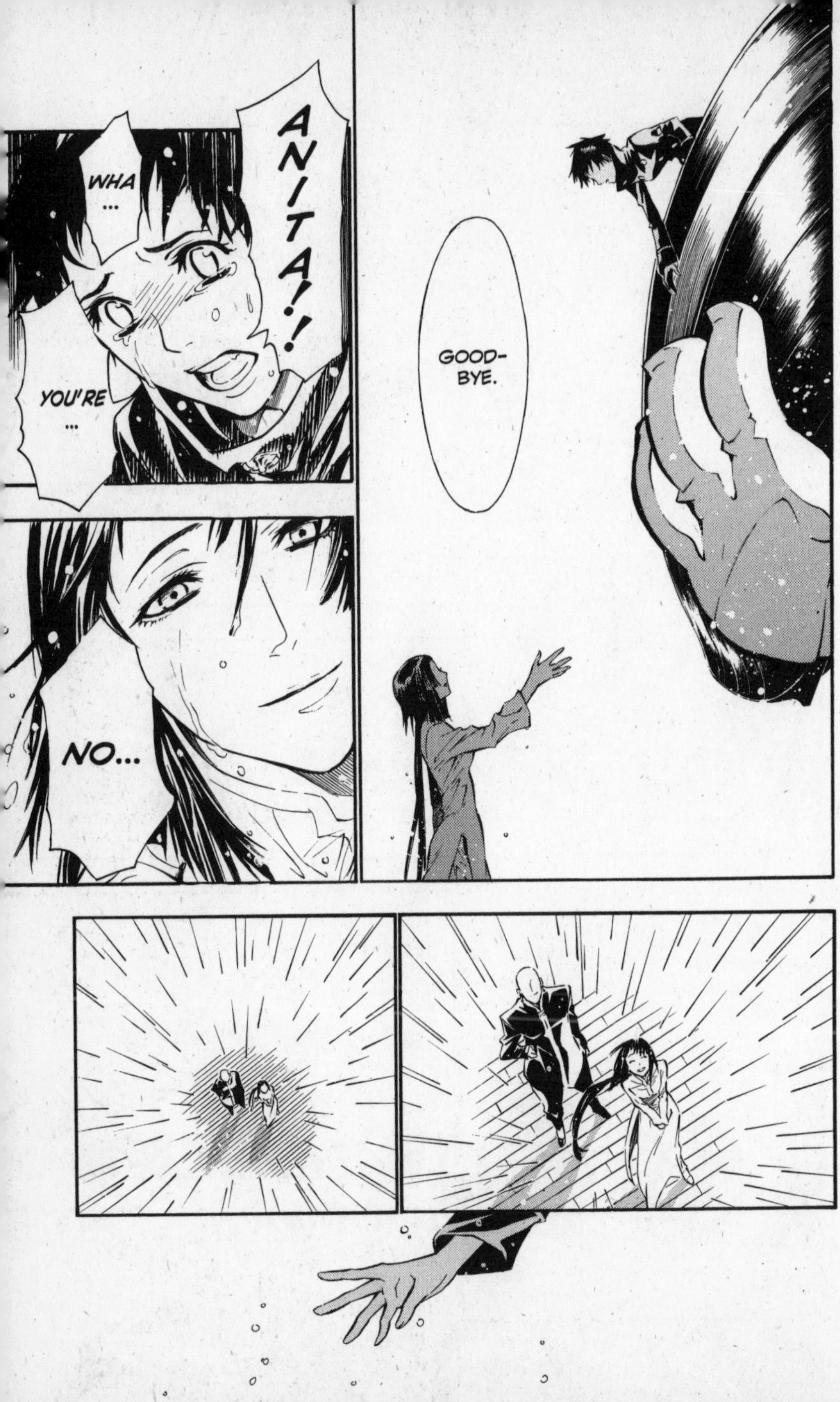
GOOD-BYE.
ANITA!!
WHA...
YOU'RE...
NO...

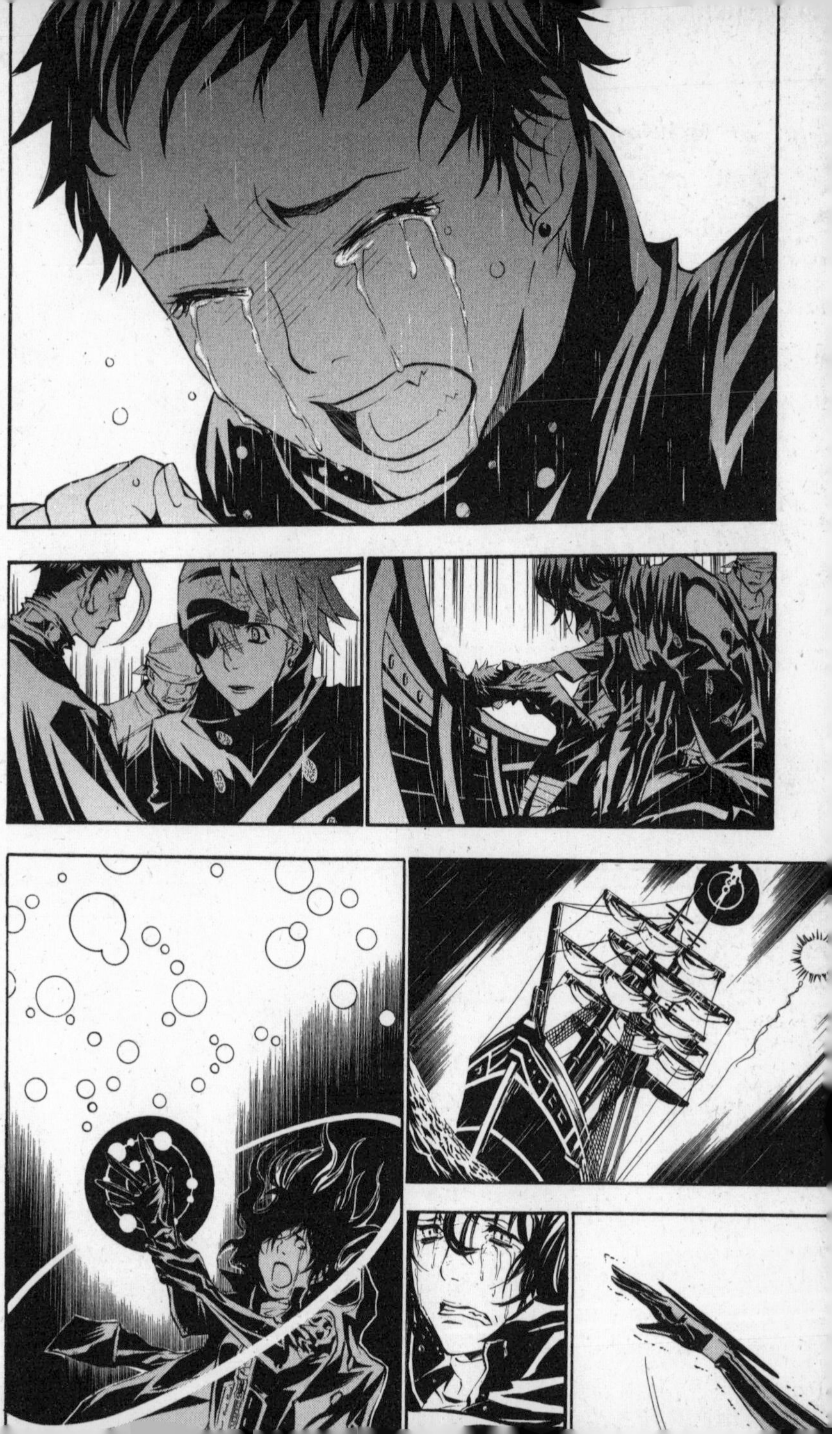

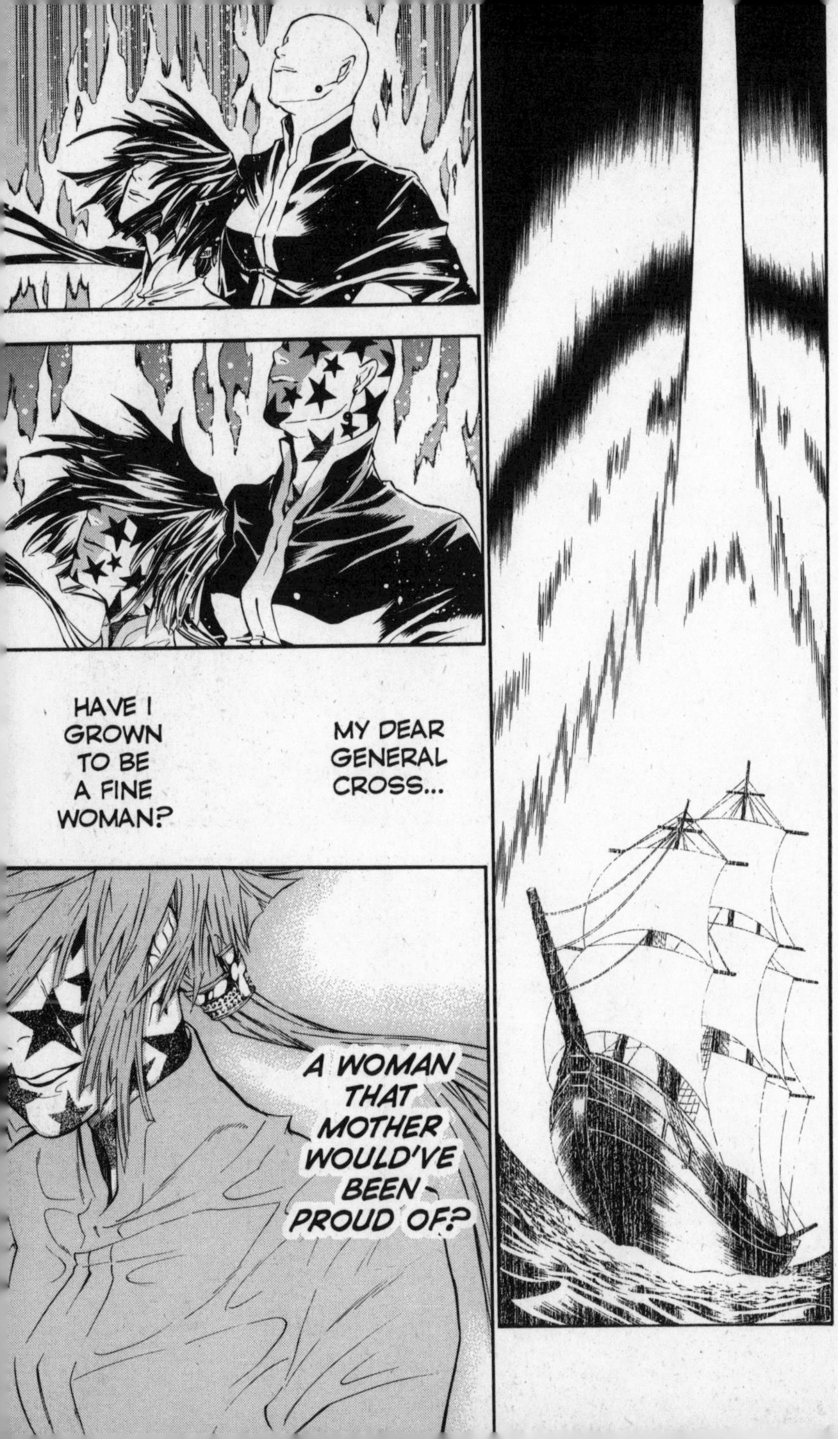
MY DEAR GENERAL CROSS...
HAVE I GROWN TO BE A FINE WOMAN?
A WOMAN THAT MOTHER WOULD'VE BEEN-PROUD OF?

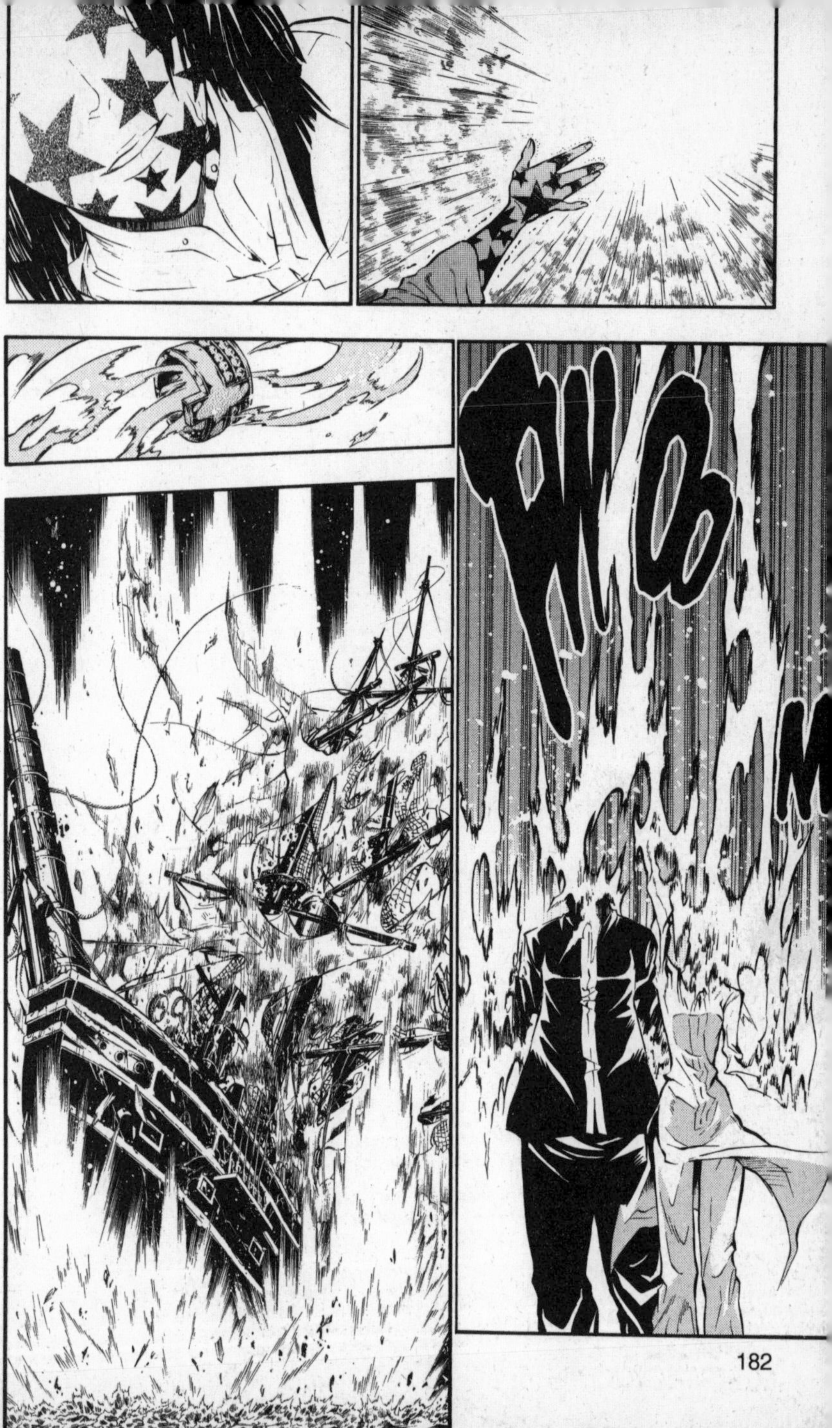
PWOOM

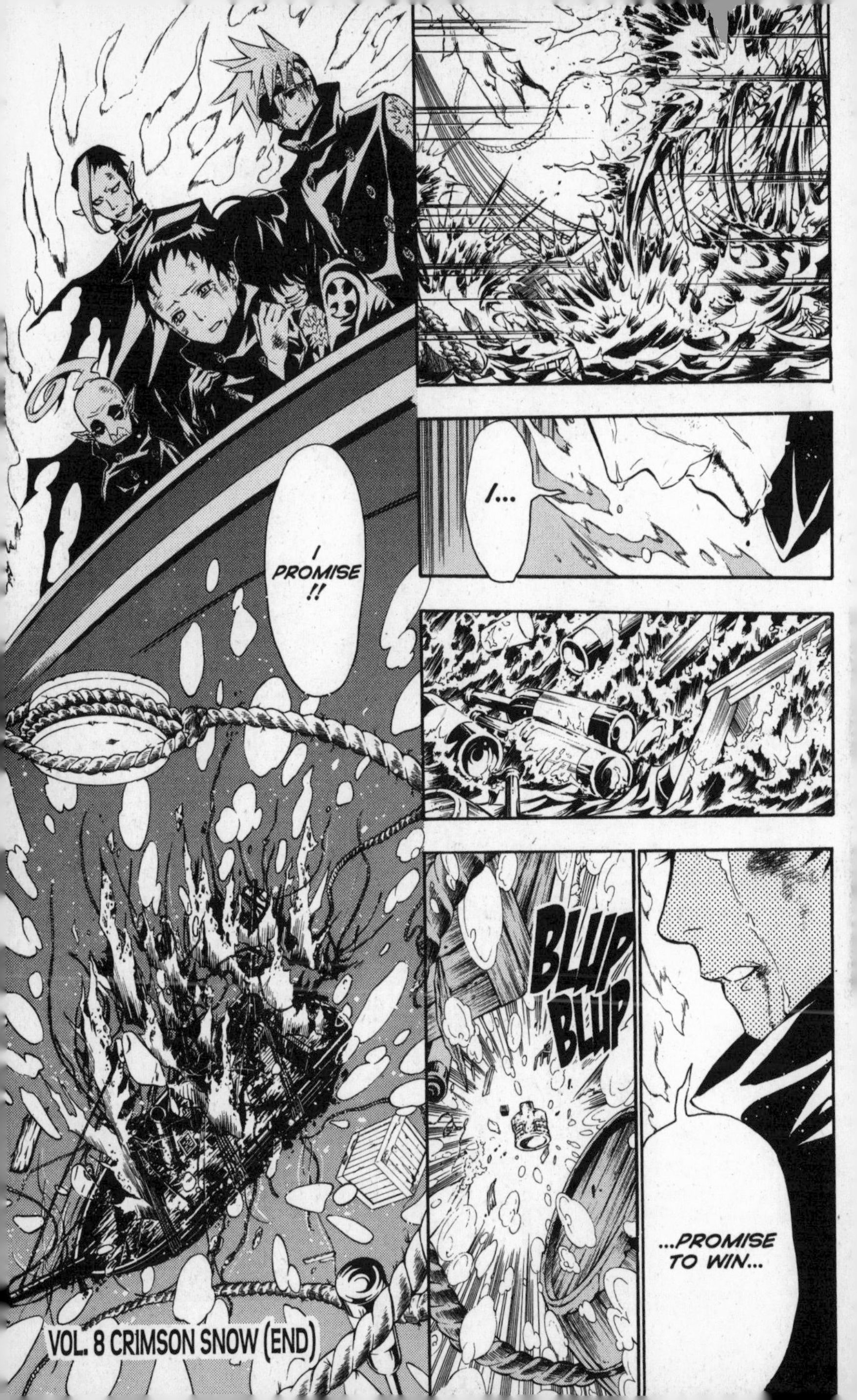
I...
...PROMISE TO WIN...
BLUP BLUP
I PROMISE !!
VOL. 8 CRIMSON SNOW (END)

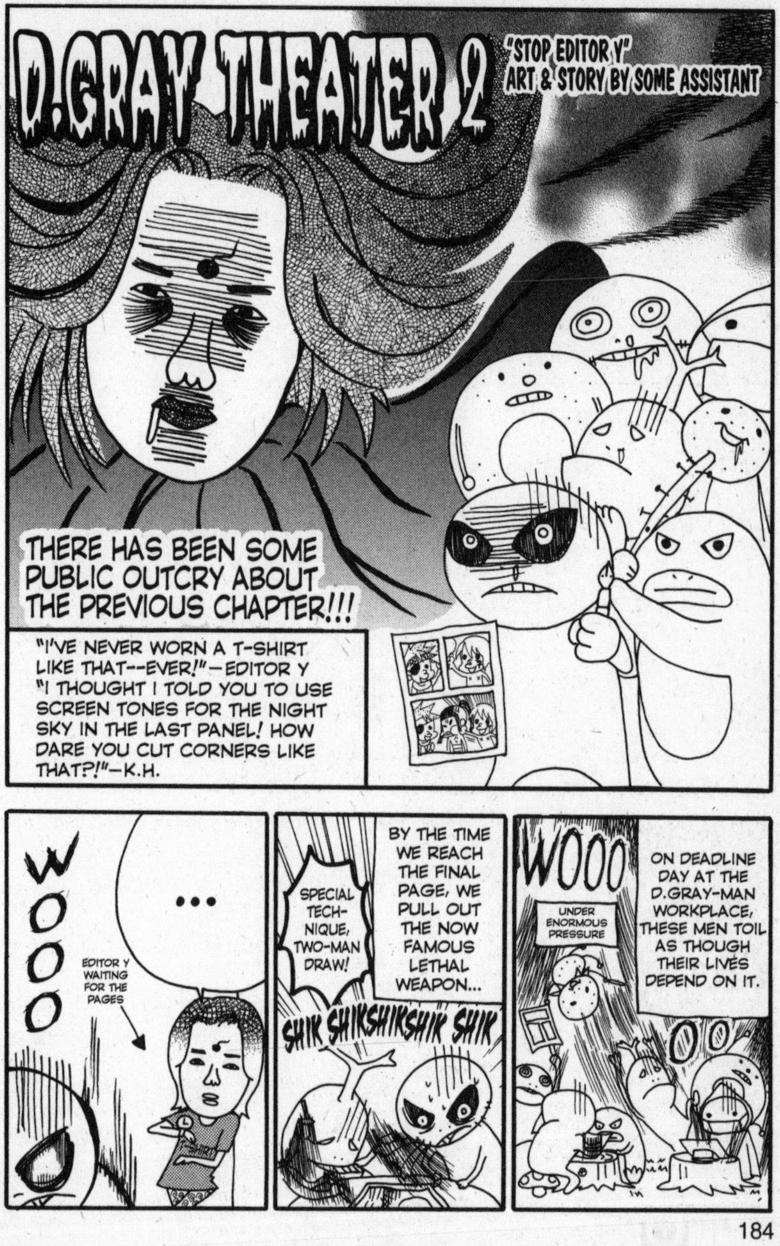
D.GRAY THEATER 2
"STOP EDITOR Y"
ART & STORY BY SOME ASSISTANT
THERE HAS BEEN SOME PUBLIC OUTCRY ABOUT THE PREVIOUS CHAPTER!!!
"I'VE NEVER WORN A T-SHIRT LIKE THAT--EVER!"—EDITOR Y
"I THOUGHT I TOLD YOU TO USE SCREEN TONES FOR THE NIGHT SKY IN THE LAST PANEL! HOW DARE YOU CUT CORNERS LIKE THAT?!"—K.H.
ON DEADLINE DAY AT THE D.GRAY-MAN WORKPLACE, THESE MEN TOIL AS THOUGH THEIR LIVES DEPEND ON IT.
WOOO
UNDER ENORMOUS PRESSURE
BY THE TIME WE REACH THE FINAL PAGE, WE PULL OUT THE NOW FAMOUS LETHAL WEAPON...
SPECIAL TECH-NIQUE, TWO-MAN DRAW!
SHIK SHIKSHIKSHIK SHIK
WOOOO
...
EDITOR Y WAITING FOR THE PAGES

READ THIS WAY

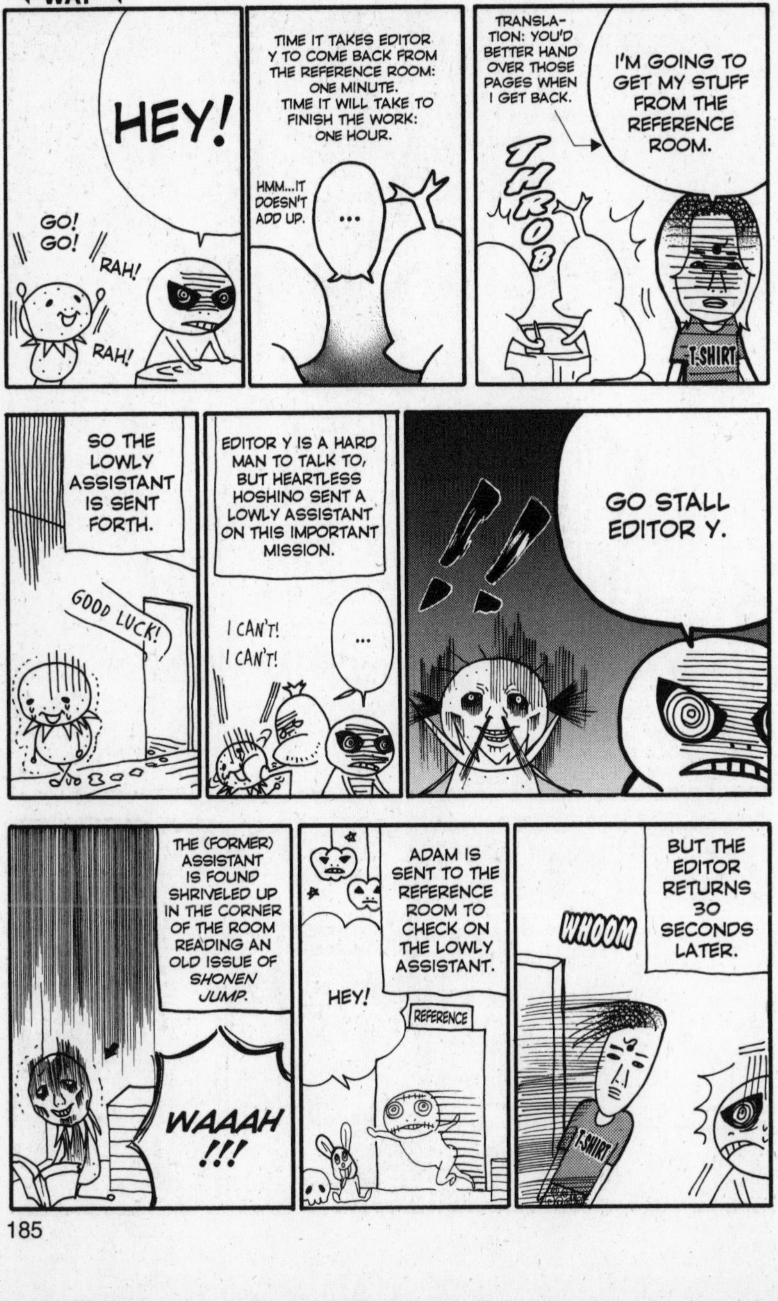

I'M GOING TO GET MY STUFF FROM THE REFERENCE ROOM.
TRANSLATION: YOU'D BETTER HAND OVER THOSE PAGES WHEN I GET BACK.
THROB
TIME IT TAKES EDITOR Y TO COME BACK FROM THE REFERENCE ROOM: ONE MINUTE. TIME IT WILL TAKE TO FINISH THE WORK: ONE HOUR.
...
HMM...IT DOESN'T ADD UP.
HEY!
GO! GO!
RAH!
RAH!
GO STALL EDITOR Y.
EDITOR Y IS A HARD MAN TO TALK TO, BUT HEARTLESS HOSHINO SENT A LOWLY ASSISTANT ON THIS IMPORTANT MISSION.
...
I CAN'T! I CAN'T!
SO THE LOWLY ASSISTANT IS SENT FORTH.
GOOD LUCK!
BUT THE EDITOR RETURNS 30 SECONDS LATER.
WHOOM
T-SHIRT
ADAM IS SENT TO THE REFERENCE ROOM TO CHECK ON THE LOWLY ASSISTANT.
HEY!
REFERENCE
THE (FORMER) ASSISTANT IS FOUND SHRIVELED UP IN THE CORNER OF THE ROOM READING AN OLD ISSUE OF SHONEN JUMP.
WAAAH!!!

IT SEEMS THAT NO ONE CAN STOP EDITOR Y. BUT JUST WHEN EVERYTHING SEEMS LOST...
OH, I FORGOT SOME PAPER-WORK IN THE OTHER ROOM.
T-SHIRT
SWP
I'M GOING TO GO GET IT NOW. (WHEN I COME BACK, YOU'D BETTER HAVE THOSE PAGES READY.)
SHIVER
TOMP TOMP
PURE TORTURE
T-SHIRT
JUST AS HOSHINO IS ABOUT TO GIVE IN TO DESPAIR, SOMETHING CATCHES HIS EYE...
WILD EYE
AN EVEN MORE HORRIFYING SIGHT.
ENTRANCE
A-ADAM?
...
...
STEP ASIDE, PLEASE.
BUT ADAM TURNS TO EDITOR Y.
WIP
THWAP
...
SILENCE
...
SILENT COMMANDS BEING SENT
SAY SOME-THING!
DRAW IT OUT!
SAY ANY-THING!
COMPLI-MENT HIM!
...

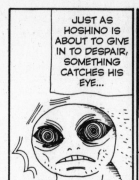

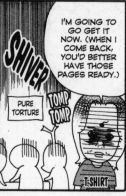

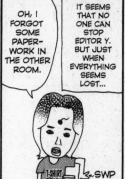

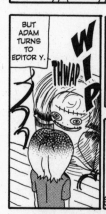

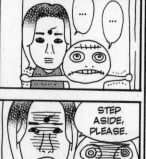

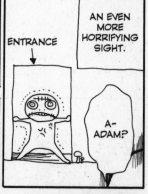

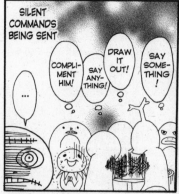

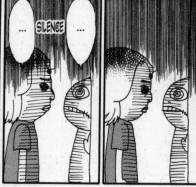

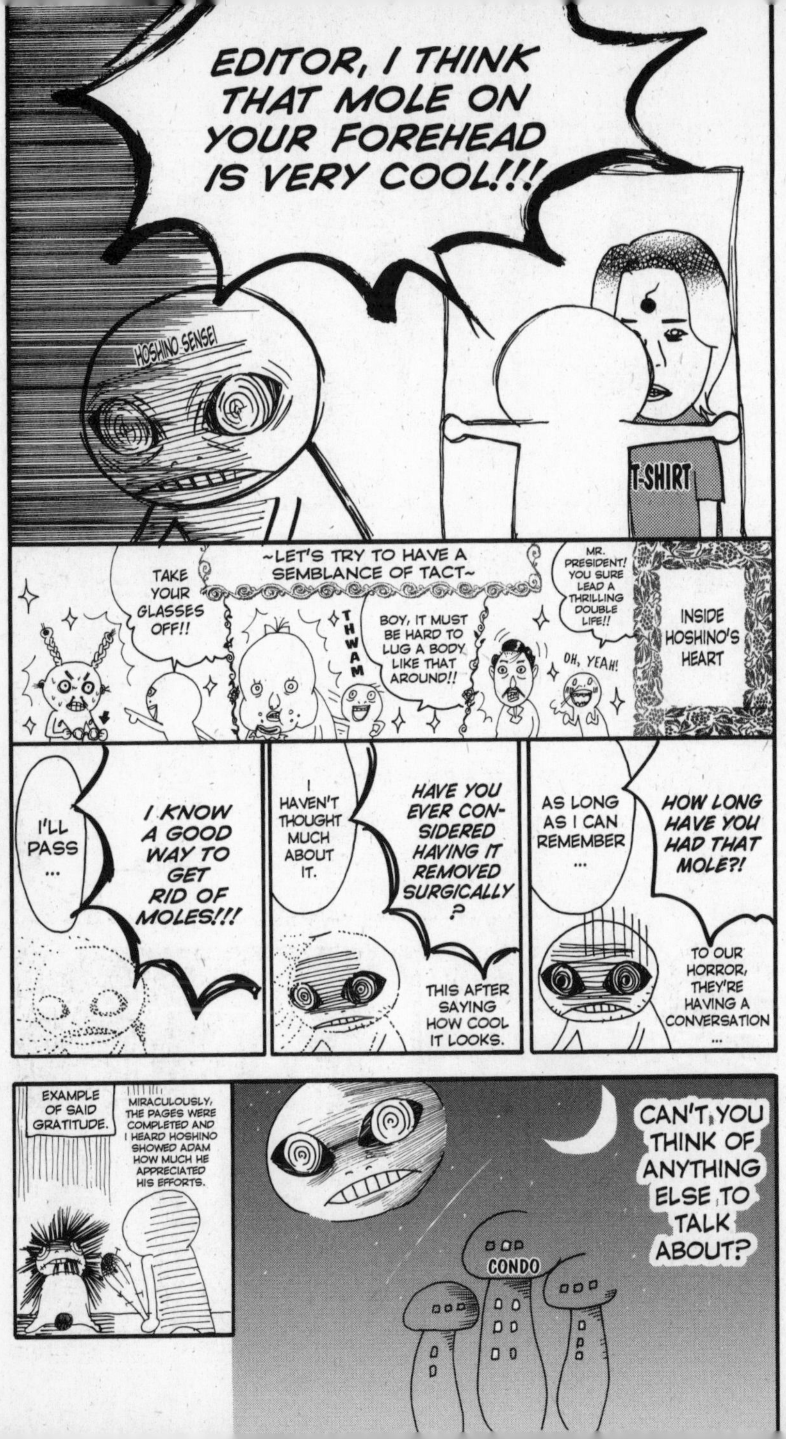
EDITOR, I THINK THAT MOLE ON YOUR FOREHEAD IS VERY COOL!!!
T-SHIRT
HOSHINO SENSEI
INSIDE HOSHINO'S HEART
MR. PRESIDENT! YOU SURE LEAD A THRILLING DOUBLE LIFE!!
OH, YEAH!
~LET'S TRY TO HAVE A SEMBLANCE OF TACT~
BOY, IT MUST BE HARD TO LUG A BODY LIKE THAT AROUND!!
THWAM
TAKE YOUR GLASSES OFF!!
HOW LONG HAVE YOU HAD THAT MOLE?!
AS LONG AS I CAN REMEMBER ...
TO OUR HORROR, THEY'RE HAVING A CONVERSATION ...
HAVE YOU EVER CON-SIDERED HAVING IT REMOVED SURGICALLY ?
I HAVEN'T THOUGHT MUCH ABOUT IT.
THIS AFTER SAYING HOW COOL IT LOOKS.
I KNOW A GOOD WAY TO GET RID OF MOLES!!!
I'LL PASS ...
CAN'T YOU THINK OF ANYTHING ELSE TO TALK ABOUT?
CONDO
MIRACULOUSLY, THE PAGES WERE COMPLETED AND I HEARD HOSHINO SHOWED ADAM HOW MUCH HE APPRECIATED HIS EFFORTS.
EXAMPLE OF SAID GRATITUDE.

IN THE NEXT VOLUME...

Allen's former colleagues head to Edo, where the Earl is reported to have set up shop. The Earl, meanwhile, has gained access to a great artifact that he wastes no time putting to use. He's assigned a squad of Akuma to infiltrate the Asia Branch of the Black Order, capture Allen, and bring the former Exorcist to him—in tiny bits, if necessary!

Available Now!

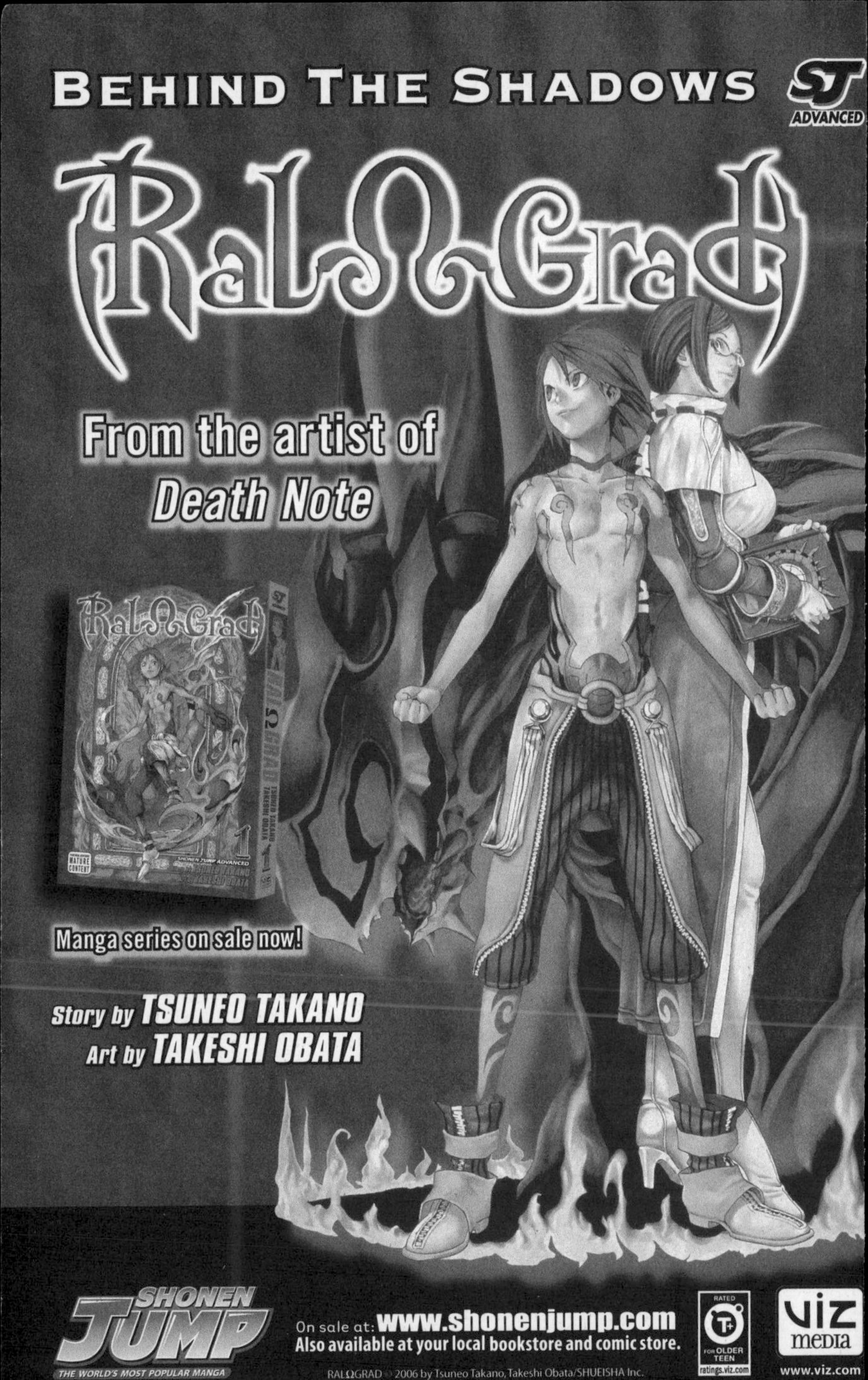
BEHIND THE SHADOWS
SJ ADVANCED
RalΩGrad
From the artist of Death Note
Manga series on sale now!
Story by TSUNEO TAKANO
Art by TAKESHI OBATA
SHONEN JUMP
THE WORLD'S MOST POPULAR MANGA
On sale at: www.shonenjump.com
Also available at your local bookstore and comic store.
RATED T+ FOR OLDER TEEN
ratings.viz.com
VIZ media
www.viz.com
RALΩGRAD © 2006 by Tsuneo Takano, Takeshi Obata/SHUEISHA Inc.